PARALLEL PUBLIC

PARALLEL PUBLIC

EXPERIMENTAL ART IN LATE EAST GERMANY

SARA BLAYLOCK

THE MIT PRESS
CAMBRIDGE, MASSACHUSETTS
LONDON, ENGLAND

The MIT Press would like to thank the anonymous peer reviewers who provided comments on drafts of this book. The generous work of academic experts is essential for establishing the authority and quality of our publications. We acknowledge with gratitude the contributions of these otherwise uncredited readers.

This book was set in Arnhem Pro and Frank New by Westchester Publishing Services. Printed and bound in the United States of America.

Library of Congress Cataloging-in-Publication Data

Names: Blaylock, Sara, author.
Title: Parallel public : experimental art in late East Germany / Sara Blaylock.
Other titles: Infiltration and excess
Description: Cambridge, Massachusetts : The MIT Press, [2022] | Revision of the author's thesis (doctoral)—University of California, Santa Cruz, 2017. | Includes bibliographical references and index.
Identifiers: LCCN 2021005682 | ISBN 9780262046633 (hardcover)
Subjects: LCSH: Arts, German—Germany (East)—Experimental methods. | Arts and society—Germany (East) | Art and state—Germany (East)
Classification: LCC NX550.6 .B59 2022 | DDC 700.943/1—dc23
LC record available at https://lccn.loc.gov/2021005682

10 9 8 7 6 5 4 3 2 1

for Ari,
as always and especially in a pandemic

CONTENTS

INTRODUCTION

Born into Socialism

In its October 1989 issue, East Germany's leading state-run arts magazine *Bildende Kunst* (Fine art) featured a two-page, full-color photo spread on the country's first and only state-sanctioned performance art festival. Hosted by the Galerie Weißer Elefant (White Elephant Gallery) in East Berlin, the Permanente Kunstkonferenz (Permanent Art Conference) coincided with the Berlin Regional Art Exhibition, an annual showcase of art made by people in the Union of Fine Artists (Verband Bildender Künstler) who lived and worked in the capital and its immediate surroundings. In the *Bildende Kunst* publicity, which appeared a few months after the June 1989 festival, ten vignettes offer glimpses into the several dozen performances and other forms of process-oriented *Aktionskunst* (action art) that comprised the thirty-one days of the Permanent Art Conference. One image shows Else Gabriel as she sits alone in a chair with blood dripping down her hair and onto her gray coveralls. In another, Erhard Monden appears wearing a red track suit and standing completely still as he faces a wall. In the foreground of this picture, Kathleen Monden contorts her body in between the bars of a rectangular and mirrored sculpture. On the facing page, a slender Micha Brendel saws eye holes into a mask on his head.

The Permanent Art Conference represented a dramatic shift in cultural policy, particularly in the official stance of the German Democratic Republic (GDR) toward experimental forms of art. Just five years earlier, Christoph Tannert, one of the conference organizers, had been fired from a plush job in the Union of Fine Artists as punishment for publishing a text that advocated for interdisciplinarity in art in the state-run magazine *Musik und Gesellschaft* (Music and society).[1] In 1985, scores of

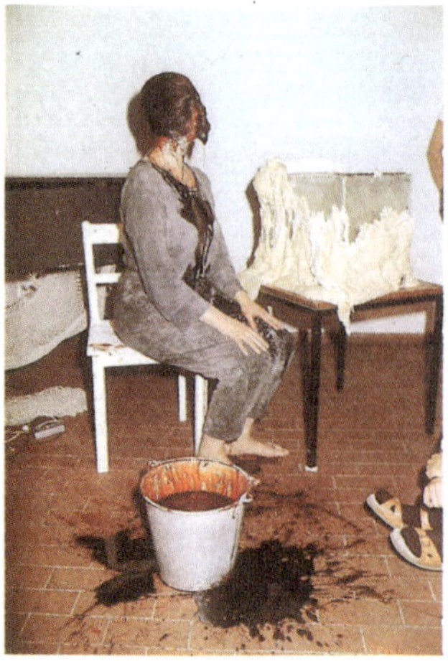

1 Else Gabriel (und Ulf Wrede) in ALIAS, Performance und Autoperforationsartistik

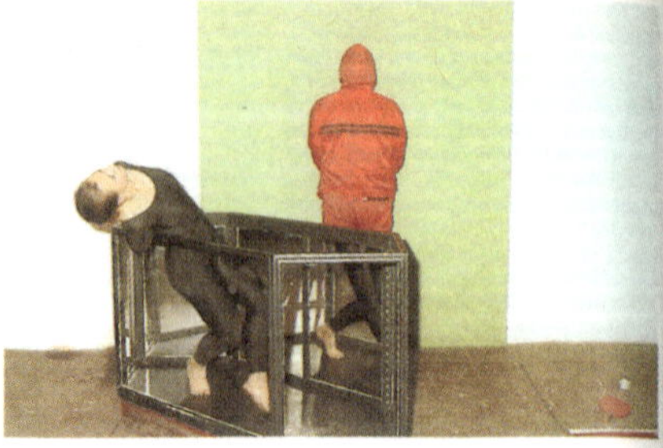

3 Erhard Monden und Kathleen Monden in WIR SIND ANGEKOMMEN HIER UND DORT, Aktion erweiterter Kunstbegriff

Permanente

Fotografien von

2 Via Lewandowsky in TRICHINEN AUF KREUZFAHRT, Performance und anonyme Rezeption

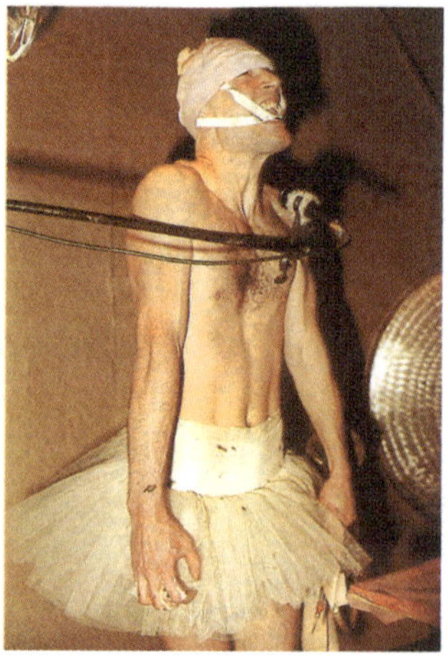

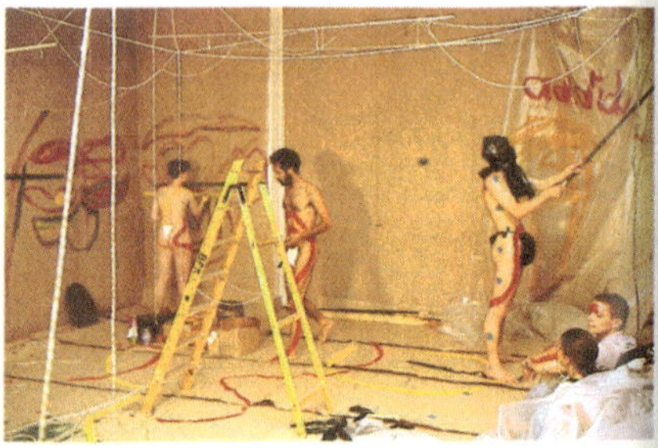

4 Cesar Olhagaray in BILDTHEATER, Kunstexperimentelle Werkstatt

5 Micha Brendel und Else Gabriel in LACHEISEN, Performance

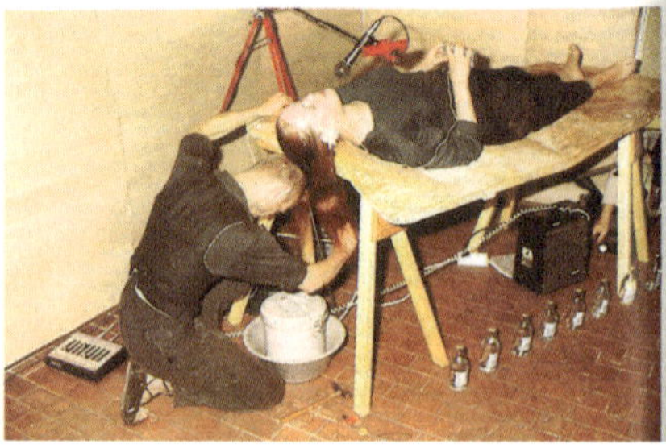

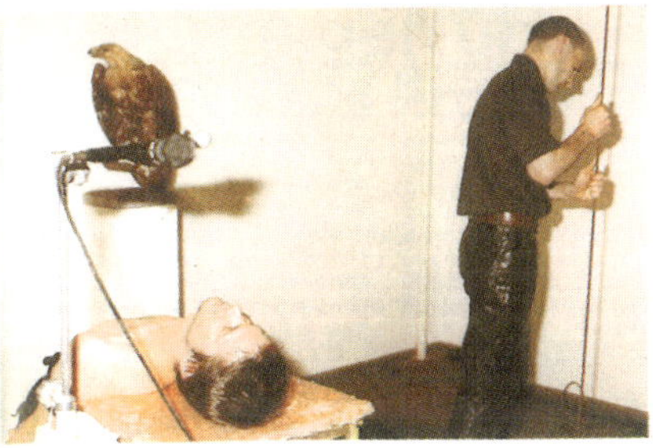

6 Durs Grünbein und Via Lewandowsky in DEUTSCHE GRÜNDLICHKEIT, Performance

Kunstkonferenz

Jochen Wermann

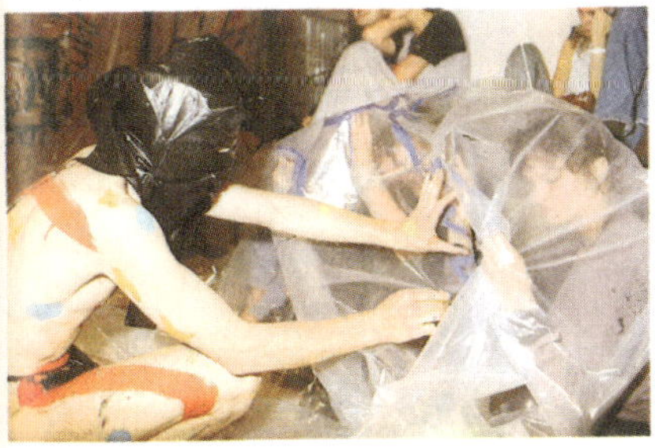

7 Cesar Olhagaray in BILDTHEATER, Kunstexperimentelle Werkstatt

8 Micha Brendel in DER MUTTERSEELENALLEINERING, Performance und Erkenntniß ART

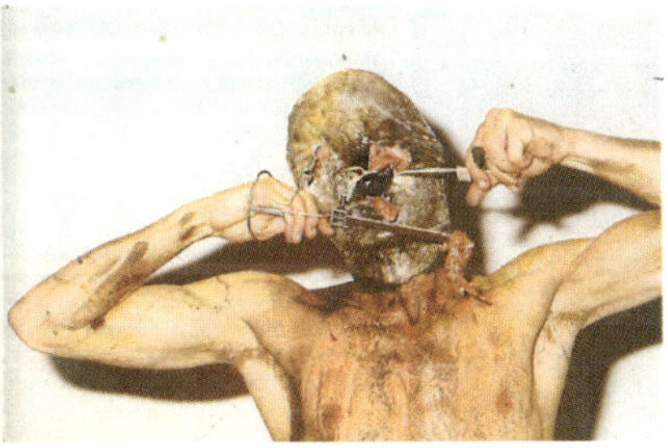

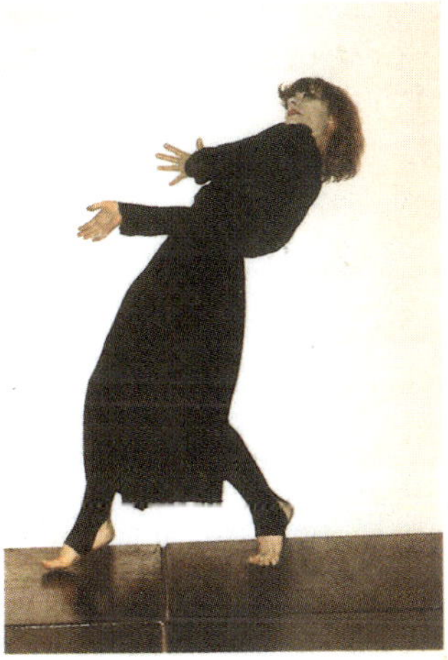

9 Hanne Wandtke (und Waldemar Wirsing), Performance Irritationen

10 Micha Brendel in DER MUTTERSEELENALLEINERING, Performance und Erkenntniß ART

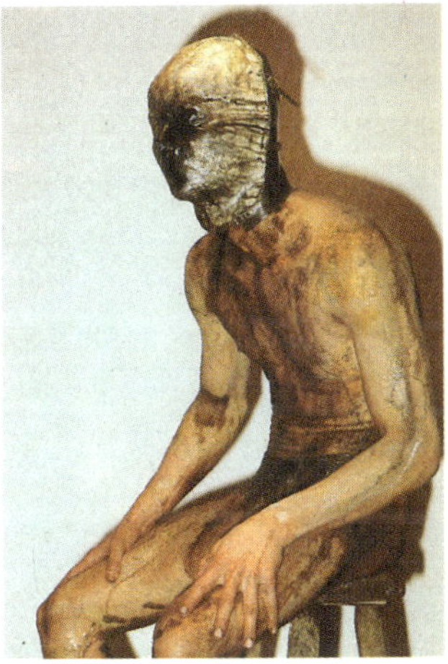

0.1

Photo spread from *Bildende Kunst* magazine (October 1989). Documentation of performances by various artists at the Permanent Art Conference, June 1989, East Berlin. Photographs by Jochen Wermann. Reprinted with the permission of Jochen Wermann. © 1989 by Jochen Wermann.

artists and organizers (including Tannert) had faced recrimination from the state in response to the Intermedia I Festival, a weekend of experimental art, film, and music that took place in a cultural center just outside Dresden. Meanwhile, support for experimental forms continued to grow among art historians such as Gabriele Muschter and Klaus Werner. In 1988, Muschter joined forces with Werner—whose longtime support of experimental forms had led to his expulsion from the SED[2] political party and the closure of his Galerie Arkade (Arcade Gallery)—to form a group of like-minded art historians who shared the objective of reforming the artists' union. The group—which included Barbara Barsch, Ina Gille, Andreas Hüneke, Henry Schumann, and Tannert—drafted a manifesto, which Barsch presented at the tenth Union of Fine Artists congress in 1988. The text in part urged that the organization begin a scholarly examination of the performance art movement in the GDR. In response, the union commissioned Tannert and the art historian Eugen Blume to compile an East Berlin-based history of performance art and other live art forms, which fell under the blanket term *Aktionskunst*.[3] Their list demonstrated both the history and the increasing significance of process-oriented art for the GDR's youngest generation of artists, and inspired the Union of Fine Artists to support and help disseminate the form. For 1989's Permanent Art Conference, cultural officials ceded the entire month of June in one of the GDR's most high-profile galleries in its capital city to a contingent of artists whose work could not have been further afield from the socialist realism that had defined the foundations of the GDR's cultural and political agenda. The event was hosted, publicized, and archived entirely on the dime of the state. Although no other experimental art event had ever received such publicity in the GDR, the scope of the Permanent Art Conference, including its visibility, was actually foreseeable, even inevitable. Demonstrating that inevitability is a core aim of this book.

By 1989, artists and organizers had been chipping away at the foundations of state culture for years. Examining how experimental artists infiltrated the communist Germany's cultural garrisons reveals that the strategies they used were not acts of subterfuge, but discernible ploys: the novel and conspicuous use of the body in performance art or photography that challenged conventional modes of representation; the Super-8 film cameras that artists employed to record themselves; the typewritten pages, photographs, and silkscreens that appeared in independent publications; the gathering places that turned enclaves into spectacles. Artists infiltrated state culture by meting out its excesses. They tested the hard-line intolerance of cultural innovation advertised by cultural bureaucracy. They hedged their bets on the threats of state security forces, and won. They identified with and sought approval from each other, even as they benefited from the advantages of the state culture whose approval they foreswore, but whose financial incentives they enjoyed. In their dedication to creative autonomy, experimental artists exposed a core vulnerability in state power—namely, its reliance on a unified national culture to reflect its communist ideology.

Without an adequate analysis of these artists as dissenters and witnesses, subjects and agents, we will continue to miscalculate the role culture played in the GDR's rapid decline. This book rewrites the history of experimental art in late East Germany by analyzing photography, performance art, film, publications, and galleries in both tacit and direct relation to public life. It thus defines the scene as a parallel public to reveal how artists engaged with the state to both exceed and expose its core disjunctions. Across seven chapters and a coda, the text focuses on people who used body-based practices like photography, film, and performance art to create new vocabularies for representation, which they then shared through independent networks of distribution and display. Uniting the metaphorical surface of the body with the literal surface of print and film, artists and filmmakers exceeded the restrictions on mobility and exchange imposed on them by Cold War geopolitics. And yet, even as artists, publishers, and gallerists scorned conventions of official cultural production, they did not hide from state authorities in the way one might expect, particularly given how thoroughly the secret police (the Ministry for State Security, or Stasi) monitored the scene. Instead, artists undermined state authority through forthright rather than covert projects that redefined the space of culture. Guileless, adaptive, and persistent, artists proved to be wily targets, immune to the conventional tactics of state control. That immunity, I argue, is symptomatic of a systemic problem of state culture, which by the 1980s could no longer dictate, let alone maintain, a coherent nation.

By the Cold War's final decade, the East German government's inability to produce a collective public significantly frayed its power. The work of experimental artists not only diagnosed a weakening state, but also served as its antidote: a mirror and a foil to official culture. The GDR's experimental scene produced an alternative public—a parallel public—with commitments to art, community, and interdisciplinarity that state socialism had sought but failed to inspire. This irony, really an inversion of state socialist principle, lies at the heart of this book.

PREMISES FOR EXPERIMENTATION

The Permanent Art Conference is a culminating moment in the history of experimental art in the GDR. If not for the fall of the Berlin Wall on November 9, 1989, more events of its scale and scope would have certainly taken place within the official cultural sector. Given the high profile the event enjoyed, restrictions that the Union of Fine Artists and cultural bureaucrats had placed on festival organizers—such as a prohibition of West German artists from the program—would very likely have been eased for future events. In fact, during the Permanent Art Conference, artists who had already found a way to work around this limitation set the course for these relaxations. A parallel program that featured people from West Germany ran at rg, a collective studio/gallery organized by the performance artist Erhard Monden and the mail artist and Union of Fine Artists graphic designer Robert Rehfeldt, among others.[4] These kinds of adaptations and innovations, coupled with a robust roster of exhibitions, screenings, and live events, as well as key participation by people officially aligned with the state's cultural institutions allowed the experimental scene to thrive. Neither the cultural nor the surveillance armature of the state could curb the rise of this artistic scene. Acting largely with indifference to state power, artists and organizers also became a moving target for the secret police. Even when the Stasi was present, actions that would have earlier justified police response became increasingly defensible as the list of contributors with an official stamp of state approval grew.

Tension existed essentially from the GDR's beginning between cultural authorities who sought to define a national culture and artists who sought both to resist and to influence the official aesthetic program. The first known work of performance art took place in Rehfeldt's East Berlin studio in 1953. No documentation of *Ich bleibe in der DDR* (*I'm Staying in the GDR*) exists, but it is described as essentially a lecture, in which Rehfeldt appeared before an audience of friends and declared his commitment to building a communist culture in the GDR.[5] Responding to a consequential brain drain of artists and intellectuals who sought to escape the cultural provisos and material privation that defined East Germany, Rehfeldt expressed a familiar attitude among the experimental artists of his generation; even the most unconventional artists embraced the ideology of communism and took seriously their role in shaping the GDR through cultural production. This position held well into the 1970s. Some key figures of this study—including the organizer Tannert, the writer, artist, and activist Gabriele Stötzer,[6] the filmmaker Gino

Hahnemann, and the gallerist Gerd Harry "Judy" Lybke—also elected to stay in the GDR rather than seek emigration papers to move West. In contrast to Rehfeldt, they were motivated not by an attachment to communism but by more localized and personal factors. Both Tannert and Lybke advocated for a unique and globally significant East German scene. Stötzer—after a yearlong imprisonment for participating in a public protest against the 1976 expatriation of the beloved singer Wolfgang Biermann—stayed so she could advocate for the country's maligned subjects, particularly women.

Paradoxically, the value that experimental artists held for their place in the world as creative people mirrored the value that the GDR's official mandate placed on culture. Although they did not seek to advance a specific political agenda, artists had internalized an almost utopian idealism about art's possibilities that was in part indebted to the national culture within which they had been raised. Also influential were the world-building agendas of the historical (and especially German) avant-garde, from Die Brücke to Dada. Of course, as the critic and philosopher Boris Groys has demonstrated, Stalinist aesthetics were themselves premised in—and, in his estimation, actualized—the promises of the avant-garde, particularly its agenda to collapse art and life.[7]

With Germany's modern art legacy in mind, East German artists approached the creative process as a philosophical enterprise with the objective of obtaining greater personal autonomy. Their hope for pure or authentic expression seems at times naïve, even quaint, when set against the backdrop of postmodern artistic practice emerging concurrently in the West. And yet in the GDR we witness the dissolution of the other side of the debates over aesthetics and politics that produced the formalist aesthetic which defined the Cold War West. Just as abstraction quickly degenerated into an armature of commercial culture, the political ambitions of the Eastern Bloc fell into the trap of kitsch that the art critic Clement Greenberg predicted.[8] In both the capitalist West and the communist East, the strict ideological agendas imposed upon cultural production—that is to say, the suggestion that there could ever be a uniform and universal vision for globalized culture—followed a similar path that led to a more critical form of culture. In the West, that criticality manifested in an anticonsumerist aesthetic philosophy with a significant influence on public life. Art and cultural historians have long admired, critiqued, and theorized this contribution. In the East, experimental artists likewise drew attention to the inconsistencies and hypocrisies of a universalizing cultural vision. Their impact, including their art's representation of the false consensus underpinning the collective identity upon which the power of the state depended, has yet to be taken seriously. To that end, *Parallel Public* occasionally introduces ways that experimental practice in the late GDR also referred back to modernist histories and questions of subject formation in culture that are meaningful beyond the East German context. The history of the GDR's experimental art complicates the definitions of art practice in the post-World War II era, even as it renews them. This book uncovers how a culture born of modernism but raised in state socialism pursued on its own terms many of the same issues central to what has come to define artistic practice in the West.

ARTISTS OF THE 1980S

To be clear, artists working in experimental but socialist-minded modes before the 1980s also largely rejected the scripted politicized art of "typical" socialist realist aesthetics. After Joseph Stalin's death in 1953, even state-sponsored artists in the GDR were not required to meet the idealism of his orthodox cultural philosophy.[9] Nevertheless, by the 1980s, for the vast majority of artists an amorphous set of individualized aesthetic ambitions had long replaced a shared hope for a communist-minded world. The literary scholar Wolfgang Emmerich's identification of three generations of East Germans offers a clear timeline for this artistic drift from the GDR's official, ideological center.[10] East Germany's first generation adhered most faithfully to the socialist realist doctrine, including its attack on aesthetic formalism. These people were generally already middle-aged or older at the end of World War II. The second generation, born between 1915 and the late 1930s, was willing to participate in building a socialist state, but was nevertheless critical of it. The third generation had all but abandoned the political idealism of socialism, and chose instead to work not only independent of but also largely indifferent to its credo. To wit, the writer Uwe Kolbe describes the condition of being "born into" (*hineingeboren*) the GDR's state socialism as the unifying hallmark of his generation.[11] In his framing, Kolbe underscores East Germanness as an accident of birth, rather than the opportunity for self-actualization that governmental leaders had continued to claim it to be. His term is in fact literal, referring explicitly to people born around the time of the Berlin Wall's surprise erection in 1961. These are the subjects of this study.

Those born into the GDR came to adulthood during a period of marked social strain that undermined the authority of the country's leaders as well as the surety of its ideological foundation. While actually celebrated by some artists as an opportunity to produce a communist culture unadulterated by the influence of capitalism,[12] the Berlin Wall (officially called the "anti-fascist protection rampart") had lost its allure by the 1980s. By the time this generation entered early adulthood, East Germans had witnessed the public censure of a series of visionary artists who had sought to recast socialist culture in a more globally minded mold. Among the most impactful of these crisis moments in state culture was the Eleventh Plenary Session of the SED. At the December 1965 meeting, officials censored nearly all feature films of the year and fired a number of important figureheads deemed responsible for their content.[13] The twelve condemned films are today regarded as some of the GDR's finest and are also held up as examples of the pinnacle of socialist film.[14] Hope for a renewed progressive and dialogical mass culture came in 1971 when Erich Honecker, the newly minted SED party chairman, promised to maintain a "tabooless" cultural order.[15] That hope was short-lived. As noted above, in 1976 Honecker summarily reversed course when he expatriated the beloved singer-songwriter Wolfgang Biermann while he was on a legally sanctioned concert tour in West Germany. For many East Germans, Biermann represented the contribution that the communist Germany could make to world culture. His censure thus shook the country to its core. Honecker defended his decision, claiming that Biermann had become "involved in a smear campaign against the Socialist Order which was organized abroad."[16] Unsurprisingly, the evidence for this alleged subterfuge amounted to typical political doublespeak that served to justify governmental authority and suppress its contestation.

The expatriation of Biermann resulted in the first-ever public outcry against the government to be made jointly by key cultural figures. Over one hundred writers, including the world-famous Christa Wolf, Heiner Müller, and Jurek Becker, as well as other cultural role models like the film star Manfred Krug, wrote an open letter condemning Honecker for exiling Biermann. Calling the move autocratic, the signatories demanded an open dialogue. A public conversation never transpired. Instead, the letter writers received threats of punishment, including loss of professional memberships and positions in the Writers Union (Schriftstellerverband) or proscription from future opportunities. Becker and Krug soon left the GDR; many more followed suit. The "Biermann Affair" triggered a loss of confidence in state culture among a generation of younger artists who no longer believed that the government would manage, let alone initiate, a progressive or artist-led communist culture in East Germany.[17] This was a decisive event for the *hineingeboren* generation represented in this book. In fact, whereas few of the well-known signatories of the Biermann letter ultimately faced real recrimination, younger people who campaigned in solidarity with them were severely disciplined. The first and sixth chapter of this text both illuminate how Gabriele Stötzer's yearlong imprisonment for gathering signatures on her college campus in support of Biermann led her to reject political activism in favor of writing, filmmaking, and performance art. Stötzer's turn away from politics is emblematic of her generation. Many had lost confidence in the government's willingness to cooperate with its citizenry, let alone the artists it claimed to support. Observing a similar shift away from centralized politics among experimental artists in other Eastern Bloc countries, the art historian Klara Kemp-Welch summons the Czech activist Václav Havel when she calls this tendency an "antipolitical" stance. As opposed to the apolitical, the antipolitical refers to what Havel described as "politics outside the sphere of power."[18] Also a dissident writer, Havel was known in the GDR for his political activism. Though they were reviled by the state, his texts appeared in East Germany's independent magazines, including in the Leipzig-based *Anschlag*, which is discussed in the seventh chapter of this book. Importantly, the rejection of state politics in favor of more localized forms of political representation was not unique to artists. Numerous studies on public life in East Germany and the Eastern Bloc demonstrate that disaffection from state politics defined the Cold War's final decade.[19] What artists did was represent that disaffection. In this regard, their production of a parallel public is not so much countercultural or dissident as it is anti-idealistic and realistic.

"ENGINEERS OF THE HUMAN SOUL"

The GDR—like the rest of the Eastern Bloc—adopted socialist realism as its official aesthetic. This politico-aesthetic cultural philosophy united art and culture to the ideological vision of communism. Cultural policy was then political policy. The "realism" of socialist realism was meant to be new, critical, and—counterintuitively—antinaturalistic. "Unlike naturalism," the historian Régine Robin writes, "the new realism is not limited to being a copy, a photograph or reality; it is not simply constative, but depicts reality in its dynamics, its movements, its development. It is not limited to fragments but seeks the *totality* of the social relationships of an era."[20] As a totalizing aesthetic, socialist realism was inherently idealistic and aspirational, providing a narrative of history that glorified the proletarian and a view of the present always one step ahead of reality. All visual objects were thus meant to not only reaffirm the national vision, but to construct it.

The GDR inherited the formal structure of its cultural bureaucracy, as well as the socialist realist doctrine, from Soviet powers in the immediate post-World War II period of occupation.[21] Mirroring projects in place in the Soviet Union since the October Revolution, which had sought to bring art equally to the masses regardless of location, East Germany's ruling party poured money into establishing cultural centers across the country. The government sustained its interest in these spaces and included them in new apartment complexes and building renovations alike. As a Stasi report on Berlin-based cultural centers compiled in the 1980s attests, the quantity of these centers was not insubstantial. National policy had long supported the arts. During the Soviet occupation (1945–1949), artists actually benefited from a law that permitted "qualified scholars, engineers, and artists" to receive the class one ration cards ordinarily reserved for "heavy laborers and workers in hazardous trades."[22] East German officials continued to prioritize cultural workers even after it achieved its own autonomy in 1949. Funds for artists were ample, making it possible for those admitted into the Union of Fine Artists (as well as those in training at art schools) to earn comfortable incomes and to reap housing, material, and even travel benefits otherwise unavailable to the average citizen. Artists earned these kinds of rewards because they were expected to lead a cultural renewal through the adoption and dissemination of communist ideology in their art—to be, in Stalin's famous dictum, "the engineers of the human soul."[23] Importantly (and ironically), state-mandated support for artists contributed to the success of experimental practice in the 1980s. Specifically, artists came to understand how they could benefit from the GDR's cultural system without compromising their creative integrity.

DEFINING OFFICIAL CULTURE

By the 1980s, the status quo had remained essentially the same since the establishment of the GDR in 1949. Public life was still defined by ritualized (essentially obligatory) cultural events that reaffirmed a homogeneous national identity. From a May Day celebration to a brigade brass band to the regularly scheduled art exhibitions

I n h a l t s v e r z e i c h n i s

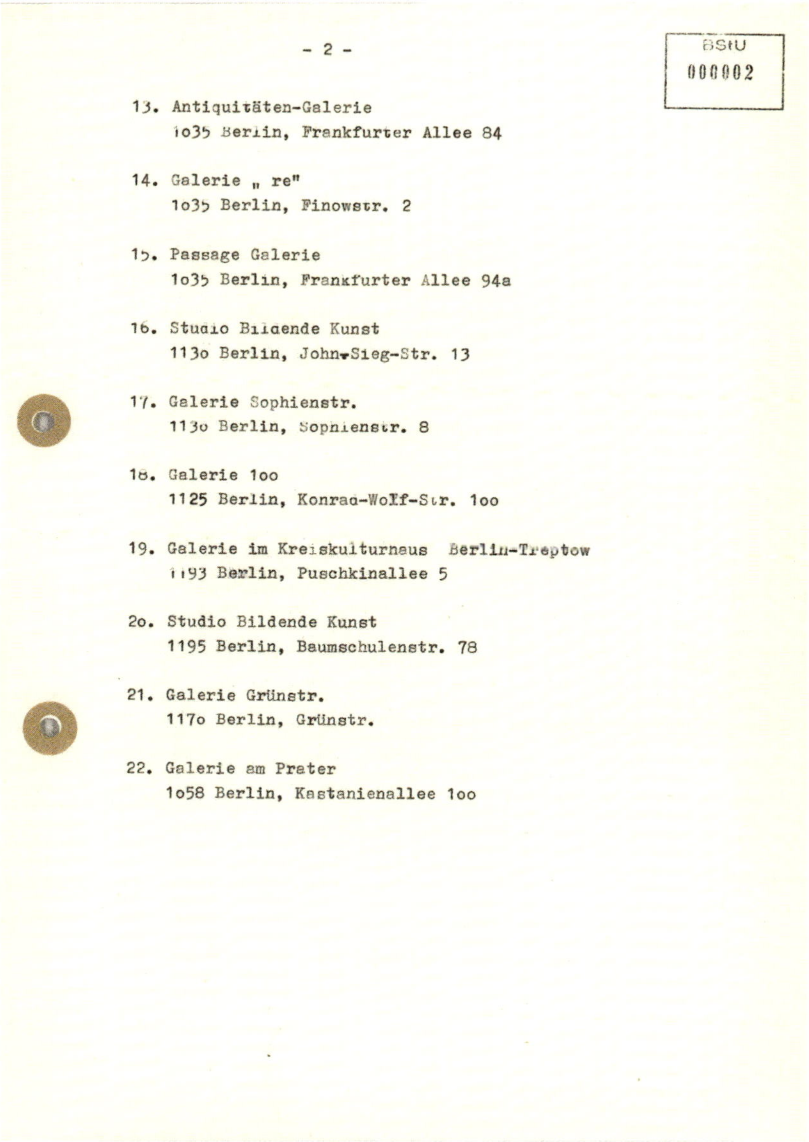

BStU
000002

13. Antiquitäten-Galerie
1o35 Berlin, Frankfurter Allee 84

14. Galerie „ re"
1o35 Berlin, Finowstr. 2

15. Passage Galerie
1o35 Berlin, Frankfurter Allee 94a

16. Studio Bildende Kunst
113o Berlin, John-Sieg-Str. 13

17. Galerie Sophienstr.
113o Berlin, Sophienstr. 8

18. Galerie 1oo
1125 Berlin, Konrad-Wolf-Str. 1oo

19. Galerie im Kreiskulturhaus Berlin-Treptow
1193 Berlin, Puschkinallee 5

2o. Studio Bildende Kunst
1195 Berlin, Baumschulenstr. 78

21. Galerie Grünstr.
117o Berlin, Grünstr.

22. Galerie am Prater
1o58 Berlin, Kastanienallee 1oo

0.2

"Inhaltsverzeichnis" (Contents). BStU, MfS, HA II, Nr. 33928, 1–2. Reprinted with the permission of the Bundesbeauftragte für die Unterlagen des Staatssicherheitsdienstes der ehemaligen Deutschen Demokratischen Republik via the Stasi Records Act (StUG) § 32.

organized by the Union of Fine Artists, mass culture was exceedingly predictable. Over the decades, even as participation in such events remained constant, the investment in the politics they represented waned considerably. In his research on the late Soviet Union, the anthropologist Alexei Yurchak calls this the "performative shift": over time, participating in the rituals of public life in state socialism became more important than believing in the ideological meaning of those rituals.[24] Similarly, the historian Mary Fulbrook describes East Germany as a "participatory dictatorship." The "somewhat oxymoronic expression," she writes, "is intended to underline the ways in which the people themselves were at one and the same time both constrained and affected by, and yet also actively and often voluntarily carried, the ever changing social and political system of the GDR."[25] Voluntary compliance does not, however, equal a cowed or frightened public. Rather, a person's decision to attend a public event often reflected a calculation of future benefit more than a shared ideological commitment. Through her research on mass culture in the GDR, the historian Esther von Richthofen demonstrates that cultural functionaries, artists, and average citizens alike all recognized that influence or gain in society required active participation in public life.[26] Some people simply kept up appearances, others located spaces where oversight was weak or—even better—where those in charge were sympathetic and allowed for more dynamic engagement with culture. Citizens could then root out other meanings or possibilities for themselves—including for their own benefit—from within official culture to the effect that "participants and functionaries determined the nature of cultural activity" often not just at a remove from but in contradiction with an official national agenda.[27]

Of course, superficial participation does not equal political resistance. As Yurchak writes, "the ability of a sign to break with context in itself is politically and ethically neutral, until invested with new meaning."[28] In fact, he argues that the "immutable and predictable aspects of state socialism, and its creative and unpredictable possibilities became mutually constitutive," and that state culture "actually *enabled* the emergence of diverse, multiple, and unpredictable meanings in everyday life."[29] This view rightly acknowledges that the government anticipated the possibility that people would find ways to work the system for their benefit. As Richthofen demonstrates, an increasing governmental tolerance of leisure activities went hand in hand with greater oversight and incorporation of these activities into organized cultural life.[30] It is thus equally no surprise that the Ministry for State Security shifted course on its surveillance operations in the wake of Honecker's "tabooless" society, as well as in response to the uproar against the Biermann expatriation. In 1976, it began its so-called *Zersetzung* (corrosion) strategy, which targeted the private lives of individuals.[31] The simultaneous emergence of more private-oriented forms of culture and the enlistment of neighbors, friends, lovers, and family members to spy on these activities as *Inoffizielle Mitarbeiter* (unofficial collaborators, or IMs) reflects a calculated governmental response to a transforming citizenry.

Yet perfunctory engagements with official culture ought not call into question the sincerity of the GDR's experimental art scene. Understanding how the East German citizenry on average dealt with public life as a prerequisite for rather than as a satisfaction of personal fulfillment helps to explain the context within which experimental artists emerged in the 1980s. They too had ritually performed the duties of public life. From attending universities to receiving degrees that gave them legitimacy and social standing to applying for membership in the artists' union, these activities were entry points to creative autonomy with positive outcomes akin to those enjoyed by a person who attended a May Day celebration to garner favor with a supervisor. Such performances of public life occasioned cultural gains that could be bartered privately, on one's own terms.

Indeed, the reality of individual experience demonstrates that artists following a path to professionalization in the GDR had far greater autonomy than the rules of cultural bureaucracy would seem to have allowed. Take for instance the art academy. Invitation to study at one of the GDR's four art schools was extremely competitive.[32] In 1986, only 6 out of 107 applicants received entry into the Weißensee Academy of Art (Weißensee Kunsthochschule) in Berlin.[33] However, some areas of study were easier to enter than others; painting, for example, remained a prized subject, while set design did not. This hierarchy of media, embedded in the aesthetic credo of socialist realism, unintentionally opened up possibilities for creative autonomy, as is clearly demonstrated by the history of the Auto-Perforation Artists, who met as set design students at the Dresden Academy of Fine Arts. The second chapter of this book examines these artists, as well as their impact on the formation of the performance art movement that would inspire 1989's Union of Fine Artists-sponsored Permanent Art Conference.

Disciplinary differences as well as the influence of individual instructors diminished the efficacy of the many layers of bureaucracy put into place to monitor and curate arts education and production. For example, under his directorship of the Leipzig Academy of Fine Arts (Hochschule für Grafik und Buchkunst), the painter

Bernhard Heisig established a tradition of learning and teaching modern art styles and history. In her book on Heisig, the art historian April Eisman demonstrates that the painter—who by all accounts reaped the greatest benefits of the state's support—faced regular controversies in response to his advocacy for experimental forms of art, as well as for artists who produced and taught them within the Leipzig school.[34] While directing the art academy, Heisig hired the neoexpressionist painter Hartwig Ebersbach who himself went on to mentor the artist Hans-Joachim Schulze, with whom Ebersbach later established the experimental art collective Gruppe 37,2 (Group 37.2). In the early 1980s Gruppe 37,2 presented a series of public performances across the country, thus contributing to the profusion of collectively made and experimental forms of art that came to define East Germany in its later period. In 1981, Schulze also became the first of Ebersbach's students to defend an experimental artwork as his thesis project. It bears mentioning that Schulze ultimately left the GDR in 1986, stating that "there was nothing more to fight for."[35] In late 1983, he had been placed under house arrest after organizing an action painting event at the Freie Deutsche Jugend (Free German Youth) club in Leipzig-Grünau, which he had recently been hired to revitalize. Had Schulze possessed the international notoriety that Heisig, and to some extent Ebersbach, enjoyed, he might have overcome this humiliation. It also seems certain, given the history to follow, that had Schulze created his work only a few years later, he would not have faced the same challenges.

The example of three generations of artists producing unconventional, "experimental" artwork from within state-run institutions begs an important question: What did "experimental" mean in the context of the art of the GDR? Endorsements by or within the bureaucracies of official culture certainly muddy the definition of "experimental," as well as the division between so-called official and unofficial culture. The Leipzig case is one of many instances of the entanglement of official and unofficial culture evident in the GDR's final decade. The impossibility of dividing these two seemingly adversarial arenas has inspired scholars of the Eastern Bloc, including East Germany, to define the interstitial space where experimental art emerged as a "second public sphere."[36] The term in this context helps to theorize more accurately the uncertain dominion that official culture had over the GDR's artists. Moreover, the idea of a "parallel public" draws attention to the ways in which artists used the apparatuses of official culture (that is, the "first public sphere") to advance their own agendas. In this book, then, the concept of a parallel public embraces the "second public sphere," while also maintaining the centrality of average—that is to say, official—public life to the development of experimental forms of art in late East Germany.

My use of the term "parallel" also relates to the performance theorist and artist Bojana Cvejić's suggestion that the art of the Eastern Bloc be read "parallel" to art of the West. "Parallelism," she writes "reveals the difference in the use of art, not in aesthetic categories of form and style."[37] Her framework of seeing art as an instrument, rather than a dialectic in conversation with western art practices, defines Eastern Bloc experimental artists as engaged in a process of problem solving or problem posing, which draws from all available artistic modes to articulate, resolve, or simply work through an idea.[38] Cvejić underscores that adaptability and flexibility—both in terms of the process of making art and in its presentation and consumption—define an aesthetic impulse visible across the art of the Eastern Bloc. Parallelism places art made in state socialism outside the metrics of aesthetics used to evaluate art from the West, allowing art from the Eastern Bloc to be the same, but different. Defining the art of the GDR within its contextual specificity is a central objective of this book. In this regard, *Parallel Public* describes the ways in which East Germany's experimental art scene ran parallel to both the GDR's official public (including, but not exclusively, in relation to state culture) and global contemporary art, both consciously and unconsciously.

THE POLITICS OF AESTHETICS

Experimental artists comprised what Christoph Tannert calls a *Notgemeinschaft* (emergency society), which existed primarily for the sake of itself.[39] The politics of their aesthetics comprised an explicit rejection of politics as advanced by the state: mass-organized, ideological, utopian, communist. And although—to think again with Havel via Kemp-Welch—to be antipolitical is not necessarily to be apolitical, it is nevertheless a tacit objective of this text to differentiate artistic experimentation from the very concentrated efforts of activists involved in 1989's civil rights movement who challenged state power through public demands for a more democratic GDR. Yet a hard line does not need to be drawn between the two; some artists certainly defined themselves as political activists. Gabriele Stötzer, for example, played an instrumental role in preventing the full-scale destruction of the East German government's secret police files, while the filmmaker and poet Gino Hahnemann participated in the gay rights movement. Nevertheless, civic-minded, actionable politics did not directly inform the art of even these two makers.

A tendency to define official culture in opposition to unofficial culture in both the literature and, more importantly, the popular conception of the Eastern Bloc has come at the expense of understanding the agency that artists could claim even within state-sanctioned spaces.[40] Homogenizing the motivations of experimental artists has caused some of the finer points of creative individuation to be missed. These artists were not necessarily consciously working to build something against the state. Rather, they were people working side by side, responding to like frustration and privation that produced and reinforced an aesthetic cohesion. With the Germanist Anna Horakova, who argues that East Berlin poets "contradict rather than confirm their stated claim to *Aussteigertum* (outsiderness), or utter disassociation from the East German state,"[41] I likewise resist descriptions that categorize or reduce an often-contradictory scene into binaries of official versus unofficial culture. Allowing for the state to be an ontological category that artists *dealt* with, but did not necessarily directly challenge, opens analysis in two directions. First, it allows for descriptions that include the ways that artists consciously considered their cultural condition as contingent, something that could be distressed and weakened through critical practice. As Horakova writes, the Prenzlauer Berg writers' "poetic and visual practices evince an actively engaged attitude towards [the state] by formally mimicking the political and cultural context from which they emerge."[42] This form of critical citation was also relevant to East Germany's visual artists. Second, recognizing official culture as a shared interest helps to move experimental art from the margins of East German culture to its center. In reality, for experimental artists, adaptability—including the willingness to move fluidly between official and unofficial culture—defined an important line of defense, which also opened up new modes of creativity.

As noted above, *Parallel Public* focuses on body-based and/or interdisciplinary practices, as well as the modes of distribution and display, which fortified and expanded the reach of the experimental scene. Many artists have been omitted here for the sake of clarity. To this point, historiographies of East Germany's experimental art have tended to be more exhaustive than argumentative, with Paul Kaiser's collaborative work with Claudia Petzold (*Boheme und Diktatur in der DDR*, 1997) and his recent expansion (*Boheme in der DDR*, 2016) among the most significant texts. Exhibitions at both art and history museums have led the research into the experimental art of East Germany (in fact, Kaiser and Petzold's 1997 text is an exhibition catalog). Major curatorial projects have followed *Boheme und Diktatur*'s attention to regions; the titles of recent catalogs reflect this tendency: *Revolution im geschlossenen Raum. Die andere Kultur in Leipzig 1970–1990* (edited by Grundmann, Michael, and Seufert, 2002); *Ohne uns! Kunst und alternative Kultur in Dresden vor und nach '89* (edited by Eckhardt and Kaiser, 2009), and *Zwischen Ausstieg und Aktion. Die Erfurter Subkulture der 1960er, 1970er und 1980er Jahre* (edited by Büchner and Knorr, 2014). Other groundbreaking studies are media specific, as evident in the leading texts such as Claus Löser's monograph on experimental film, *Strategien der Verweigerung* (2011) or Uwe Warnke and Ingeborg Quass's edited volume on the independent publishing scene, *Die Addition der Differenzen* (2009). New approaches are emerging. For example, the Germanist Seth Howes's book *Moving Images on the Margins: Experimental Film in Late Socialist East Germany* (2019), which unites small-guage film work to the GDR's history of performance art, does much to demonstrate the fluidity of genre that defined experimental forms of art in late East Germany. A necessary amount of attention has been paid to gendered aspects of the experimental art scene; I am indebted to the pathbreaking research of art historians such as Susanne Altmann, Bettina Knaup, Angelika Richter, and Beatrice Stammer.

In contrast to the majority of these studies, my book is deliberately not encyclopedic, region-based, or media- or gender-specific, but is rather driven by my objective to demonstrate, through well-detailed case studies, the breadth of experimental practice in the late GDR, as well as the clever organizational strategies that supported it. As a caveat—or disclaimer—I would like to add that my omission of the concurrent neoexpressionist painting movement, which took hold in East Germany's art schools in the 1980s, is also intentional. I decided that the subject of painting, which would require a detailed accounting of East Germany's academy system as well as its artists' relationships to the history of German modernism across the twentieth century, necessitated a different set of methodologies. In short, the subject of abstract painting merits its own book. To be sure, it is with some hesitation that I signal the presence of this movement only here in an introduction. Clearly, as many examples outlined in the chapters that follow demonstrate, painting influenced a variety of artists and also contributed to multiple explorations of media—from performance art to film. I advise interested readers to examine the literature on East German art mentioned above, as well as the exhibition catalog for the 2016 show *Gegenstimmen. Kunst in der DDR 1976–1989* (*Voices of Dissent: Art in the GDR*), in which painting across generations figures prominently.

A NOTE ON SOURCES

In addition to the artwork itself, *Parallel Public* draws from four major sources: (1) interviews with more than two dozen artists, art historians, writers, and organizers; (2) artist-made publications; (3) official reports by the Union of Fine Artists, including articles from its flagship publication *Bildende Kunst*; and (4) Stasi surveillance records. This combination of sources provides an impression of how the collapse of the GDR, including revelations about the extent of spying, has complicated the experimental art scene's narrative of creative autonomy as well as the state's vision of its own hegemony. Although recent texts written in the fields of East German history and literature urge a more nuanced methodology,[43] foundational scholarship on the art of East Germany has read these materials in isolation or contestation. In contrast to this tendency, I bring the multiple, often-conflicting sources of personal anecdote, official and private discourse, and surveillance records together to demonstrate the entanglements of unofficial and official culture. For example, I read texts written by members of the Union of Fine Artists as records of both the art and the art historian to ask how the author's interpretation relates to his or her attachment to ideology, aesthetic theory, and attitudes about art's political function. Stasi reports by private citizens who secretly reported on people to the secret police—IMs—likewise offer a second perspective from people who had some kind of personal relationship with the person they observed. Sometimes IM accounts are careful and even seem motivated to protect or praise the people or events under observation. Other times, they are vitriolic and dismissive, written by people whose motivations, unlike the union records, are less easily defined. I interpret the ambivalence of the Stasi sources as a partial explanation for the agency that experimental artists claimed under unpredictable conditions of observation and judgment. I follow, particularly, the guidance of the historian Konrad Jarausch who wrote in 2014: "The endeavor of discerning the actual role of the [Ministry for State Security] needs to free itself from the dialectic of exaggeration by its former victims and belittling by its erstwhile members and strive instead to determine exactly what the Stasi did or did not do."[44]

Even more concretely, secret police reports actually add material details about an event that were not elsewhere adequately recorded, such as an odor or the temperature of a room. For an example of this application of a report written by an IM, see the second chapter's discussion of the Auto-Perforation Artists' exhibition *Menetekel*. In fact, the sociologist Karl-Siegbert Rehberg—a leading scholar of the art of East Germany—has advocated for the use of the Stasi's "Summary Reports" (*Sachstandberichte*) in interpretations of these experimental artists. He writes that these texts "on the 'operational findings in the work on observed people (*OV-Personen*)' were written in great detail, and have today proven themselves to be precise descriptions of art actions."[45]

The motivations of Stasi spies are obviously suspect. It is thus impossible to calculate the accuracy of their reports. In fact, the historian Jens Gieseke has demonstrated that Stasi officials altered their texts to please their superiors.[46] To that end, in addition to reading secret police reports in conjunction with other primary sources, I carefully look at these texts for recurring themes, cyclical thinking, and redundancies, which I interpret as shortcomings in the power of the secret police. This method is inspired by postcolonial scholars who, in the words of Ann Laura Stoler, advise reading the archives of colonial powers "along the archival grain."[47] In other words, preoccupations and repetition—that is to say, conspicuous content—reveal vulnerabilities that will otherwise go unrecorded. In the case of the GDR, reports reveal a surveillance state essentially spinning its wheels. For example, officers responding to a report on a screening of a film with "antisocial" tendencies may have requested further observation, but rarely demanded direct or punitive action. In general, my research reveals a state power still beholden to a vision of proletarian conversion therapy, as the police apparatus believed artists could be set on a better path through exposure to ideology. When this did not work, the Stasi took little action other than sending more IMs to monitor the scene. In short, the hundreds of pages of state surveillance that I have consulted confirm that, yes, the Stasi was present in often unanticipated numbers, but that in fact their presence rarely impacted the experimental arts scene of the late GDR. My perspective will be considered controversial by many; it is well documented that leading figures in the literary scene, which often intersected with the visual arts, reported on the activities of their friends to Stasi heads.[48] Nevertheless, my research demonstrates a far from clear-cut relationship between the Stasi's tactics of information gathering and its capacity to control artists. Here the necessity of reading a Stasi report in conjunction with other sources is illuminating.

By taking seriously the state-made records that have traditionally been interpreted as evidence of oppression, I reveal the tenuous foundations of governmental power. This vantage may help to explain the rapid decline of the state after the dramatic fall of the Berlin Wall in November 1989. It will certainly help to clarify some of the reasons the experimental art scene was so varied as well as why its artists so quickly disbanded after German unification; demonstrating the former is a recurring theme throughout this book, and the latter will be addressed in its concluding chapter. Importantly, even if it seems unusual within research on East German art, my method aligns with the shift among leading historians of the GDR, including Konrad Jarausch and Mary Fulbrook, who long ago moved away from theories of totalitarianism or dictatorship and toward social or people's histories.[49] It likewise follows a trend in scholarship on the art of the Eastern Bloc that highlights citizen agency and the nuances of people's relationship to state power.[50]

Because the work I study scarcely exists in public archives or museums, access to original artworks, films, publications, and documentation must be obtained through personal relationships. The oral histories that I have collected as part of gaining access to private archives uniquely shape my conclusions. Each person I spoke with has provided me with primary material, including artworks, publications, and personal effects, otherwise unavailable in the public record. Else Gabriel, Gundula Schulze Eldowy,[51] Gabriele Stötzer, and Christoph Tannert were particularly forthcoming; their presence in this text reflects that engagement. My most important private archives have been the ex.oriente.lux collection of East German experimental film, organized by the filmmaker and film historian Claus Löser, and the EIGEN+ART archive, held and organized by the gallery's founder and director Judy Lybke. Important public archives have included the Akademie der Künste, especially its Gino Hahnemann Archive, to which the now deceased artist's longtime partner, Matthias Fischer, provided me unrestricted access. My personal relationships have also enabled me to work with records of Stasi surveillance, as permission from each person observed is required to work with the secret police files. I have acquired these through interviews conducted between 2012 and 2016 in Germany, and subsequent contact with many subjects described in this book.

ORGANIZATION AND CHAPTER OUTLINE

Parallel Public analyzes the tension between state culture and lived reality by defining East Germany's experimental art scene as a form of public life. Case studies become the lens through which to understand how artists both internalized state discourse and critiqued or retooled it for their own creative purposes. I have selected my examples for a number of reasons. First, they demonstrate the fluidity between official and unofficial culture that foregrounds my understanding of experimentation in the art of East Germany. Second, the examples reflect the vast range of practices that comprised the experimental scene, and which spanned the interconnected regions of the GDR. Further examination of any of the artists, events, galleries, or publications will reveal many more stories and points of connection.

This book begins its examination with artworks that at first seem to conform to the popular image of a totalitarian East Germany. Addressing this head on, and through the GDR's most notorious bureaucracy, chapter 1 examines Stasi-inspired artworks by Verena Kyselka, Christine Schlegel, Cornelia Schleime, Else Gabriel, and Gabriele Stötzer as reflections of a not altogether disempowered experience at the hands of the Ministry for State Security. All five artists share a common experience of being equally angered and puzzled by the contents of their files. By using excerpts, recontextualization, and restaging, Kyselka, Schlegel, Schleime, Gabriel, and Stötzer highlight aspects of their empowerment and everyday autonomy, which the Stasi may have observed and recorded, but which it could not hamper. Their artworks make plain, in short, that the ambitions of the state security system must be distinguished from its achievements.

In the GDR, cultural policy explicitly advanced the communist ideology, and all visual representation mapped the political. Artists who worked with the human form, in particular, drew attention to the ways in which the individual body had been sacrificed in service of the social body. Chapter 2 argues that artists confronted state expectations of the perfected socialist body by developing new modes of body-based expression—whether in photographic representation or in performed activity. Thomas Florschuetz's *Körperbilder* (*Body Portraits*), a series of self-portraits, symbolize the experience of self-alienation through a visual rupture in the figure. The Auto-Perforation Artists took the contradiction of real and imagined life to an extreme in performances that put their bodies at the limits of comfort and dignity. I describe these projects as allegorical and extremely visceral representations of the mental anguish that these artists diagnosed as catastrophic to the GDR's prosperity. In truth, defining East Germany's experimental art in opposition to an oppressive state offers only partial insight. This chapter ultimately wrangles with the imprecision of an allegorical interpretation by illustrating how an artistic reference to state oppression does not translate to a confession of victimization.

Simultaneous to a corporeal turn in photography and performance art was the ascent of an increasingly incisive form of portrait photography, as well as a commitment to self-documentation on Super-8 film. Chapter 3 examines these coinciding developments through two case studies. As opposed to chapter 2, which analyzes artists who consciously reveled in an aesthetic of agony to contrast with the idealism of the country's official culture, Gundula Schulze Eldowy and Cornelia Schleime offer another vantage point on the GDR's social makeup. Both used mainstream technologies of photographic reproduction—the still camera and the Super-8 film camera—and brought them to mainstream spaces—from public parks to factories—as well as private domestic interiors. State socialist ideology claimed to collapse the division between public and private life, and thus expected a clear ideological continuity across work and home life, public engagement and leisure. Schulze Eldowy and Schleime thus document the discrepancies between the state ideal and lived reality. This work of representation is about more than inserting the marginalized into a homogeneous visual field. The active public participation in the creation and consumption of Schulze Eldowy's photographs and Schleime's experimental films suggests that the citizens of the late GDR had become more critical of the machinations of mass culture. East Germany's national culture had come to be understood as a superficial and ritualistic obligation, rather than an inspiring and stabilizing force. Schulze Eldowy and Schleime thus represent a changing and increasingly critical attitude toward a centralized economy of representation.

Chapter 4 examines the work of a progenitor of the experimental film scene. In particular, Gino Hahnemann's films represent moments of communion and conviviality across several of East Germany's least accepted social strata. Writers he knew from East Berlin's experimental literature scene acted alongside friends he had made from the circus school. Visual artists, as well as teenagers bound together in a small gay scene, shared space in ways not generally witnessed in either conventional or experimental GDR society. As instruments of advocacy, Hahnemann's films contributed to his efforts to normalize homosexuality through art (as well as poetry). Importantly, he organically united that aim of advancing queer visibility with a sincere interest in Germany's cultural legacies, by making films that drew from historical icons like Goethe and historical places like the Charlottenhof Palace in Potsdam. As a writer and a filmmaker, as well as an artist and a gay man, Hahnemann also represents the interdisciplinarity and intersecting identities that were a hallmark of his generation of makers.

Chapter 5 focuses on the importance of multimedia practice and collaboration to the cohesion of the experimental scene. Setting these attributes in relation to the state's official definitions of both artistic medium and the collective, I examine how experimental artists challenged the aesthetic categories around which state policy sought to organize its public. Indeed, the impulse to compartmentalize artistic practice is the twin of the impulse to delineate the ideal socialist subject. The core case study of this chapter is the Intermedia I Festival, which took place in June 1985 at a state cultural center. The text uses the multimedia practices of several artists, with a particular focus on Lutz Dammbeck, to illustrate how artists worked across media as a way of exceeding the limits of culture imposed upon them by the state.

Chapter 6 continues the previous chapter's examination of multimedia and group-oriented artwork through an analysis of the collaborative work made by the Künstlerinnengruppe Exterra XX (Women Artists Group Exterra XX), an art collective located in the city of Erfurt. A unique but nevertheless crucial example of a union of art and politics in the experimental art scene, the collective of several dozen participants began first out of a need for women to gather and create art and ultimately led to the most significant political action undertaken by East German artists: the storming of Erfurt's Stasi headquarters in December 1989. The chapter explores another dimension of the Women Artists Group's essential figurehead, Gabriele Stötzer, who is first introduced in the book's first chapter. A former political prisoner turned artist, Stötzer demonstrates the potential radicalization—specifically a grassroots and creative one—that a disaffection from organized political life could inspire.

The final case study in chapter 7 describes how East Germany's experimental artists produced an alternative platform for sharing ideas and assembling, effectively contesting the state's monopoly on public life. While galleries became physical gathering spaces, a robust network of independent publications expanded the reach of experimental artwork by creating printed matter that could pass from hand to hand. This chapter describes how the publication *Anschlag* and the gallery EIGEN+ART, both based in Leipzig, shared a vision for a critical culture that was globally oriented. It likewise demonstrates how the work of one emboldened that of the other. By concluding the book's primary historical content in a discussion of modes of production and distribution, I emphasize how reliable and adaptable sites of exchange had the potential to make the East German cultural underground viable and impactful both within and beyond its own geographic confines.

In a coda entitled "There Is No East German Art without East Germany" I consider some of the reasons for the relative absence of this country's Cold War cultural history from contemporary scholarship, curation, and museum collections, in

Germany and beyond. The lack of interest in the art of East Germany, despite a robust and growing field of research and exhibitions on art from Central and Eastern Europe in the state and postsocialist eras, may be explained in part by the artists' intentional, and natural, distancing themselves from their past. At the same time that new examinations of the experimental art of the late GDR draws out similarities to other parts of the Eastern Bloc, a reevaluation of this art on its own terms actually helps to complicate and redefine its own specificity.

1

"NEGATIVE-HOSTILE ATTITUDES"

Artists Work Their Stasi Files

The Ministry for State Security (Stasi) dominates the popular image of East Germany. Narratives of foreign subterfuge, a collection of smell samples, interpersonal denunciation, and high-profile citizens profiting through their complicity with a surveillance state titillate and make for fascinating melodrama. However, concerns over the centrality of the Stasi in the historicization of East Germany have likewise resounded, entering public discourse prominently in 2006 when Florian Henckel von Donnersmarck released his Stasi-inspired drama *Das Leben der Anderen* (*The Lives of Others*). The East German actor Henry Hübchen, for example, denounces the film as a "fairy tale, American style," and critiques von Donnersmarck for overgeneralizing and simplifying the relationship between East German citizens and their Stasi observers.[1] In contrast, Hübchen says that "the Stasi was not just an organ of intimidation; it was despised, mocked, and ridiculed more than anything."[2] Stasi-inspired artworks by Verena Kyselka, Christine Schlegel, Cornelia Schleime, Else Gabriel, and Gabriele Stötzer[3] reveal the kind of nuanced, not altogether disempowered attitude about the Stasi that Hübchen describes. All five artists share a common experience of being equally frustrated, irritated, and bemused by the contents of their files. Through the methods of excerpting, recontextualizing, and restaging, Kyselka, Schlegel, Schleime, Gabriel, and Stötzer highlight aspects of their empowerment and everyday autonomy, which the Stasi may have observed and recorded, but which it could not hamper. Their artworks show that the ambitions of the state security system must be distinguished from its achievements.

It is significant that all five artists are women. In fact, all Stasi-inspired artworks to date have been made by women. The interest they paid to their files stands in inverse proportion to the actual attention the Ministry for State Security paid to female artists. Though a substantial academic study of gendered aspects of Stasi observation has yet to be conducted,[4] anecdotal evidence resoundingly reveals a bias against women artists. This is particularly evident in the Stasi's lack of coverage of women (which is itself symptomatic in general of East Germany's male-dominated culture, in general). For example, in comparison to her three male collaborators, Else Gabriel had far fewer reports made on her, even though she was also a core member of their performance art collective, the Auto-Perforation Artists. The omission reflects a systemic problem, namely an underestimation of women's contributions in areas outside the home. In her 2019 book on experimental art by women artists in the late German Democratic Republic (GDR), the art historian Angelika Richter foregrounds her discussion by pointing to the country's gender imbalance. Although the government took direct measures to achieve equality for women, she writes that these steps prioritized women's economic standing and were "not aimed at a fundamental criticism of supposedly 'innate' gender difference and traditional gender hierarchies."[5] Myra Marx Ferree, a sociologist, writes that although the significance of "equal treatment of women and men in an employment-centered way of life . . . as a social norm should not be underestimated . . . in the East, such evidence of formal equality was used to repress any discussion of gender inequality and to persuade women that the problems they continued to experience were their personal shortcomings."[6] Importantly, the government's dismissal of women's complaints about the GDR's gender inequality helped to spur the development of a grassroots and locally organized feminist movement in the late 1980s. The Stasi ultimately also misrecognized (or willfully refused to acknowledge) the galvanizing power of women-centered activism. Stötzer, a former political prisoner turned artist and writer, observes that the secret police paid no attention to the multitude of meetings that her artists' circle had with activists in the late 1980s.[7] The Stasi file projects that she, Kyselka, Schlegel, Schleime, and Gabriel have made reveal that the state security system was more interested in women's domestic or personal concerns than in the impacts of their activities. Of course, the contents of Stasi records, in general, have often been found to be resoundingly trivial. Nevertheless, it should come as no surprise that a state surveillance operation would underestimate the cultural or social value of women. The files demonstrate that the license to observe women as a matter of national security was in fact a thinly veiled permission to stalk them.

STASI FILES AS BIOGRAPHICAL APPROXIMATIONS

Passed in December 1991, the Stasi Records Act made the GDR's state surveillance files publicly available for the first time.[8] The Ministry for State Security had been dissolved less than two years earlier in January 1990. The opening of these files—seventy miles of which remain in state-run archives today—exposed not only their contents but the functioning of the GDR's most oppressive apparatus of governance. Revelations included the important role played by citizen spies, known as unofficial collaborators (*inoffizielle Mitarbeiter*, or IMs) whose reports on colleagues, neighbors, friends, family members, and lovers revealed just how much the East German state relied on betrayal to maintain its authority. The surveillance files made plain that, as historian Jens Gieseke observes, "a form of power-conscious statism had become the core of the Stasi's identity."[9] The realization that average people had contributed to that corruption put citizens at odds with one another. Uncovering the revelations of familial or collegial duplicity became an obsession for many.

According to Gieseke's 2014 book, since 1992, approximately 1.5 million people have requested to see their surveillance files, with an average of 85,000 to 100,000 new applications made per year since 2005.[10] Gieseke puts these numbers into perspective: "If the number of applications (which includes West German and foreign applicants) is measured against the approximately twelve million adult inhabitants of the GDR in 1989 or the approximately six million individuals listed in the central files of the MfS (about one-third of whom were not residents of the GDR), it is clear that the tide of applications will not be ebbing anytime soon."[11] These statistics, which do not account for requests from journalists or scholars, reveal a considerable fascination with the history of state surveillance in the GDR. Gieseke, however, cautions that this interest may be out of proportion. He suggests that the attention paid to the Stasi files has overshadowed the impact of other institutions and protagonists, including the ruling SED[12] party or the judges and state prosecutors of the political justice system. The historian Konrad Jarausch similarly critiques the fixation on the Stasi, which he believes "has fostered a sort of tunnel vision that sees the hand of the secret service everywhere, even where it was not."[13] "Seeing the world only through the eyes of Stasi perpetrators or victims," he warns, "runs the risk of retrospective exaggeration and ignores the relative normalcy of life around them."[14] This is not to suggest that the Stasi's impact should be reduced or relativized. Nevertheless, the tendency to treat the Stasi files as "a veritable fountain of truth" is not only methodologically

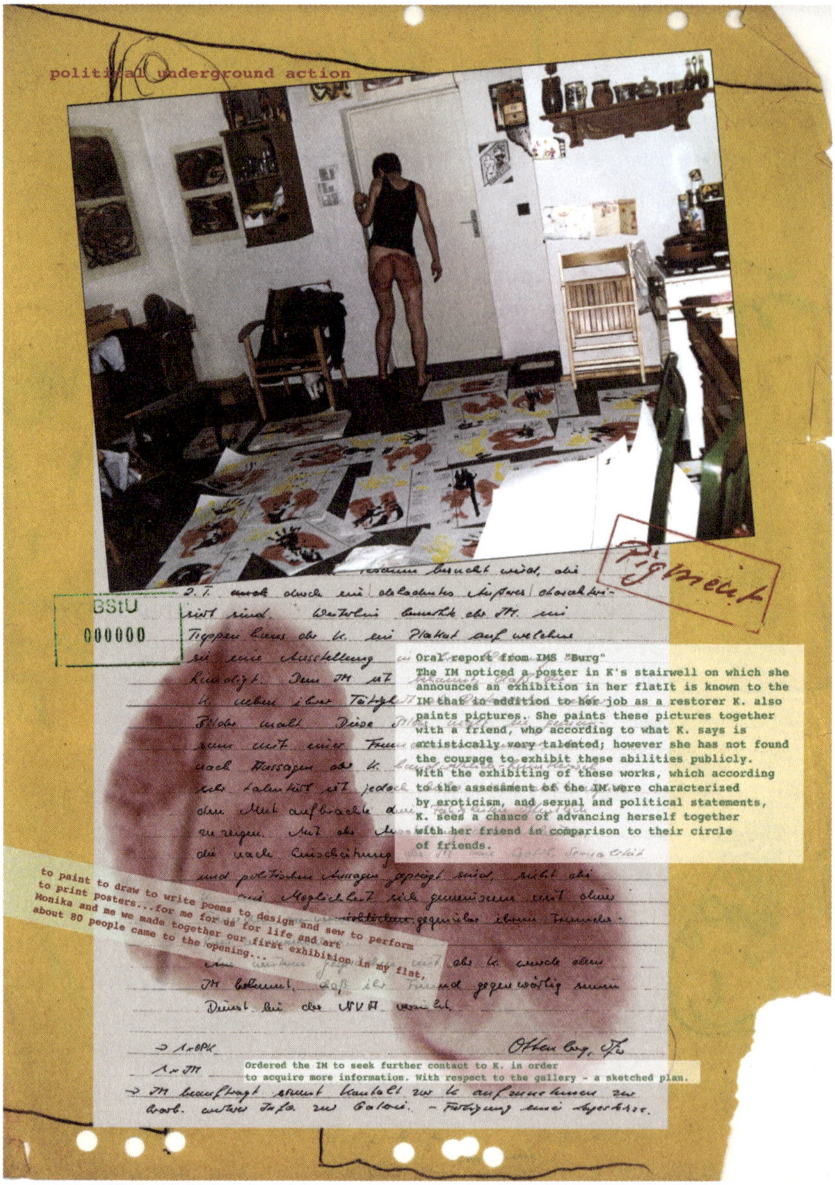

1.1

Verena Kyselka. From the series *Pigs Like Pigments*. 2007. Collage images. 100 × 70 cm. Reprinted with the permission of Verena Kyselka. © 2007 by Verena Kyselka.

unsound; it also exaggerates, and even mythologizes, the reach and impact of East Germany's secret police.[15]

Artistic uses of Stasi files expose them as motivated and prejudicial records of a person's life, records of suspicion, or even fantasy, rather than reality. Verena Kyselka's series of C-prints *Pigs Like Pigments* (2007) takes its title from the code name assigned to her surveillance file, "Pigment." The 100 x 70 cm digital collages layer photocopies of her original Stasi file with translations into English and photographs of herself in the distant past, including images taken of her during the time of her observation. The artist explains that "in *Pigs Like Pigments* I reconstruct the real facts that lay behind the contents of my Stasi file."[16] Through this project, Kyselka ultimately seeks to demonstrate "how ordinary everyday life can be falsely interpreted as subversive activity, recorded and filed, to be used as evidence against you."[17]

Christine Schlegel's series of collages *Eingeschweißte Überwachung* (*Shrink-Wrapped Surveillance*, 1999) similarly codifies the surveillance files as a surreal biographical approximation. The artist combines typewritten excerpts from her file with magazine cutouts, snapshots, and drawings. After pasting these on a canvas backing, she seals them behind melted clear plastic. The project mimics the pages of an artist's sketchbook or journal, an impression solidified by a 2001 reproduction of *Shrink-Wrapped Surveillance* in book form. The publication includes a text by Schlegel in which she describes her experience consulting the files: "I found it compelling to read a biography written from secret observations by a spy—to learn something about myself from voyeurs."[18] Like many others, Schlegel acknowledges that fabrications and embellishments make these accounts both unreliable and largely unverifiable. Her project does not account for these deceptions, but rather inhabits them visually. Her excerpts are cut from the pages of her file and placed seemingly at random among an assortment of images. Black-and-white photographs, fields of color, small paintings in rich acrylic paint, ink drawings, and magazine cutouts all share a muted beige, black, and brick-red color palette that complements the smudged and yellowing paper of the Stasi file photocopies. The "satirical and Dadaistic" content of these pages, Angelika Richter observes, reveals "the banal, absurd, and at the same time hazardous record of her person" that the texts contain.[19] *Shrink-Wrapped Surveillance* eludes easy definition of that hazard. The observations certainly represent a threat to personal sovereignty. The record is also hazardous insofar as its contents, which have been drafted by partial and at the time unsuspected observers, are fundamentally fragmentary and thus

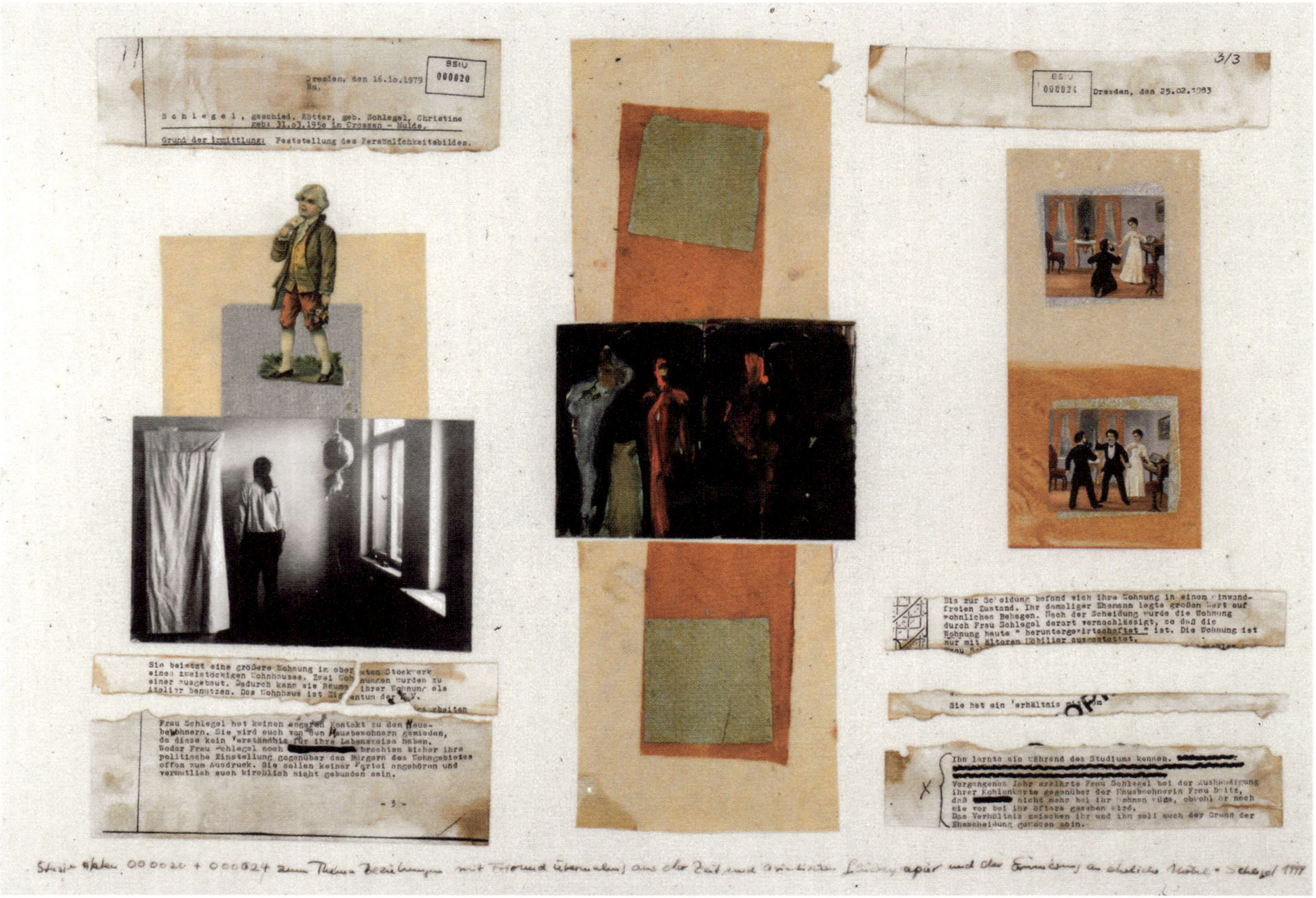
BSIU 000020
Dresden, den 16.1o.1979
Hu.
S c h l e g e l , geschied. Kütter, geb. Schlegel, Christine
geb: 31.o3.195o in Crossen - Mulde.
Grund der Ermittlung: Feststellung des Persönlichkeitsbildes.
Sie beisetzt eine größere Wohnung im obersten Stockwerk eines zweistöckigen Wohnhauses. Zwei Wohnungen wurden zu einer ausgebaut. Dadurch kann sie Räume ihrer Wohnung als Atelier benutzen. Das Wohnhaus ist Eigentum der KWV.
Frau Schlegel hat keinen engeren Kontakt zu den Hausbewohnern. Sie wird auch von den Hausbewohnern gemieden, da diese kein Verständnis für ihre Lebensweise haben. Weder Frau Schlegel noch [redacted] brachten bisher ihre politische Einstellung gegenüber den Bürgern des Wohngebietes offen zum Ausdruck. Sie sollen keiner Partei angehören und vermutlich auch kirchlich nicht gebunden sein.
- 3 -
BSIU 000024
Dresden, den 25.02.1983
3/3
Bis zur Scheidung befand sich ihre Wohnung in einem einwandfreien Zustand. Ihr damaliger Ehemann legte großen Wert auf wohnlichen Behagen. Nach der Scheidung wurde die Wohnung durch Frau Schlegel derart vernachlässigt, so daß die Wohnung heute " heruntergewirtschaftet " ist. Die Wohnung ist nur mit älteren Möbiller ausgestattet.
Sie hat ein Verhältnis
Ihn lernte sie während des Studiums kennen. [redacted]
Vergangenes Jahr erklärte Frau Schlegel bei der Aushändigung ihrer Kohlenkarte gegenüber der Hausbewohnerin Frau Beitz, daß [redacted] nicht mehr bei ihr wohnen würde, obwohl er noch wie vor bei ihr öfters gesehen wird.
Das Verhältnis zwischen ihr und ihm soll auch der Grund der Ehescheidung gewesen sein.

untrustworthy. As if in a mirror, Schlegel's randomly chosen images reveal the surveillance files to be erratic and unmethodical through her inversion of their bureaucratic order. "The reading of my files was such a curious experience," she reflects, "that I found myself leaving the archive with tears of laughter streaming down my face."[20] Important in Schlegel's work, and evident in the projects to be described below, is the simultaneous ability for the artist to both laugh at and feel a need to work through an often-unhappy past. Schlegel, for example, learned that a longtime partner spied on her for many years. She was also not immune to the observations of the experimental art scene's most infamous informer, the poet Sascha Anderson.

The revelations about Anderson's lengthy and multifaceted work with the Stasi are well-storied and continue to bear a significant impact on how the GDR's experimental culture has been written into history.[21] Soon after they were first opened to public viewing in 1992, the files uncovered that Anderson—a leading organizer of East Berlin's Prenzlauer Berg poetry scene—had spied on his friends for fifteen years, including after his emigration to West Berlin in 1986. Though others in the tightly knit circle of experimental artists worked as Stasi operatives, including the poet Rainer Schedlinksi, none offered as much information as Anderson. None were, moreover, as pivotal to that scene as he. Yet the Germanist Julia Hell describes the attention to Anderson as "overdetermined," and suggests that the focus on him distracts from a more troubling systematic refusal to critically engage the GDR past, writing: "He has become a screen for the projections of his fellow citizens, the projection of all the small acts of betrayal and cowardice and accommodation that were required in the East."[22] Importantly, Hell frames her critique within the context of what she calls the "incomplete project of GDR research," which she identifies as a symptom of the ideological, rather than historical, relationship to East Germany that pervades contemporary German society.[23] Rather than being sensationalized or wholly discarded, she argues, the artists who worked as Stasi spies ought to be examined as a kind of East German-specific creator. Paraphrasing Anderson's

1.2

Christine Schlegel. From the series *Eingeschweißte Überwachung* (*Shrink-Wrapped Surveillance*). 1999. Collage images. 50 × 70 cm. Reprinted with the permission of Christine Schlegel. © 1999 by Christine Schlegel.

contemporary, the writer Jan Faktor, she concludes her essay: "Who else was in the position to experience what Anderson did? The answer is, no one."[24]

To wit, the extent of Anderson's spying, including the entanglement of his work on behalf of his friends (as a writer and an organizer) and against them (as a spy), suggests that his behavior was driven by a compulsion to be significant. By Schlegel's account, discovering that Anderson had worked as an IM did not surprise her: "Sascha understood very well how to humiliate people quickly and exactingly before generously offering them his help."[25] That it turned out he had played both sides—as both advocate and adversary—conformed to his personality. Yet Anderson's deception has come to symbolize the imprecise allegiances of the experimental scene as a whole.[26] Comprised of people driven to foment cultural innovation in the GDR, a multiregional network of artists and organizers likewise oriented themselves largely beyond their context. Many (in fact, nearly all those described in this book) planned to and ultimately did leave East Germany. Particularly for writers, Anderson's betrayal has further entrenched long-standing fractures that ran through an already tentative allegiance of creators. The impact of his surveillance, however, cannot explain the relative lack of appreciation for the history of the experimental art scene, as evidenced by the near total absence of this artwork from museums and galleries outside Berlin or the former East German territory, as well as the scarcity of scholarship on the subject of experimental art from the GDR written in any language but German. Indeed, as with the above-noted suggestions that a focus on the Stasi surveillance files has led to an imbalanced account of the influence of the Ministry for State Security on East German society, the fascination with Anderson has come at the expense of more careful historicizations of the GDR's unofficial culture.

Like Schlegel, many have communicated an intellectual or psychological curiosity in Anderson, who has come to symbolize the latent, but not always immediately impactful, corruption of East German society. The painter Cornelia Schleime, once Anderson's closest friend, dedicated much of a semiautobiographical text to unpacking his deception and has spoken frequently about it.[27] She is a central figure in the 1994 film *Betrayal* (*Verrat*), a Swedish-made documentary that offers a psychological portrait of Anderson in large part through the painter's eyes.[28] Early in the film, Schleime prepares for her first visit to the Stasi Records Archive in Berlin. She is well aware of Anderson's work as an IM. Standing before a mirror with a set of wigs, she carefully styles herself to best match the occasion. She elects to go with something "more natural," in this case without a wig. Schleime is intrigued, rather than downtrodden: "What he's done is fascinating. Fascinating and terrible at the same time. And what's more exciting in life than something that's fascinating and terrible at the same time?" After spending some time in the archive, Schleime walks through a dusky Berlin while processing the contents of her files with the film's narrator and chief investigator, Björn Cederberg, a person with whom both she and Anderson share a long friendship. The film's climax occurs when Cederberg surprises Anderson in a Roman restaurant with a visit from Schleime. It is clear that this is their first encounter since he had been exposed as a Stasi mole. Schleime slightly softens the ambush. She asks Anderson to explain his impulses, even tells him that his "observations were precise and psychologically accurate." In response, he gives a sheepish smile. This is not to say that Schleime offers Anderson her forgiveness; his actions are irredeemable, but nevertheless intriguing, revealing the inner workings of a very broken person. In the film, Anderson describes a reliance on East Germany's secret security forces to not only validate but craft his experience: "Part of my life was a response to my Stasi work. The hyperactivity and exaggeration in my behavior. The wish to do the opposite of what was expected was connected with my experiences with the Stasi." Anderson's work as an IM provides an exaggerated example of the influence of context on identity, in this case both his and that of the scene he played a pivotal role in cultivating.

Of course, Anderson was not the only person guilty of spying on his friends. The most high-profile spy among visual artists was Ralf-Rainer Wasse, a photographer who documented the *plein air* activities of Clara Mosch. Arguably East Germany's earliest and most influential experimental art collective, Clara Mosch was active between 1977 and 1982 in and around the city of Karl-Marx-Stadt, where it also ran an eponymous independent gallery partially under the auspices of the Union of Fine Artists. Raising the presence of Stasi moles within the experimental art scene underscores the impossibility of a clean division between state and unofficial culture. It does not, however, prove that the government could influence experimental culture. Observation and presence do not equal control, or even impact. Schedlinski, in defense of his work as an IM, claims his reporting to the Stasi steered authorities away from a clearer understanding of the scene.[29] Without overstating the case, Schedlinski's suggestions about the idiosyncrasies of IM reports do align with how others have interpreted the content of their surveillance files. EIGEN+ART gallery director and founder Gerd Harry "Judy" Lybke likewise notes a pattern of fabrication or deescalation in the reports that comprise his lengthy file: "The Stasi people sometimes left something out of the reports, sometimes invented things.

We were not allowed to seem too dangerous, nor too harmless, otherwise we would be shut down. They clearly did not want that. The gallery, these openings, this was a super job for them. There was always something going on, always a good feeling."[30] Lybke's anecdote demonstrates that Stasi reports need to be critically analyzed and should not be taken at face value. It also suggests that the motivations for spying resist easy summation. With a reported 173,000 IMs at work for the Stasi in 1988–1989, the only thing "typical" of a spy was his gender: about 85 to 90 percent of them have been identified as men.[31]

OUTRAGE AND IRONY

It is significant that Cornelia Schleime's *Stasi Series*, a grouping of fourteen self-portraits paired with excerpts from her surveillance file, addresses this history through themes that entwine outrage with irony. Officially titled *Bis auf weitere gute Zusammenarbeit, Nr. 7284/85* (*Until Further Useful Collaboration, Nr. 7284/85*), the *Stasi Series* rehearses the vocabulary of the GDR's secret police, at once underscoring the categorical oppression of the secret police, while mocking the sincerity of that system.[32] Created in 1992 and 1993, in the months after the East German state's secret police files were first made public, Schleime describes her project as "a way for me to free myself from this trauma."[33] While scores were trapped by the past as it came surging back in the files—"It was the only thing that anyone was talking about!"—the artist says she needed to do something productive with the crisis.[34] Journaling on the experience in the early 1990s, she wrote: "This permanent looking backward makes me the most sick. I have better things to do with my time. I want to continue working on my new paintings, but now I am choked. It's not enough that they betrayed people. Now they're stealing time, too."[35] Yet Schleime also describes humor as a primary impulse for the *Stasi Series*: "Alongside my very human

1.3

Cornelia Schleime. *Bis auf weitere gute Zusammenarbeit, Nr. 7284/85* (*Until Further Useful Collaboration, Nr. 7284/85*). 1993. Photograph on silkscreen. 100 × 70 cm. Reprinted with the permission of Cornelia Schleime. © 1993 by Cornelia Schleime.

Elstermann

120

Der Bundesbeauftragte für die Unterlagen des Staatssicherheitsdienstes der ehemaligen Deutschen Demokratischen Republik Postfach 1199, O-1086 Berlin

VP.-Inspektion Mitte
Volkspolizeirevier- 4

Berlin, der 24.10.1983

Der Bundesbeauftragte für die Unterlagen des Staatssicherheitsdienstes der ehemaligen Deutschen Demokratischen Republik Postfach 1199, O-1086 Berlin

KOPIE

Protokoll

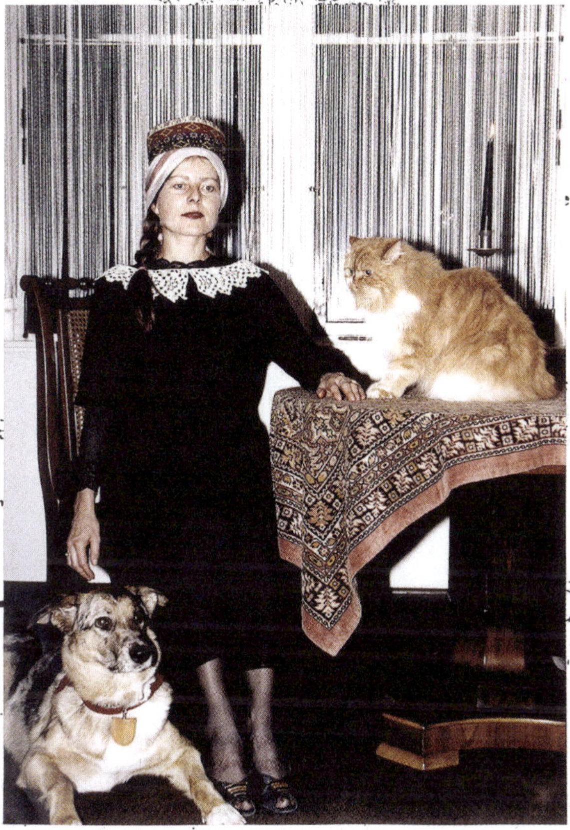

...polizei-
...ntoilette.
...aus-
...-und
...cheinung
Erschei... ...tiv in
sein s...

...OPIE

Die Wohnung ist notdürftig mit alten Möbelstücken, was modern wirken soll, eingerichtet.
Ihre äußere Erscheinung ist mit der Aussattung der Wohnung in Abstimmung gebracht worden und "Soll" ebenfalls sehr modern aussehen.

Der Bundesbeauftragte für die
Unterlagen des Staatssicherheitsdienstes
der ehemaligen
Deutschen Demokratischen Republik
Postfach 1199, O-1086 Berlin

Im Wohnhaus ist die zu Ermittelnde den Mietern nicht bekannt, nur der /KP.

[redacted] und

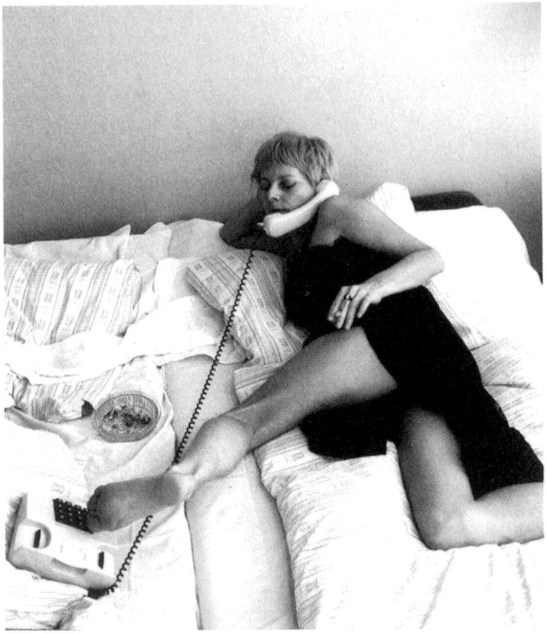

Die Sch. soll in ihren Beuf auch ganz gut verdienen.

Die Ermittelte ist gut gekleidet, sie trägt auch "Westkleidung".

einen Freund hat man im Haus noch nicht gesehen.

feelings of disappointment, I came back to my sense of humor and made my work about the files."[36]

Motivated by a desire to expose the "perverse" banality of the Stasi's observation of her, Schleime claims to have intentionally omitted more political texts, including reports on her art practice.[37] The excerpts she chooses from her file range from assessments of her external appearance ("modern and Western") to the time and manner of male visitors ("just for fun") to her self-isolation ("she maintains no contact with her neighbors"). The series alternates between portraits that embody an idealized image of an East German woman and ones in which the artist appears as a woman lost to the wiles of capitalism. In the former, Schleime plays the woman the Stasi wanted her to be, at least in principle. In the latter, she becomes the woman the Stasi wanted, in fact, *needed* her to be—the citizen fallen to western decadence who only the GDR could save. Here was the enemy incarnate, the proof the Stasi required to justify its own existence. Through this project, Schleime effectively ridicules the state security system, identifying the superficiality of their ideological premises, while at the same time unfailingly bearing witness to a power differential that placed her in sightlines that she could not escape (let alone anticipate). To this end, the *Stasi Series* explicitly targets not only Anderson's work as an IM (she uses at least two excerpts from his reports) but all of the citizen spies who reported on her. In an introductory caption, she writes: "This work could only have been realized with the help of the GDR's Ministry for State Security and its many collaborators, who contributed in painstaking detail to these texts. To them I am thankful." Importantly, Schleime does not profess a unilateral critique of those collaborators; in her autobiographical novel *Weit Fort* she writes about a housemaster who lied about her in obligatory reports to the Stasi. Perhaps motivated to protect Schleime from the law, the woman had lived through the Gestapo and thus knew "what denunciation can mean."[38]

Beyond the texts themselves, Schleime also offers a sharp and empowered revision of her biography. If at first compelled by the contents of her files, the artist

1.4

Cornelia Schleime. *Bis auf weitere gute Zusammenarbeit, Nr. 7284/85* (*Until Further Useful Collaboration, Nr. 7284/85*). 1993. Photograph on silkscreen. 100 × 70 cm. Reprinted with the permission of Cornelia Schleime. © 1993 by Cornelia Schleime.

nevertheless moves quickly away from these observations by posing herself in the way she wants to be seen. Her self-reimagining is done in double. She is both a character in the Stasi-scripted drama of her life and a person today looking back at and rewriting that narrative. Certainly, a dimension of analysis that considers the multiple roles a person would play in an oppressive society would be appropriate here. That would align with Anderson's above-noted confession that his activity with the Stasi influenced his behavior. It also may be interesting to compare how Schleime's clothing choices conjure the absurd disguises the Stasi would don while on the job.[39] Nevertheless, beyond an allegory for state oppression, this analysis suggests instead that Schleime used her Stasi file as a means to record herself as an active agent in a moment when she could quite naturally (that is to say, unapologetically) have succumbed to victimization. The *Stasi Series* is thus not only about Schleime working through her history of oppression at the hands of the East German state; it is also about her deciding to reframe the narrative around what it meant to not just live through but excel in and then move past an environment that aimed to destroy her spirit. In this sense, the project refers to both the time of the GDR and the time of working through the GDR—that is, the immediate postreunification period, when victimization and traumatization dominated the stories about East Germany. The *Stasi Series* is thus a kind of farewell or transitional gesture, a work that acknowledges a history quite seriously—why else use the files?—while at the same time not allowing that history to place Schleime in a state of suspension.

Similar to Schleime, Else Gabriel created a work with an excerpt of her surveillance file that highlights the ways in which the Stasi focused on her external appearance to interpolate her into its surveillance system. In *Stalabile Anlage* (*(Un) Stable System*), first installed for the 2016 *Gegenstimmen* (*Voices of Dissent*) exhibition held at the Martin-Gropius-Bau in Berlin, the artist has scaled up a single A4-sized page from her surveillance file to the size of a wall. She places six black-and-white photographs over this oversized paper, whose top and bottom ends roll in on themselves against the wall and onto the floor. The photographs are taken from three series of Gabriel's artworks from 1986: *Warte—an On* (*Wait On*), *One way speed limit*, and *Puppen* (*Dolls*). All were made while Gabriel was active as a performance artist and filmmaker, notably as part of the Auto-Perforation Artists. Fastened to the wall and onto the paper is a magnifying glass, which hangs from a long string. To the left of this is a roll of paper, recalling both toilet paper and the rolls of paper that were stationed outside of the doors to apartment buildings in East Germany. People would tear scraps from these rolls and leave notes for neighbors and friends,

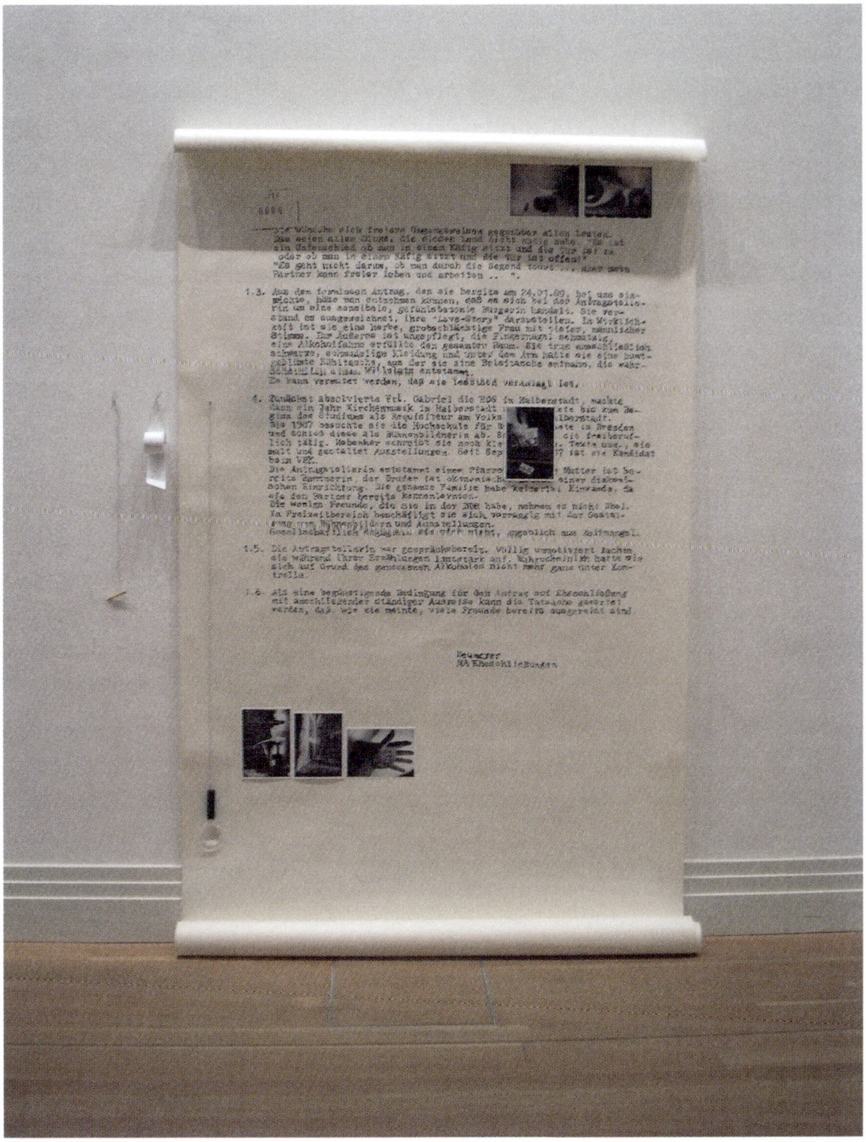

1.5

Else Gabriel, *Stalabile Anlage* (*(Un)Stable System*). 2016. Reprints of black-and-white photographs (*Warte—an On* [*Wait On*], *One way speed limit*, *Puppen* [*Dolls*]) and documont, magnifying glass, and notebook. Reprinted with the permission of Else Gabriel. © 2016 by Else Gabriel.

affixing them to the door. The visual reference to a message board offers some context for the file Gabriel has excerpted, suggesting that the information it contains has been derived whole or in part by an IM who had close ties to her. The text from 1989 is the fourth and final page of a report on Gabriel's petition for a marriage license to wed a man in West Germany. The appeal, if granted, would give her the right to legally emigrate from the GDR. Though the state ultimately approved the marriage application, the contents of the excerpt come from a moment in the midst of Gabriel's application process. The report dwells on derogatory description: "She is unkempt, her fingernails are dirty, a scent of alcohol on her breath is pervasive. She wears almost exclusively black, tattered clothing and under her arm she carries an insulated bag decorated in bright flowers, from which she extracts a briefcase that probably came from the trash." "It can be supposed," the assessor concludes, "that people assume she is a lesbian." The text recalls the excerpts from similar reports that Cornelia Schleime appropriated in her *Stasi Series*, for example these sentences taken from the excerpt she pairs with a black-and-white image of herself sprawled across an unmade bed: "The Sch. also apparently earns a lot of money in her profession. The investigated is well dressed. She also wears 'western clothes.' No one in the house has seen a boyfriend yet." In both instances, a misogynistic Stasi evaluates these women against metrics of normative female appearance, including the expectations that such appearances have for a person's love life. As either gay or single, neither Gabriel nor Schleime conform to correct womanly behavior in the eyes the Stasi. The interest in their romantic relationships also reveals a strategy regularly employed by the secret service. The Stasi often looked to partners, using them for information gathering, meddling with the stability of a relationship, or leveraging the significance of that partnership as a means to depress their target. For example, Schleime's boyfriend, the painter Ralf Kerbach, received his approval to emigrate two years before she received hers.[40]

Particularly illuminating in Gabriel's *(Un)Stable System*—and again, this bears out in Schleime's project as well—are the ways in which the arguments against granting a citizen's request for a marriage license, permission to emigrate, and so forth relied so heavily on subjective details that had no clear political consequence. There appears to have been no method to the Stasi's ever-increasing data collection, which hit its maximum in the 1980s, when 60 percent of files were produced.[41] Jens Gieseke concurs: "What [the Stasi] lacked was the will and the mental equipment to undertake a critical analysis of the underlying causes of the deficits and problems it uncovered in East German society, beyond the mere formulation of additional security needs."[42] Had it not led to the suffering of so many, the GDR's Ministry for State Security would be remembered today as an incompetent and irrational perversion.

REGARDING THE SPIES IN HER MIDST

Gabriele Stötzer has long led in efforts to expose the corruption of the East German government through its surveillance operations. As an artist, a writer, and a former political prisoner, she has consistently approached these efforts with a candor that combines vulnerability and irony. In 2014 Stötzer worked with the Stasi Records Agency on a publication of excerpts from her extensive Stasi surveillance file.[43] Around this time, she began to hold public readings of these records across Germany and beyond. Combining rote recitation with music, Stötzer was accompanied by an opera singer as she read from her files during a 2016 performance at Zurich's historic Cabaret Voltaire. As observed by the Slavicist Sylvia Sasse, the performer "voiced [Stötzer's] Stasi-alleged offenses with characteristic trill, the fear expressed in the language metamorphosed into shrill sounds."[44] Sasse refers to the following excerpt to emphasize the "mantra-like, almost incantatory repetition" of the file's prose: "The negative-hostile attitude of the person in question, as well as her objectives of disseminating hostile ideas and affiliating herself with other similarly negative-hostile persons as sympathizers, is apt to aid the achievement of the objective of the hostile centers of the political underground in the GDR."[45] Read in isolation, the repetition of the word "hostile" (here translated from various uses of the word *Feind*) exposes the Stasi as an inarticulate and single-minded institution. The original German reveals the reliance on the various grammatical forms of "hostile" as a kind of substitute for meaningful description: "feindlich-negative Grundeinstellung" (negative-hostile attitude), "feindliches Gedankengut" (hostile ideas), "feindlich-negative Personen" (negative-hostile people), "Feindzentren" (hostile centers). The repetition of these words served to justify Stötzer's yearlong imprisonment for "defamation of the state" (*Staatsverleumdung*) in 1976. Her crime: gathering signatures on a college campus to protest the highly controversial expatriation of the singer-songwriter Wolfgang Biermann. Stötzer would more than get the last word, however. Today she is not only one of the most vocal witnesses to East German state oppression, and specifically that driven by the Stasi; she was also one of five women who initiated the first occupation of a Stasi headquarters in

December 1989—an action that prevented the planned full-scale destruction of the East German state's surveillance files.

Although she would not see them until after the Stasi Records Act passed in 1991, the contents of Stötzer's surveillance file revealed a formidable presence of IMs in her circle of artists and friends. From these documents, she now knows, for example, that an acrobatic punk, whom she enlisted to "tackle" the most phallic symbols in Erfurt for her Super-8 film *Spitze* (*Summit*, 1986) had worked as a Stasi mole under the name "IMB Breaky."[46] In the film this man, Peter Krause, scrambles over the Ehrtal Obelisk; he climbs an arched entryway to St. Mary's Cathedral; he hangs from ropes and rolls down the stairway leading up to the medieval church. In a November 2019 short documentary created for German television, Stötzer describes Krause's Stasi work in passing, and professes a greater interest in the significance of the film to her: "For me [the phallic symbolism] was a kind of wall, something that could fall. For me, that was a kind of resistance film."[47] Importantly, Krause would appear in another one of Stötzer's solo films, entitled *Kentaur* (*Centaur*, 1988). The recurring presence might on its surface suggest the Stasi's calculated deployment of a vetted collaborator. In reality, however, it is more likely that Krause returned to Stötzer on his own volition.

In the documentary, Stötzer discusses the presence of another IM in one of her photo books. This time that presence is somewhat circuitous. A spy working for the Stasi (Hans Kostial, alias "IMB Konrad") compelled Stötzer to take photographs of a vulnerable young person—a man known as Winfried who enjoyed dressing in women's clothing.[48] Having both participated in a drawing circle organized by the artist Heike Stephan, Kostial and Stötzer had known each other for some time. She welcomed his offer to introduce her to Winfried, whom both she and Kostial refer to as a "transvestite." In a report to the Stasi recorded on September 9, 1984, Kostial in fact describes Stötzer's response to his offer as "feverish."[49] Well aware of her art photography, Kostial furnished her with a few photographs of Winfried. The images, which Stötzer calls *Fangfotos* (entrapment photos),[50] document him in various states of undress and while wearing typically "female" clothing. Winfried's poses are intentional. In one image, he looks back at the camera while standing in heels, donning a belted rain jacket, a matching purse on a chair to his left. In another Winfried smiles while seated with his legs crossed under a short black lacy dress. In still another, he gazes downward while balancing on one leg and disrobing. Winfried clearly desired an audience. Stötzer was happy to support him. Of course, she could not know that the Stasi had sent Winfried to her because it hoped to catch her taking pornographic images. As Stötzer reflects, "The work I made with Winfried was of course a completely different kind of photography, something authentic. Even today these images have real impact."[51] Winfried appears in several parts of one of Stötzer's photo books, the *Mackenbuch* (*Book of Defects*, 1985). The book combines multiple series of sixteen A4-sized black-and-white photographs, each depicting one person, or at most three people, as stills in thematic and often sexually provocative action. Stötzer appears topless in half of the *mit Fell* (*With Fur*) sequence; two men and one woman cavort in long leather trench coats in *Männerträume* (*Dreams of Men*); a man and a woman strike sixteen fashion-inspired poses in *schwarz-weiß* (*Black-and-White*). The *Book of Defects* includes several sequences of scenes shot outdoors, but Stötzer has staged most of her scenes indoors as in a commercial studio, posing her models against a plain white or black backdrop. These interior shots tend to be more candid, and frequently contain people who have partially or almost completely disrobed.

Among the book's most intimate series are the images of Winfried. In descriptions of this model Stötzer uses the pronouns "he/him." The following description maintains these pronouns, as well as the artist's own labeling of him as "trans." In *Trans in schwarz* (*Trans in Black*) and *Trans in weiß* (*Trans in White*), this person appears in various states of undress in black or white clothing. In each picture, he wears signature female clothing items, including a skirt, heels, and a dress. Stötzer's subject appears coy and demure in some images; in others, he stares right into the camera lens; in many, a contrapposto stance shot from the front or back reveals his anatomy. These pictures, especially in which genitals are exposed, are strikingly clear and uninhibited. Stötzer poses her trans muse not only in the clothes but in the roles traditionally assigned by sex. In *Trans Mutterkind* (*Trans Mother-Child*), the model appears with a woman whose androgynous dress and obscured form make it often difficult to differentiate her from her partner. The models simulate sex acts on and under a table, with the sixteen-image sequence concluding in a shot of a person crouched on the piece of furniture. The posture makes it difficult to discern whether this is a man or a woman. The table reappears in *Trans mit Küchenutensilen* (*Trans with Kitchen Utensils*), a series that invites comparisons to Martha Rosler's 1975 *Semiotics of the Kitchen*. Stötzer couches her references to women's domestic duties more in sexual activity than Rosler does in her foundational work of feminist film. In *Trans with Kitchen Utensils*, Stötzer's kitchen dweller begins with pots and

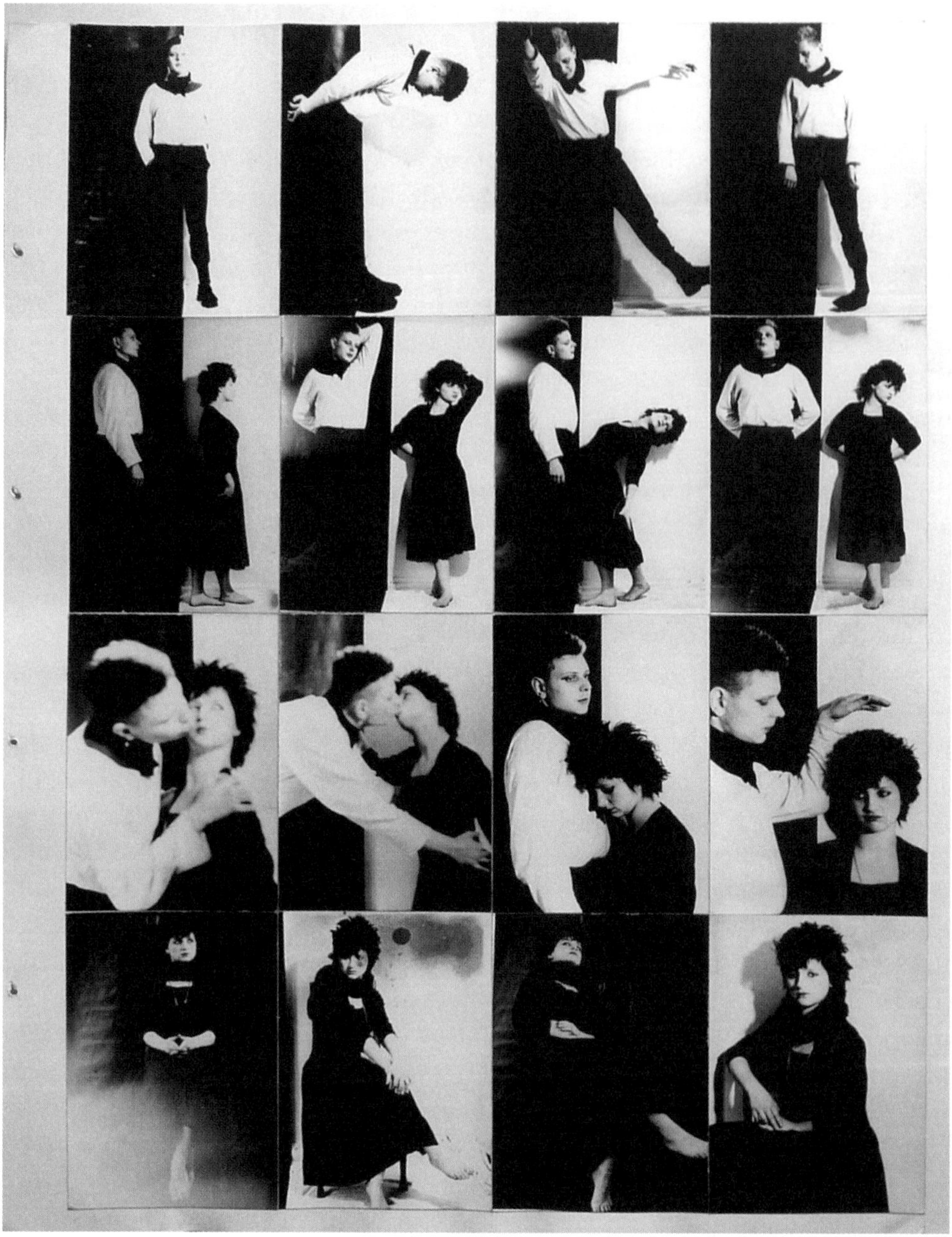

pans, but quickly returns to the nude and seminude poses of earlier scenes in the book. The sequence's concluding image, in which the model sways flirtatiously in a floral print blouse and miniskirt, suggests that Stötzer's reference to the kitchen is, indeed, more metaphorical than Rosler's—a kind of symbolism for the multitude of gendered behaviors that come to define a woman. To this end, the *Book of Defects*' series of photographs *Trans als Mann* (*Trans as a Man*) illuminates perhaps most explicitly the attitude Stötzer and her sitter had toward his presumed "defect." The model appears naked aside from a pair of black strappy heels. In three images, he dons or doffs the footwear; in two others, he gently draws a black knee-high stocking up his leg; another still shows him kissing his right knee, which he has brought to his mouth with a hand pulled against the thigh. In the majority of the remaining photographs, the model sits on a wooden dining room chair. The heels stay on, and a pair of black underpants are sometimes shed. He is at first demure, crossing his legs, and even turning away from the camera as he shields the left side of his face. The final four photographs of *Trans as a Man* are his most assertive; the model splays his legs wide in three images, and once completely exposes his genitals. The trans becomes, or rather performs, a man.

The *Book of Defects* as a whole is an exercise in intimacy. This is commonplace in Stötzer's artistic practice, and in fact reveals the impact of her experience as a political prisoner. "When I got out of jail," she explains, "I felt so many unspeakable things, things women don't express. So, I depicted them using women."[52] The discovery that one of her most willing, if insecure, models had been sent to her studio by state security seems not to have surprised Stötzer: "The secret police thought I was perverse anyway, so they sent me a mole[53] who was struggling with his identity and wanted me to photograph him. I called him 'trans.' He was clearly meant to get me to make pornographic pictures, to incriminate me." Such a manipulative deployment was in keeping with the Stasi's strategy of *Zersetzung* (corrosion), a

1.6

Gabriele Stötzer, *schwarz-weiß* (*Black-and-White*) from the *Mackenbuch* (*Book of Defects*), 1985, Black-and-white A4 photographs on board, 45.5 × 60 cm, Reprinted with the permission of Gabriele Stötzer. © 1985 by Gabriele Stötzer.

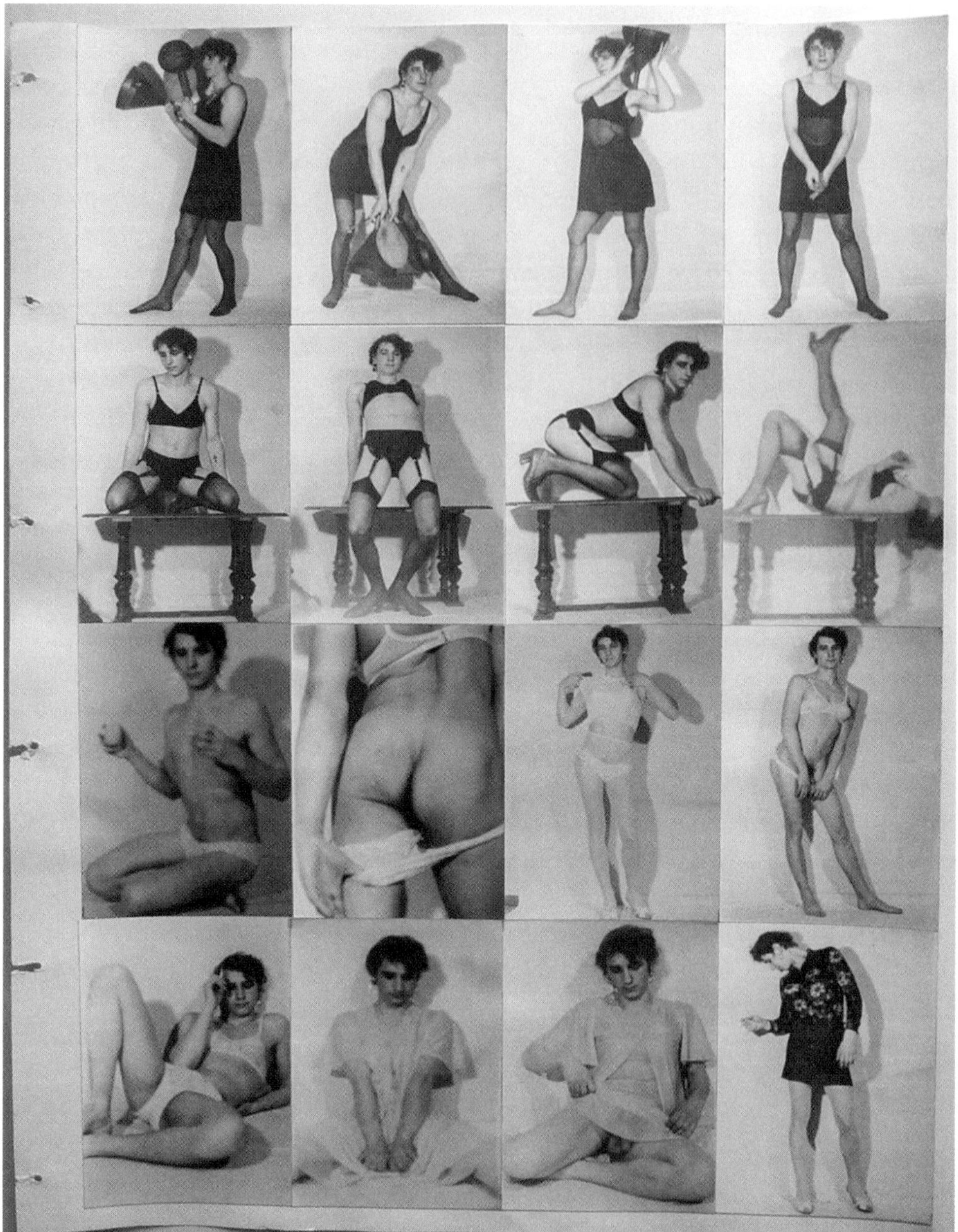

method adopted in 1976 to produce insecurity within relationships and to denigrate a person's reputation.[54] Importantly, *Zersetzung* also allowed for discrediting information to be "untrue, yet believable and irrefutable, and therefore equally discrediting."[55] The young man was thus sent into the confidence of Stötzer's studio (really her home) to inspire her to engage in an illegal activity. The accusation that she made pornographic photographs never actually appeared in her file, suggesting that the images were themselves not deemed inflammatory enough for legal action. Stötzer's experience also contrasts the Stasi's purported desire in the 1980s to, as the literature scholar Alison Lewis has suggested, not only guide artists to truly become the "engineers of the soul" that Stalin had envisioned, but to be those engineers themselves.[56] As the case of *The Book of Defects* demonstrates, the Stasi's influence on artistic production could actually work in the inverse.

Without wishing to minimize the conspiratorial, deceitful, and ultimately self-absorbed (and often personally beneficial) work of many unofficial collaborators, it nevertheless matters that Stötzer holds a fairly nuanced, even at times sympathetic, view of IMs. Frequently the Stasi's "selected person" would already be under some kind of observation by the Stasi, which would lead to information "that could be used to place that person under pressure" to collaborate.[57] Stötzer cites as an example the painter Ralf Klement who was sent to the army reserves as punishment for holding *plein airs* in the countryside outside of Erfurt, and was only allowed to return home after he agreed to work as an IM. Stötzer may have been more disappointed in the betrayal of her friend Peter Krause, had the punk scene not been so rife with IMs. Again, the reality is more complicated than at first appearance. Punks were frequent Stasi and police targets. They also often readily signed up to report on their scene to the secret police in exchange for favors and material goods. With an abiding "futureless" or anarchic vision of the world, punks were nevertheless unreliable and unrepentant sources who often lied or otherwise misguided their Stasi handlers.

1.7

Gabriele Stötzer, *Trans mit Küchenutensilen* (*Trans with Kitchen Utensils*) from the *Mackenbuch* (*Book of Defects*), 1985. Black-and-white A4 photographs on board, 45.5 × 60 cm. Reprinted with the permission of Gabriele Stötzer. © 1985 by Gabriele Stötzer.

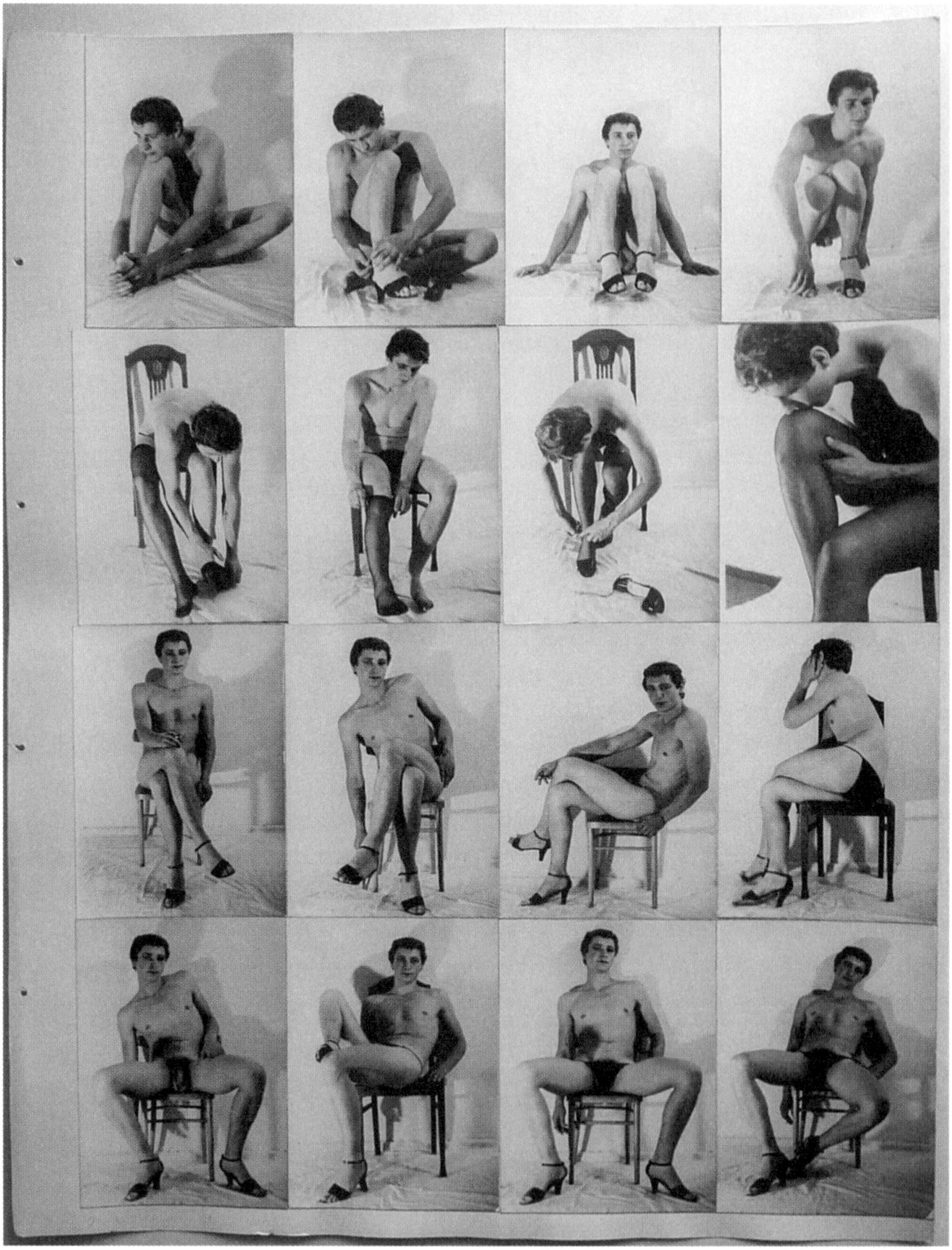

Thus, even though the police habitually rounded up punks for arrest and *pro forma* banned them from public spaces or sent in Stasi agents to devise ways to break up bands and other alliances, this flexing of state muscle appears to have amounted in most cases to a hassle, rather than the physical or psychological menace it was meant to be.[58]

Stötzer's empathic attitude about the motivations for Stasi spying, despite the real impact of that spying on her life, is perhaps what has led her to bear witness to her experience of state oppression with such candor and humor. In fact, both the artist's visual and literary work on her Stasi and prison experience have been unremitting, a fact that testifies to the enduring and complicated psychological impact of the experience. In early 1990, Stötzer returned to the jail in Erfurt where she had awaited trial for five months. The photographer Bernd Hiepe took a series of pointed photographs of her in her cell. In one she appears peering through the waist-high window in her thick cell door through which guards had delivered food. Her hands reach through this opening, held apart in a gesture of offering and supplication. Physically confined by the frame of the window, Stötzer looks vulnerable. Around this same time, in collaboration with her friend Thomas Werner, who had been charged with her for gathering signatures in support of Biermann, she made *Zelle 5* (*Cell 5*, 1990). The five-minute color video depicts Stötzer in the cell she had inhabited in Erfurt's remand jail. She appears cradling a loaf of bread, smearing it with butter and jam, and tearing it apart into crumbs, which she then places with great care in and around her cell. The art historian Ulrike Bestgen interprets Stötzer's crumbling of the bread as "an elemental symbol."[59] The bread motif in *Cell 5*, including its function as a kind of ersatz baby, illustrates a sustained interest in the gendered East German experience. Importantly, Stötzer's year of incarceration, and in particular the seven months she spent in a woman's prison, expanded her understanding of the East German state's abusive treatment of its least privileged citizens. As will be described in detail in the sixth chapter of this book, Stötzer's

1.8

Gabriele Stötzer. *Trans als Mann* (*Trans as a Man*) from the *Mackenbuch* (*Book of Defects*). 1985. Black-and-white A4 photographs on board. 45.5 × 60 cm. Reprinted with the permission of Gabriele Stötzer. © 1985 by Gabriele Stötzer.

artistic practice reveals a confidence in art as a means of building community and political solidarity.

This chapter has illustrated some of the ways that artists used their Stasi files to expose the dysfunctionality of the East German state. While certainly notes of victimization remain present, and are even at times foregrounded, a sense of gloom and despair do not dominate in these artworks, which excerpt, recontextualize, and restage the archives their makers were never meant to see. In contrast, through these projects, Kyselka, Schlegel, Schleime, Gabriel, and Stötzer invite their audiences to consider the ways that East Germans, and especially artists, persevered in the face of a constant threat of observation. This book has begun with a selection of these Stasi projects as a means of challenging the common conception of a high-functioning security state that irreparably debilitated East German artists. Yes, the threat of oppression was very real. Nevertheless, the lasting impacts of state authority were less decisive than might be expected. The remainder of the text seeks to demonstrate this fact. Let these initial pages thus serve as a reminder of an oppressive context. Let them also remind readers that East Germany's experimental artists exceeded—and redefined—that context. Theirs is a history of creative self-determination.

2

THE BODY IN RUINS

Photographs by Thomas Florschuetz and Performances by the Auto-Perforation Artists

In the German Democratic Republic (GDR), cultural policy explicitly advanced the communist ideology and all visual representation mapped the political. Artists who worked with the human form, in particular, drew attention to the ways in which the individual body had been sacrificed in service of the social body. The work of Thomas Florschuetz and the Auto-Perforation Artists provides case studies for an influential aesthetic of corporeal ruin that united photography and performance art. The immediate relationship between these media and the body intensified the radicality of these artworks within the East German context. Unlike painters who regularly coded subversive content into their canvases, artists who directly thematized or used the body could not hide behind their media.[1] In fact, they did not wish to hide at all.

The photographer Florschuetz made the dissonant experience of living in the GDR tangible in a series of self-portrait collages—the *Körperbilder* (*Body Portraits*)—in which he split and then reassembled his body into preternatural poses.[2] Through performances that reveled in pain, disgust, and symbolic materials, the Autoperforationsartisten (Auto-Perforation Artists)[3] made tangible the psychological impact of the state's official definition of the East German subject on both individual and collective experience. While certainly other creative and biographical impulses are legible in the artwork of Florschuetz and the Auto-Perforation Artists, the relationship between their projects and state authority remains salient. Their photography and performance art thus aligns with the popular understanding of life in East Germany: oppressed, agitated, coerced, and disturbed. That conception is embraced here. In truth, defining the GDR's experimental art against an oppressive state offers partial, and not altogether false, insight. That being said, this chapter ultimately wrangles with the imprecision of an allegorical interpretation by illustrating how an artistic reference to state oppression does not translate into a confession of victimization.

SPELLING THE BODY: THOMAS FLORSCHUETZ'S REASSEMBLED SELF-PORTRAITS

Dissected into six square black-and-white photographs, Florschuetz appears twice in an untitled *Body Portrait* from 1985. The first body consumes the leftmost four panels. Its right eye strains to remain open as the face squeezes against a bare shoulder. The second adjacent panel completes the head; its enlarged size bulges and swells. The jaw disappears into the folds of the neck. Two squares beneath the head and shoulders complete a figure. Clenched fists awkwardly hook upward and fade into smooth forty-five-degree angles that meet where the torso ends in the upper frame. This diamond-shaped trunk appears fixed and unmoving, rendering the twisting of the head and arms connected to it more animate—grotesque in that animation, exceeding formal and biological bounds. The figure at once recoils and prepares pitifully to guard itself with a spastic defense. The apprehension of this body contrasts the second, more abbreviated one found in the image's two rightmost panels. This time the head in the upper frame begins at the bottom, shot from just at the chin. The perspective accentuates jagged and discolored teeth, the peak of a nose with flaring nostrils, and a head, which dissolves into a white abyss. The body is completed below the lower jaw by a hand reaching down with thumb, index, and middle finger from the top of the frame, poised as errant limbs that recall the roots of an extracted molar.

Though disjointed and out of proportion, the figures nevertheless conform to the conventional logic of the human body: one head, one base. At nearly five feet wide and more than three feet tall, with each of its six pieces claiming an equal 50 × 50 cm share, the photograph has a commanding presence. Yet these bodies seem babyish, vulnerable, and weak. Florschuetz's self-imposed distortion of the body clearly signals an internal and psychological turmoil. The image's high contrast tone and blindingly white background render its distortions at once surreal and clinical, as if the figures have been prepared for inspection and scientific study. The *Body Portraits* are indeed rooted to questions of how photographic process or a unique photographic language influence a resulting image. Florschuetz explains

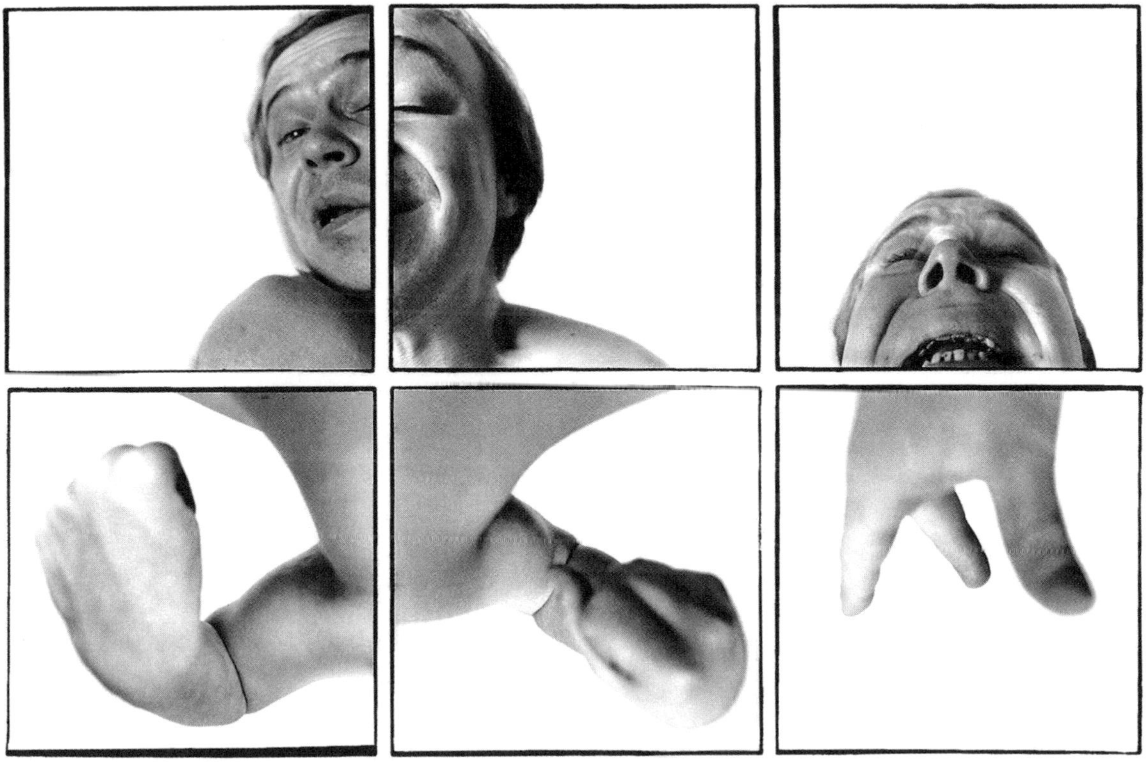

2.1

Thomas Florschuetz. Untitled (*15.XI.85*) from the *Körperbilder* (*Body Portraits*) series. 1985. Silver-gelatin prints, each 50 × 50 cm. Reprinted with the permission of Thomas Florschuetz.

his process: "What you do to make an image is really a very minimal gesture, a very minimal expenditure. It is the picture itself which makes something happen. So, you sit in front of the camera. You spell something out, speak certain words that will stay there."[4] Chance abides in a logic organized around a series of controls: the camera itself, which was medium-format and so produced a specific size of image, the range of motion possible within the diminutive size of the artist's East Berlin studio apartment, and the access he had to his own body, as well as the choices he could make about which parts of that body to show. Florschuetz succumbs both to his chosen medium, the still-photography camera, and to his context, an old and unrenovated apartment in Prenzlauer Berg, a working-class neighborhood in the GDR's capital city.

Florschuetz's *Body Portraits* are at once expressive, even agonistic, and highly methodical. The photographs reveal the artist's curiosity about how the production of an image ascribes it meaning. He is drawn to, but wary of the camera's presumed objectivity. By highlighting the camera as a technology, Florschuetz implies photography's vulnerability to context, manipulation, and instrumentalization. His approach contrasts significantly with that of the GDR's conventional photographic culture. East German photographic theory promoted the idea of what the art historian Sarah James calls "seeing photographically."[5] This utilitarian view of the medium maintained that photography possesses a visual and symbolic clarity that can instruct and educate its viewers. Berthold Beiler, a preeminent photography scholar in East Germany, claimed the medium's function was to provide an "aesthetic education."[6] That education was meant to be universal as well as eternal. Photographs, he explained, "do not just enormously influence the visual, emotional and rational worldview of their viewers. Rather, at the same time they produce . . . an enduring image memory of mankind."[7] The futurity and grand scale of Beiler's thinking mirrors central tenets of socialist realism—namely, its requirement that art and visual culture be progressive and oriented to a unified collective vision.[8] Though the medium had certainly become increasingly more subjective over time (see, for example, the work of Arno Fischer, Roger Melis, and Evelyn Richter), East German photographic culture nevertheless maintained a documentary premise that prioritized representational realism and uncomplicated messages over individual expression or formal experimentation. In contrast to this, Florschuetz set his camera on the very conventions of photographic representation. Expressly, the formal inquiry of the *Body Portraits* is rooted to questions of how photographic process or a unique photographic language influence a resulting image. By working exclusively with the human body, specifically his own, Florschuetz obscures the language of the highly loaded genre of portrait photography, questioning its claim to realism both formally and methodologically. His *Body Portraits* illustrate the visceral, incorporated experiences of living in East Germany's "real existing socialism." His interest in producing a unique photographic style through the genre of portraiture, and especially self-portraiture, demonstrates a conceptual disavowal of the conventions of normative East German culture. "Seeing photographically," Florschuetz visualizes the psychic distress that has pervaded East German society; these are documents of that suspension.

Plötzliche Heimkehr (*Sudden Return Home*), a vertical diptych from 1985, visualizes social and personal delay as a domestic crisis. In the top image, Florschuetz lays his left cheek against the camera lens. His profile consumes only half of the frame. The photo's white background bleeds into the place where his nose ought to be. The tension in his forehead and eyelids indicate the physical discomfort required to capture his bony jowl up close. Here Florschuetz's facial structure becomes a quality for formal inspection. The darkness that traces below the white mound of his cheek emphasizes its comparatively large size. His eyes are shut and mouth slightly open, giving him the appearance of a person in a gesture of supplication or at the moment of death. Beneath his face, a triangle of shoulder connects to the frame below, in which a forearm extends into a fist clutching a piece of taught rope. If this is the right forearm, it has been shot from the front, as if the hand grips the rope to pull something toward itself. If the image is shot from behind, then the rope held by the left hand supports the figure as it jumps improbably forward. Maybe it is being pulled, hoisted up an incline; Florschuetz's leaning profile might also suggest that the clenched fist is a brake. Read as a whole, the arm is the single appendage of a silent, sleeping, dreaming, or lifeless head pendulating its way up the angled rope. The work's title, *Sudden Return Home*, partially disambiguates the photographs. The adjective "sudden" implies a lack of preparation. This return home is undesired, not chosen. The image's ambivalence reflects deferment, stasis, and enclosure.

And yet that agony is itself simultaneously constrictive and constructive. When reflecting on the experience of working in a condition of cultural constraint, Florschuetz explains: "That was definitely also the most exciting part—really the fundamental condition or the fundamental premise—that you did not make what you did not want to make. . . . The need to find a language for yourself was always in one way

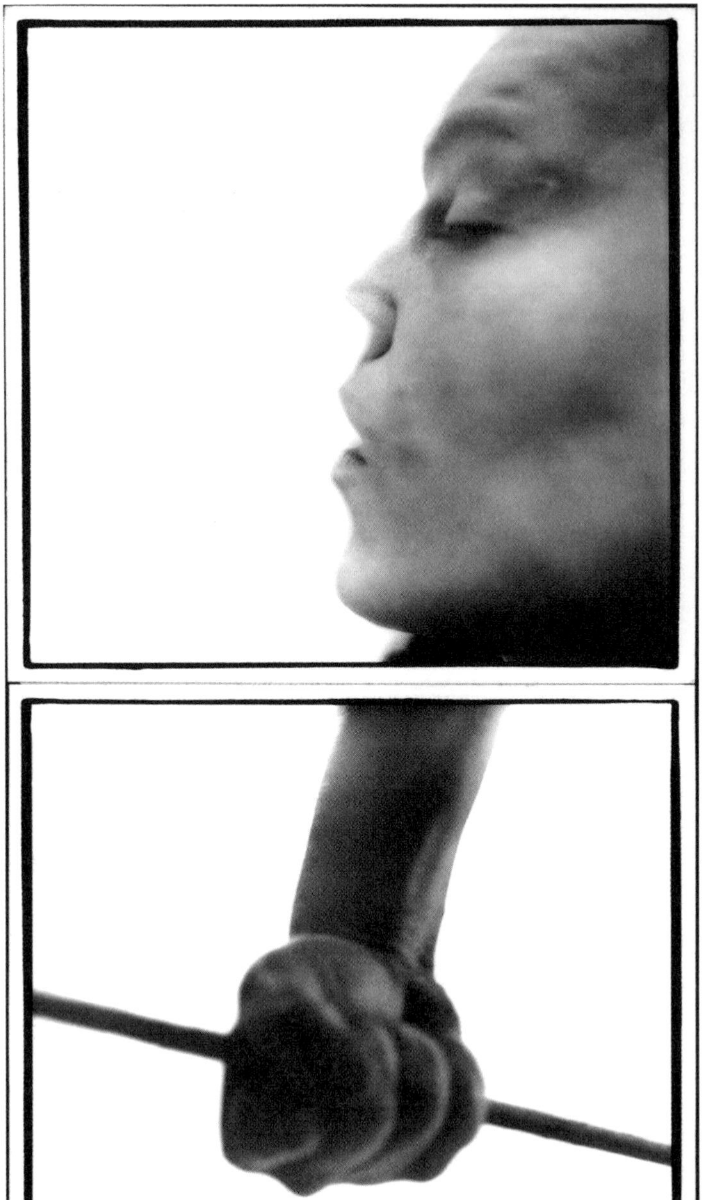

or another the primary concern."[9] Of course, the drive for self-expression is fundamental to artists in any context. Here Florschuetz's exuberance may surprise. He enthusiastically describes the limited material and working conditions of the late GDR as a stimulus for creativity. The painter and filmmaker Cornelia Schleime—who also lived in East Berlin—has shared a similar sentiment. A few years after she emigrated to West Berlin, she appeared in a 1988 documentary describing the city she had just left as having a frantic creative energy, where the "main point" was "to keep moving," that is to say, to learn new modes of expression and to reinvent oneself through new media.[10] Schleime's turn from painting to film will come into focus in this book's next chapter.

Like Schleime, Florschuetz socialized and collaborated with several artistic circles, including the experimental poetry scene of the Prenzlauer Berg. Writers, many of whom Florschuetz would photograph for another series of black-and-white portraits, engaged in language play, in particular through texts that upended grammatical convention. "Against speech, with speech,"[11] as the writer and leading figure of the scene Gerhard Wolf would explain, this aesthetic represented more than experimentation with form or sound, though the concrete poetry of Dada artists like Hugo Ball was an explicit reference.[12] Writers disrupted grammatical conventions as a means of drawing attention to the nonsense of the politicized speech and texts that dominated East German culture. Similarly, Florschuetz and others, like Micha Brendel, also renowned for his work with the Auto-Perforation Artists, reimagined the official language of portraiture through clear and deliberate distortion. Staging his own body over and over again, Florschuetz's critique is not so much autobiographical as it is organized around a consistent visual language. His identity is secondary to the fact of his body, as such. Although his face appears in nearly every *Body Portrait*, it is never identifiable. He splits the naked figure into its most utilitarian parts, into the units that labor: head, arms, legs, hands, feet, and shoulders. Printed, he reassembles them, spells the alphabet of the body to emphasize its inherent utility or to invent novel uses for the body in pieces.

2.2

Thomas Florschuetz. Untitled (*Plötzliche Heimkehr*) (*Sudden Return Home*) from the *Körperbilder* (*Body Portraits*) series. 1985. Reprinted with the permission of Thomas Florschuetz. © 1985 by Thomas Florschuetz.

THE SHELTERED MAN

The self-incisions of Florschuetz's *Body Portraits* may be interpreted as visualizations of the Marxist philosopher György Lukács's anxieties about the alienation of the human subject in industrialized labor, which he describes in his 1923 *History and Class Consciousness*. Lukács argues that when the individual body is subordinated to its function, it becomes a quantifiable object. As the body is parceled out in the service of labor, the individual's humanity is lost: "[I]t freezes into an exactly delimited, quantifiable continuum filled with quantifiable 'things'—the reified, mechanically objectified 'performance' of the worker, wholly separated from his total human personality: in short, it becomes space."[13] Just as Lukács identified a parallel problematic in both capitalist and communist labor practices, which produced similar conditions of the "atomization of the individual,"[14] Florschuetz's contorted and disfigured bodies invite us to consider the distance between the East German state's fantasy of a satisfied laboring public and its lived reality. In what seems now like an affirmation of his conclusions, Lukács would famously recant *History and Class Consciousness* after receiving pushback from communist party leaders who envisioned an emancipated but still industrialized proletariat. His original critique of the trappings of industry nevertheless remains foundational to critical theory, which in its earliest moments targeted both the exploitation of capital and the woes of a technocratic form of communism, like that employed in East Germany. Indeed, the philosopher Michel Foucault argues that the laboring body is disciplined toward efficiency and predictability, and produces "docile" subjects.[15] Although he was critiquing capitalism, Foucault was certainly aware of concurrent critiques of the kind of bureaucratic socialism operative in the GDR, where significant hierarchies of leadership worked in combination with state surveillance to pacify the population. While the arms of the law targeted and criminalized deviance, the GDR's official culture functioned as a tool of state legitimation, deployed to normalize and make inarguable a central and homogeneous vision for the "new socialist man."[16]

Historian Greg Eghigian names the East German subject *Homo munitus*: the sheltered or defended human. He expands on those material and metaphorical defenses, writing that the *Homo munitus* describes a "people historically repressed and denied access to happiness by the walls and overly protective political system ostensibly designed to defend them."[17] Referred to in official texts as the "anti-fascist protection rampart," the Berlin Wall symbolized the most concrete and obvious way the state circumscribed its public through an ostensible gesture of protection. The wall was thus meant to demarcate both a physical and a mental space. The heads of the ruling SED[18] political party were apparently quite attracted to human psychology and produced a "vast literature and an array of policies concerned with making sense of and dealing with deviance."[19] An obvious paternalism saturated that hope, with the effect that individual decision making and personal agency were disincentivized, and often criminalized. Conformity was praised; it was also required to make even the most basic social or professional advancements. Deviance, in turn, came to equal not just a personal moral failing, but a threat to national security. Self- and interpersonal policing thus bolstered the mechanisms officially in place to observe the East German population. Looking more specifically at East German photography, then, one might consider again the status of art and visual culture, which aspired to—as the Secretary of the Union of Soviet Fine Artists would explain in 1953—"represent reality in its revolutionary development, in its most progressive appearances."[20] For Eghigian, writing after Foucault, the East German government manipulated its public by coddling and training it to believe in a "medical and scientific management of normality and abnormality."[21] Reality was thus predicated on a predefined, regulated, and internalized vision of the real.

The *Body Portraits* intervene in the expectation for photographic "realism" in two ways. First, they call attention to the processes that produce those norms, namely, the technology of the camera. As the art historian Karin Thomas observed in 1987 of these images: "For Thomas Florschuetz the photographic medium is no longer simply reproduction and interpretation of a given reality; rather, he uses . . . the potential within the art form to create a different, meta-empirical reality."[22] The new perspective on reality presented by the *Body Portraits* amounts to more than a formal or aesthetically driven alternative. Instead, it underscores the despotic premises that shape the East German state's claim to reality. Florschuetz's distortions of the body, moreover, draw attention to the government's reliance on a recursive and affirmative visual culture. In their attention to portraiture as a process of seeing and constructing an image, the *Body Portraits* summon to mind the ideological techniques used by the state's own photographic production. However, these images record a body that has submitted to the photographic mechanism, which has rendered it hyperdocile, malleable, entirely subjected—an empty vessel. At the same time that they underscore the mechanics of a photograph's production, the *Body Portraits* submit to the privileged access granted by the technology of the camera. Through framings that cut and smash, gawk and inspect, sever and contort, the viewer is given free access to angles of a person otherwise unavailable.

In this respect, Florschuetz's East German viewers indulged in the experience of inspection that in fact constantly threatened them.

It may seem at first incongruous that Florschuetz received support from the Union of Fine Artists, which was the GDR's central arbiter of the fine arts. In accepting him into their organization in 1984, union officials formally recognized Florschuetz's artistic merit. In fact, he counts among some of the first autodidacts (that is to say, people without any formal education in their craft) to be admitted to the professional association. In part through union-sanctioned exhibitions abroad, Florschuetz also earned notable interest in his photography from people outside the GDR. Perhaps they were drawn to the agony of his imagery; perhaps that agony conformed to their vision of an East German existence. It is worth noting that Thomas, a West German art historian, published her remarks on the *Body Portraits* in the English-language magazine *European Photography*, based in West Berlin. Her interest in Florschuetz contributed to the growth of his reputation, which ultimately helped to facilitate his illegal emigration in February 1988. Essentially, Florschuetz never returned from West Germany, where he had been installing an art exhibition. Clearly, union officials—who answered to the GDR's ruling SED party leadership—had not factored in this possibility when they granted Florschuetz permission to show his work abroad. Though a more complex narrative underlies these events, it matters that the state's consistent underestimation of experimental artists, combined with the calculated risks those artists would take to advance their creative pursuits, would come to benefit a great many. Both unintentional and deliberate support for experimental forms of art in late East Germany were perhaps no more emphatic (and unlikely) than in relation to the bloody, gutsy, noisy, and willful aesthetic of the Auto-Perforation Artists.

POOR LITTLE SAUSAGES

The sounds of loud experimental music spill out of the Academy of Fine Arts in Dresden onto the Brühl's Terrace, a grand pedestrian walkway overlooking the Elbe River. After one passes through the art school's two heavy wooden doors, a steam of smoke and sweat engulfs the air. Hundreds of people occupy the floors and halls of the academy. It is February 1986 during *Fasching*, the school's annual Carnival celebration, a costume party of epic proportions that will span three evenings. In the foyer, a spectacle is underway. Six performers fill a raised stage. Four guide

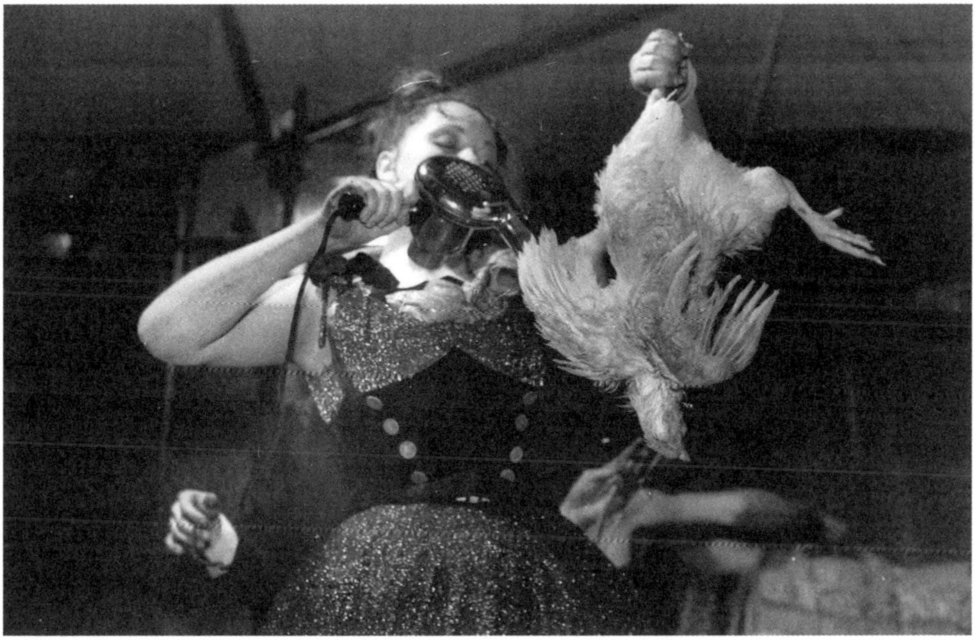

the action.[23] They are the Auto-Perforation Artists—Micha Brendel, Else Gabriel, Rainer Görß, and Via Lewandowsky. The stage is set for one of their first group performances, *Spitze des Fleischbergs* (*Top of Meat Mountain*). Ropes, metal bars, and sheets of spotted and checked acrylic tablecloth rise from floor to ceiling. Roughly describing a kitchen or a home, *Top of Meat Mountain* is a campy exaggeration of East German domesticity. Each artist plays a specific role, spontaneous in action, but nevertheless foregrounded by rigorous conceptual preparation.[24] Dressed in a German *dirndl* with bosomy floral smock gathered tightly to her waist by a black

2.3

Else Gabriel in *Spitze des Fleischbergs* (*Top of Meat Mountain*) by Micha Brendel, Else Gabriel, Rainer Görß, and Via Lewandowsky. Hochschule für Bildende Künste, Dresden, February 1986. Performance. Photograph by Andreas Rost. Reprinted with the permission of Else Gabriel and Andreas Rost. © 1986 by Andreas Rost.

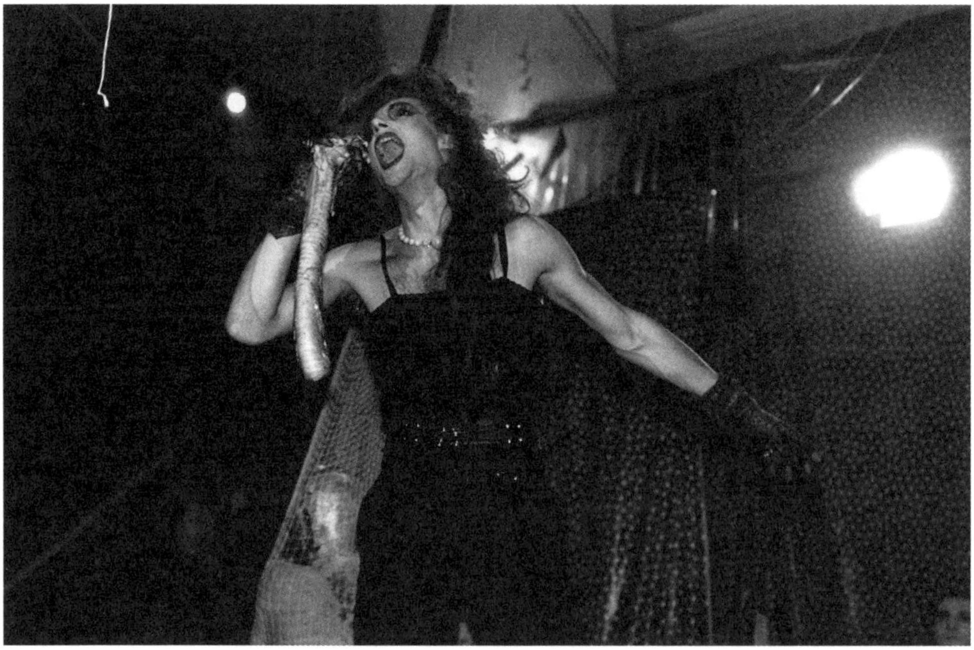

bodice, Gabriel uses a hairdryer to desiccate the feathers on a dead chicken. The gleam of the metallic instrument contrasts with the exaggerated femininity of Gabriel's traditional dress. In her right hand she grips the bird's right leg assuredly. The gesture underscores the affectation of her role as a good German woman. Lewandowsky's contribution to the performance likewise counters the idealist image of the "new socialist man." He wears a long red wig, dramatic stage makeup, jewelry, and short fingerless gloves made of lace. The black leather strapping at

2.4

Via Lewandowsky in *Spitze des Fleischbergs* (*Top of Meat Mountain*) by Micha Brendel, Else Gabriel, Rainer Görß, and Via Lewandowsky. Hochschule für Bildende Künste, Dresden, February 1986. Performance. Photograph by Andreas Rost. Reprinted with the permission of Via Lewandowsky and Andreas Rost. © 1986 by Andreas Rost.

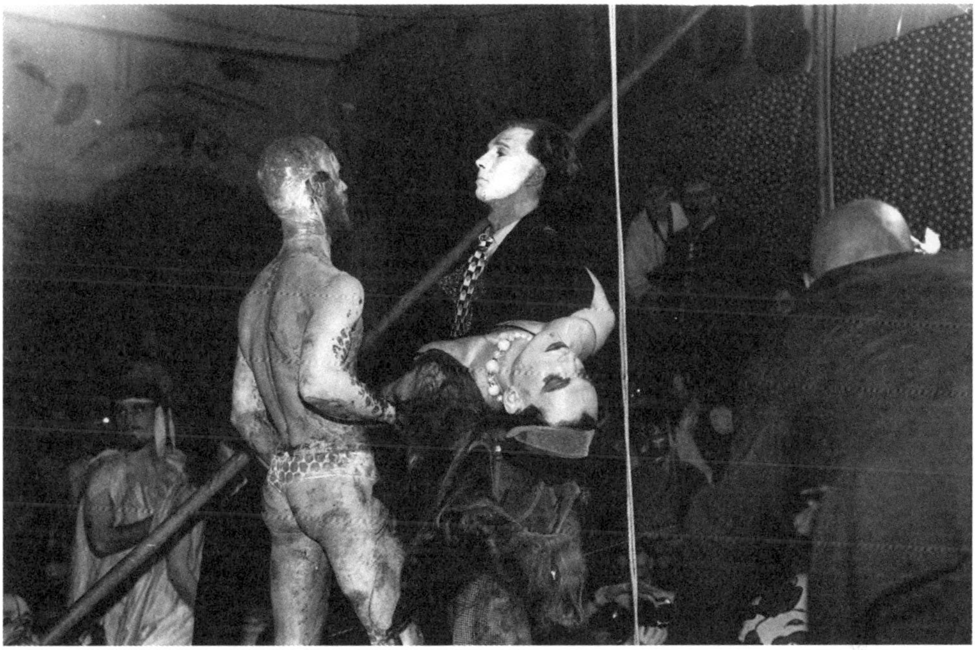

his waist both amplifies his long, thin frame and suggests fetishistic sexual play. During the performance, Lewandowsky belts into a microphone to which he has attached a cow's gullet, whose long and slack raw flesh resembles a phallus. Elsewhere, he takes a more submissive pose. Bending his weight into the outstretched arms of Brendel and Görß, Lewandowsky appears enraptured, maybe exhausted. His companions stare into one another's eyes. Brendel's state of undress is a vulgar foil to Lewandowsky's mannered mimelike appearance. Brendel, whose small body

2.5

Micha Brendel, Via Lewandowsky, and Rainer Görß in *Spitze des Fleischbergs* (*Top of Meat Mountain*) by Micha Brendel, Else Gabriel, Rainer Görß, and Via Lewandowsky. Hochschule für Bildende Künste, Dresden, February 1986. Performance. Photograph by Andreas Rost. Reprinted with the permission of Micha Brendel, Via Lewandowsky, Rainer Görß, and Andreas Rost. © 1986 by Andreas Rost.

is stenciled with the hexagonal pattern of chicken wire, appears at times turning a large white hoop, his lips stiffly opened to the guttural incantation of a long vowel. This "tantrum"[25] culminates in an automatic painting made from splatters of green liquid feces that Brendel methodically drips onto a canvas from a punctured animal's intestinal tract. The performance concludes after all four artists black out from exhaustion.[26]

If performance art is the GDR's resounding experimental form, then the Auto-Perforation Artists may be its signature artists. They are certainly its most conspicuous. The four artists that formed the group's core united around a shared aesthetic of self-harm, as the name they would adopt in 1987 suggests. Brendel, Gabriel, Görß, and Lewandowsky were less collaborators than they were coconspirators; their work is resoundingly individualized even when presented in group form. Indeed, each artist pursued a solo artistic path. Rather than providing a comprehensive overview of the vast Auto-Perforationist aesthetic, this chapter's focus on a few of the artists' most memorable and public-facing projects highlights the ways their work communicated a message of shared social frustration.

The Auto-Perforation Artists's apocryphal origin story illustrates how gaps in East Germany's cultural bureaucracy quickened the unraveling of centralized control over fine art production in the 1980s. Brendel, Gabriel, and Lewandowsky met in 1982 when they began as set design students at the Dresden Academy of Fine Arts. In their second semester, their lead instructor, Günter Hornig, fell ill and had to leave the school. Despite the vacancy, the students still pursued their course of study, but were left essentially unsupervised in their basement studios. Brendel, Gabriel, and Lewandowsky took the opportunity to band together. By 1984 Rainer Görß had entered the school and joined the trio. Their mischief-making, which reached its fever pitch in a 1987 group thesis project, would fundamentally redefine the future of art in the GDR. Their first target, the art academy itself, became an unwitting—and almost accidental—host.

The group's first major appearance took place on May 20, 1985, when Brendel, Gabriel, Görß, and Lewandowsky staged an exhibition and performance entitled *langsam nässen* (*wet slowly*). As would be the case in their performance art to come, each artist appeared individually on stage. In fact, despite their adoption of the group moniker Autoperforationsartisten in 1987, the artists always maintained the primacy of the individual.[27] The art historian Claudia Mesch has interpreted this attention to individuation as a rejection of the superficial rhetoric of collectivity that pervaded official culture.[28] She suggests that the artists' abject use of their bodies "was also [intended] to make plain that their concern was an extensive investigation of the self and its boundaries in a society that forced a notion of collectivity upon its citizens."[29] In *wet slowly*, the artists engage in a kind of parallel play, inhabiting space where their interactions are minimal and often punctuate their division. For example, Görß communes with a broken wall, while Brendel is described as using milk and sugar cubes to "play with separation."[30] Gabriel later takes the cubes to spell out and then set aflame the title of the performance. Meanwhile, Lewandowsky, naked and draped in a rose-printed cloth, crawls across the room. Here Lewandowsky would first present his interest in ideas of sexuality, childhood, fear, terror, as well as libidinous energy and destructive fantasy. More than any East German artist who identified as male, Lewandowsky explored the contours of his masculinity in vocabularies that today would be described as gender-nonconforming.[31] Appearing regularly in dresses, tutus, leotards, and other typically "girlish" clothing, Lewandowsky also experimented with taboo human and animal substances, like feces, vomit, entrails, bones, hair, and dust. Brendel, who frequently appeared in the leather and bindings typical of sadomasochistic clothing, also considered personal mythology in his work, in which he regularly employed organic materials like blood and sperm, as well as toxic ones like turpentine and resin. He described his aesthetic pursuit as an effort "to experience pain, to see blood flow, to smell the bowels emptying, to hear the brain burst."[32] Görß likewise engaged in painful or awkward genital manipulations in works that investigated male sexuality and fertility. More typical of his aesthetic, however, was an interest in language and information processes.

The only woman in the group, Gabriel bore her femininity as a material. In some works, she might appear bare-breasted or in a bosom-accentuating piece of clothing. In others, she might experiment with materials with strong domestic connotations. Bread dough was a regular medium, but so were pests (including a pet rat named Elke). Combined, these materials conjure the abject underbelly of domestic labor that the homemaker seeks to tame. Gabriel explains the intersection of material, performance, and concept in the Auto-Perforationist artwork:

> On the one hand these were the things at hand, what was just lying around. And on the other hand, this was also certainly another kind of provocation, because the GDR always made itself out to be the "workers and farmers state" where everyone had it so good. We showed, both with the performances themselves and the materials we used, that we are all poor little sausages and we will show ourselves as poor little sausages. We are pathetic creatures who are very far removed from the triumph of socialism.[33]

Gabriel's recourse to food to describe East Germans is symbolic—a gibe at the state's promise to satisfy the essential needs of all of its citizens. The Auto-Perforation Artists' work disavowed the image of the public as propagated by the GDR's state socialism by performing an interpretation of a degraded reality in the extreme. They defined the abject, the marginalized, and the crushed as the true face of communism. Auto-Perforationist artwork reflected simultaneously the alienating experience of a single body working to escape constraint and the totalizing effects of that constraint on the community of the East German public. In fact, in tandem with a unique and groundbreaking aesthetic, the group deliberately concentrated on spaces controlled by official culture to great effect.

As a training ground for those in whose hands the state would entrust its future representation, the East German art school was an exaggeratedly ideological space. Marxist-Leninist art history and obligatory party celebrations or commemorations supplemented studio courses. Public events included an explicit, albeit often incoherent, communist agenda. In fact, the official list of organizers of the 1986 Carnival where *Top of Meat Mountain* appeared includes a state-appointed faculty member from the Marxist-Leninist department.[34] It can be assumed that this Dr. Seltmann added some ideological touches—perhaps an opening speech, which would have been typical at such an event. The Auto-Perforationist performance may at first have seemed incongruous, even impossible. Yet it took place not once but three times—staged each night of the 1986 Carnival. As it did every year, the event offered the entire student body the opportunity to present new and in-progress work with seemingly little oversight. Dr. Seltmann either did not see the Auto-Perforation Artists' performance or did not care to be held accountable for its presence at an event he was meant to supervise. Punting responsibility is, of course, a mainstay of bureaucracy. Beginning with the *Top of Meat Mountain* omnibus performance—with a name as inscrutable as the actions themselves—the Auto-Perforation Artists continued to hide in plain sight. Their efforts would quickly take on greater risk.

DEFENSE ON THE OFFENSE: THE AUTO-PERFORATION ARTISTS RESHAPE THE ART ACADEMY

It is July 3, 1987. Hundreds of onlookers crowd a basement room in the Dresden Academy of Fine Arts. A cloth-draped Gabriel spastically jabs at the keys of a typewriter. Perhaps she strikes the keys in unison with a soundtrack. In the film version

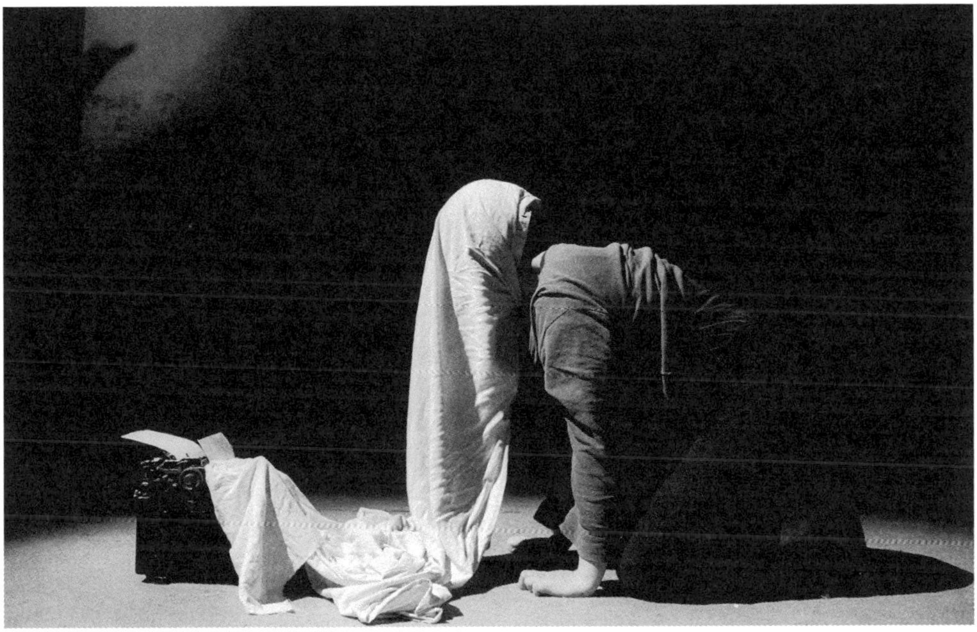

of *Herz Horn Haut Schrein* (*Heart Bone Skin Shrine*, 1987),[35] the sound ranges from high-pitched noise to a MIDI-style version of the key theme in Ravel's *Bolero* to rhythmic incantations of "Nein Nein Nein Nein" (No no no no). The chant references a work by the West German artist Joseph Beuys,[36] whose socially engaged performance art, as well as his interest in the GDR, had long captured the imaginations of East Germany's experimental artists. In *Heart Bone Skin Shrine*, the reference to Beuys extends respect to the artist, who had died in January 1986, while also cunningly undermining the clear misgivings state cultural officials held toward

2.6

Else Gabriel in *Herz Horn Haut Schrein* (*Heart Bone Skin Shrine*) by Micha Brendel, Else Gabriel, and Via Lewandowsky. Hochschule für Bildende Künste, Dresden, July 3, 1987. Performance. Photograph by Werner Lieberknecht. Reprinted with the permission of Else Gabriel and Werner Lieberknecht. © 1987 by Werner Lieberknecht.

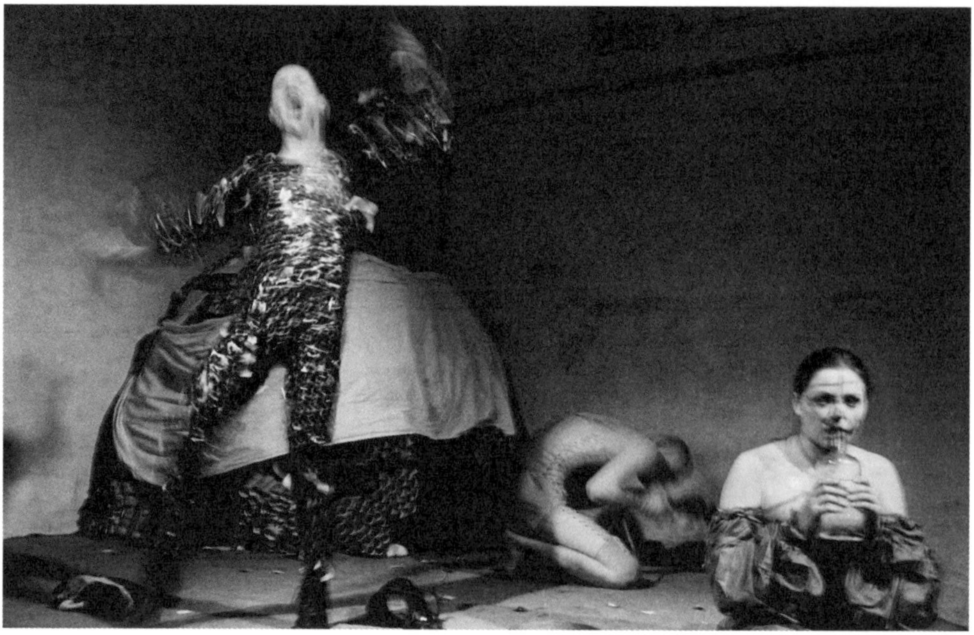

him. Indeed, the poet and regular Auto-Perforationist collaborator Durs Grünbein interprets the chant "as a rejection of the hegemonic mode of art education, and also as a warning call for the future."[37]

Well into the performance, Gabriel recites another text, perhaps the words she has typed out. Now uncovered, she is loosely swaddled in the red cloth, which slips gradually down her body to reveal her breasts. In general, she stands apart from her two collaborators, at times overseeing the action, at times directing it. Brendel

2.7

Micha Brendel, Via Lewandowsky, and Else Gabriel in *Herz Horn Haut Schrein* (*Heart Bone Skin Shrine*) by Micha Brendel, Else Gabriel, and Via Lewandowsky. Hochschule für Bildende Künste, Dresden, July 3, 1987. Performance. Photograph by Werner Lieberknecht. Reprinted with the permission of Micha Brendel, Via Lewandowsky, Else Gabriel, and Werner Lieberknecht. © 1987 by Werner Lieberknecht.

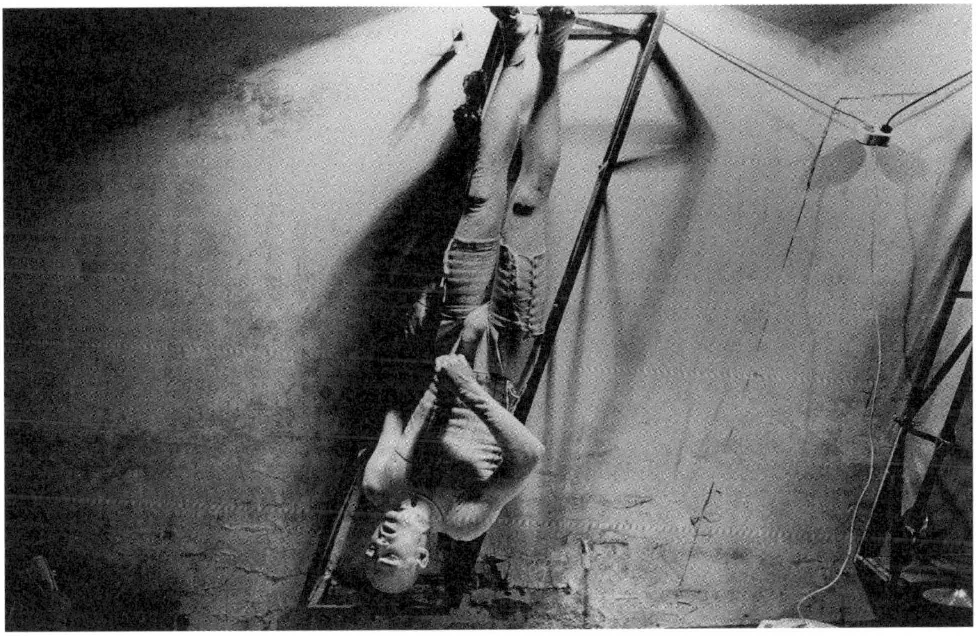

taunts and play-fights with Lewandowsky, his "masochistic counterpart."[38] Their interactions are as homoerotic as they are animalistic. Each man seems to wager the other as a competitor-companion, someone with whom he can cohabit this strange, otherworldly stage. Lewandowsky appears in a characteristically gender-nonconforming outfit: a pink corset holds tight to his torso. His legs are covered to the thigh in shorts of similar fabric that lace up along the sides. Underneath this soft armor, he wears a body suit the khaki color of his bald head and flesh. Brendel

2.8

Via Lewandowsky in *Herz Horn Haut Schrein* (*Heart Bone Skin Shrine*) by Micha Brendel, Else Gabriel, and Via Lewandowsky. Hochschule für Bildende Künste, Dresden, July 3, 1987. Performance. Photograph by Werner Lieberknecht. Reprinted with the permission of Via Lewandowsky and Werner Lieberknecht. © 1987 by Werner Lieberknecht.

is Lewandowsky's aggressive contrast. His hair tightly shorn—at times covered with a wrestler's chin strap—he wears black from head to toe. An overlayer made of neatly tessellated photographs of two eyes on black ground covers his pants and top. At the beginning of the performance, Brendel stands in a corner whipping himself lightly. Later, he engages the audience, speaking directly to them or peering at them through binoculars. He and Lewandowsky eventually wrestle their way into a domed structure made of bent metal covered in empty toilet paper rolls. Gabriel joins them. Inside this chamber the action is barely visible; a bright light is turned on, while the rest of the performance space goes dark. The remainder of the spectacle involves a series of violations: The two men force water into Gabriel's mouth through a tube until she begins to gag. Later Brendel uses this same tube as if to suck Lewandowsky's brains from the crown of his head. The final phase of *Heart Bone Skin Shrine* begins when the artists are affixed by their feet to wrought-iron coffins. They bang on instruments and shout. Görß, who helped to cage them, now frees each one from his or her rack. The lights go dim. The sounds of an electric drill fill the room as the artists mount three plaques, each engraved with the words "*für Herz Horn Haut Schrein*" and one performer's name, to the wall. Their territory marked, the performance ends.

Brendel, Gabriel, and Lewandowsky each took turns off stage, where they wielded a motion picture film camera and recorded the event. At least two other documentarians, including Karin Wieckhorst and Werner Lieberknecht, took still photographs. These documentary measures help to explain the notoriety of this work, as well as of Auto-Perforationist art more generally. A methodical approach to self-archiving was typical of the experimental art scene, a defensive strategy that reflects a prophetic—or apocalyptic—view of the East German state. For the Auto-Perforation Artists, documentation likewise contributed to the evidence they could use to defend their claim to artistic significance both in and beyond the GDR. A seven-minute promotional version of the *Heart Bone Skin Shrine* film served this purpose.[39]

The art academy could not have anticipated the renown the Auto-Perforation Artists would enjoy today, let alone the reputation they would gain or the influence they would harness in their time. In fact, officials did attempt to curb the visibility of their now-famous thesis project. Although Brendel, Gabriel, and Lewandowsky received permission to present a joint defense, academy officials stipulated that each student produce individual thesis projects. Lewandowsky received unequivocal praise for his design concept for the Heiner Müller play *Anatomie Titus Fall der Rome. Ein Shakespeare-Kommentar* (*Anatomy Titus Fall of Rome: A Shakespeare Commentary*).[40] For her solo work, Gabriel also dealt with Shakespeare, creating a set design for *Romeo and Juliet*, for which she received a barely passing grade of four.[41] The three artists' joint defense was a sober event, closed to the public, as per academy custom. In contrast, *Heart Bone Skin Shrine* attracted an audience of several hundred people, despite the school's attempts to minimize its visibility by scheduling it in a basement gymnasium. According to Gabriel, the three artists were promised but never received a grade for their elaborate performance of *Heart Bone Skin Shrine*.[42] An evaluation that used the metrics of a more conventional set design thesis may have been possible, because as the Germanist Seth Howes observes, the performance's forays into theater and dance actually "exemplif[ied] the kind of work that scenography students were supposed to supplement with a built environment."[43] While both sides compromised, the art academy faculty's decision to permit the group project had clear benefits for Brendel, Gabriel, and Lewandowsky, who all had much to gain with official diplomas in hand. Obliged to state leadership to graduate as many of its students as possible, the Dresden school's leadership would have caused a greater stir by expelling or failing the three artists than by giving them this unprecedented opportunity. Investing in a student was not taken lightly in the GDR. Art students were promised three-year appointments after graduation as part of their candidacy period for membership in the Union of Fine Artists and were also promised art contracts, which would supplement their state-subsidized artist income. The schools only admitted as many students as it had positions or art contracts, which were themselves designed based on the numbers of anticipated graduates. School bureaucracy was thus deeply tied to the national economy, and in particular the high rates of postgraduation employment. For the artists, a completed degree meant professional status and made them eligible to apply for membership in the Union of Fine Artists. In fact, Brendel, Gabriel, and Lewandowsky would use their thesis defense as part of their argument for the acceptance of performance or action art as an official fine arts category in the union. Fighting for this right, and winning, ensured that even a person schooled in set design, considered a handicraft, could be eligible for the substantially better benefits of a person who had studied something deemed "fine art."[44] Görß would actually benefit from even greater concessions to his chosen course of study when in 1989 he defended the Dresden Academy of Fine Arts' first ever multidisciplinary thesis. However, Görß's work—an installation and performance series involving multiple contributors—was ultimately deemed an exception by the school's faculty council. Nevertheless, as Howes writes, "Görß's unprecedented dual degree at the Academy attests [that] he and his fellow Autoperforationsartisten put pressure on the customary ways of teaching, making, and exhibiting art in the GDR, breaking down disciplinary boundaries and confronting audiences with unaccustomed material."[45]

CONFRONTING A NATIONAL CRISIS THROUGH BODILY AND EMOTIONAL EXCESS

Writing under the pseudonym Anita Kenner for the West Berlin-based arts magazine *Niemandsland* (*No Man's Land*), the curator Christoph Tannert described the unintelligibility of East Germany's performance art as a deliberate and context-driven choice: "In view of the mechanisms of surveillance—which are oriented toward transparency—these performers invest their works with private myths. They commit themselves to obscurity by using cryptic layers of meaning."[46] By equating the "transparency" of state surveillance with the deliberate nonsense of the Auto-Perforation Artists, Tannert underscores the disingenuous foundations of East German government. The group's signature self-abuse—what Durs Grünbein refers to as "Protestant rituals"—reveals a multifaceted set of impulses native to the East German context.[47] On the one hand, self-sacrifice is fundamental to communism; on the other, it defines a premise of Protestantism, the historic and still dominant religion in the region. The Auto-Perforation Artists thus fused presocialist with contemporary identifications. This union of religious and political influence suggests that the willingness of East German citizens to accept and adapt to a paternalistic and scolding government reveals a longer history. Importantly, the East German Protestant church played a decisive role in the formation of the activist groups that ultimately rose up against state leadership in 1989.[48] Nevertheless, the East German psychologist Hans-Joachim Maaz critiques the church's typically neutral view of the state, writing that "in reality, with their encouraging words and authoritative advice and help, [church leaders] reinforced the widespread dependent and depressive attitudes and character structures of many members of the congregations."[49] As opportunistic as it was welcoming, in Maaz's view, the "church in socialism" preyed on the need of the East German public for places of free expression without actually giving those people the means to act autonomously—that is to say, to truly rebel.

In East Germany, physical restraints amplified the psychological consequences of a heavily bureaucratized state. Walled in, East Germany was, in Maaz's words, "a tremendous cage . . . a stable and secure enclosure of perfect control and training . . . oriented toward performance and obedience."[50] Here Maaz uses the disciplinary object of the Berlin Wall as a physical manifestation of a chronic *Gefühlsstau* (emotional blockage) that plagued East German society. According to his theory, this blockage formed in response to the immense pressures placed on people to conform to social expectations, leading to an inability to process complex emotions or to confront or reconcile the contradiction between state ideology and lived reality. The Auto-Perforationist performances penetrated this emotional impasse by forcing a self and system reflection. In a country that Gabriel once described as "so dead that the only thing you could do was laugh about it,"[51] these artists confronted their dissatisfaction through hyperbolic disruption, inversion, and abuse. Citing Maaz, the art historian and curator Eckhart Gillen, originally from West Germany, interprets these artistic moves as "shock techniques," devices aimed not only at reviving a lifeless or passive public, but also at redefining the East German citizen positively: not as a self-effacing and oppressed subject but rather as a discerning and agitated citizen.[52] Identifying a loss of confidence in the arts as a generational problem with devastating consequences for all echelons of East German society, he writes: "In contrast to many artists in the GDR who tried to spread their belief in a better socialism within the real existing socialism, their public remained without consolation, alternative, or hope. [The Auto-Perforation Artists] blew apart the familiar but unspoken consent of the alternative art scene."[53] Gillen's final observation is of particular importance: the Auto-Perforation Artists challenged rather than succumbed to the communal sense of frustration that had come to define a young and disaffected population. By creating what Gillen calls "uncertainty, fakes, farces, and confusion," they produced alternatives for a counterpublic that had grown to identify with its own marginalization.[54] Rather than lamenting, protesting, or creating a detached alternative to a fractious environment, the Auto-Perforation Artists produced works that sought to define alienation as a source of power and union. In so doing, they exposed a core vulnerability of state power. If no one believed in the new socialist man which they had been trained to emulate, the *Homo munitus* would cease to exist.

BAD OMENS: THE AUTO-PERFORATION ARTISTS, BIOPOLITICS, AND THE STASI

"You should live a clean and respectable life and be mindful of your family."
The Ten Commandments of the New Socialist Man (1958)

The Auto-Perforation Artists deliberately subverted acceptable uses of the body so as to draw attention to the docile subjects upon which the state's claim to authority depended. Good East Germans were clean and upstanding, and not only self-regulated but also monitored their families, and by extension their friends, neighbors, and colleagues. The Auto-Perforation Artists hyperinstrumentalized their bodies, highlighting their participation in a wider subjectification while simultaneously drawing attention to the threat to individual sovereignty that the East German state had perpetrated. By turning their bodies into fleshy material, they inverted the vision of the ideal East German while subversively actualizing it: malleable, without identity, submissive, and moldable. And yet their performed submission to state ideology revealed the undesired consequences of the GDR's biopolitics. As if anticipating Maaz's diagnosis of systemic *Gefühlsstau*, the Auto-Perforation Artists made evident that psychological decay, and not social harmony, had come to define the East German's shared condition.

A penchant for allegory is perhaps best revealed in one of the Auto-Perforation Artists' last group projects, the exhibition *Menetekel*, which took place in Dresden's state-run Galerie Nord (Gallery North) in early 1989. The title, which means "bad omen," offers some translation of a large and provocative installation that included moldy wallpaper, shards of glass, beef shanks, an industrial-strength magnet, and a toy-filled aquarium, among other things. Ironically, *Menetekel* portended a likely assured future for Brendel, Gabriel, and Lewandowsky, who submitted the exhibition in their application to full membership status in the Union of Fine Artists. The "bad omen" thus points to a cheeky critique of the GDR's cultural conventions, specifically, the experimental forms that would soon dominate state culture. Yet *Menetekel* has a wider scope. The exhibition's materials make symbolic but crystalline reference to an impending social disaster.

2.9

Installation views of *Menetekel* by Micha Brendel, Via Lewandowsky, and Else Gabriel. Galerie Nord, Dresden, January 8–February 18, 1989. Photographer unknown. BStU, MfS, BV Dresden AKG PI, Nr. 69/89, 6. Reprinted with the permission of the Bundesbeauftragte für die Unterlagen des Staatssicherheitsdienstes der ehemaligen Deutschen Demokratischen Republik via the Stasi Records Act (StUG) § 32.

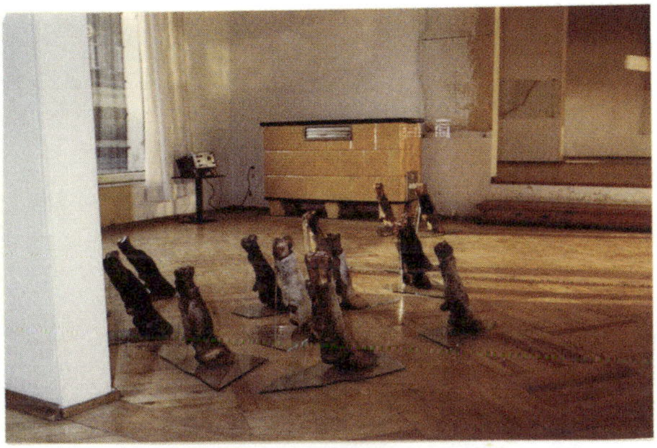

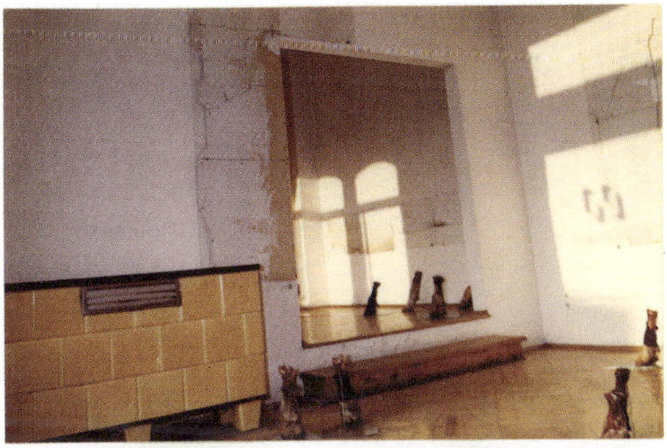

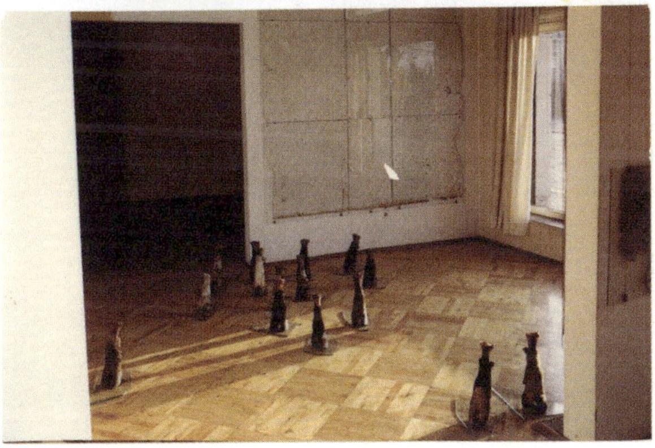

BSTU
0007

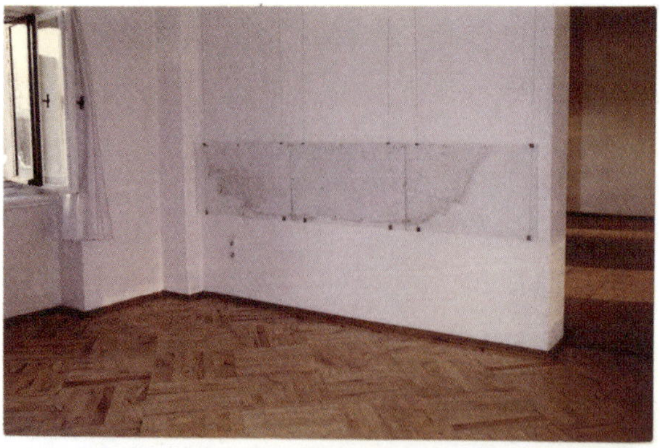

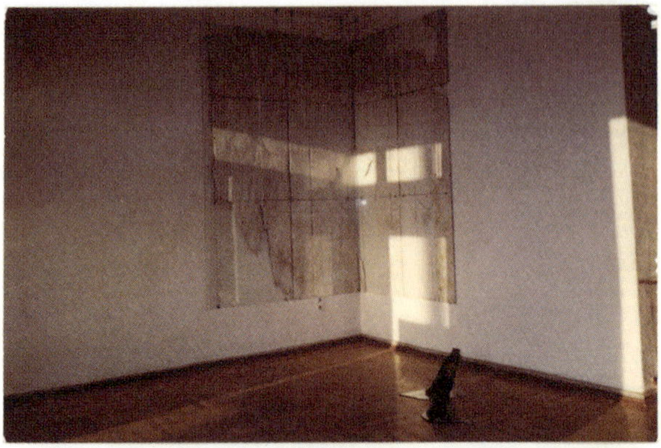

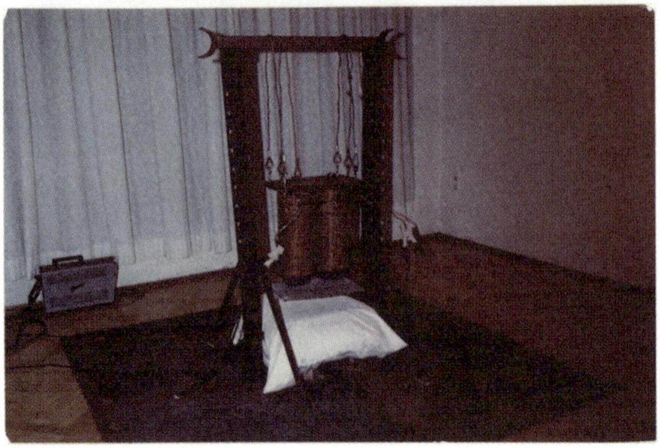

A high-pitched buzz emanates from a cluster of speakers installed in the ceiling of one of the gallery's entry rooms. A rhythmic *CLANG!!!————dunk—dunk* amplifies off the walls from an unseen source. Assembled across the parquet floors of the Galerie Nord's two large, street-facing rooms, the feet of twenty-five cows severed at the hock joint adhere to individual shards of clear glass. The elegant slope of each hoof as it leads to the leg makes the amputated limbs appear poised to move, as if the bodies of a grazing herd had suddenly detached themselves and hobbled away. Torn and mildewing remnants of wallpaper from a recent émigré hang on the walls above the cow's feet and are protected behind glass. The sheets of paper almost appear to be scars along the comparatively clean walls they adorn. They are both memorials to the continued loss of community members to the "free West" and reminders of the material realities that drove them away. The phantom animals march toward the gallery's two other spaces: the first is a large room, darkened due to its drape-covered windows; the other, more of a corridor, is abundantly lit with fourteen red heat lamps. In the larger room, an industrial strength magnet lifts and lowers a piece of lead. The mechanism is guillotine-like, with two oppressive-looking coils of coppery wire powering the crude animation of lead smacking up from the force of the magnet and then gently releasing as the pull subsides. The ominous rhythm that greets the *Menetekel* visitor finds its source here. Back in the entry room, red light spills in from the narrow corridor. At the end of the passage stands a rectangle of white light. Once approached, the rectangle reveals itself to be a water-filled aquarium in which the artists have placed a group of eight plastic figurines, a mixture of construction workers and farmers. This is the workers' and farmers' state in miniature. Inanimate and caged in a watery capsule, the toys are posed as if working the sand beneath their feet.[55]

2.10

Installation views of *Menetekel* by Micha Brendel, Via Lewandowsky, and Else Gabriel. Galerie Nord, Dresden, January 8–February 18, 1989. Photographer unknown. BStU, MfS, BV Dresden AKG Pl, Nr. 69/89, 7. Reprinted with the permission of the Bundesbeauftragte für die Unterlagen des Staatssicherheitsdienstes der ehemaligen Deutschen Demokratischen Republik via the Stasi Records Act (StUG) § 32.

BSTU
0005

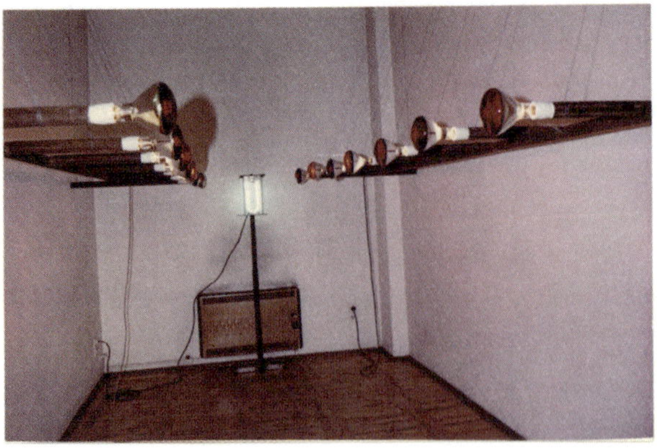

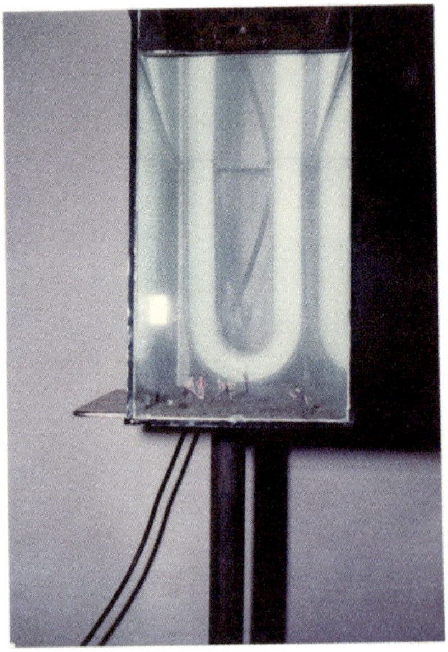

The Ministry for State Security (Stasi) took a special interest in *Menetekel*; its records are, in effect, the state security's own bad omen. The photographic documentation that has been used here to illustrate the exhibition reveals a curious and exacting gaze. But the documentation is rote, revealing a surveillance operation without strategy or direction. An examination of texts from the reports on *Menetekel* further illustrate a foundational failing of state power, what the historian Jens Gieseke identifies as a lack of "will and the mental equipment to undertake a critical analysis of the underlying causes of the deficits and problems it uncovered in East German society."[56] Writing under the alias "Nora Steege,"[57] a classmate at the Academy of Fine Arts reports: "The rooms in the Galerie Nord were consumed by such a stink from the cow's feet that you were glad to leave the exhibition. Nevertheless, in terms of the work's theme, the smell also works as a kind of provocation."[58] Elsewhere, Steege further details *Menetekel*'s sensations: "The exhibition presents the visitor with various kinds of stimuli. Optical and acoustic impacts are directed at the viewer through several kinds of materials and objects. These stimuli are in part nauseating, as in for example the overdose of warmth upon entering the 'Red Light District,' or through excessive noise caused by a very strong magnet."[59] Itself a kind of violation, the activation of the viewer's body reflects the exhibition's unsubtle messaging. The metaphorical body is violated in multiple ways: the amputated limbs of the beasts of burden symbolize the East German public who were valued by the state as an expendable instrument; the lead that smacks uncontrollably into the magnet summons the public's endless cycle of exploitation; and finally, the figurines who dig at the land in the flooded aquarium recall the trap of the proletarian sycophant. Sound, smell, and feel make these metaphors tangible, visceral.

2.11

Installation views of *Menetekel* by Micha Brendel, Via Lewandowsky, and Else Gabriel. Galerie Nord, Dresden, January 8–February 18, 1989. Photographer unknown. BStU, MfS, BV Dresden AKG PI, Nr. 69/89, 5. Reprinted with the permission of the Bundesbeauftragte für die Unterlagen des Staatssicherheitsdienstes der ehemaligen Deutschen Demokratischen Republik via the Stasi Records Act (StUG) § 32.

353

Abteilung XX Dresden,den 22.2.89

I n f o r m a t i o n
d e s IMS"Nora Steege" zur Ausstellung "MENETEKEL"

Ich besuchte auftragsgemäß die Ausstellung von Görß,Lew., Brendel und Gabriel in der Galerie Nord.Das war zwei Tage vor der Schließung dieser Ausstellung.
Die vier Genannten waren nicht selbst anwesend.
Hauptsächlich das 5.Studienjahr unserer Fachrichtung hat ebenfalls die Ausstellung besucht.Folgender Grundtenor wird bei den anschließenden Diskussionen sichtbar:
Das Gesamtkonzept der Ausstellung "MENETEKEL" wird als lächerlich und kurios angesehen.Gewertet wird die Ausstellung als "andersartige Sache".Deshalb findet sie auch bei den meisten Besuchern einen Anklang,weiles eben etwas anderes ist.Hinterher wird dann die Ausstellung belächelt.
Das beabsichtigte und für den sachunkundigen Besucher unbewußte Ziel der Ausstellung - Darstellung der Reize in verschiedenen Arten - wird erreicht.
In der Ausstellung werden die unterschiedlichsten Formen von Reizen auf das Individuum dargestellt.Durch verschiedene Materialien und Gegenstände werden optische und akustische Reize beim Betrachter erzeilt.Diese Reize werden z.T. widerlich dargestellt.Z.B. durch eine "Überdosis" Wärme beim betreten der "Rotlichtstraße",oder durch übermäßigen Knall (erzeugt durch starke Magnete).
Die Reize werden also auf eine sehr unangenehme Art provoziert bzw.dargestellt.
Dabei ist diese Art der Ausstellung auch nichts neues.Die Grundidee stammt von Richard Wagner,der im vorigen Jahr eine ähnlich gelagerte Ausstellung in Berlin-West durchführte, natürlich auf höherem Niveau.
Durch die Kuhfüße wurde in den Räumlichkeiten der Galerie Nord ein derartiger Gestank verbreitet,daß man froh war,die Ausstellung zu verlassen.Aber vom Thema her gesehen ist eben der Geruch auch eine Art Reiz.
Die Ausstellungsobjekte waren so angelehnt,daß eine eindeutige politische Wertung bzw.Zielstellung der Ausstellung erkennbar war.Selbst für Leute,die ein ausgeprägtes Kunstverständnis besitzen,war es schwer,den künstlerischen Inhalt mancher Objekte zu deuten.Man hatte den Eindruck,daß der politische Aspekt in den Vordergrund dieser Ausstellung rückte.
Alle dargestellten "Kunstwerke" sind mehrdeutig.Dabei kam es den Autoren an,die Besucher kopflastig zu belasten.
Man kann also sagen,daß so eine Art auch von den Studenten abgelehnt wird.Dabei weiß man,daß Görß in einer Gruppierung um Brendel integriert ist und sie sich selbst als etwas besonderes sehen.Unterstrichen wird dies auch durch die besondere "Würdigung" durch Tannert.
Daß die Autoren der Ausstellung nur auf ihr eigenes Image bedacht sind,verdeutlicht die Tatsache,daß sie am Ausgang der Ausstellung eine Liste anbrachten,auf der alle Betriebe und Institutionen vermerkt sind,die sie bei der Ausstellungsausstattung unterstützten.Diese Art ist absolut ungeläufig ,sie bezwekken damit,damit die Leute sehen,wie großzügig und anerkannt ihre Kunst ist.

Bureaucrats employed both direct and indirect strategies to condemn the exhibition and its artists. Neither made a difference. Officials tried once to close the exhibition for hygienic reasons when a cow's hoof began to rot. After the artists used ten bottles of disinfectant and attained the approval of a sympathetic veterinarian, *Menetekel* remained open.[60] The Stasi's official report on *Menetekel* reveals a pointed anxiety over the significance of the exhibition both within its own walls and in terms of its implications for East German public life, in general. The title of the report alone reveals the melodrama that underpinned the operations of the GDR's state security apparatus: "Young artists, whose attitudes and activities have led them to escape the [proper] influences of society, and who possess a provocative political charater."[61] Advocating that a political reeducation would be their most effective measure to curb creative production and influence, the Stasi ultimately suggested that the artists "be furnished with a practical artistic skillset through education. Therein they will receive the appropriate partners who will guarantee a positive political influence."[62] This reversal, of course, was not only improbable, but impossible. Too much had happened. By 1989, Brendel, Gabriel, and Lewandowsky had already received their diplomas, and the *Menetekel* exhibition would soon give these artists full entry into the artists' union.

It matters that these artists did not simply work within a cultural underground comprising furtive locations with secret handshakes. In fact, as this book seeks to demonstrate, such spaces did not really exist in the GDR. The Auto-Perforation Artists in particular demonstrate the insistence of the country's experimental artists on creating work with purpose and impact in mind. These artists were in fact advocates, even activists, leading a charge begun in their pathbreaking thesis defense to legitimate performance art within East Germany. Their efforts—in terms

2.12

"Information des IMS 'Nora Steege' zur Ausstellung 'MENETEKEL.'" ("Information on the Exhibition 'MENETEKEL' from the IMS 'Nora Steege'"). Dresden, February 22, 1989. BStU, MfS Dresden AOP 2784/90/1, 391. Reprinted with the permission of the Bundesbeauftragte für die Unterlagen des Staatssicherheitsdienstes der ehemaligen Deutschen Demokratischen Republik via the Stasi Records Act (StUG) § 32.

of both the consistency of their art practices and the attention they paid to formal channels of bureaucracy—helped convince the Union of Fine Artists to establish a performance art working group, led by Christoph Tannert and Eugen Blume. This new status eventually led to the inclusion of the art form as a valid category and ensured that performance artists (even those schooled in a handicraft like set design) would receive the union's highest-level benefits. Brendel, Gabriel, and Lewandowsky spearheaded the efforts for that kind of professional validation.[63] It is significant that all three would exit the GDR, emigrating in the wake of change that perhaps came too slowly for them. Performance art was a way out: first from the GDR's mandatory social body and finally from the geographic confines that defined them as East Germans in the first place.

AN IMMINENT END

Just four months after the *Menetekel* exhibition closed, the first—and only—performance art festival organized under the official auspices of the Union of Fine Artists opened in East Berlin. Called the Permanente Kunstkonferenz (Permanent Art Conference),[64] it ran from May 29 to June 30 in the state-run Galerie Weißer Elefant (White Elephant Gallery). It featured more than twenty performances, lectures, and film screenings, and ran parallel to the Berlin Regional Art Exhibition.[65] Produced just a few weeks before both Gabriel and Lewandowsky would legally exit the GDR, the Auto-Perforation Artists' contributions, which were more solo than collaborative, represent a dual disaffection from both the socialist state and the group. Gabriel's performance, *ALIAS/Die Kunst der Fuge* (*ALIAS/The Art of the Fugue*), in particular, signals a need for excision from East Germany—of both her person and of the Auto-Perforationist art form that she had helped to establish.

2.13

Else Gabriel in *ALIAS/Die Kunst der Fuge* (*ALIAS/The Art of the Fugue*) by Else Gabriel and Ulf Wrede. Galerie Weißer Elefant, Berlin, June 17, 1989. Performance. Photograph by Jochen Wermann. Reprinted with the permission of Else Gabriel and Jochen Wermann. © 1989 by Jochen Wermann.

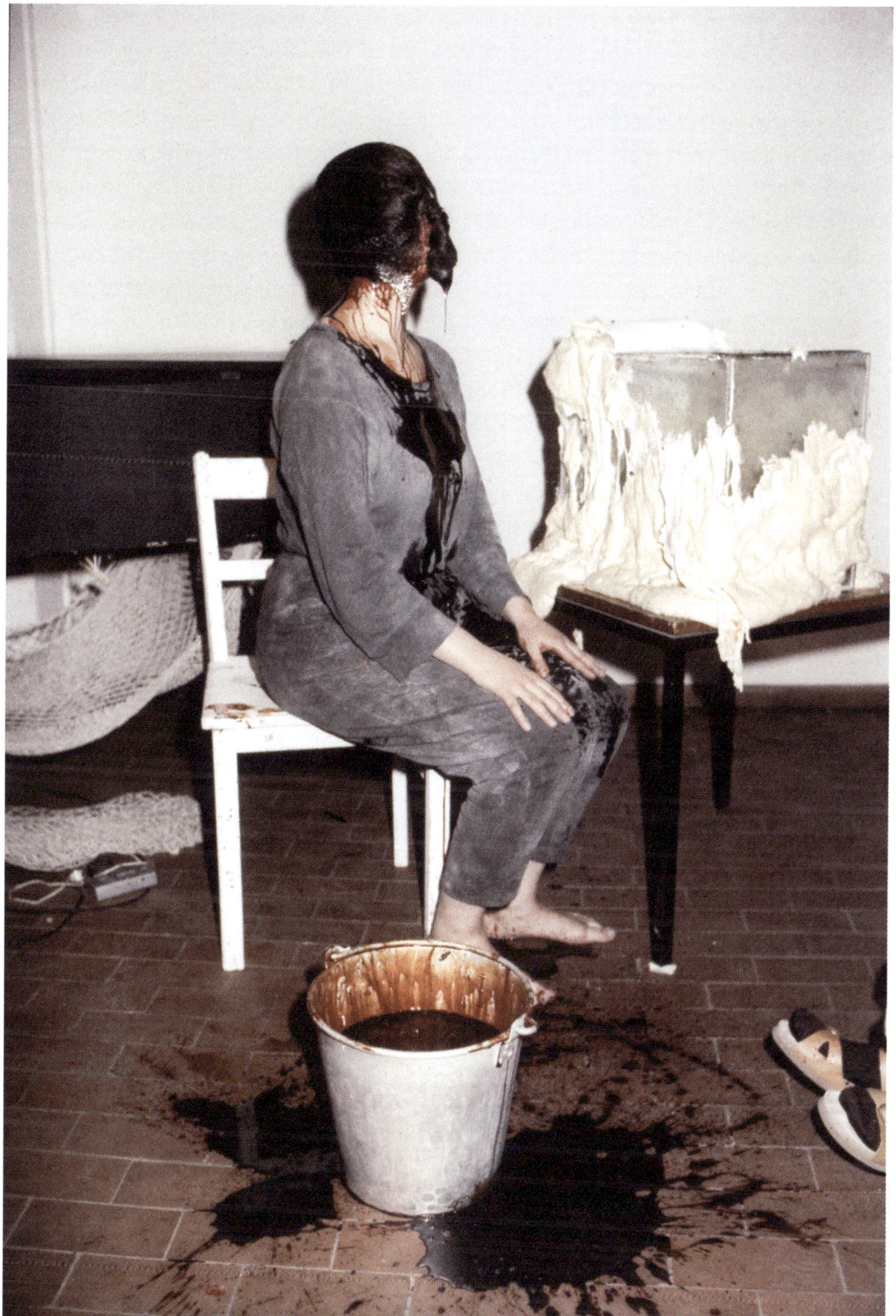

The stage is set with a metal bucket, a chair, and an aquarium loosely draped in bread dough that stands to the left of a grand piano. Ulf Wrede, Gabriel's collaborator, enters the room first. He mills gummy bears and raw beef through a meat grinder and into a pan. After setting the concoction on a burner, he sits at the piano bench and begins to play. Wrede performs a fugue masterfully; the performance is part of his thesis project, which will grant him entry into the music profession. After he is done, Gabriel's voice is heard from beneath the piano. She recites a text whose words are difficult to discern. After some time, she crawls out from her hiding place. Dressed in gray coveralls, she has pulled her hair to the front of her face in a bun, obscuring her eyes and nose. She kneels to the ground. Wrede pours the warm and bubbling meat-candy mash into the metal bucket, which unbeknownst to the audience is full of day-old pig's blood. Without warning, Gabriel dunks her head into the vessel. After a few seconds she emerges. Long, thick streams of the sticky mess drip from her hair. She takes a seat next to the aquarium and tears the cover of dough aside. A swarm of flies is released into the air. Behind her, someone turns on a fan so that the stench of blood, sugar, meat, and dough spreads into the hot and overcrowded gallery. Gabriel waits for her audience to leave. Eight minutes pass. The blood begins to coagulate, sticking her feet to the ground. Her gaping spectators are finally roused when a woman begins to retch. The performance is now over. In reflecting on these grueling minutes, Gabriel recalls that she understood the passivity of her audience as a sign that the Auto-Perforationist artwork had become an institution.[66] The abject aesthetic she and her collaborators had cultivated as a means to shock and even madden their audience out of a state of complacency had been normalized. The group members had themselves become disciplinarians who captured a docile audience, inuring them to the discomfort of witnessing a body in ruins. The end was near, not just for the group, but for the country, which would enter a decisive period of civil unrest just a few months later.

Whereas looking to the art under discussion in this chapter does not (and should not) demonstrate a clear link with East Germany's 1989 revolution, it nevertheless offers some insight into the feelings of frustration that had inspired a disaffected body politic to rise up and demand change. Importantly, the bodies represented in the artworks analyzed in this chapter are ordinary—"poor little sausages." The exhausted, overextended, deformed, frustrated, abject body is elevated as a shared cultural condition, perhaps *the* unifying identity of the East German population. Florschuetz's fragmented image and Gabriel's blood-soaked head share a common humanity. These are not aberrant figures, but everyday ones. The next chapter of this book will examine even more closely the representations of the GDR's ordinary citizens—as well as its outcasts—through the social photography of Gundula Schulze Eldowy[67] and the Super-8 film work of Cornelia Schleime. Their work, as well as that of Florschuetz and the Auto-Perforation Artists, thus redefines commonality, replacing the imposed image of a consummate communist public with one that is broken and disfigured. And in that breakage, power resides.

3

THE TABOO OF THE ORDINARY, THE VALOR OF THE MISFIT

Photographs by Gundula Schulze Eldowy and Films by Cornelia Schleime

Simultaneous to the corporeal turn in photography and performance art was the ascent of an increasingly incisive form of portrait photography, as well as a commitment to self-documentation on Super-8 film. This chapter examines these coinciding developments through the photographs of Gundula Schulze Eldowy[1] and the films of Cornelia Schleime which, like the photography of Thomas Florschuetz and the performance art of the Auto-Perforation Artists, may serve as allegories for the frustrating experience of living in the German Democratic Republic (GDR). Whereas Florschuetz and the Auto-Perforation Artists consciously reveled in an aesthetic of agony to contrast with the idealism of the country's official culture, Schulze Eldowy and Schleime offered another vantage point on the GDR's social makeup. Both used mainstream technologies of photographic reproduction—the still camera and the Super-8 film camera—and brought them to mainstream spaces—from public parks to factories—as well as private domestic interiors. State socialist ideology claimed to collapse the division between public and private life, and thus expected a clear ideological continuity across work and home life, public engagement and leisure activities. But Schulze Eldowy and Schleime document the discrepancies between state ideal and lived reality. By using modes of self-documentation that the government had encouraged its citizenry to adopt, from hobby photography to home filmmaking, they took advantage of readily available materials while also subverting their intended purposes.

These artists—like others discussed throughout this book—all sought to share their work with an audience, and to thus change the circumstances of cultural production along the way. Sometimes a broad audience may have readily identified with the artwork, as was the case with Schulze Eldowy's candid shots of neighbors or hard laborers, which today offer an expanded and sympathetic documentation of everyday East Germany in its final decade. For Schleime, whose films record artists, punks, and random people who attracted her interest, the identification was more exclusive, specific to the circles of social misfits she ran in. Her films are records of the GDR's caste of deviants, an underclass that state authority had sought to contain through written and unwritten laws of exclusion. In fact, the work of both artists adds new subjects of representation to a visual record of East Germany, which had otherwise prohibited their entry. But this work of representation is about more than inserting the marginalized into a homogeneous visual field. The active participation in the creation and consumption of Schulze Eldowy's photographs and Schleime's experimental films suggests that the citizens of the late GDR had become more self-aware and more critical of the machinations of a mass culture that aimed to discipline them into predictable and "docile" subjects.[2] East Germany's national culture had come to be understood as a superficial and ritualistic obligation, rather than an inspiring and stabilizing force. Schulze Eldowy and Schleime thus represent a changing attitude toward a centralized economy of representation.

BEARING WITNESS: THE PORTRAIT PHOTOGRAPHY OF GUNDULA SCHULZE ELDOWY

Her name is Tamerlan. She is sixty-six, but aged well beyond these years, seated on a park bench with her legs wide apart, both casual and confrontational. She leans forward in her seat, calling out to her viewer with her mouth open in an enigmatic expression of simultaneous indignation and amusement. The black-and-white photo conceals the color of the thick overcoat that covers her slim upper body to bare knees. The black of her eyes, set in shadow by a furrowed brow, renders

3.1

Gundula Schulze Eldowy. *Tamerlan, Berlin* from the *Tamerlan* series. 1979. Silver-gelatin print. Reprinted with the permission of Gundula Schulze Eldowy. © 1979 by Gundula Schulze Eldowy.

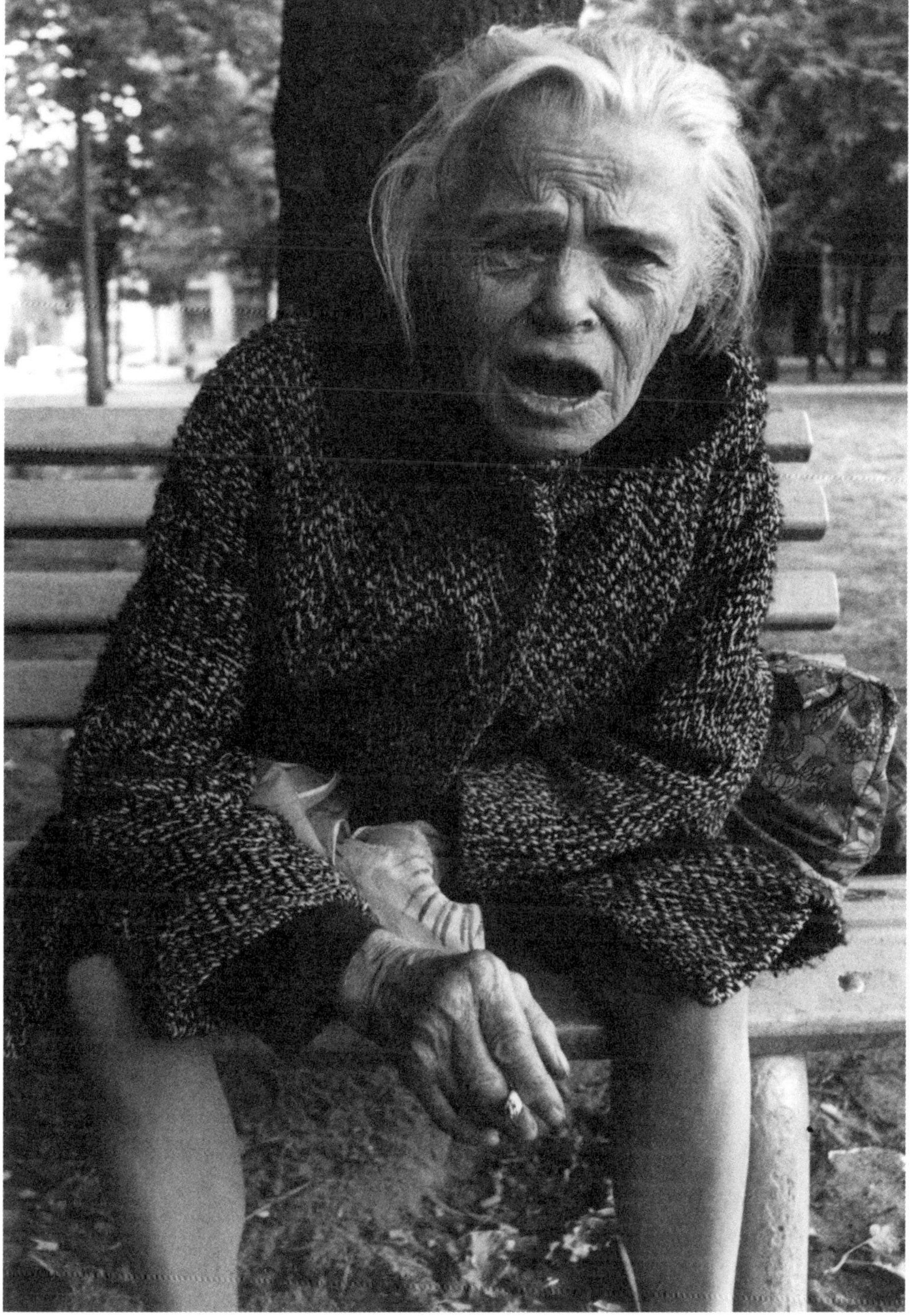

her gaze imprecise—its reach arcing the entirety of the photo's vertical frame. A cigarette is crushed deeply into the crevice of the second and third fingers of her right hand. Behind her, blurred tree leaves and a stretch of grass reveal this to be a summer day. A second, less confrontational image shot from above records a pause in Tamerlan's spoken exchange with her photographer, Gundula Schulze Eldowy. Tamerlan appears passive, her look distracted as she directs her gaze to the ground before her feet. A slight hint of a smile renders her mood once again hard to discern. The photo is framed as a swirl that envelops the woman, almost cupping her but for the horizontal cut of the park bench that extends off frame. Lightly blurred bushes in the upper left carry the viewer's eye toward and then around a tree that intersects Tamerlan's back. Footprints guide this movement to her toes peeking through plastic sandals and lead finally to an unseen object that holds her attention off-screen.

These images document Schulze Eldowy's first meeting with Elsbeth Kördel, whose husband gave her the pet name Tamerlan after a song he loved from the 1920s. The chance encounter in the East Berlin neighborhood of Prenzlauer Berg in 1979 began an eight-year collaboration. Schulze Eldowy photographed Tamerlan—a retired postal worker—until 1987, producing more than two dozen images that follow her through a series of carnal ends: amputations that progress from her toes to knees to lower to upper legs, the death of her boyfriend Erwin, as well as the slow decline she shared with her nursing home companions. Tamerlan is one of dozens of people Schulze Eldowy photographed between 1977 and 1990. In these portraits, the photographer gazes earnestly into the faces of her neighbors, looking to document a shared history buried beneath the rhetoric of the East German state's mandatory collectivity. This analysis is dedicated to a selection of portraits from Schulze Eldowy's black-and-white series *Berlin in einer Hundenacht* (*Berlin on a Dog's Night*, 1977–1990). The photographer made a second, nearly simultaneous color series *Der große und der kleine Schritt* (*The Big and the Little Step*, 1982–1990), for which she traversed the East German nation to create a generic overview of a city and its infrastructure: "From the dance hall in the hospital, the anatomy room in the slaughterhouse, from there into the ballet school, the opera, on to the factory floor, into the delivery room and finally the graveyard."[3] My choice to focus on portraits from the Berlin series is twofold. First, black-and-white photography was not only more common, but commonplace in the GDR.[4] Second, the portraits exemplify a portrait photography movement underway in East Germany at the time of Schulze Eldowy's studies in the early 1980s and during her entry into the profession of photography thereafter. Significant here are the ways that Schulze Eldowy traversed both official and unofficial culture to share a vision for how to represent or document East Germany in ways authorities deemed at times acceptable, at other times contentious.

In terms of material, noncolor photography makes multiple references to photographic practices specific to East Germany, where shooting and printing in color were a near impossibility for most people. Schulze Eldowy printed her color series in West Germany at the famous Niggemeyer Studio. A West Berlin boyfriend, as well as professional contacts with the studio, enabled this exchange. Encounters with officials ultimately made her wary of potential threats to her creative autonomy, and Schulze Eldowy eventually began hiding film negatives in her bedpost.[5] She later learned that a friend—whom she described as "the person to whom I was closest"—had been informing on her to the Ministry for State Security (Stasi), and that the agency not only undertook secret searches of her Berlin apartment, but also aimed to plant incriminating materials in her home.[6] This duplicitous entrapment strategy was, of course, not unusual, and reflects the corruption that undermined the GDR's claim to be a democracy. Most of the photographs Schulze Eldowy exhibited in East Germany were on black-and-white film, which she could easily process herself. Because artists could develop and print monochromatic film in home or private studios, the advantage of working independently also afforded a level of protection from authorities who regularly confiscated or made duplicates of photographs processed in state-run studios. Schulze Eldowy even muses that the Stasi has the most comprehensive collection of her GDR-era photographs—a suspicion that could likely bear out for others, as well. In fact, in 1992, Schulze Eldowy discovered a great many photographs in her Stasi file. The images, vintage prints from her color series, *The Big and the Little Step*, had been confiscated by border guards when a friend attempted to bring them back East after they had been printed in West Berlin. Schulze Eldowy's requests for the return of these precious images have been denied. "The images," she explains, "now belong to the Federal Republic of Germany."[7]

In terms of content, *Berlin on a Dog's Night* ponders the impact of the then-recent experience of two world wars on this major German city, and sets it in relation to the vision of communism, which obscured rather than remedied this trauma. Fascinated by this place which "swallows its inhabitants without mercy . . . covers them under a cloak of forgetting, layer by layer,"[8] Schulze Eldowy photographed dilapidated surroundings and dilapidated people—focusing on how the city's wartorn history had produced its public. She stuck to Prenzlauer Berg and Mitte, two wall-adjacent neighborhoods where a poorer population, including working-class and immigrant families, had historically lived. Proximity to the Berlin Wall made the area undesirable for development. Cast off from the GDR's ambitious building plans, these neighborhoods contained a high percentage of unrenovated buildings, many still scarred from the firestorms of World War II. In no small part owing to this state of neglect, these are also the places where East Berlin's experimental art and literature scene ultimately established itself. But Schulze Eldowy was unconcerned with artists and considered herself to be an outsider, even to this scene.[9] Instead, she photographed longtime residents: Tamerlan, a couple down the hall in their wedding finery, the alcoholic mother with babe in arms, a nearly blind mail carrier. She wanted to photograph the ordinary realities of her less-than-perfect neighbors, to show a reality ignored by the ideals of state socialism.[10]

In the introduction to the 2011 publication of *Berlin on a Dog's Night*, Schulze Eldowy frames her black-and-white series with compassionate curiosity: "How can so many people live in the most degrading circumstances? With this question in mind I approached and listened to them. I experienced their stories, for I was living beside them, became one of them."[11] Pathos may have inspired these photographs, and helps to explain their immediate pull. Who could not be moved by Tamerlan, whose frame literally shrinks before our eyes in a series of photographs that record a succession of amputations? Yet Schulze Eldowy's subjects engage her camera, asserting agency and self-awareness, which the photographer also sometimes details in firsthand accounts. This is not to say that she glorifies her subjects. To the contrary, a rawness permeates these images. An introductory text to the *Tamerlan* series describes the woman's sad and often miserable life. Letters she pens to Schulze Eldowy—whom she calls her "little girl"—likewise reveal that monotony and despair consumed Tamerlan's final years, which she spent in a nursing home. Schulze Eldowy records the potential horrors of aging, dramatized through the speed of Tamerlan's decline, made so physically apparent in her loss of limbs. Coupled to these images of Tamerlan are portraits of her nursing home neighbors—toothless, bedridden, their faces marred by age spots, and eyes watery and sunken. An elderly couple embrace on a park bench. Their kiss and crooked fingers are heartfelt and tender, but their advanced age renders the image almost surreal, as themes of romantic love are generally reserved for the young. The *Tamerlan* series embraces the challenge of humanizing marginalized subjects, in this case the elderly, who, if Tamerlan's letters are any indication, led isolated lives of agonizing predictability. "That's the end of the day," she writes to her "little girl." "After that, blessed sleep.

I wish it was forever. And, every day the same." The point here is not to dwell on misery, but rather to allow these photographs to bear witness to the lives of people left to expire in much the same way they would have if they had lived elsewhere, including in a capitalist context. In addition to ageism, Schulze Eldowy likewise documents the ableism that state socialism had failed to eradicate. "Officially," she says, "the communists had declared that there were no social problems anymore, and I personally had learned of such an unbelievable poverty and abjection from these people. And I showed it exactly how I had lived it."[12] Framing financial and emotional hardship as a consequence of societal expectations that were impossible to achieve, Schulze Eldowy's images opposed the claims of economic prosperity and social harmony that official culture promoted.

Details that surround the *Tamerlan* series reveal that self-awareness and a desire to engage motivated the woman's participation in her documentation. Schulze Eldowy's portraits illustrate both the compassion of their maker and the desire of their sitters to be seen. A series of nudes, taken from the thesis project she successfully defended in 1984 at Leipzig's Academy of Fine Arts (Hochschule für Grafik und Buchkunst) reveals that reciprocity. The series comprises a range of body types: a man gently clutches his pregnant wife in a narrow room flanked by a bed and a piano; an older woman sits assuredly in her dining room; a young woman wearing eyeglasses with thick lenses sits with her knees drawn in front of her—a coy smile is made enigmatic by the two stuffed animals set behind her and a frilly dressing gown carefully framing her breasts. In nearly all of the nude portraits, the subjects stare back into the camera with eyes that range from self-assured and intimidating to innocent and sweet. None of the subjects are particularly striking—not overly beautiful, not ugly, but all average—that is to say, ordinary. All appear in their own homes with objects that are personal and familiar. Writing on the emergence of a new form of nude photography in the 1980s, including Schulze Eldowy's contribution, the historian Josie McLellan observes that when artists took "as their subjects men, children, the old, the overweight and the physically disabled, not only did their photographs point out the hypocrisy of mainstream nude photography, but they also drew attention to the regime's social and economic failures."[13] And yet Schulze Eldowy's subjects are not failing. They may be frail in some cases, but they are not destitute. Nevertheless, when taken in the context of a highly idealistic and instrumentalist image culture, the uniqueness of her subjects is plain.

Schulze Eldowy drew inspiration from the photographers Henri Cartier-Bresson, Diane Arbus, Paul Strand, and Robert Frank; Frank actually mentored her for

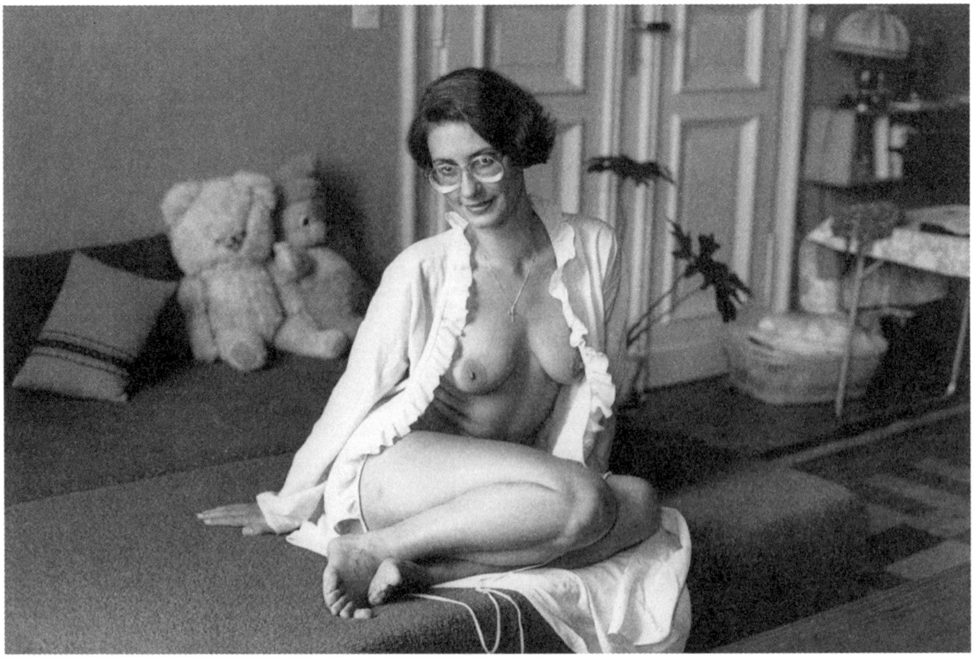

several years after they first met at an East Berlin gallery in June 1985. These influences partially explain the candidness of her portraiture, as well as the high contrast and deep pools of dark black; both are aesthetic signatures of the live or straight photography that helped to define an international style of documentary photography in the post-World War II era. Schulze Eldowy would have gained exposure to work by Cartier-Bresson, Arbus, Strand, and Frank, as well as the MAGNUM studio they associated with, through professors during her studies at the Academy of Fine Arts in Leipzig, as well as later through the French Cultural Center, which opened in East Berlin in 1984. She ultimately profited greatly from the support of

3.2

Gundula Schulze Eldowy. *Leipzig* from the *Aktporträts* (*Nude Portraits*) series. 1985. Silver-gelatin print. Reprinted with the permission of Gundula Schulze Eldowy. © 1985 by Gundula Schulze Eldowy.

Frank; their mentoring relationship would bring her to New York City shortly after the fall of the Berlin Wall.[14] Of course, photographers in East Germany had long continued Germany's legacy of photographic innovation, and drew from both pre-Cold War German examples and contemporaries from France, West Germany, and the United States, in particular.[15] Influential makers from the GDR included Evelyn Richter, Arno Fischer, and Roger Melis, who sought to move beyond the didactic figures prevalent in early East German photography, while still abiding by a socially responsible documentary ethic. In fact, Schulze Eldowy studied with Richter and Fischer in Leipzig. Although the collective practices that had been so central to them did not inspire her or other young photographers to work collaboratively, the efforts made by artists like Richter, Fischer, and Melis to free photography from the grips of state-oriented documentation resound in the images made by their students and admirers.

THE TABOO OF THE ORDINARY

Although East German photographers had begun early on to advocate for more variety and complexity in the country's photographic culture,[16] Schulze Eldowy represents a generation of makers—including Karin Wieckhorst, Ute Mahler, and Harald Hauswald—even less willing to compromise or bend to state doctrine. Photographers in the 1980s saw the gap between lived and represented reality as a cultural crisis that could be addressed photographically. Their works enact a politics of what the visual culture scholar Nicholas Mirzoeff names "countervisuality," which offers an alternative to a dominant mode of seeing or understanding the world by not just imagining but actualizing its alternative through new modes of representation and ways of inhabiting space that demand to be acknowledged.[17] Countervisuality recalibrates the power of vision by redefining both what is worthy of being seen and who is worthy of doing the seeing. These alternative visions assert "the right to look, [which] claims autonomy, not individualism or voyeurism, but the claim to a political subjectivity and collectivity."[18] Mirzoeff's focus on the binding quality of countervisuality returns this discussion to a more expansive vision of an East German public in two ways. First, the process of producing an alternative way of seeing the world requires the participation and acknowledgment of another: "You, or your group, allow another to find you, and, in so doing, you find both the other and yourself."[19] Countervisuality thus emerges through connection and reciprocity.

Not conjured or imposed, countervisuality instead awaits recognition. Tamerlan is a familiar subject, as are the somewhat lumpy bodies of Schulze Eldowy's nude subjects. Yet their excision from East Germany's visual culture shrouds their existence in shame. By photographing them, Schulze Eldowy relieves her subjects of this humiliation and redefines normalcy beyond the ideal. Second, Mirzoeff's tandem concept of "the right to look" calls this recognition a right and an action. The right to look redefines what is and can be seen. It also redefines who can do the seeing—both in terms of the taker of the image (the photographer) and the origin of the image (her subject). By offering alternatives to normative representation, Schulze Eldowy's photographs deauthorize the authority of "real existing socialism." They destabilize its premises of equity in representation and mutual benefit for all East Germans by inserting new but familiar stories that make evident the failings of the state socialist system. This is the taboo of the ordinary.

Schulze Eldowy's images of work most clearly visualize that taboo. Her *Arbeit* (*Work*) series—a set of sixteen photographs from the Berlin project—is exemplary in the subtlety of its visual and symbolic inversion of worker photography, a genre popular throughout East Germany's four-decade history. In spite of their ubiquity, by the 1980s it would have been difficult to find anyone who took seriously the images of harmonious workers churned out by official culture. Schulze Eldowy's images thus visualize a fundamental irony: laborers were not only still alienated from their labor; they were uninspired by the heroic projections imposed upon them by the state.

Schulze Eldowy explains that she took her photographs of workers because she wanted to see for herself how the people she lived among made a living. Because she could only enter the worksites with the requisite permission of the Union of Fine Artists, Schulze Eldowy prepared herself to meet the hostility of her chosen subjects. The workers she met did not regard artists highly because, as she put it, "[artists] fall to their knees for the state."[20] They were bitter toward the government because they knew that it was not invested in the working class, but nevertheless required an image or ideal of workers to maintain its legitimacy.

The workers' response to Schulze Eldowy reveals their critical awareness of a clear, known failure of official culture to actually fulfill its promise to the proletarian. For a brief time between 1959 and 1964, a nationally organized socialist cultural program known as the Bitterfelder Weg (Bitterfeld Path) had initiated collaborations between artists and laborers.[21] Programs like Bitterfeld aimed to fulfill a central tenet of Marxist-Leninist culture, namely its ambition to eradicate the class distinctions entrenched in bourgeois culture by collapsing the division between art and everyday life. The irony of Bitterfeld is that it worked too well as a tool for educating artists on the harsh realities of the labor they were meant to valorize.[22] Artists became more attuned to the experience of the subjects of (and audience for) their work. They translated the reality of untidy or inconsistent economic policy or cultural and class inequality onto the pages, canvases, and films of the era, which began not only to shed the layers of socialist realism's dogma but also to critique the state.[23] Although the government shuttered the Bitterfeld program in 1965 just six years after it began, artists still could rely upon government contracts or allowances to enter worksites. Decades later, when Schulze Eldowy came on her own volition, she nevertheless also had to gain access to the factories through official permission from the Union of Fine Artists. It makes sense, then, that she recalls that the workers she wished to photograph "were of course not very open to me at first, because they thought that I had been sent by the state. . . . None of the artists went to the factories, only the state or party lackeys did, and of course they thought I was one of them, because no one else came!"[24] Here, we see how Schulze Eldowy's process—her desire to know workers, to meet them on their level—informed her practice. In fact, it took several weeks for her to gain the trust of her subjects. She had to crawl into and around machinery to prove her sincerity. Of course, she was also a woman entering a world of men. Her presence in the factories thus summoned the inherent contradiction between the state's proclamation of gender equality and the reality of East German society.

Women do occasionally appear in Schulze Eldowy's *Work* series. However, with the exception of one photograph that shows a man and a woman on a break from work in a rubber factory,[25] women are not included in scenes of hard labor. In fact, the sexes are segregated in all but one other image, which is also the most joyful of the series. A man in a white hat and smock clutches and kisses a similarly clothed woman. They stand between a trough of a white viscous material—likely food—and a pile of neatly stacked boxes. Long pathways of fluorescent bulbs illuminate the large room. A pretty line of tiles along a wall softens the space and indicates that this is an industrial kitchen installed long before the minimalist interiors of communism had taken hold. Two other images show women in more banal—if no less taxing—work environments. In one photograph, a woman is shot from behind as she bends down to clean a service elevator. In the other, two women clean vats of small fish. One appears in the background intent at her work; the other bears a tray of marine creatures and looks, unsmiling, at Schulze Eldowy's camera. Her left eye

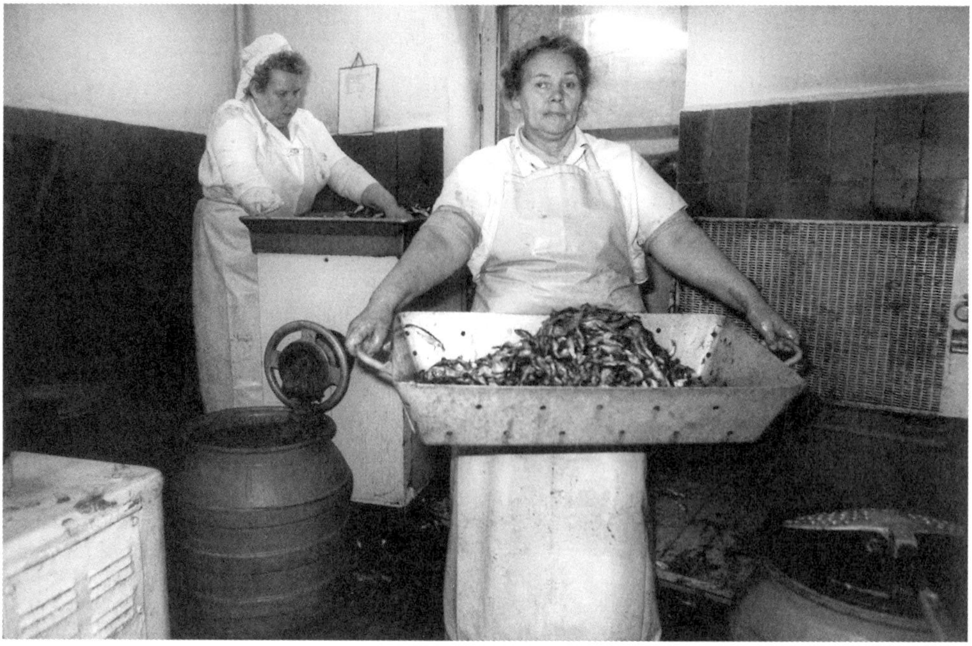

vacantly fixes on her viewer. Her right eye, which is amblyopic, migrates toward the periphery.

The remainder of the *Work* portraits capture men in the midst of hard labor. These images cast machines as bodily appendages or illustrate the precautions a person must take to complete the tasks of heavy industry. One striking portrait draws attention to the conditions of labor through an image that quite viscerally inverts a standard-issue image of worker heroism. In *Andreas, der Rußkönig* (*Andreas, the King of Soot*), a man exhausted and covered in filth takes a moment of rest from the vile task of treating rubber with a mixture of coal and chemicals. Married and of

3.3

Gundula Schulze Eldowy. *Erfurt* from the *Arbeit* (*Work*) series. 1987. Silver-gelatin print. Reprinted with the permission of Gundula Schulze Eldowy. © 1987 by Gundula Schulze Eldowy.

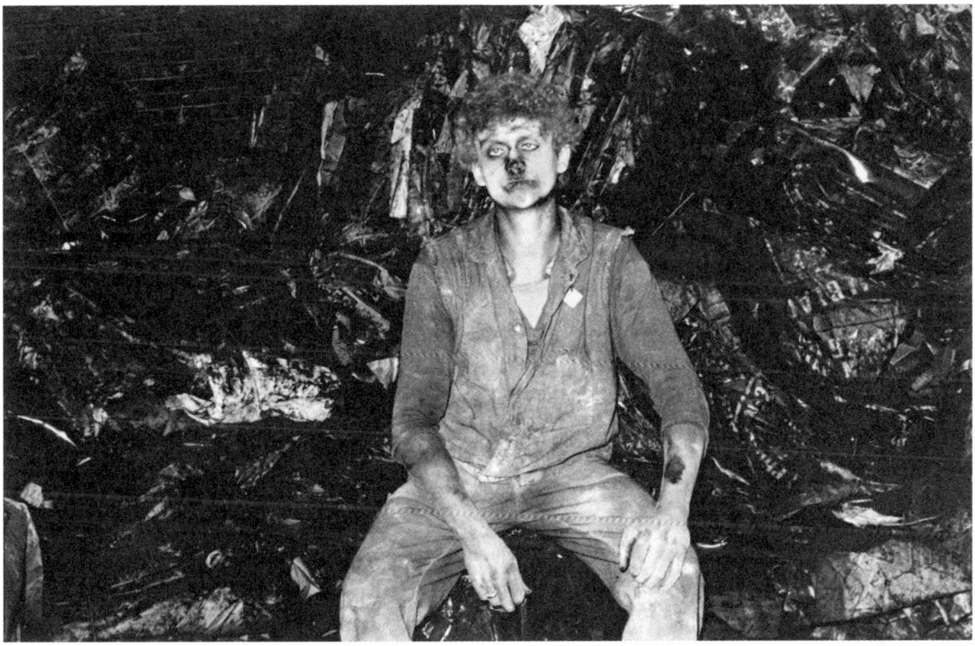

unknown age, Andreas's identity as a laborer (rather than a derelict) is revealed only by the essay Schulze Eldowy has written to accompany her portrait.[26] Slumped over, he appears weary and distant. Schulze Eldowy assigns him ironic regalia: he is a king in the socialist state. But Andreas looks more like a wayward clown than a king, with face made up in coal dust and curly hair frizzed by the steam of the factory. Dark circles weigh his eyes heavily downward. They are rimmed with ash, marks that Schulze Eldowy describes as permanent: "Despite daily showers I will never get rid of it," Andreas complained to her.[27] His nose, barely visible but for some gentle smudges of white skin, and his mouth, deeply recessed by black grime, reveal an

3.4

Gundula Schulze Eldowy. *Andreas, der Rußkönig* (*Andreas, the King of Soot*) from the *Arbeit* (*Work*) series. 1985. Silver-gelatin print. Reprinted with the permission of Gundula Schulze Eldowy. © 1985 by Gundula Schulze Eldowy.

extreme exposure to contaminated working conditions. His body is clothed in soot-covered overalls. Gaps of skin still clean indicate that he has unbuttoned several layers for this break, rendering the concentration of filth on his breathing, speaking, and eating orifices all the more alarming. Dehumanizing labor cannot erase the traces of the body. To the contrary, hard labor highlights the limitations of the human body. Andreas's orifices are vulnerable. The grime on their surfaces mark the places where he has swallowed, inhaled, and absorbed toxic filth. A cavernous backdrop of a room consumed by a heap of black, crumpled, and reflective material mirrors his polluted interior. This is the worker king on his throne.

Schulze Eldowy's photographs of workers recall critical images of labor that emerged in cities across Western Europe and the United States at the turn of the twentieth century. In a period of rapid urbanization, many were suspicious of not only the unfamiliar anonymity of city life but the reliance those cities had on hard labor and especially factory work. One prime example is the work of Lewis Hine, a sociologist and documentary photographer. Hine's campaign to record the conditions of child labor in major American factories in the early twentieth century was instrumental in changing these laws in the United States. Of course, Schulze Eldowy never sought the scale or social messaging that Hine achieved. Nevertheless, both shared the spirit of using the camera to document the underbelly of a society literally built on the backs of humans.

In important ways, Schulze Eldowy may be more closely aligned to the Weimar-era photo essays of August Sander, but in the inverse. In *Antlitz der Zeit* (*The Face of Our Time*), his totemic work from 1929, Sander sought to collect every type of person in German society. The project was heavily schematic and based on his idiosyncratic system of classifications and stereotypes. In a way, Schulze Eldowy's ironically titled "king of soot" really contests Sander's logic, which mirrors that later pursued by East Germany's photographic culture. In fact, as the art historian Sarah James has demonstrated, Sander's typologizing portraiture actually laid the groundwork for East Germany's divisive and compartmentalized form of photographic culture, and ultimately became a standard reference for photographic theory. James's research on Berthold Beiler demonstrates that a critical, but nevertheless faithful relationship between the photographic theorist and the Weimar photographer prevailed in the GDR. Beiler created what James describes as a visual "training atlas" on Sander,[28] which became standard material for the study and practice of photography in the GDR. He also discussed the artist in nearly two dozen articles that spanned a period from 1961 to 1989. As James explains, "For Beiler, Sander's typologizing series and the sober, frontal style of his photography . . . provided a central model for the photographic representation of social life through portraiture and, by proxy, a crucial means of photographically fashioning the socialist self."[29] In fact Sander's series included figures like the communist revolutionaries Erich Mühsam and Paul Frölich who would become important icons in East German culture.[30] His method of typologizing ultimately conformed neatly to socialist realism's penchant for visualizing "the typical," that is to say, the "essence of a particular social force . . . the 'ideal' and the universal."[31] Schulze Eldowy deliberately made worker portraits that contrasted with the idealized or typologized images of labor that populated official culture. In looking through her images, one is struck by the way they replace the ideological union imposed upon the East German public by the state with a more organic, everyday one. Schulze Eldowy's focus on the body, moreover, underscores the lived experience of East Germany as a material ordeal actually inscribed on the faces and bodies of the public.

Official photographers in East Germany typically cleaned up the reality of hard labor by emphasizing pleasure, satisfaction, leadership, and everyday heroism in the workers they posed before the lens. To take one example, an untitled image that appeared in the professional magazine *Fotografie* in 1986 by Thomas Kläber, a recent photography school graduate, depicts an unnamed laborer installing a natural gas pipeline somewhere in Ukraine. Most conspicuously, this worker's face and clothing are spotless. His pose is similarly sanitized. His hands rest in a snug waistband, emphasizing his slightly chubby body (considered the ideal body type for a worker).[32] His back right foot leans slightly forward on its toes, as if the photographer has caught him in motion. In contrast to Schulze Eldowy's image of Andreas, the backdrop is clear and open: a gas main to the man's right directs the image back along a road that winds toward a receding horizon of buildings. These are documents of a future in the making. The laborer's expression is uncomplicated, dull, and ironically lifeless compared with the acute exhaustion legible in Andreas's entire body. Unnamed, the pipeline worker likewise remains indistinct within a wash of proletarian subjects. Presented in a magazine within a photo essay awkwardly titled "Eine Bewährungsprobe für Fotografen" (A test of one's worth for photographers), Kläber's photograph was ostensibly a requirement for his professional advancement. The portrait is one of seven images that document work and life at the natural gas pipeline. The location is described in a short introductory text as a "central youth subject [*Jugendobjekt*]," suggesting that the motif was a standard pedagogical tool in photography. The text praises the benefit such "socially

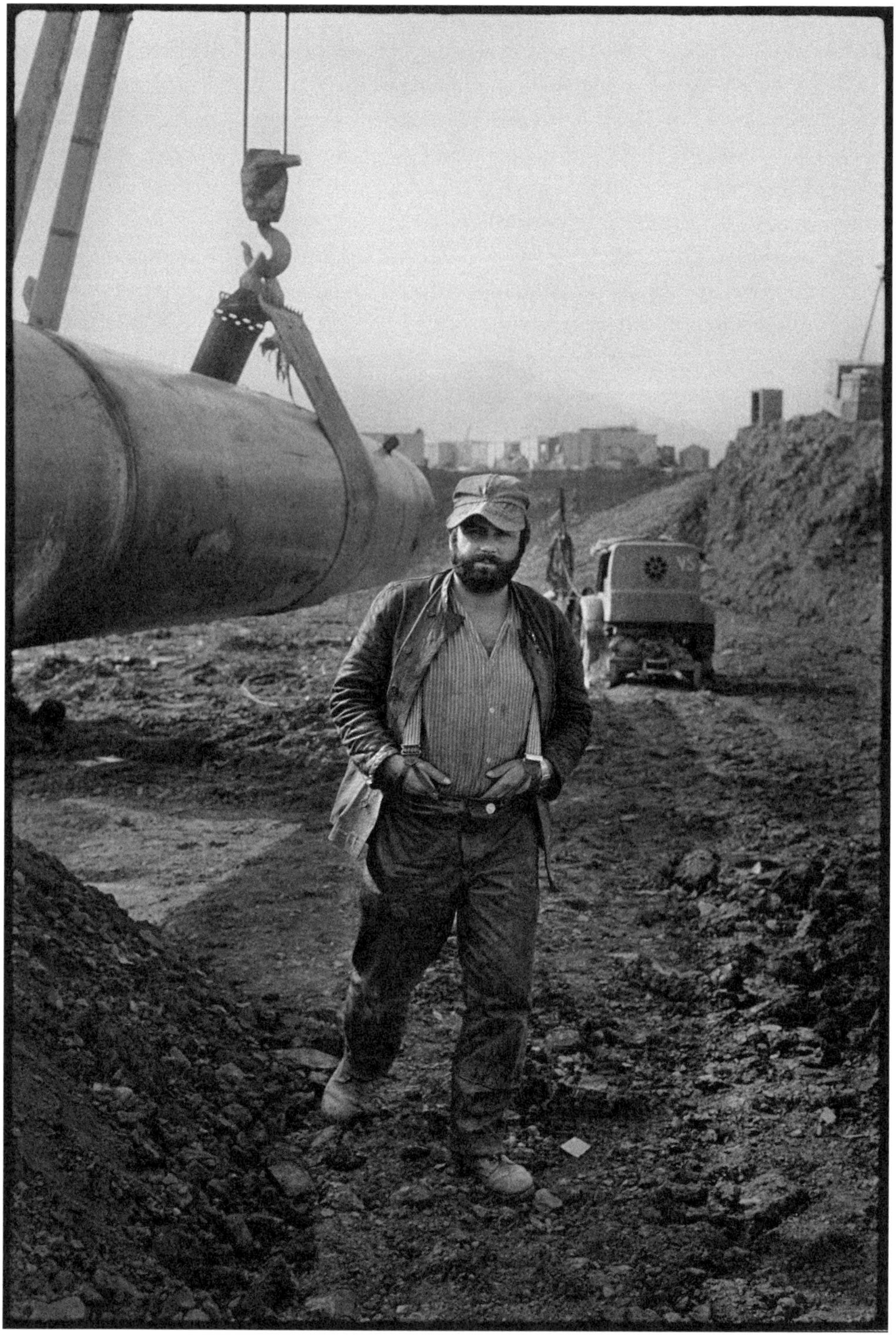

responsible assignments" had on the country's photographers in training.[33] A similar agenda for the magazine's East German readers is implicit. Intention is rendered sentimental in the images, which dramatize hard labor at the expense of a greater realism. In contrast, Schulze Eldowy's photograph of Andreas visualizes the physicality of hard labor through its toll on the body. There is no idealism projected onto Andreas. His plight is both a familiar and taboo subject. This kind of sensitivity to the realities of labor is not only absent in Kläber's portrait; it is carefully concealed.

Importantly, photographs by Schulze Eldowy also appeared on occasion in the state-run *Fotografie* magazine. For example, two landscape photographs from the *Der Wind füllt sich mit Wasser* (*The Wind Fills with Water*) series in her Berlin project appeared in a 1981 issue. At the time, Schulze Eldowy was a student at Leipzig's Academy of Fine Arts. The text she wrote to accompany the two photographs makes no suggestion of her student status or the context of the photographs within the larger *Berlin on a Dog's Night* project. This detail—not to mention the publication of her images in the state-run magazine, a prestigious venue for any GDR photographer—demonstrates the porosity of the borders between official and unofficial culture. Kläber, for his part, likewise pursued a more critical practice not represented in the image reproduced in *Fotografie*. That a publication could be supportive and selective is not unique to East Germany; however, that selectivity points to an important facet of the history of photography in the GDR. The curator Christoph Tannert compellingly suggests that photography in East Germany should be divided not by whether it was journalistic or artistic, but rather by whether it was published or unpublished, "because there were also journalists that could not get anything published."[34] Acceptable photography was thus a question not of style but of the photograph's perceived political position.

Worker photography remained quite popular even in the 1980s, especially as a reliable theme for the *Auftragskunst* (contract art) that many students at state art academies and members of the Union of Fine Artists received. Because the East German state identified itself so strongly with the proletariat, contract images were

3.5

Thomas Kläber. *Untitled/Erdgastrasse* (*Natural Gas Works*). 1983. Photography. Reprinted with the permission of Thomas Kläber. © 1983 by Thomas Kläber.

often idealistic, even fetishistic. These images comprised a significant portion of East Germany's dominant and repetitive visual culture. During the final decades of the GDR, the state's attachment to a proletarian identity had, nevertheless, withered into superficial posturing—a systemic, but conscious, self-deception. The historian Mary Fulbrook observes that although at this time more people than ever, particularly those in top positions within the party, were claiming a working-class identity, a unified proletarian community had been strategically disempowered: "But while the notion of the 'working class' was almost grotesquely expanded in GDR official ideology, in what might be called the 'lived experience' of East German workers there was an uncoupling of many of these features, and a dissolution of 'class' bonds."[35] An inflated use of the image of the working class had replaced actual engagement with the needs of the working class, including addressing the difficult labor conditions that Schulze Eldowy documents in her series on work.[36] The sociologist Wolfgang Engler identifies a similar problematic in his description of East German society as an *arbeiterliche Gesellschaft* (workerly society): "Rarely has a political system held its subjects on such a short leash, the responsibilities of its most important class more harshly reduced, its idealism more harshly tested as this one. . . . And seldom has leadership in modern times incapacitated the working class for so long and to such an extent, while at the same time depending on it."[37] Whereas the worker was consistently heroized and remained the leading prototype for the ideal East German citizen, the working class had very little political agency—that is, of course, until it claimed it in 1989.

When Schulze Eldowy first exhibited her black-and-white portraits in 1983 at the state-run Galerie Sophienstraße 8 (Gallery 8 Sophie Street) in East Berlin, a man who passed through during installation reported the photos to the Stasi, whose national headquarters were located just around the corner. On the day of the opening, a man and a woman from the governing SED[38] party came by. The photos of Tamerlan in various stages of amputation brought the woman to tears as she exclaimed: "Hopefully this will never happen to us!"[39] The man, who Schulze Eldowy suspected of working for the Stasi, pulled her aside to congratulate her on the exhibition. Nevertheless, he explained that he and his colleague had come to withdraw some of the images from public display. They asked for her suggestions. She selected an image of a middle-aged naked man and a few other portraits, electing to save photographs she considered more politically charged, including ones of people at public marches. She felt these images of "acceptable" public life possessed an irony that her colleagues would be able to discern. Today she says that she would have removed these more explicit images, and kept those of everyday people on the wall.[40] In the context of an official gallery, especially one just blocks away from the GDR's central intelligence agency, representing the average East German citizen as a flawed and ambiguous subject had a starker defiance than any political image, regardless of sarcastic intent.

As the essayist Susan Sontag writes, even the most banal images can be as powerful as the most explicit ones: "Those occasions when the taking of photographs is relatively undiscriminating, promiscuous, or self-effacing do not lessen the didacticism of the whole enterprise. . . . Images which idealize . . . are no less aggressive than work which makes a virtue of plainness."[41] Here Sontag warns that manipulation is easily embedded in images that seem otherwise ordinary: what seems familiar has been made to be familiar. In contrast to this, because her subjects are so plain, and thus unextraordinary—not heroes, but also not victims—Schulze Eldowy's photographs of ordinary people reveal the fallacy of East German culture's claim to be "typical." Her records of everyday life in the GDR act as substitutes for the socialist state's art and visual culture, which in its preference for idealistic fantasy over reality rendered the common man invisible. These are portraits of East Germany, but as it did not want itself to be.

THE VALOR OF THE MISFITS

The impulse to record a world that was otherwise absent from normative East German culture also inspired artists to pick up the camera. Super-8, a low-gauge and soundless motion picture film stock that was readily available in the GDR, became a preferred medium among the country's experimental artists. In contrast to Schulze Eldowy and other photographers whose portraits of everyday people filled a conspicuous visual gap in the GDR's economy of representation, artists like the painter Cornelia Schleime used the film camera to explore and record the country's manifestly unordinary populations. Schleime's films, in particular, record people who sought to stand out. These are subjects who intentionally upended convention; theirs is the valor of the misfits.

Schleime was a painter prior to being a filmmaker. Her turn to film was not all that unusual for fine artists in the 1980s. An investment in multiple media—an aspect of the experimental scene outlined in the fifth chapter of this book—was paramount at that time, a proactive move that reflects a moment of excited, even frantic,

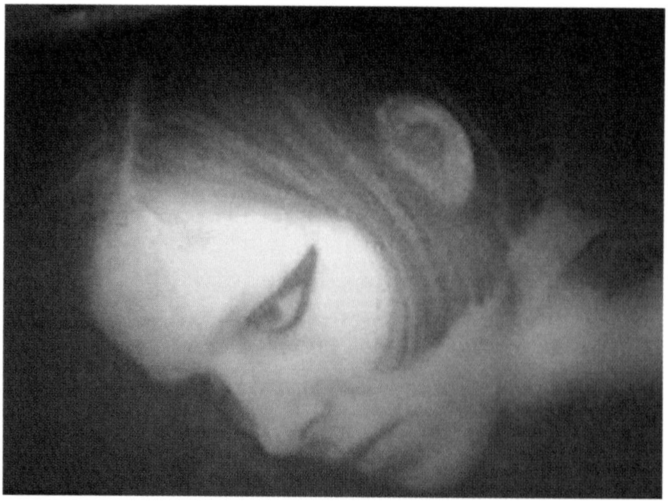

exploration of the self and artistic possibility. Schleime's first film, *In der Sanduhr* (*In the Hourglass*, 1982), recorded in the courtyard of an old tenement building in East Berlin, depicts an artist sharing space and ideas with friends. The elaborate costuming and masks that appear in the eleven-minute work bear the marks of a recent venture to the East German village of Hüpstedt where Schleime and Gabriele Stötzer,[42] who appears in the film, had just worked side by side on a series of self-portraits. Several of these and other "self-stagings" incorporate a wrapping motif that would be central to Schleime's third film, *Unter weißen Tüchern* (*Draped in White*, 1983).

The mood of *Draped in White* is uncertain—disconcerting and unstable. Its dimly lit and sparsely furnished environment is bleak, even without the enigmatic props that Schleime has staged. Unlike her three other GDR-era films, *Draped in White* follows an intelligible narrative. It begins with the delicate plucking of a finger harp and a backlit image of a woman and a man alone in an apartment. They smoke

3.6

Cornelia Schleime, *Unter weißen Tüchern* (*Draped in White*). 1983. Super-8 film, 9 min. Reprinted with the permission of Cornelia Schleime. © 1983 by Cornelia Schleime.

and pace gloomily around the space, which is nearly empty but for a dreamy installation of translucent white woolen cloths that hang from the ceiling. The woman appears with a veil on her head and smiles. Schleime speeds up and slows down the frames of her film; its soundtrack follows suit. The sound abruptly turns dissonant; the recording now plays backward. The woman changes into a white dress, suggesting that she is preparing for a wedding; her future husband also now wears white. After a quick shot along a quiet sunlit harbor where the couple stand with another man, the film returns to the apartment. It is now lit by the gloomy dusk of winter, and a light snowfall animates the window. White bandages affix three people to a wall. They appear as cocoons, or insects trapped in sticky webs, or growths bulging through plaster. Their faces are painted completely white, their eyes are thickly lined, and their mouths are deeply red. A postcard depicting a large ship at sea that Schleime has overpainted with a milky black figure breaks the scene irregularly. The bride reappears, now wearing all black; she wears dramatic makeup. She crouches among a pile of yellow apples set on the ground before the trapped bodies and combs the pelt of a white rat. No exchange between the woman and her bandaged companions ensues. The mood shifts. The soundtrack grows increasingly frantic and the people slip out of their cocoons. They frolic around the apartment; the bride looks increasingly troubled. She suddenly appears affixed to a door, which swings open and shut. She holds an apple in her hand. It drops, returns, drops, returns, repeatedly. The soundtrack remains dissonant. The film escapes this cyclonic nightmare and ends at the harbor, where the camera lingers on a tree hung with large sardines. The woman turns to her husband, who is smoking. She smiles faintly.

The art historian Angelika Richter interprets *Draped in White* as a "visual metaphor for the restrictive situation of the GDR's state socialism," particularly for its artists, "whose hands are tied" by this context.[43] The metaphor also extends to allegory; this may be a "filmic self-portrait," as its creation coincided with the emigration of Schleime's longtime boyfriend, the painter Ralf Kerbach. In Richter's interpretation, the bride who agonizes as she waits for her groom represents Schleime, who was then experiencing a similar "condition of existential disappointment and forced standstill."[44] The nine minutes of *Draped in White* bear the artist's imprint—a reflection of her dreamy aesthetic, a translation of raw emotion into creative object: "Whenever life got too intense, I'd pick up the camera."[45] The soundtrack, which Schleime would have performed live at a film screening, is improvisational and reflects the influence of the noise-punk band she was in at the time, Zwitschermaschine (Twittering machine). In a decades-long career as an

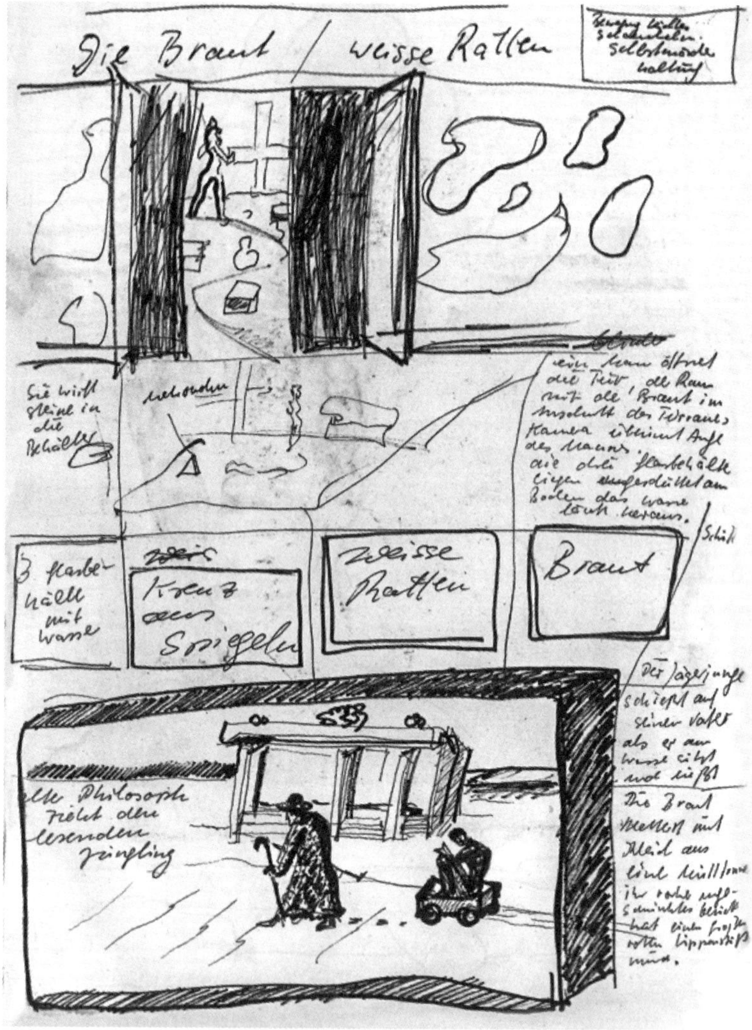

3.7

Cornelia Schleime. Film sketch for *Unter weißen Tüchern* (*Draped in White*). 1983. Ink on sketchbook paper. Reprinted with the permission of Cornelia Schleime. Image provided by Claus Löser. © 1983 by Cornelia Schleime.

artist, Schleime has dedicated only about two years to the moving image, all in the lead-up to her emigration to West Berlin. She was, however, an original player in the Super-8 film scene that boomed in 1980s East Germany, which saw nearly fifty people create approximately 150 films between 1976 and 1989.[46] Schleime made five of her six Super-8 films between 1982 and 1984,[47] with the sixth begun in the GDR, but completed in West Germany.[48] Her turn to the medium came after cultural authorities made exhibiting her paintings untenable, and essentially illegal from 1981 onward. The Stasi had begun a surveillance operation against her in 1979. The contents of these files, which she would contemplate in her 1993 *Stasi Series*, reveal a state government intent on humiliating and demoralizing her.[49]

Determined to emigrate by legal means, Schleime's move to the camera also reflects her anticipated escape from the GDR. Films, which are more portable than paintings and can be made with borrowed equipment, accommodated the twenty-four-hour window granted émigrés upon approval of their *Ausreiseantrag* (exit application). In fact, the Super-8 films, along with a box of photographs, are nearly all that remain of Schleime's GDR-era art. She lost more than ninety paintings in her move. Entrusted in the care of her friend Sascha Anderson—later revealed to have been a Stasi informant—their whereabouts (or fate) remain unclear to this day. The Super-8 films thus act as an archive of the artist's final years. As the film historian Claus Löser writes, they fill a void, "at least partially, since numerous motifs from the lost paintings can be found in the films, and they help us to bridge the gap to the artist's current creative period."[50] The wrapping that is *Draped in White*'s namesake is, as noted above, a signature image in the self-portrait photographs Schleime made in 1981 and 1982, but also reappears in later paintings (see, for example, *Liz II*, 1997). The overpainting of watercolors inserted in between *Draped in White*'s filmed sequences likewise return in Schleime's postcard and travel diaries from the early 1990s, as well as in a recent series of self-stagings (see, for example, *Augenwinde* [*Eye Winds*], 2019). The artist, in fact, returns regularly to the performance portraits, which she began making in the early 1980s. Thus, a clear trajectory exists between the work Schleime made in the GDR and that which she has made subsequently.

FILM AS SPEECH ACT

Schleime's brief interest in film reflects more than a pragmatic response to an adverse situation. Rather, the Super-8 film medium provided both creative and social openings. "There was so much going on. How could you go to your studio and paint? It just didn't work," she reflects in a documentary made by fellow émigré artist Lutz Dammbeck in 1988. Quite simply, she explains, "I wasn't able to transfer all I was living into a painting."[51] Working in Super-8 also guaranteed contact with a network of like-minded makers and consumers. Artists shared cameras and other equipment, and also appeared in each other's projects. Film screenings brought people together and facilitated future artistic exchange.

At the beginning of his comprehensive study on Super-8 films in the GDR, *Strategien der Verweigerung* (*Strategies of Refusal*), Löser proposes that "the very act of filming was a political undertaking."[52] Elaborating on his definition of these cinematic "strategies of refusal," he quotes the art historian Rüdiger Thomas who describes the politics of the 1980s experimental scene thus: "Even if this autonomous art had wanted to appear above all as apolitical, its political explosiveness lay precisely in the ways artists insistently ignored the state, which had become completely irrelevant to them."[53] This chapter seeks to expand upon this idea of "insistent ignorance" through the filmmaking of Schleime, whose works on Super-8 rejected the classifications and categories authorities cited as a means of exerting and legitimizing their power. In short: her films aestheticize and, in so doing, normalize deviance.

Schleime began working with film shortly after she was prohibited from exhibiting in 1981. Film stock was cheap and readily available, cameras could be easily shared, and—contrary to the usual impression of the GDR—filming in public posed few risks. Moreover, because film is a generally communal object—both in its making and in its presentation—working in this medium secured Schleime the audience the state had sought to deny her: "I didn't want to lock myself up at home and bumble around, just making paintings by myself," she reflects.[54] Schleime wanted to reach people, to communicate with them, and thus "smuggled"[55] her films into as many public forums as she could. The process of making a film also facilitated a kind of contact that made the present moment more interesting. Schleime describes how sexual intrigue in part fueled her final film, *Das Puttennest* (*Den of Cherubs*, 1984): "I saw this guy in a café and asked my friend, 'Woah, how do I get to know *him*?' I just went up to him and said that I thought he was interesting and that I make films, and so on."[56] Film as flirtation; film as seduction.

That seduction was manifold, both a means to gain personal fulfillment and a ploy against the authorities Schleime suspected of watching her: "I always hoped that the Stasi was sitting in and that they would say to themselves: 'Schleime is

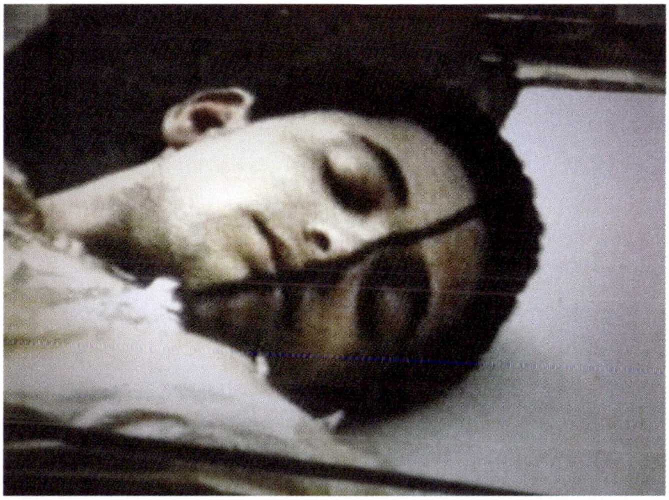

making such garbage, we have to let her go to the West.'"[57] The anticipated threat of observation motivated her to make work that could be deemed morally and physically repugnant: "That's why I made such provocative things," she reflects, "like that one with the meat. I thought I had to do something really disgusting to get them to let me out."[58] Here she speaks of her fourth film, *Das Nierenbett* (*Bed of Kidneys*)—a twelve-minute color film from 1983, in which raw meat plays a pivotal role. In its opening shot, a naked woman appears on a bed. She is accompanied by a man cut off at the head, as if he were trapped in the middle of black sand. The woman proffers herself with a silver tray of meat. Later, she sits at a table and consumes the flesh, while chicken feathers blow and land on her meal. The carnal themes culminate in a brief, but potent scene: The man is now whole. Naked, he is strapped on an old army cot covered in rotting meat. Random snips of images flicker through the film at varying speeds, sometimes animated in stop motion.

At times, quite literally buried in Schleime's abject scene is a call to be seen. Scipio, the young man who played the film's main protagonist, was, as the artist

3.8

Cornelia Schleime. *Das Nierenbett* (*The Bed of Kidneys*). 1983. Super-8 film, 12 min. Reprinted with the permission of Cornelia Schleime. © 1983 by Cornelia Schleime.

recalls, "totally fascinated with the idea of getting tied to the heap of rotting meat."[59] In this film, Scipio is a young man: slight, attractive, mixed race, and queer. His willingness to lie prone on a bed of flesh, and to reportedly enjoy it, suggests a bevy of emotional realities, for which he—as an underrepresented minority in East German society—may have been seeking a form. Scipio's name is likely a *nom de plume* that celebrates his race through its revival of the legend of a third-century BCE Roman general from West Africa. Perhaps Schleime used his brown-skinned body, unusual within the GDR, to add another character to her cast of misfits. Her fascination with Scipio would have reflected the racialized exoticism of the black body that pervaded East Germany's supposedly racially equal society. McLellan has called this a "clumsy logic which associated blackness with primitivism."[60] In truth, Schleime's use of Scipio's body in *Bed of Kidneys* is conspicuously erotic, a marked difference from the aloofness and indifference embodied by her other male actors. In contrast to these traits commonly associated with masculinity, Scipio is feminized with makeup, tight clothing, or no clothing whatsoever. At the risk of minimizing the possible victimization of a racialized body, it may be more important to entertain here the possibility that Scipio saw Schleime's film as an opportunity to put his racial difference, as well as perhaps his gender fluidity, on display. He returns in other projects, notably in the films of Gino Hahnemann, which will be discussed in this book's next chapter. East Germany's experimental film may be understood as a kind of speech act—an assertion of personhood that could be shared across multiple publics. As Schleime's expectation that there would be Stasi surveillance at her film screenings suggests, many people did not fear having larger publics, even potentially threatening ones.

Bed of Kidneys bears a latent affinity to methods of abject critical practice that consumed the experimental art scene in the 1980s. Essentially, from the self-abuse in the Auto-Perforation Artists' performances, films, and installations to the metaphorically divided body in Thomas Florschuetz's self-portraits to the portrait photography of hard laborers by Gundula Schulze Eldowy, visualizing devastation at the most intimate level of the body became an important tactic for artists to both differentiate themselves from the norm and to identify the GDR's internal hypocrisies. For Schleime, the meat in *Bed of Kidneys* is one part of the film's "card catalogue of images"[61]—sculptural heads, people wrapped in bandages, pigeons, feathers, a person dressed as a horse. Her film may thus be understood as a regurgitation of internal decay—a psychological burlesque and horror show.

Schleime's final GDR-era film, *Das Puttennest* (*Den of Cherubs*, 1984), records a crumbling reality, teetering between a dissociative documentary of some of East Germany's spaces of leisure and a loose and dreamy narrative that ends in unexpected violence. Its twelve minutes begin in Potsdam. The remains of cherub sculptures—putti—litter a gated-in, overgrown park at the Sanssouci Palace.[62] In the next sequence, now in black-and-white, two punks walk along the shore of the Baltic Sea on the north coast of East Germany. Thereafter, a conveyor belt drops buckets rhythmically into the water beside a quarry. The film moves from color to monochromatic stock and back again, an aesthetic choice that accentuates the dreamy atmosphere provided by its soundtrack, a downtempo version of Erik Satie's first *Gymnopédie*. The plodding of this well-known minimalistic and melancholic composition nevertheless contrasts with the frequent changes of Schleime's loose arrangement of images. Scenes move rapidly from the space of the palace to the seashore to random sites of industry: the quarry, a set of railroad tracks. The camera lingers only on the faces of Jens Ernst Tukiendorf and Christian Duschek, known as Spinne. Jens and Spinne hang out along the water, drinking and smoking. They brood, but scarcely interact. Their conspicuous appearances give form to their ennui: Jens's hair is spiked to a crest; Spinne's falls languidly in his face. Black eyeliner exaggerates his wistful gaze. Others enter the scene at random. People cavort in the rolling waters of the Baltic Sea. The putti return, shot at high angles that give them a sinister look exaggerated by the high contrast of low-quality Super-8 film. This den of cherubs oversees a parade of visitors shot through the lattices of a thick iron gate. Young soldiers in the national army walk to morning exercises. An elderly man laboriously moves his wheelchair forward with hand cranks. As we near the film's end, an unexplained drama cuts through the pensive but aimless atmosphere. Jens bludgeons a previously unseen man five times with a makeshift weapon. Spinne falls victim next as Jens strikes him with a guitar case.

Den of Cherubs is a loose interpretation of an apocryphal story: into "the decay of cultural heritage," Schleime reflects, "weaves the story of Cain and Abel."[63] The film documents the GDR in a state of suspension and contradiction. The buckets at the quarry fill, empty, refill in a mindless and plodding rhythm. The palace stands, but crumbles. It is an icon of the bourgeois hypocrisy and cultural concessions that underlay the justifications for East Germany's "real existing socialism." The seashore is both an escape and a last stop—a site of spontaneous pleasure and unexpected

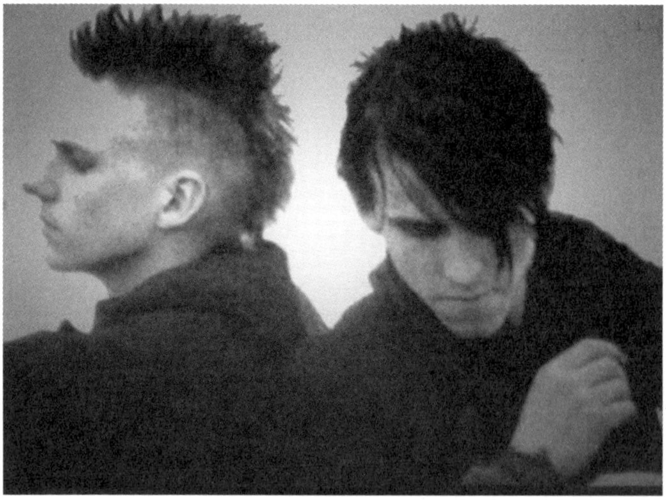

violence. In fact, Schleime's punk aesthetic, and specifically her use of punks and other undesirables in her films, doubles the attention to the loss of state power.[64] Her punks embody the undoing of socialist principles; this is their salient message. Their dress, hair, and makeup literalize that defiance: Jens and Spinne are unmistakably different from the norm. They are the GDR's intended sacrifices—individuals whose autonomy the state sought to punish, subdue, and eradicate through a heavy-handed culture. They are not just insistently indifferent; they are products of a country that now teems with mutant citizens.

The Stasi devoted considerable resources to observing this new genus of human—the punk—treating the group as an aberration rather than an outgrowth of the GDR's failed collective experiment. A short excerpt from a surveillance video of punks reveals power that is uncertain and performed, rather than effective. The low-fidelity ninety-six-second color video shot from a slow-traveling vehicle captures three vignettes of young misfits drunkenly occupying a city street. The two Stasi men patrolling them

3.9

Cornelia Schleime, *Das Puttennest* (*Den of Cherubs*), 1984, Super-8 film, 12 min. Reprinted with the permission of Cornelia Schleime. © 1984 by Cornelia Schleime.

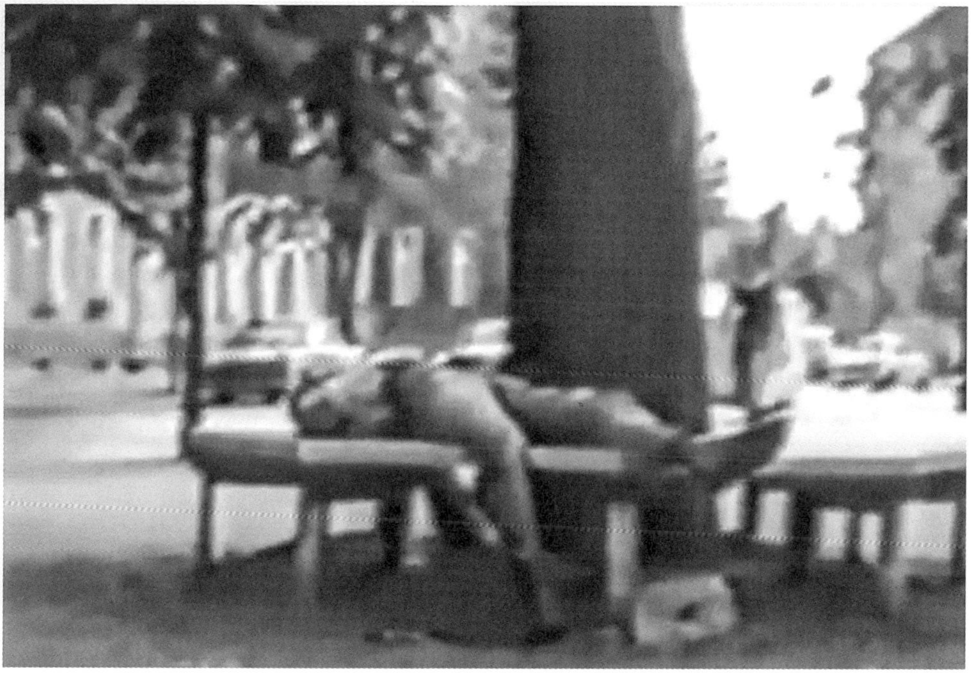

are a captive audience. First: Three punks rest along the street curb—two are seated, one lies on the sidewalk. The camera operator firmly commands his driver to stop. The camera pans around them in a gentle C-curve as the vehicle hugs the sidewalk. With faces now obscured, the three people are recorded from multiple angles and in close-up. They acknowledge the camera, moving their heads wearily to meet its gaze. One appears with hands raised in a gesture of exasperation that is almost confrontational. Second: Cut to a man lying along a bench encircling a tree planted in a cobblestone sidewalk. A man in shorts passes by, glancing briefly at the sleeping figure. The camera

3.10

"Farewell Comrades! Stasi watching punks," YouTube video, 1:36, from a 1989 Stasi surveillance video, posted by "FarewellComrades," February 23, 2012, https://www.youtube.com/watch?v=sLehmoEH7lE. Screengrab reprinted with fair use.

operator chides, "A pile of puke right next to him. Niiiice," as he zooms his recorder in on the messy substance. The man is left undisturbed, as is his vomit. Third: The video concludes with a lone punk on whom the camera lingers for the span of a full minute. We first spot him through the front windshield of a parked car as he retches along the side of the road. The Stasi men continue to spy on him, trailing him at a distance of several feet as he stumbles along the sidewalk. Two women pass. The clatter of an engine and a bit of light traffic fill the soundtrack and the two men in the car scarcely speak. The beleaguered punk pauses at a garden wall and leans his head in his arms. "Move ahead a bit," the camera operator commands. As the man begins to walk again, the camera pans left and the car remains stationary. A group of young people gathers at the end of the block; another three cross the street.

Not a work of art, the Stasi video nevertheless has an intentionality in its production that makes it more than a mere document. Specifically, the bemused narrator who (predictably) relishes the superlative power he enjoys from his patrol car gainsays the film's presumed objectivity. The sequence reveals a kind of fanciful, if bored, behavior that is both interesting to watch and also highly predictable in the context of an overly inflated and humdrum bureaucracy. How many more Stasi officers were sent out to report on this kind of scene that morning in 1989? And what was their task, but to furnish evidence for the continued necessity of a moral authority to cruise the streets? Their cameras offered no strategy—not even effective intimidation—to remedy the apparent social dysfunction of young men vomiting in public tree wells. Today, the video is a record of a typical summer morning in a GDR city—punks litter the streets with themselves and their effluvia. Passersby are unfazed. The Stasi workers stay safely ensconced in their bureaucratic bubble. They gape and gawk at the life forms whose population and power grow in inverse proportion to the secret police's own waning influence.

The evocative (and rare)[65] example of Stasi video surveillance is brief, but nevertheless records several concrete examples of a world that "insistently ignored" state power. These punks take up the space they are meant *not* to claim. The threat of state power deployed to contain them fails to make them go away. They remain seated on the curb; they still spike their hair upright; they vomit indiscriminately. The Super-8 film scene of the 1980s GDR, moreover, demonstrates that there were in fact cameras looking back at the oppressor, and they were wielded by people not cowering in corners, but tramping through the street. Not always with glue in their hair, but sometimes, as Schleime recalls, wearing gas masks.[66] It is this looking back—this claiming of the right to look—which begins the political annunciation that Löser and Thomas identify as foundational to the experimental culture of late East Germany. Yet experimental film is more than an act of disregarding the state; it is an intentional affront. Social outcasts film each other and name it art. Experimental film is thus a double offence: both a disregard for Stasi looks and a disregard for the very purpose of that observation—to craft, curate, and produce a like-minded collective cohered around state culture.

The examples of films by Schleime explored here represent a coincidental, and even co-constitutive, movement to create new forms of self- and collective representation that were also essential to Schulze Eldowy's portrait practice. Both artists explored new ways of seeing East German society. Whereas Schulze Eldowy trained her camera on ordinary people, Schleime aimed hers at society's misfits. Both artists offer supplements to the GDR's image culture. Yet this is not their signature move. More important are the social relationships—the acts of recognition—that their works documented, facilitated, and distributed.

4

MAKING A SCENE

Films by Gino Hahnemann

The foundational thinking of scholars on East Germany's experimental art and literature scene has centered on *Selbst-Behauptung* (self-assertion) as both a galvanizing force and a solution to the limitations of official culture.[1] In tandem with this self-assertion, artists held a commitment to producing an autonomous culture that ran parallel to, and sometimes at an intersection with, mainstream society. This culture is particularly well evidenced in the proliferation of people working in small-gauge film. By the mid-1980s, as the Germanist Seth Howes has observed, "independent experimental filmmaking had grown from an activity pursued by just a few isolated artists to an artistic practice embraced by dozens of filmmakers who formed superregional networks and founded filmmaking collectives along with parallel institutions [like publications and annual film festivals] for exhibiting and discussing their work."[2] For many who participated in this "ciné boom," as the film historian Claus Löser has called it, filmmaking became an intense, if temporary passion.[3] The sheer quantity of films produced in the German Democratic Republic's (GDR) final fifteen years—approximately 150, by Löser's count[4]—reflects the depth of this media Zeitgeist. Film was thus not just an artifact or document; it was a cultural practice of history-making, or better said, of scene-making.

For many filmmakers, the temporal and fluid qualities of Super-8 made it the only medium that could adequately translate experience. The artist Cornelia Schleime, whose works this book's previous chapter discussed at length, explains that she found film to be more "communicative" than painting because it allowed her to go out in the world and meet people.[5] This chapter centers on another artist,

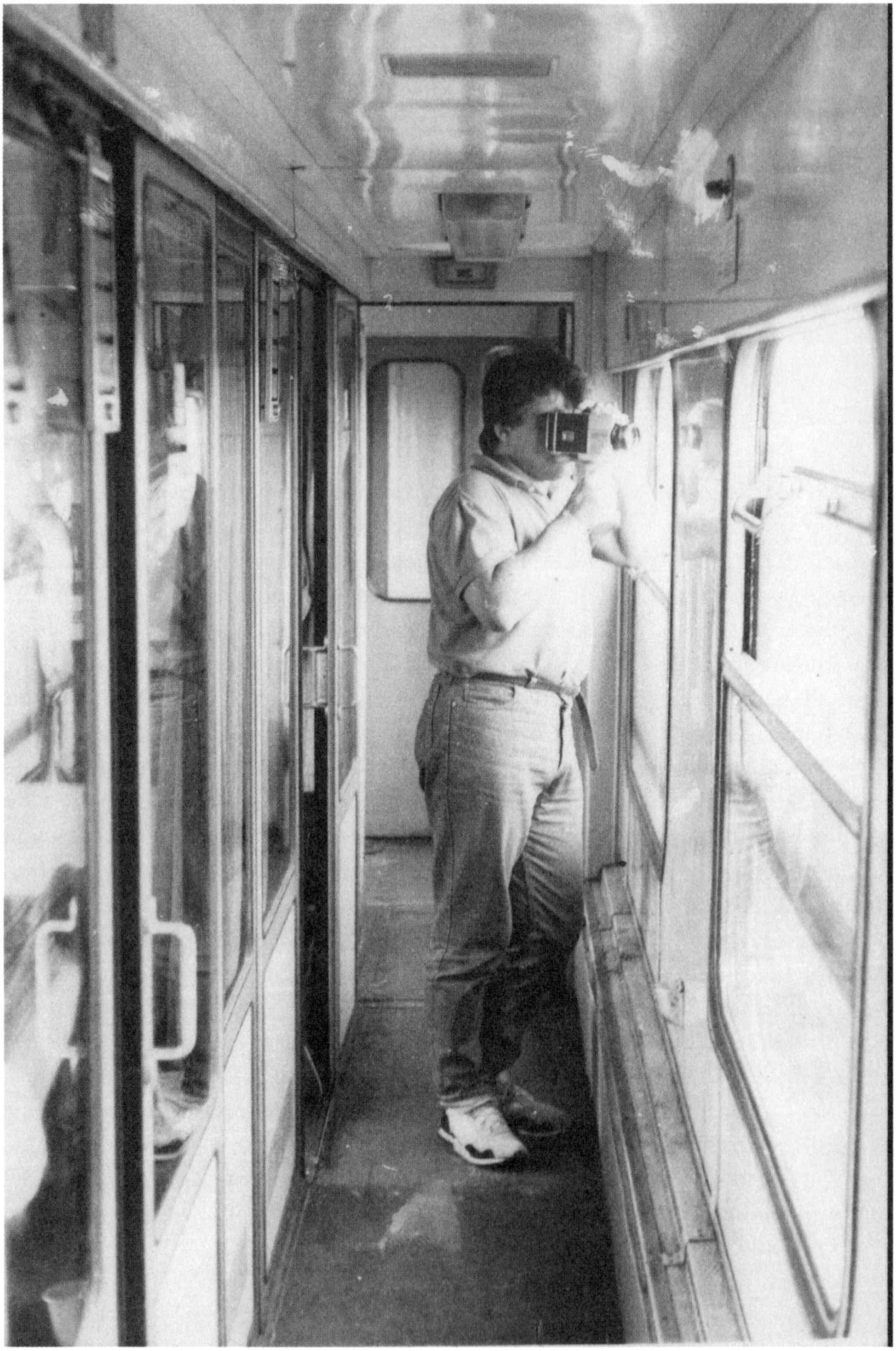

Gino Hahnemann, who actually inspired Schleime's turn from painting to film.[6] Like hers, Hahnemann's films represent moments of communion and conviviality. In fact, Hahnemann excelled in inspiring people from various social strata to convene: his films record and commingle members of the literary, art, gay, and youth scenes. Particularly noteworthy is the way he organically united his efforts to normalize homosexuality through films (and poetry) with a sincere interest in Germany's cultural legacies, from historical icons like Goethe to historical places like the Charlottenhof Palace in Potsdam. If Schleime exemplifies what Howes describes as the "more abstract repertoires"[7] of painters and other artists who used film to supplement their studio-based practices, Hahnemann represents a second, more context-specific tendency among filmmakers who worked in narrative and especially literary adaptation. Although he did not participate in the amateur film clubs where a host of creators got their start (including the now highly regarded German film director Andreas Dresen), Hahnemann shared the ethos of professionalism that permeated them. This is evident in the length and complexity of his films, as well as in the carefully detailed film treatments and production documentation he assembled for nearly all of his thirty-one GDR-era films.[8] As a writer and a filmmaker, as well as an artist and a gay man, Hahnemann also represents the interdisciplinarity and intersecting identities that were a hallmark of his generation of makers.

Although he did not allegorize the state in his films and he did not address—let alone consciously consider—the presence of oppressive authorities in his films in the way Schleime claims to have done, Hahnemann nevertheless cites the limitations that no artist could avoid in the walled-in country as a creative catalyst: "I did not feel physically, but culturally constrained in the GDR, also with regard to film. I finally said to myself: just make your own cinema."[9] He called these films "GINO KINO." The thirty-one Super-8 works Hahnemann made between 1982 and 1990 range from short four-minute romps (as in *Seusslitz-Bourrée*, 1983) to carefully planned narratives that ran upward of twenty-four minutes (as in the *Goethe Project*, 1989).[10] Their quantity and range signal their maker's professionalism; no doubt,

4.1

Gino Hahnemann films from a train. Ca. 1986. Photographer unknown. Akademie der Künste, Berlin, Gino-Hahnemann-Archiv, no. 251. © 2021 by Matthias Fischer.

S E U S S L I T Z • B O U R R E E

Super 8 SCHWARZWEISS Sep.Ton
Länge: 3 Min.35 Sec. KOSTEN: 5o,-M
Kamera: Hahnemann Lomo 214
DREHZEIT/ORT: 24.8.83 Seußlitz bei Dresden
MUISIK: Bach, Bourrée aus Ouverture d-dur BWV 1o68 (Suite Nr.3)
DARSTELLER: Junger Mann-Egon Naumann
Die drei Grazöösen-Conny Schleime, Axel Zumbach, ?
Drei Putten - ? ? ?
Alter Mann - ?

SEUSSLITZ: Sächsisches Elbedorf an der Landstrasse Meißen-Riesa mit Ausflugsgaststätten in Weinbauernmanier, ein paar Läden, einem nach 1725 von Georg Bähr (Frauenkirche Dresden) projektierten Schloß, das jetzt Altersheim ist und dem beredte Gartenparterre zur Seite liegen, die am jenseitigen Hang in sechs gemauerten Terrassen mit eingeschossigem Pavillon (Heinrichsburg) kontra-punktiert sind.

BOURRÉE: Altfranzösischer Gesellschaftstanz aus der Auvergne des 16./17. Jahrhunderts, der schnell in höfischen Kreisen Liebhaber findet und den Komponisten des zeitgenössischen Ballettschaffens, der Oper und der instrumentalen Suite den meist auftaktigen, synkopierten "Bourrèe francaise" abverlangt.

S E U S S L I T Z • B O U R R E E 24/8/83

he would have worked in higher-quality film stock had it been available to him. A fastidious and detail-oriented maker, Hahnemann created film treatments for even short projects like *Seusslitz-Bourrée*. These plans reveal the research he conducted in preparing his films, particularly those which consider Germany's cultural legacy. Nearly all of the GINO KINO films consciously display their maker's homosexuality, with gay identity sometimes quite deliberately foregrounded and at other times woven into a narrative in ways that are conspicuous but nevertheless not underscored. When questioned about the apparent centrality of homosexuality in the poetry he wrote at the same time he was making films, Hahnemann explained that "the gay aspect [of my work] is simply a theme. I am describing a scene . . . I do not see myself as a gay author or that I only write for a queer audience. There is my existence as a writer and there is my gay identity. One will influence the other, even though there are a lot of connections regardless, [drawing attention to them] is not my ambition."[11] He is gay and fascinated by German culture. He is an experimental artist and a devout humanist. He is no starstruck champion of cultural heroes; instead, he destabilizes their authority in works that queer them—literally and figuratively.

FILMIC ARCHITECTURE: HAHNEMANN RESCRIPTS EAST GERMANY'S SPACES OF CULTURE

A self-trained and highly productive filmmaker, Hahnemann is both a signature voice of the GDR's experimental film scene and an artist whose variety of works prevents simple summary. What is it that he wishes to summon in his viewers? A desire for the past; a reverence for cultural precedent; an appreciation for the multiple kinds of subjects who may attach themselves to local history; an advocate for gay identity and presence? All and yet not one of these aims are prioritized in his films. A signal achievement of GINO KINO may be the consistency in which it reshapes

4.2

Gino Hahnemann. Film treatment for *Seusslitz-Bourrée*. 1983. Typewritten on paper. Akademie der Künste, Berlin, Gino-Hahnemann-Archiv, no. 22. © 2021 by Matthias Fischer.

the GDR's cultural habitus, specifically its spaces of history. The mixture of historical reference, homosexual elements, and musical and visual anachronisms creates a space of film (its architecture) that is both familiar and estranged.

An early work, *Römische Bäder* (*Roman Baths*, 1982), exemplifies the ways in which Hahnemann documents and at the same time repurposes space. A series of buildings set in a grand park shot from multiple angles cycle through the fifteen-minute color film. Its setting is the Charlottenhof Manor, a grand estate tucked within the Sanssouci Palace grounds in Potsdam. The soundtrack alternates between synthesized New Age music and a voice explaining the history of the place. The narrator pays special attention to Frederick William IV of Prussia, who commissioned the architectural ensemble that is this film's namesake. Karl Friedrich Schinkel, a beloved neoclassical and neogothic architect active in the late eighteenth to mid-nineteenth centuries, designed the space in the model of ancient Italian villas. The speaker intones: "The Charlottenhof was a Christmas gift from King Frederick William III to his son King Frederick William IV in 1825." Details accumulate as in a filmstrip for tourists or schoolkids: "In 1827 there was also a plan to make a pumping station for the Charlottenhof's Italian-style fountains on the east side of the castle. Hence, in 1828 one was erected for the main garden house . . ." The dullness is almost farcical.

A break comes unexpectedly. A naked man bends over a pond unmoving, and the homoerotic innuendo of the Roman bathhouse becomes the film's unequivocal overtone. The film next captures a series of sculptures, mostly the round curve of buttocks and calves carved in stone. The dry narration drones on. The naked man returns with greater regularity. The camera alternates between scanning the musculature of the statues and that of the naked man. The film moves across the seasons: snow blankets trees in one shot; ducks glide across a pond in another; later, fountains burst upward against a sunlit background. The film ends dreamily, its history incomplete. Final moments linger on the man as he walks naked out of the palace pond. The music swells and abruptly ends.

4.3

Gino Hahnemann. Film treatment for *Römische Bäder* (*Roman Baths*). 1982. Typewritten on paper. Akademie der Künste, Berlin, Gino-Hahnemann-Archiv, no. 22. © 2021 by Matthias Fischer.

R Ö M I S C H E   B Ä D E R

Super 8, Farbe, Separater Ton,   Länge: 16 Min.   Kamera: Hahnemann

Drehzeit/Ort: 2.4.82, 3o.5.82, Okt.82 Röm. Bäder und angrenzende Anlagen im Park Charlottenhof (Potsdam Sansouci); Febr.83 Winteraufnahmen Röm. Bäder und Friedhof Bornstedt, Orangerie.

Material: 8 Kassetten a 15 Meter   Filmkosten: 18o,-M

Fertigstellung 28.7.1983

Text und Sprecher: Hahnemann   Gesang: Frank Baer

Darsteller: Axel Zumbach (Faun und Hofgärtner)

---

aus einem geplanten "kommentar zur architektur meiner Kollegen" entstand eine essayistische fiktion über ein muster romantischen klassizismus'

weil ich an der architektur meiner kollegen nichts zu kommentieren fand

die in Bild und Ton einer an Wissenschaftlichkeit orientierten Betrachtungsweise trotzt, die sich in Römischen Bädern gewaschen hat.

Fehlende Handlung und eine Bauklötzchen-Dramaturgie können auch in Zukunft den Film erweitern und es schadet nicht, Bilder herauszuschneiden.

Mein S p i e l -Film.

Tatsachen werden zur Fiktion. ~~Zusammenhänge werden gewittert~~ Wittern Zusammenhänge. Trennendes wird vereint. Neue Wirklichkeiten entstehen aus Mangel oder Überschuß an Parteilichkeit.
Die Fiktion sitzt der Wirklichkeit auf den Versen.

---

kein film g e g e n schinkel.
mich interessiert das verhältnis kreativität zu lebensbewältigung.
an jedem menschen.

ICH KANN DIE HEILIGEN KÜHE DER ARCHITEKTUR NICHT DEN THEORETIKERN ÜBERLASSEN; NOCH NICHT.

TRAUMHAFTER klassizismus Römischer
b   ä   d   e   r

Mein Film und die Architektur haben keine Schauseite. Von jeder Seite zu betrachten. Von innen und außen. Malerische Wirkung in der Landschaft. Derjenigen des Parkes Charlottenhof/wie der des (Amateur)films.

Shot in 1982, *Roman Baths* was one of Hahnemann's first Super-8 films. Before making the film, Hahnemann had studied architecture and had worked in this profession until he was "discovered" on the streets of East Berlin and became a fashion model. With clear correspondence to the filmmaker's biography, the film's attention to architecture and its incongruous ending may be construed as a miniature self-portrait—the gay architect turned filmmaker unites his lifestyle with his professional expertise. Hahnemann's reflections on the film reveal a kind of bombastic identification with the Charlottenhof architects: "From a planned 'commentary on the architecture of my colleagues' emerged an essayistic fiction about an example of romantic classicism."[12] Further in the *Roman Baths* film treatment, Hahnemann's notes reveal deeper investments in charting a relationship between cinema and architecture. Naming a desire to translate the multiple dimensionality of architecture and the built environment into cinematic form, he writes: "Both my film and architecture have no right side. You need to look from every side, from the inside and the outside. Painterly effects [populate] the landscape: within the park of the Charlottenhof Manor, just like within this (amateur) film."[13] Here, Hahnemann's placement of the word "amateur" in parentheses betrays both his professional ambitions and his modesty.

Hahnemann echoes Sergei Eisenstein—whom he may indeed have read—who wrote that "at the basis of the composition of an architectural ensemble is the same 'dance' which is at the basis of film montage."[14] That dance is the movement of the viewer, who makes sense of cinematic space by taking in what the film and media historian Giuliana Bruno calls "spectatorial movements."[15] Bruno's reading of Eisenstein leads her to define film as "geographic,"[16] insofar as it leads its spectators along an imaginary path: "a spectatorial voyage [inherited] from the architectural field, for the person who wanders through a building or a site also absorbs and connects visual spaces."[17] Hahnemann's film, which invites his viewer to "site-see" the Charlottenhof palace at the accelerated speed that film permits, literalizes Bruno's metaphor of a multisited cinema as a kind of architectural space.[18] Of course, his film is quite didactic, even ham-fisted or (knowingly) "amateur." The bodies Hahnemann inserts into the landscape—what he calls his "painterly effects"—direct his spectator to a specific narrative about architecture and the use of romantic space as a welcoming one for gay men.

Bruno concedes that filmic frames are more than "directional arrows"; they are "mobilized territories, mappings of practiced places," that have been "transformed by an open relation of movement to events."[19] Hahnemann's film draws attention to the historical valence of the palace grounds. In the late 1970s, Sanssouci Palace became a site of a renewed (and state-sanctioned) interest in Prussian history. King Frederick II (aka Frederick the Great), who had been a reviled figure under the GDR's first SED[20] party chairman, Walter Ulbricht, received a revised materialist/ Marxist historicization in 1979 in the blockbuster book by the East German historian Ingrid Mittenzwei (*Friedrich II. von Preußen. Eine Biographie*). In a recent article by the historian Christoph Dieckmann, Mittenzwei is quoted as reflecting that Prussian history was a part of collective memory that could not be repressed. Her book gave East Germans permission to explore these familial and national roots.[21] A revisionist view redefined the castle as a monument to the great achievements of the eighteenth-century working class, and Frederick the Great as a congenial employer.[22] Importantly, the second SED party chairman, Erich Honecker, had a special affection for Frederick the Great, which he imparted to the East German public by reinstalling the king's statue on East Berlin's main thoroughfare, Unter den Linden, in November 1980. The king, as well as his favorite architect Schinkel, were thus enshrined as parts of the GDR's revised *Kulturerbe* (cultural heritage), itself a kind of socialist rehabilitation of a German *Heimat* (homeland). It is worth remembering that Cornelia Schleime also filmed *Das Puttennest* (*Den of Cherubs*) at the palace. Her 1984 film does not indulge the fantasy of Sanssouci, but rather documents its vanishing. For her, the Charlottenhof palace is East Germany's metaphorical and literal tomb. Hahnemann, on the other hand, plays with this space, and makes it a site of fantasy. His film retools the propaganda of the architectural ensemble of the GDR to map new possibilities—both detours and escape routes. Still, as a film that is as carefree as it is monotonous, *Roman Baths* represents the simplicity of indulging in form: the directions in which it travels point to beauty, nice-looking things, and the passing of time.

BEING SEEN BY MAKING A SCENE

Shortly after making *Roman Baths*, Hahnemann would make two other works at another of the GDR's prized locations from the country's incongruous, though nevertheless venerated, aristocratic past. Both *Seusslitz-Bourrée* (1983) and his *Hölderlin Project* (1984) were filmed at the Seusslitz palace, located about twenty-five miles northwest of Dresden. The four-minute *Seusslitz-Bourrée* features a frolic through the palace grounds, all structured around the waking dream of a long-haired and flamboyant man. He dances, scampers, and climbs around the gardens. His joyful, if somewhat unskilled, pirouettes lead him to the palace's grand outdoor staircase and patio, where he joins hands with three other dancers, including Schleime. Three naked children dance in a circle—a fountain come alive—as the adult friends waltz in merry affectation of the palace's former amusements.

The second film for which Hahnemann would use the Seusslitz palace as a backdrop is his *Hölderlin Project*, a nineteen-minute work with an official title that is as long and winding as its contents: *Ein Zeichen sind wir, deutungslos, und haben die Sprache in der Fremde verloren* (*We Are a Sign, Meaningless, and We Have Forgotten Our Language in Exile*). Friedrich Hölderlin's biography is secondary in this film, with the nineteenth-century German lyric poet more a loaded reference than a source of content. This is a "scene" film, that is to say, a film about being seen. Some of the experimental art and literature circle's most prominent figures lead the cast. In addition to Schleime, who appears in the film as Diotima, the poet-spy Sascha Anderson plays the lead role of Hölderlin. The film's main settings—the Seusslitz castle grounds along the Elbe River and Wilfriede Maaß's ceramics studio—likewise draw connections across temporalities and cultural actors. The former, a key site for the Dresden romantics, is reincarnated in the latter, a locus point for East Berlin writers and artists in the 1980s.[23]

A loose drama, *We Are a Sign* begins with Hölderlin floating lit red candles in the Elbe. Candles recur throughout, a rather pat symbol of the artist showing his followers the light. The refrain to the Rolling Stones' "Lady Jane" repeats on a loop, knit between the droning organ of Philip Glass's *Koyaanisqatsi*, "Spy in the Cab" by the post-punk band Bauhaus, and a song by Anderson's music group Fabrik (Factory). The soundtrack renders a psychedelic tone to the film that in another context might have come across as affected. As Löser has observed, the music almost seems to anticipate the film's hidden farce: "Spy in the Cab" plays as Anderson, the experimental scene's greatest betrayer, shuffles along as angst incarnate.[24] But Hahnemann's film is earnest—secure and unselfconscious in its yearning to communicate a feeling of admiration for Hölderlin. His film bears the poet's message; by its conclusion, his candles have returned. Like Hahnemann and his circle of artist-friends, Hölderlin was underappreciated by the wider public in his time. East Germany's own official (and somewhat idiosyncratic) disinclination for romanticism had also turned the poet into a fairly obscure entity, perhaps thus contributing to his allure.[25]

We Are a Sign's loose and esoteric drama reflects the rarefied aesthetic that defined the GDR's experimental cultural scene—and in particular, its literature. The film presents a unique iconography of recurring images and actions set in an elaborate backdrop. Catching, let alone making sense of the film's many signs—to think of its title—demands an attentive and generous viewer. This is Hahnemann's poetry, similarly cryptic, put to film. Löser, a contemporary and friend of Hahnemann, critiques his recurring use of didactic tropes and long titles, which he says "betray a certain mannerism [and] affectation."[26] This is a fair critique of a highly stylized filmmaker. The profound presence of Hahnemann's practice as a writer in *We Are a Sign* is not unique to this film or this filmmaker, but rather reflects a tendency among the artists of the late GDR to inflect their work with exaggerated, but absolutely sincere, pathos and melodrama.

Whatever autobiographical elements Hahnemann may be projecting in *We Are a Sign* are amplified by the touches of nonnormative sexuality that he fluidly weaves into his film. He casts Scipio, the mixed-race youth who appeared in Cornelia Schleime's film *Das Nierenbett* (*The Bed of Kidneys*), as the author and statesman Isaac von Sinclair, and references the brief but intense friendship Sinclair shared with Hölderlin. As a dress-wearing Sinclair, Scipio mirrors Schleime, who appears in the film as Diotima, the original emissary of platonic love who becomes the object of Hyperion's desire in Hölderlin's eponymous work. The references to Sinclair are thus twinned for fans of German romanticism: on screen appears Hölderlin's actual friendship with Sinclair as well as the imagined friendship he lionized in the Sinclair-inspired character, Alabanda, who is Hyperion's trusted, if contentious, confident. *We Are a Sign*'s nineteen minutes offer few clues into these relationships. From Scipio's dress to the submissive mien Anderson takes in the young man's presence, these are not exotic, aberrant, or even explanatory moments, but participating elements that contribute to the film's unique atmosphere.

4.4 and 4.5 (following two pages)

Gino Hahnemann. Production stills. *Ein Zeichen sind wir, deutungslos, und haben die Sprache in der Fremde verloren* (*We Are a Sign, Meaningless, and We Have Forgotten Our Language in Exile*). 1984. Super-8 film, 19 min. Photographer unknown (Gino Hahnemann?). Akademie der Künste, Berlin, Gino-Hahnemann-Archiv, no. 22. © 2021 by Matthias Fischer.

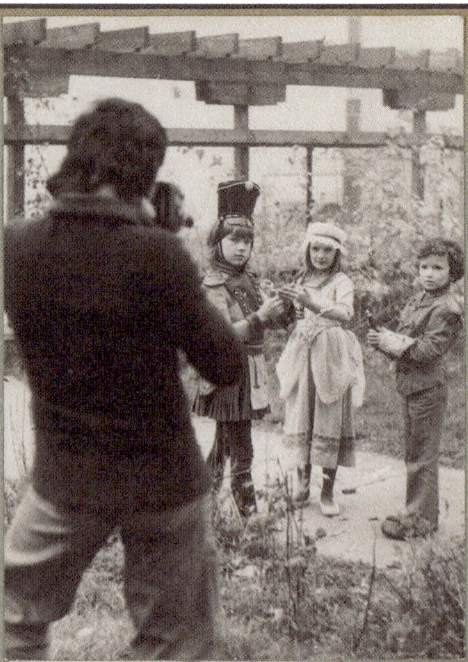
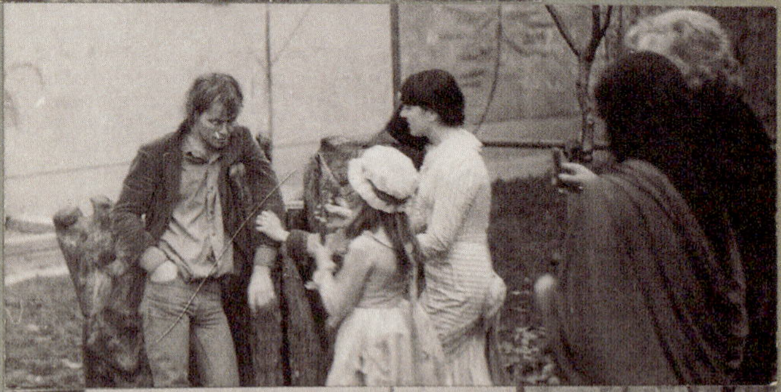
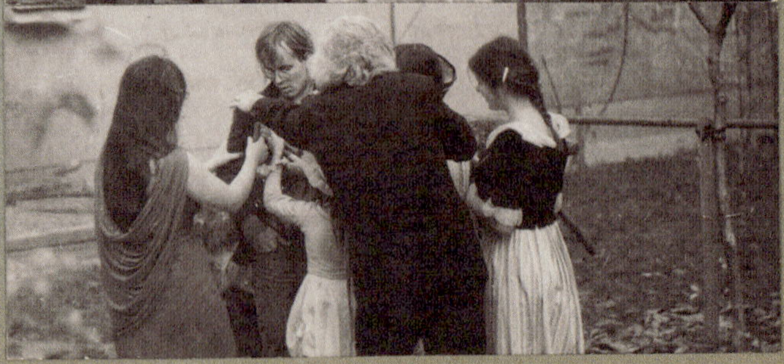

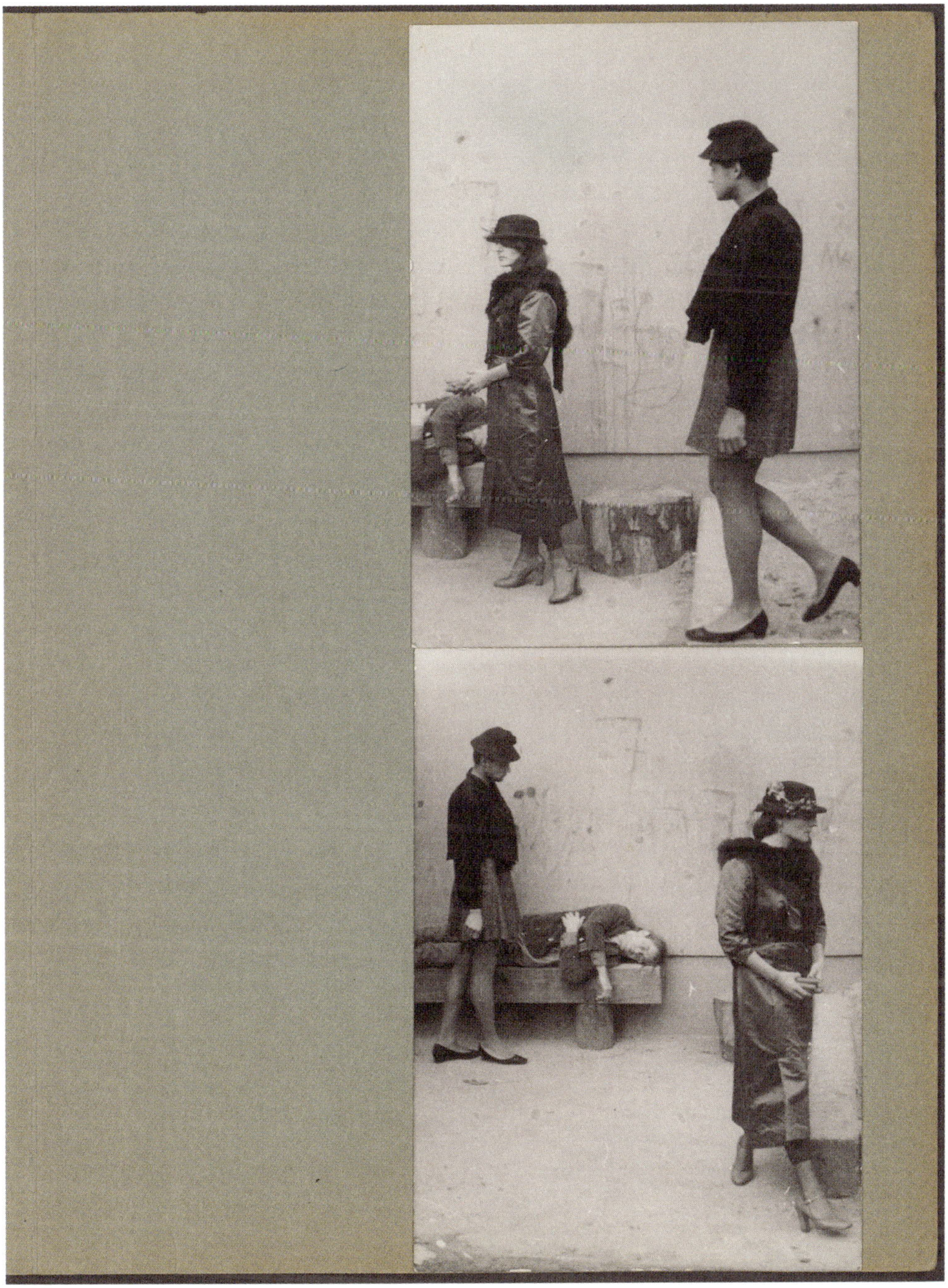

"SURREAL, POLITICAL, AND EROTIC" BIKER BOYS

Hahnemann's aesthetic complicates a simple need to be seen. His mixture of homosexual themes and homages to humanism's heroes exceeds the need for "self-assertion" that has been theorized to describe the GDR's experimental arts scene as apolitical, anarchic, and disinterested in the state. The range of screening contexts where Hahnemann's films appeared underscores their expansive social—even political—potential. He showed his films across the GDR, both in unofficial galleries and private spaces, as well as in small-scale and independently run, but nevertheless state-sanctioned programs (such as Claudia "Wanda" Reichardt's Filma Morgana film festival at the Dresden Arts Academy in 1987).[27] A gay rights working group in Dresden included his films (described as "surreal, political, and erotic") as part of its public programs ("a night of fantasy").[28] A poster for a two-night screening of Hahnemann films, organized by the Arbeitskreis homosexuelle Liebe (Homosexual Love Working Group) in Jena introduced his films with the disclaimer: "Whoever comes here for entertainment cinema, and who wishes to be amused for an hour and a half, will be disappointed. Gino's works are not really films, but more collages of painterly and dramatic elements that document and reconstruct real and fictional worlds. The audience members must thus trust the unusual contents and messages of these short films."[29] Though unlisted in the program, the films that appeared may have included *Kaspar Hauser Stirb* (*The Death of Kaspar Hauser*, 1983), an eight-minute reinterpretation of the famous myth of the nineteenth-century German youth who claimed to have been raised in complete isolation and without language. Discovered in his teens, Hauser was nearly without speech, and though some believed he had an aristocratic origin, others thought the orphan had been raised by animals in the wild. Hahnemann's reinterpretation of the apocryphal tale, which ended in Hauser's untimely death just five years after he had been

4.6

"Zwischen Fantasie und Wirklichkeit. Filmische Collagen. Gino Hahnemann" (Between Fantasy and Reality. Film-Collages. Gino Hahnemann). November 27 and 28, 1987. Poster. Lutherhaus. Akademie der Künste, Berlin, Gino-Hahnemann-Archiv, no. 283. © 2021 by Matthias Fischer.

Wer hier unterhaltsames Kino erwartet mit der Hoffnung, sich eineinhalb Stunden amüsieren zu können, wird sich schwer enttäuscht sehen. Genaugenommen handelt es sich bei Ginos Arbeiten nicht eigentlich um Filme, sondern um Collagen aus bildnerischen und dramaturgischen Elementen, Dokumentationen und Rekonstruktionen realer und fiktiver Welten. Der Zuschauer muß dabei VERTRAUEN WAGEN zu den ungewöhnlichen Inhalten und Aussagen dieser Kurzfilme.

ZWISCHEN

FANTASIE

UND WIRKLICHKEIT

FILMISCHE COLLAGEN

GINO HAHNEMANN . BERLIN

DO. 20.°° . 27.11.+28.11.

FR. 20.°° . LUTHERHAUS

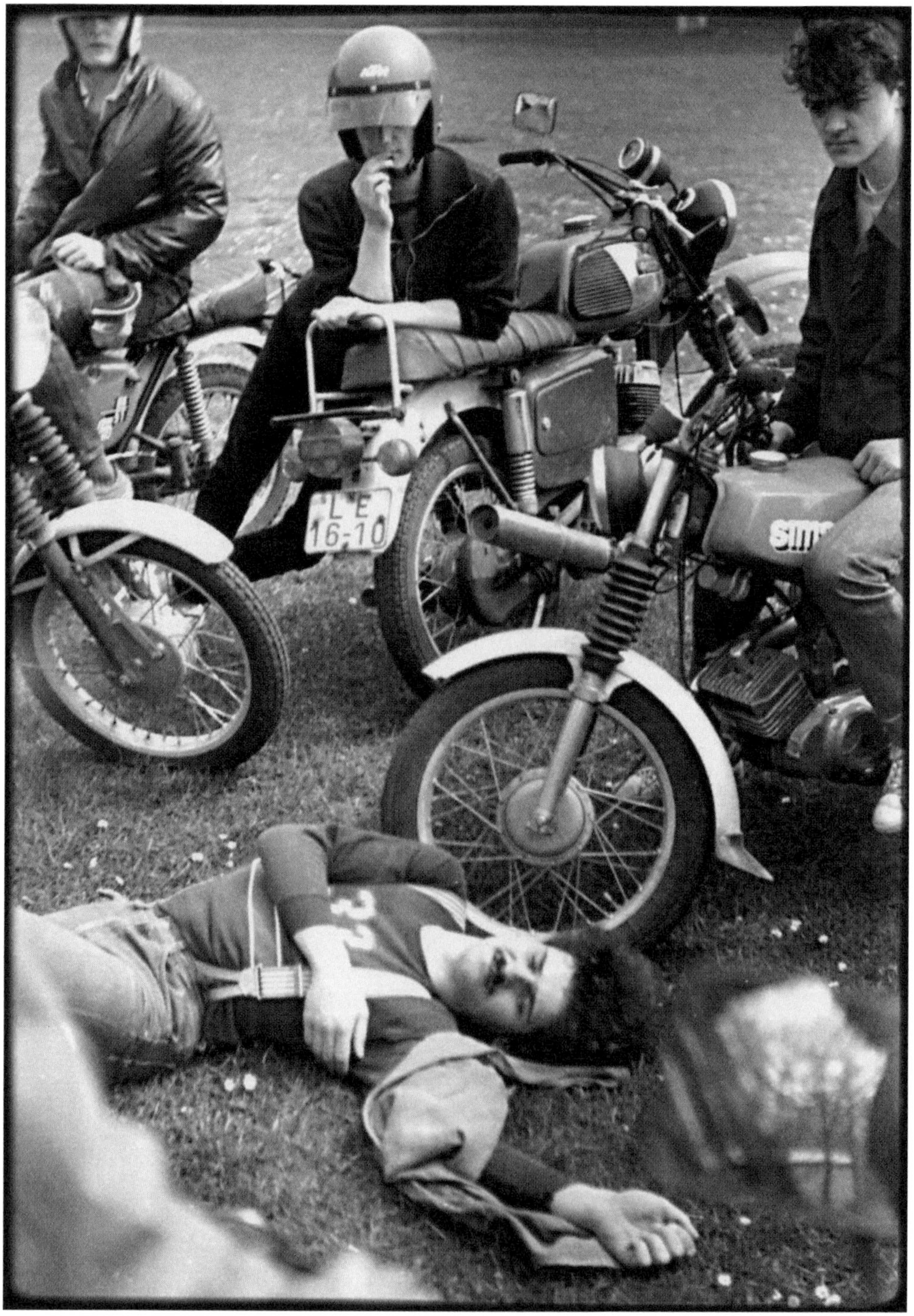
L E
16-10

reunited with human society, embraces the wild and animalistic characterization of the young orphan. He also turns Hauser into a Tom of Finland-style biker boy, whose life seems to begin and end in a trash dump where he ravages raw meat.

Perhaps *Harte Romanzen* (*Hard Romance*, 16 min., 1984) appeared at the gay rights meetings. This film, like *The Death of Kaspar Hauser*, visualizes a real-life motorcycle gang of gay men. They ride together and convene in a field where they chase and torment a young mustachioed man on foot. He returns home, nurses his wounds, and later administers care to his boyfriend, who has been struck by a delivery truck while riding with the bikers. Recovered, the two men rejoin their group of biker friends in a public park. His presence now welcomed, the man with the mustache clambers over the structure around which the motorcycle gang gathers. A quotation, which Hahnemann attributes to the Russian author and translator Boris Pasternak, concludes the film: "The extent to which we are all human rests in the people whom we have loved or the possibility we have had to love. All of us."[30] Liner notes suggest that Hahnemann filmed *Hard Romance* in the village of Apolda, located just outside of Jena where he spent his childhood. It thus documents a location where his sexuality may have once proved hazardous. As an adult, he returns and documents the gay men who, as his liner notes taunt, "do not exist in Apolda." It bears mentioning here that Hahnemann was an orphan, adopted into a family of intellectuals who gave him the name Karl-Heinz Tanzyna. His self-ascribed surname "Hahnemann" embraces the German identity he had been raised with and cherished, while the first name "Gino" reflects the exotified projections he faced (and capitalized on) as a darker-skinned European man, including in his part-time work as a fashion model in the GDR.

Hahnemann united his identification with East Germany's gay community with his creative practice most trenchantly in 1989 when he designed the set for a theater production of the activist Jürgen Lemke's *Ich bin schwul. Männerbiographien in der*

4.7

Gino Hahnemann. Production still. *Harte Romanzen* (*Hard Romance*). 1984. Super-8 film, 16 min. Photographer unknown (Gino Hahnemann?). Reprinted with the permission of Matthias Fischer. © 2020 by Matthias Fischer.

DDR (*I am Gay: Biographies of Men in the GDR*), which premiered at the theater in the Palast der Republik, one of East Berlin's most important stages. Lemke describes his 1989 book *Ganz normal anders. Auskunfte schwuler Männer* (*Gay Voices from East Germany*), which inspired the *Männerbiographien* play, as "the first and last book about gays in socialism. There are no other such books in socialist countries, nor here [in the United States], nor is it any longer possible to write such a book."[31] The sober, almost stoic, description follows a thoughtful testimony about the status of homosexuality in late East Germany. Lemke focuses on the strategies toward normalizing queerness through exposure and dialogue, and describes this candor as unique to East Germany. In this sense, Hahnemann's films may be understood as reflections of a larger movement of deliberate and sincere identity politics that permeated the GDR's mainstream culture.

THE FAIRY KING KILLS THEIR DARLINGS

Hahnemann's preoccupation with German culture reflects a genuine personal curiosity that is at once characteristic of his friendship circle of writers and yet unique to his own biography and experience. In a 1990 interview, he described his interest in *Kulturerbe* (cultural heritage) at first defensively—"Why should I suppress my *Heimat* (native culture)?!"—and then suggests that this preoccupation had emerged in contrast to intention: "Even when I think that maybe I can subdue *Heimat*, which is where I come from, and which I feel good about, in the end it is just not possible."[32] Hahnemann's films maintain important consistencies with the logics of state culture. His works repurpose the *Kulturerbe* that the East German government foregrounded as a means of streamlining its citizenry. In their amorphous, subjective relation to German culture, Hahnemann's films thus connect to a layer of everyday society, where local identification met the limits of state ideology. In his use of canonical figures—like Hölderlin—and in his explorations of heritage backdrops from the eighteenth and nineteenth centuries—like castles and romantic landscapes—the filmmaker reveals a personal fascination with Germany that actually resembles that of East German cultural officials who yearned to establish socialism in relation to German culture and history. That desire, of course, explains the previously noted revival of Frederick the Great. Efforts toward making socialism more accessible to a local audience conform to Stalin's 1934 vision for culture that was "national in form, socialist in content."[33] As the musicologist Elaine Kelly writes, a nativist cultural logic was central to communist culture and "served as a method of control for the SED, encoding the GDR's foundation myths and translating them into a discourse that promoted social cohesion and collective identity."[34] Hahnemann's use of important, and sometimes controversial, cultural figures in his films thus reveals both an internalization of their significance and a revision of their uses in—or rejections by—state culture. The desire to reevaluate cultural norms is no more pronounced than in his 1989 *Goethe Project*, which was also his last major film.

Goethe's Weimar garden house—a pilgrimage site since the late nineteenth century—glimmers in the oversaturated muddy colors of low-quality Super-8 film. A series of still shots interspersed with abstract drawings by the neoexpressionist painter Andreas Hegewald picture the baroque building through the seasons. A wistful, synthetic soundtrack plays in the background. A monotone voice breaks through these whizzes and pops: "The Germans read Goethe. These learned dilettantes do not free themselves from their servile existence. I have decided not to be a better German." For his twenty-four-minute *Goethe Project* (also titled *Die Täuschung verträgt die Realität nicht*, or *Illusion Cannot Bear Reality*, 1989), Hahnemann reinterprets Goethe's most famous poem "Erlkönig" (Erlking). Its title may also be translated as "Fairy King." In the 1782 original, the fairy king mysteriously kills a child who is riding home on horseback with his father through a dank wood. In Hahnemann's refashioned version, Goethe plays the father. His costume and elegant horse have an air of eighteenth-century perfection and give him a decadent, narcissistic appearance. Goethe's longest exchange in the film is with the boy he will eventually kill. The boy, who wears a red Nike sweatshirt when he first appears on the poet's balcony, speaks and gestures excitedly toward a small color television that broadcasts the frozen home screen for the Nintendo *Ghostbusters* game. The western consumer goods seem out of place, but contemporize the poet's own dandy decadence. After slaying the boy off camera, Goethe rides with his corpse to a meadow where he leaves the body covered with an orange satin cloth. The murder ultimately inspires him to write his famous poem.

The story proceeds in a series of unconnected images: The boy comes back to life as a man who runs through the field naked, with the orange cloth flying behind him. Red paint drips down a tree. Hegewald makes his art. Goethe hosts several men in his home, draws Schiller's house, visits a horseshoer, and walks through the quiet Weimar streets. The naked man poses like the *Erlkönig* statue in Jena. The soundtrack interrupts the rhythm of images at random. The narrator oscillates between metaobservation on the film form—"By turning it into a series of

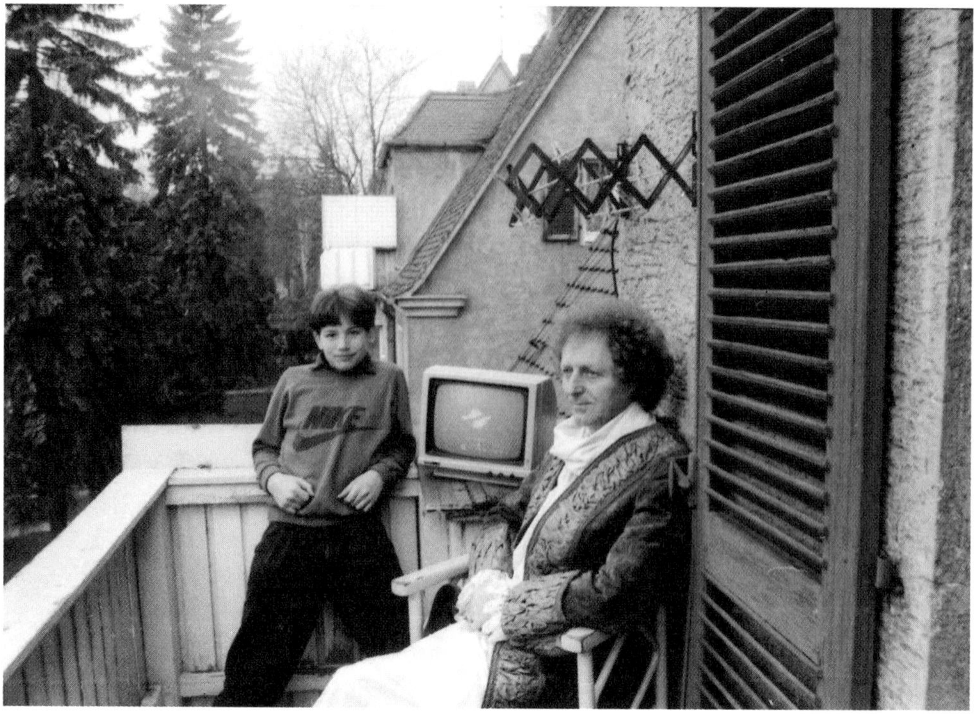

4.8

Gino Hahnemann. Production still. *Die Täuschung verträgt die Realität nicht* (*Illusion Cannot Bear Reality*). 1989. Super-8 film, 24 min. Photographer unknown (Gino Hahnemann?). Reprinted with the permission of Matthias Fischer. © 2020 by Matthias Fischer.

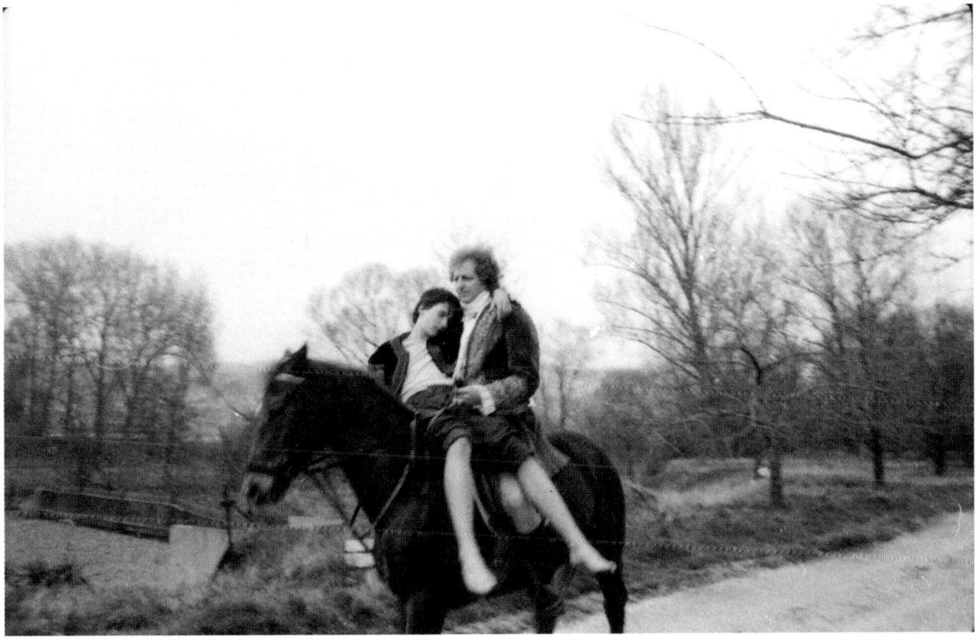

stories, cinema made the whole world unreal"—and reflections on the significance of Goethe. The words of the West German writer Hans Henny Jahnn are intoned, confronting the sincerity of the German fascination with Goethe: "He embodies all the possibilities of the German, the good and the bad—and that is his formidable danger."[35] On screen, Goethe composes a list of cultural greats: Nietzsche, Frederick the Great, Ibsen. . . . He checks them off, one by one—competitors are advised to mind their place. In the final shot, alone in his apartment, Goethe lifts a chair,

4.9

Gino Hahnemann. Production still. *Die Täuschung verträgt die Realität nicht* (*Illusion Cannot Bear Reality*). 1989. Super-8 film, 24 min. Photographer unknown (Gino Hahnemann?). Reprinted with the permission of Matthias Fischer. © 2020 by Matthias Fischer.

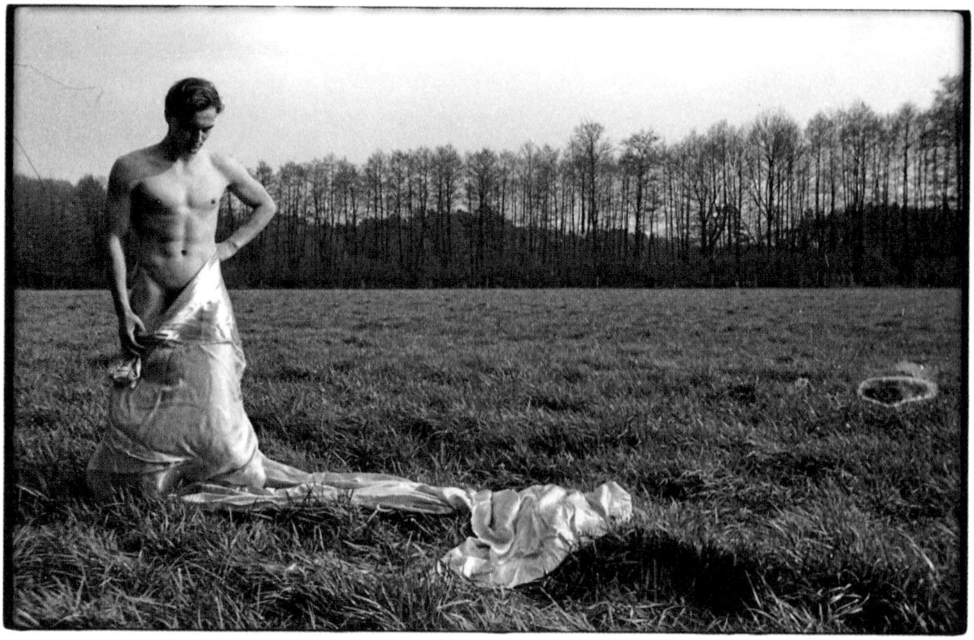

turns it to the wall and sits to face it. Is it true, as Jahnn concludes, that "the German catastrophe began with Goethe"?

The GDR's official *Dictionary of Cultural Politics* (*Kulturpolitisches Wörterbuch*) awards Goethe special status within its definition of realism. He is characterized as exhibiting a "realism with profound historicity" as well as a "qualitative realism designed in the greatest humanistic image of man."[36] In the Marxist-Leninist cultural framework, Goethe became a proto-socialist hero artist, whose historical and social sensibilities had paved the way for socialist culture. Editors of the

4.10

Gino Hahnemann. Production still. *Die Täuschung verträgt die Realität nicht* (*Illusion Cannot Bear Reality*). 1989. Super-8 film, 24 min. Photographer unknown (Gino Hahnemann?). Reprinted with the permission of Matthias Fischer. © 2020 by Matthias Fischer.

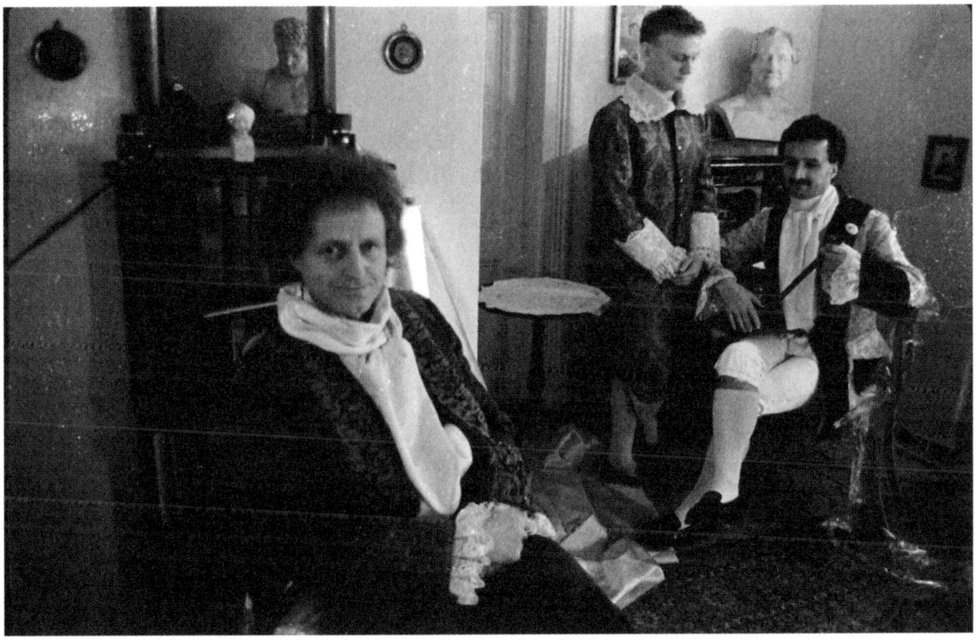

Dictionary of Cultural Politics reproduced famous lines, such as the following from *Faust*, and selectively interpreted them as pleas for communal and equitable living: "How each to the whole its selfhood gives / One in another works and lives!" Official interpretations defined Goethe's visionary humanism as an antecedent to socialist humanism, and thus enabled East Germany to claim the Weimar writer and statesman as their own. A socialist Goethe was, after all, no longer a West German Goethe. In fact, the coinciding of the GDR's official establishment year, 1949, with Goethe's two-hundredth birthday was touted as an auspicious coincidence

4.11

Gino Hahnemann. Production still. *Die Täuschung verträgt die Realität nicht* (*Illusion Cannot Bear Reality*). 1989. Super-8 film, 24 min. Photographer unknown (Gino Hahnemann?). Reprinted with the permission of Matthias Fischer. © 2020 by Matthias Fischer.

for the nation's defining moment.[37] Of course, the fact that the Federal Republic of Germany was also established in this year was strategically ignored by the East German government. Cultural officials called Goethe the "redeemer-god of the sinful German cultural heritage."[38] Here was the quintessential cultural icon for the anti-fascist Germany.

Hahnemann's *Goethe Project* represents a conflicted relationship to this "redeemer-god." The film balances critique with fascination—sketching an origin story that condemns the writer but also demonstrates his unimpeachable significance. In fact, critiques of Goethe pervaded the GDR's mainstream film and literary worlds in the 1970s. Cultural officials had long preferred Goethe's methodical classicism over the excess that is essential to the romantic tradition. Nevertheless, by the 1970s, a greater interest in the individuation that romanticism embraces, coupled with a frustration with official culture's idealistic characterization of Goethe, inspired a series of debates on the writer. Elaine Kelly summarizes the critiques that appeared in the state-run magazine *Sinn und Form* (Meaning and form) in 1975 thus: "Goethe's heroic qualities and preferencing of healthy classicism over sick romanticism were widely denounced not as evidence of a pre-socialist humanism but as the foundations of a legacy of deep-rooted arrogance and intolerance."[39] Critics emphasized Goethe's pride, including his well-documented unwillingness to support younger artists; Thomas Günther would in fact dramatize this detail in his DEFA (Deutsche Film-Aktiengesellschaft) film *Lotte in Weimar* (1975). Hahnemann's *Goethe Project* reflects the ambivalent attitude toward the writer that pervaded East German culture. Goethe is an elegant horseman and generous host, but he is also a murderer and a blowhard.

The homoeroticism that Hahnemann infuses in the film is secondary to his grappling with the figure of Goethe. This is the filmmaker's autobiographical backdrop, his *mise-en-scène*. The dance scene of the killed boy reincarnated as a muscular Adonis, the dandies who play cards in Goethe's house, the film's effeminate narrator—these are drawn from Hahnemann's everyday life, where out homosexuality was a norm and a social conduit. In his film Hahnemann grapples with Goethe as another inexorable part of his identity: "I have decided not to be a better German."[40] "For all eternity," the narrator continues, "whenever I enter the Goethe-pharmacy of this country looking for something to treat my wounds and when I visit the Goethe cinema, I will always think of the disappointments of film"; illusion cannot bear reality.[41] The Goethe cult has elevated the man and his letters to curative status with monumental consequences for the post-Nazi German people. As

Jahnn observes from West Germany: "There is no thought that he did not once have. Everyone can rely on him, but no one really calls on his greatness."[42] Hahnemann identifies the small-mindedness of cultural nationalism. He critiques it but resigns himself to it. After all this, he cannot be a better German.

SITUATING SUPER-8

Before the fall of the Wall, Hahnemann had few substantial connections to West Germans, with whom he shared a clear affinity. He also does not seem to have sought these relationships out. Nevertheless, very little documented—let alone anecdotal—evidence exists to demonstrate that West Germans were interested in East Germany's experimental film culture. In 1985, Hahnemann was one of three other artists, including Gabriele Stötzer[43] and Christine Schlegel, to be included in a GDR-specific program in West Berlin's third Interfilm Festival of experimental and independent film. The invitation was likely mediated by Cornelia Schleime and the painter Helge Leiberg, who is thanked in the film festival program. As the event's organizers state in the foreword to their program: "We are especially happy, and not a little bit proud, that we have been able to present a program from the GDR."[44] Their description of the Super-8 film scene in East Germany offers a basic explanation for the technical restrictions these three filmmakers faced. They note that the lack of access to better film stock or camera equipment has contributed to the emergence of an interdisciplinary set of film and projection practices in the GDR: "Owing to these restrictions, Super-8 film has been used primarily as an intermedial collaborative art form (film and live music, performance art, etc.)."[45] The next chapter of this text will examine closely the concept of multiple media implied in the Interfilm program. For now, the focus of analysis returns to the material constraints that helped to shape East Germany's unique brand of experimental film.

There was essentially only one kind of camera available to the average East German: the Soviet-made Quartz, which used cassette film stock.[46] Synchronized

4.12 (following two pages)

"Vorwort" (Foreword) in the Interfilm Festival program. Berlin, 1985. Akademie der Künste, Berlin, Gino-Hahnemann-Archiv, no. 279. © 2021 by Matthias Fischer.

VORWORT

60 (sechzig!) Stunden Super-8-Filme sind den Initiatoren von **Interfilm 3** zur Sichtung eingereicht worden. Eine schier unglaubliche Bilderflut, , die uns mit fast physischer Macht in die Kinosessel drückte. Die Auswahl, die wir aus diesem Angebot zusammengestellt haben, immerhin 20 Stunden, dokumentiert nach unserer 'radikal subjektiven' Ansicht den hohen Qualitätsstandard der bundesdeutschen und berliner Super-8-Filmproduktionen, obwohl mir in diesem Zusammenhang des öfteren ein Satz von Peter Nau einfiel, der einmal bemerkte, daß "das wirkliche Leben (...) oft dergestalt seinen Glanz verliert, daß man es manchmal mit dem Firnis der Fiktion wieder auffüllen muß."

Neben dieser Auswahl (an der sich Vertreter der drei Spielstellen beteiligten) freut es uns besonders, wieder auf großes Interesse bei ausländischen Filmemachern gestoßen zu sein. Die Programme aus New York, London, Frankreich und ein internationales Programm mit Beiträgen aus Austalien, den Niederlanden und Österreich legen davon Zeugnis ab. Besonders froh und ein bißchen stolz sind wir darüber, daß es uns gelungen ist, ein Programm aus der DDR präsentieren zu können. Nachdem Kontakte zu offiziellen Stellen zu keinem Ergebnis geführt hatten, fruchteten persönliche Kontakte und ermöglichten die Zusammenstellung eines Programmes von hoher künstlerischer Qualität.

War Interfilm 1 das von den Filmemachern selbst organisierte Fest, Filmstatt Berlin das von offizieller Seite (Freunde der Deutschen Kinemathek, Kultur-Senat) geförderte Fest, so kehrt **Interfilm 3** wieder zu den Ursprüngen zurück. Auch ohne Unterstützung seitens der 'Freunde' ist es den Spielstellen in Zusammenarbeit mit den Filmemachern gelungen, diese Schau des Super-8-Filmes zu organisieren. Auch die geringe Unterstützung, die der Senat in letzter Minute gewährte, konnte die Etat-Lücken nicht schließen, sodaß **Interfilm 3** noch mehr auf die Solidarität der Filmemacher angewiesen ist, denen wahrscheinlich noch nicht einmal die sonst übliche Minutenvergütung zu Teil werden wird. Wir bedauern dies außerordentlich!

Das KINO EISZEIT, schon an Interfiln 1 und Filmstatt Berlin beteiligt, möchte einen Beitrag seitens der Veranstalter für die Arbeit mit Super-8 leisten: Von Dezember `85 an wird es (zunächst) in 8-wöchigem Abstand eine Veranstaltung geben, wo jedermann seine Arbeiten auf S-8, 16mm und Video vorstellen kann (die Anwesenheit der Filmemacher/in ist allerdings Voraussetzung).

Schon oft wurde über die "imaginäre Kraft, das Ursprüngliche, die Direktheit, die politische Dimension usw." des Super-8-Mediums räsoniert, nur waren allzuoft die Filme leider nicht so, daß sie diese Prädikate für sich reklamieren konnten (was die vielfältigsten Gründe hat). Inzwischen jedoch - das ist mein persönliches Fazit von **Interfilm 3** - konzentrieren sich immer mehr Kräfte, die dem Super-8-Film einen ernstzunehmenden Platz in der deutschen Filmlandschaft erstreiten. Wenn ich hier die Bielefelder Produktionsgemeinschaften herausgreife, bedeutet dies keinenfalls eine Herabsetzung der Bemühungen an anderen Orten.

Um eine 'Ortsbestimmung' des S-8-Filmes wird es auch bei den von Reinhard Wolf initiierten Veranstaltungen zu Vertrieb und Professionalisierung von S-8 gehen. In einem weiteren Workshop "Trickmöglichkeiten im S-8-Film" wird Manfred Jelinski mit der weitverbreiteten Vorstellung aufräumen, daß Einzelbildschaltung die einzige Möglichkeit darstellt, im S-8-Film zu experimentieren. Wir wünschen den Teilnehmern an diesen Veranstaltungen viel Spaß!

Aus den **Interfilm 3** eingereichten Filmen hat das KINO EISZEIT ein Auswahlprogramm zusammengestellt, welches im Anschluß an das Fest zunächst auf eine größere Tournee (London, New York, Pittsburgh, Boston, L.A., Paris) gehen wird und im Anschluß vom KINO EISZEIT verliehen werden wird.

An dieser Stelle möchten wir allen Menschen unseren herzlichen Dank aussprechen, die unsere Arbeit an **Interfilm** 3 unterstützt haben!

Insbesondere gedankt sei:

Reinhard Wolf (KOB-8-Filmbüro)
Manfred Jelinski
Mathias Nelle (Asta FU)
Helge Leiberg
Frau Koglin (Filmbeauftragte-Senat)
Verein der Freunde der Villa Kreuzberg
Alf Bold (Freunde der Deutschen Kinemathek)
Jo Comino (London Film Coop)
Peggy Ahwesh (The Kitchen, New York)
Veronique Schlitz (Frankreich-Programm)
Monika Seeberger (dto.)

im Namen von **Interfilm 3**

Wolf Mellen

Organisiert haben **Interfilm 3:**

Jürgen Brüning, Frieder Butzmann, Heinz Hermanns, Wolf Mellen, Wolfgang Pause, Dorothee Seggewies und Bernd Vorjans

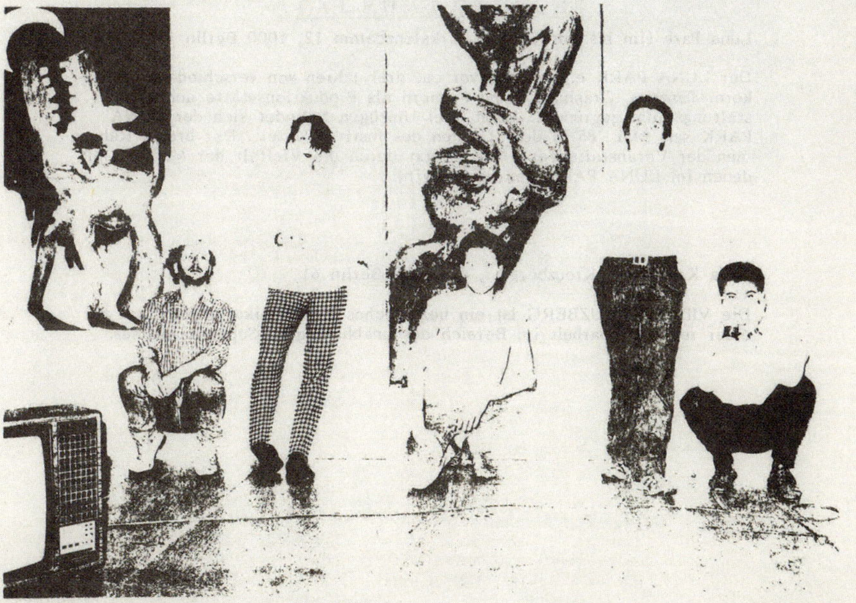

v.l.n.r.: Jürgen Brüning, Dorothee Seggewies, Bernd Vorjans, Heinz Hermanns und Wolf Mellen

DEUTSCHE DEMOKRATISCHE REPUBLIK

Zur Situation des Super-8-Filmes in der DDR:

Seit einigen Jahren werden in der DDR verstärkt Super-8-Filme gedreht, da dort unabhängiges Filmen nur in diesem Format möglich ist (Der Besitz von 35mm-Equipment ist strafbar; 16mm-Material gelangt nicht in den freien Verkauf). Die S-8-Arbeit wird allerdings durch eine Reihe von Hindernissen erschwert: Es sind nur Doppel-8-Kameras und -Projektoren russischer Bauart verfügbar, die mit 16 Bildern pro Sekunde arbeiten, Filmvertonungen sind technisch nicht möglich und auch das Kopieren fertiger Filme ist schwierig. Aufgrund dieser Restriktionen wird das Medium 8mm-Film hauptsächlich im Rahmen einer intermedialen Zusammenarbeit (Film + Live-Musik, Performance etc.) genutzt.

Die unabhängige 8mm-Szene der DDR steht im Widerspruch zu den offiziellen "Amateurfilmclubs". Aus diesem Grund finden Vorführungen i.d.R. im privaten Kreis, oder aber im Rahmen von Konzerten und anderen "Kulturveranstaltungen" statt. Einen besonderen Stellenwert haben in diesem Zusammenhang die Maler, die, zum großen Teil selbst 8mm-Filmer, gewisse Freiräume genießen und häufiger in ihren Ateliers 8mm-Filme zeigen. Die unabhängige 8mm-Szene wird von staatlicher Seite stillschweigend toleriert, da ihr keine große Breitenwirkung beigemessen wird.

Die Filme:

DIE AUSTREIBUNG AUS DEM PARADIES

Von Gabi Kachold

22 Min.

Eine konsequente Innenraumsituation, Gedankenmutationen zu dem Thema Freundschaft, Berührung, Überschneidung, Vertauschung, Verwechslung, Bindung, Bildung Trennung.

Die darstellenden Frauen sind Monique Förster und Claudia Räther und die Bilder entspringen einer zum damaligen Zeitpunkt zwischen mir und den beiden herrschenden illusionären Realität.

Der Schnittpunkt aus vergangenen Verletzungen, Verlusten
das körperliche Spüren eines unausgetragenen Leides
die Vorvergangenheit, die Ahnung und das Betreten des illusionären Raums
wer gibt ihr den Apfel der Erkenntnis, der Trennungen, der Raumzerstörung
das Paradies ist Berührung, Realität, Dasein, Verschmelzung
die erste Trennung ist der Gedanke, das Wort, die Geste von mir weg
zu den anderen hin
jedes miteinander gedankenlos gelebte ist im Nachhinein das gedankenvoll
Erstrebte
aber jeder Neuanfang beinhaltet die Fußstapfen der anderen
die Nachstellung der Bilder eröffnen uns die Taten der Vergangenheit
ich bin geprägt durch das was war
ab wann beginnt Selbstschöpfung

zur Ausstattung des Films wurde gesagt: "Strumpfhosenerotik", ein sehr zutreffender Begriff, der Moment der Unter-Rock-Raumfelder, der nicht mehr ganz Mode aber doch fast, Strips und Straps der Vergangenheit einer vom männlichen Geist bestimmten Industrie heute (nach der Strumpfhosenrevolution) pornografisches Material eines "achdaswarennochzeiten" liebedienerischen Frauenbildes. Aber der Fortschritt zieht der Frau die Hosen an, da

sound was an impossibility on the reversal black-and-white or color film sold on the consumer market. Copies of films could be made, but only through the country's state-run reproduction facilities. Reproduction was not only costly but ran the risk of exposing work to state oversight, as copies could easily land in the hands of the secret police (the Ministry for State Security, or Stasi).[47] Whereas some filmmakers may have wanted to work in other formats, 35mm film was strictly prohibited outside of professional studios, and thus nearly impossible to come by. It was less tricky but still quite difficult to acquire the higher-quality 16mm film without strategic connections to someone at the film school or DEFA studio who could provide stock, equipment, and processing. The risks of working in a more professional-grade material outweighed the benefits. Nevertheless, in an essay that appeared in the independently produced magazine *KOMA-KINO*, the filmmaker Cornelia Klauß described the impracticalities of the equipment at hand as an opportunity: "Thanks to the nightmarish quality of the copies from Johannisthal [one of the few state-run locations where motion pictures could be copied], only originals appear on the screen, including whatever possibilities might emerge, so that the films can be edited based on the mood at hand."[48] In anticipation of the fragile realities of the screening, she advised people to "film spontaneously" and to allow the "aesthetic of chance" to guide them.[49] Klauß's identification of experimental film's unavoidable lo-fi aesthetic may amount to the GDR film scene's only unifying theory. Indeed, a coherent film movement never emerged, though some did make efforts in this direction, including Klauß and Thomas Werner, who organized *KOMA-KINO* from its first issue in 1987 to its fifth and final one in 1989. "Nobody," as Schleime reflects, wanted to formalize the Super-8 scene—"everything else was already so overorganized in the East."[50] "What we did," she continues, "was just help each other as much as possible."[51] However, the impulse to care should not be overstated, as a desire to produce something autonomous and engaging indeed represented a foundational motivation for many artists working in this and other media. The

4.13

Page 1 of "Deutsche Demokratische Republik" (German Democratic Republic) in the Interfilm Festival program. Berlin, 1985. Akademie der Künste, Berlin, Gino-Hahnemann-Archiv, no. 279. © 2021 by Matthias Fischer.

turn to film also conforms to curator Christoph Tannert's characterization of the experimental culture of the late GDR as an "emergency society" (*Notgemeinschaft*).[52] Here "emergency" is not so much a reference to panic but to necessity—that is to say, adaptability and resourcefulness.

While it is tempting to place East Germany's Super-8 film scene within a western (or even an Eastern Bloc) history of avant-garde and experimental film, doing so runs the risk of imposing unrealistic cultural precedents and material realities onto the GDR. The truth is that East German artists were overwhelmingly isolated from the rest of the world. There were no independent film festivals bringing over films or film theory from the West, and surprisingly little exchange with other Eastern Bloc countries took place. In fact, in her 1987 *KOMA-KINO* essay, Klauß chose to reassure her fellow filmmakers that their lack of awareness of concurrent film cultures could be liberating. And when they do come to discover a film or director whose work bears some unintentional affinity to their own, she writes, "likely these are (unconscious?) repetitions, which is, in any case, a good sign."[53] Klauß's encouragement is heartfelt, and seems to anticipate the now well-worn critiques that the GDR's experimental art was derivative and thus inauthentic.[54]

Limited contact with western countries, including West Germany, may certainly be explained geopolitically, at least to a point. It was possible for artists from outside the Eastern Bloc to travel to the GDR on day visas to East Berlin. Foreigners could also freely travel to Leipzig during its annual trade and book fairs, as well as for its international documentary film festival, which favored politically progressive content over aesthetic innovation. The delight that West Berlin's Interfilm organizers expressed after first acquiring films from the GDR in 1985 reflects the belatedness of the efforts to grant East German artists a western audience. The festival program's attention to the material conditions of film production likewise reflect a tendency to emphasize privation and constraint over more careful examination of the content or artistic merit of art made in the GDR. It is not surprising that in 1988, the host of the first and only program of experimental film works to air on mainstream West German television likewise prioritized a description of material constraints over critical analysis of the films.[55] In short, though cross-German connections seem plausible, they were surprisingly rare and did not lead to collaborations or a consistent exchange of ideas.

Equally interesting is the lack of contact between East German filmmakers and those working in other Eastern Bloc countries. Logistical realities, including language barriers and the requirement of a visa to travel to every Eastern Bloc country

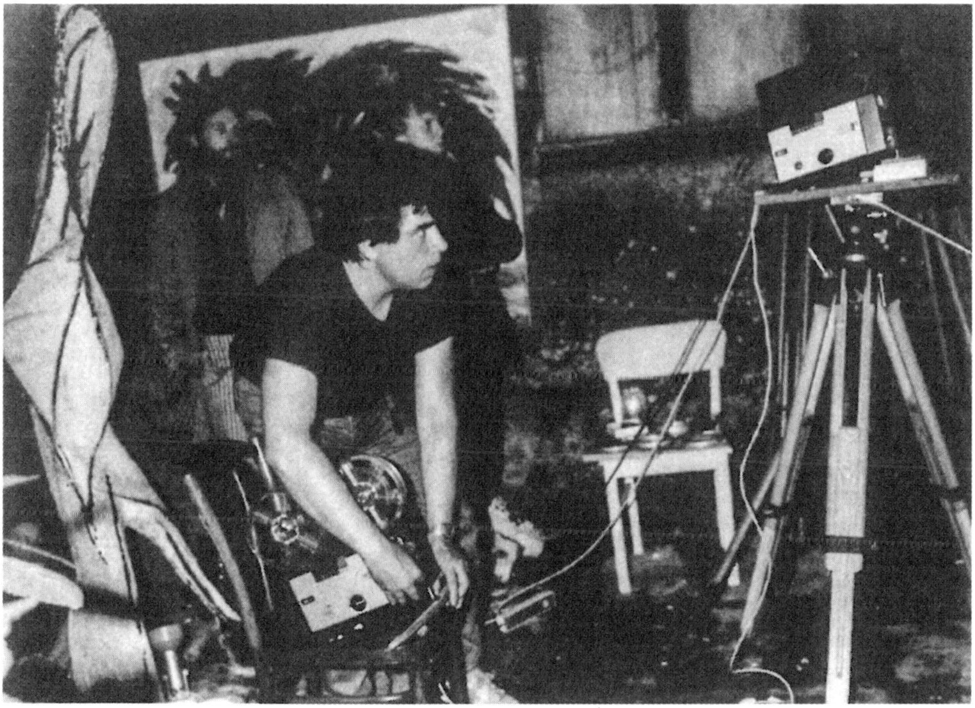

4.14

Gino Hahnemann sets up projectors at a film screening in Jena, East Germany. Ca. 1986. Photographer unknown. Reprinted with the permission of Christoph Tannert. © 1986 (?) by Christoph Tannert.

but Czechoslovakia,[56] help to explain the lack of substantial exchange, at least on the part of the East Germans. Perhaps the GDR works were too marginal or amateur for other Eastern Bloc countries, where avant-garde cinema was established enough that it could compete with the nationalized film studios. In Hungary, for example, experimental cinema had become a part of public discourse, leading even to the development of rival film schools and philosophies.[57] The Austrian-American filmmaker Amos Vogel took up this issue briefly in his 1974 *Film as a Subversive Art*, when he (falsely) observed that in comparison to other Eastern Bloc countries "no 'subversive' films exist in East Germany [that are] directed against its own establishment."[58] Vogel allowed that conditions of production—rather than artistic intention—had made a critical East German experimental film scene an impossibility: "It is not that there are no social or political problems: it is simply that the state owns all motion picture production, distribution, and exhibition."[59] Tellingly, Vogel made no mention of the short-lived era of DEFA productions that were overtly critical of state culture. The so-called German New Wave of the early 1960s ended abruptly with the near full-scale censorship of all feature films made in 1965.[60] Vogel's lack of awareness of this history reveals the effectiveness of centralized control over a global understanding of East German culture at the time of his book's 1974 release.[61]

Defining the East German experimental film scene on its own terms, particularly with regard to material conditions, thus matters greatly. Of course, the analysis of Hahnemann's films, and of Schleime's in the preceding chapter, has privileged the position of the researcher. East Germany's Super-8 film is buried piecemeal in the archive, but its live or performed quality is otherwise inaccessible.[62] The overwhelmingly obvious limitations of the digitized copies of these films (the only format readily available), including the existence of essentially one passion-project collection—Claus Löser's ex.oriente.lux archive—to contain them, underscore their objecthood. Under these conditions, the material of the film, specifically its vulnerability and ability to transform in the space of a screening, is absent. Moreover, the sound is constrained and unnaturally fixed in the digital format.

In the 1980s, filmmakers adapted their works to meet the screening site. Cafes and bars, living rooms and apartment block courtyards, gallery spaces and churches, art school clubs and state cultural centers—each setting imposed its own set of material (sometimes ideological) demands on the films. A picture of Hahnemann at a 1986 screening in Jena illustrates the lengths to which a filmmaker might stretch material circumstances to achieve a certain vision. Here, in what appears to be a double-projector setup, Hahnemenn fixes his eyes upon a screen, jerry-rigging a way to make the two projectors run to his liking. Projection equipment was notoriously temperamental. The inability to reproduce films rendered the quality of the projected material itself suspect. A broken reel meant a new edit had to be made of the one and only copy. Film was thus less a precious object than a living agent.

The sound is also skewed by the archive. For example, in his *Goethe Project* film treatment, Hahnemann lists the soundtrack as an accordion version of Erik Satie's *Gymnopédie No. 3*, but the DVD recording he released in 2006 features the electroacoustic composer Eckhard Rödger. Its recorded voiceover by Uwe Hübner noticeably pans from left to right. There is something missing here. Material conditions in the 1980s made synchronized sound impossible. So people improvised: films were designed to fit abstract scores played off a tape or performed live. Often a recited, sometimes improvisational text that did not describe or narrate the image would accompany a film. Many remember the screening space as something impossible to duplicate—these were performances where risks fell in the camp of literal, as well as aesthetic, rule breaking.[63] Cassettes, live music, or readings accompanied the films in situ. As Hahnemann's *Goethe Project* demonstrates, just what was played during a film screening is not always easy to glean. The mood of the room, the filmmaker's current taste, or the screening setup required spontaneous decision making. Certainly, the GDR's improv jazz scene, a highlight of the mid- to late 1970s and still significant into the mid-1980s, contributed to the spontaneous aesthetic of the Super-8 film screening. Indeed, screenings often facilitated live action, and films could be backdrops as much as focal points.

The material conditions that defined the form of experimental film in the GDR also defined the reality that these films sought to deconstruct, retool, and transcend. That reality is exceeded and consistently cited in the screening space. The observers observed themselves. Sometimes that looking back was literal: often the actors on screen comprised the film's public. For others in the audience, the connection to an alternative way of seeing or being seen in the landscape of East Germany was more abstract. The GDR's experimental cinema was multisensorial, marking the screening space as another site to claim material independence and autonomous practice. As multimedia events, the films were core components of an interdisciplinary context, where live music and performance completed the Super-8 object. That complexity of form, interwoven with multiple personages, makes film one of East Germany's most restless and adaptable experimental forms of culture.

5

TYPES, KINDS, AND GENRES OF ART

The Intermedia I Festival in 1985

Saturday, June 1, 1985, 6 PM, Klubhaus Coswig: Hundreds have made the short trip from Dresden to the neighboring town of Coswig to attend the opening night of the two-day Intermedia I Festival. Punks don their leather and metal chains. Jazz tramps wear the uniform of their ilk: a collarless blue-and-white-striped long-sleeved *Fleischerhemd* (butcher's shirt) and jeans. Artists, filmmakers, and musicians mingle and await their moment to showcase their work. Dozens of paintings scrawled onto the uneven surface of Roman blinds hang from the clubhouse's open-plan balcony. Festivalgoers lean on the bannister looking down at the revelers who commune below. The building is grand, a private guesthouse built in the neoclassical style in 1900 that has served as Coswig's cultural center since 1978. Fine crown molding and an elegant coved ceiling contrast with the bold and expressive paintings and raucous party attendees.

A cordoned-off area at the front of the main hall is a makeshift stage. Upon it rest a wooden shipping palette and several sculptures made from frosted plastic sheeting that the artist Lutz Dammbeck has wrapped around willow branches and wooden scaffolds. A large sheet of white paper scrawled with a list of names—STALIN, SIEGFRIED, TARZAN, HERAKLES, etc.—forms a backdrop. Suddenly all of the lights go black. A light behind the stage flickers on. A body stands backlit behind the paper screen and begins to move and contort as the sounds of the free jazz band Musikbrigade (Music brigade) swell to a cacophony.[1] The performer breaks through the paper, tearing it apart with swift jerking movements. This is Fine Kwiatkowski, a dancer with shaved head wearing her trademark performance

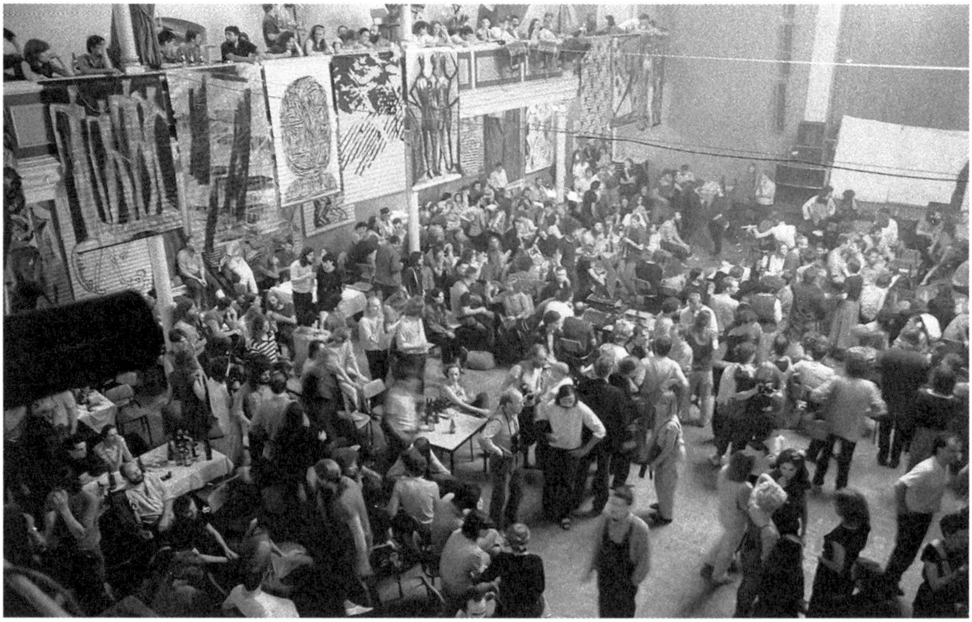

uniform: a silver skintight bodysuit that accentuates the unimaginable movements and contortions of her rail-thin body. The crowd looks on as she moves with and against the music. She dons, at times, a tall mask roughly hewn from pieces of cardboard stitched together in Dammbeck's signature style; a two-dimensional copy of one half of a head made by the sculptor Arno Breker, a favored artist in the Nazi-era, completes one side of the mask. The snarl of this face in profile, carved by Breker to convey the steadfast confidence of Hitler's Aryan fantasy, is all the more garish and frightening in this context—a clear reminder of the still-healing

5.1

Harald Hauswald. Untitled documentation of the Intermedia I Festival. Klubhaus Coswig, June 1 or 2, 1985. Reprinted with the permission of OSTKREUZ—Agentur der Fotografen GmbH. © 1985 by Harald Hauswald and the OSTKREUZ—Agentur der Fotografen GmbH.

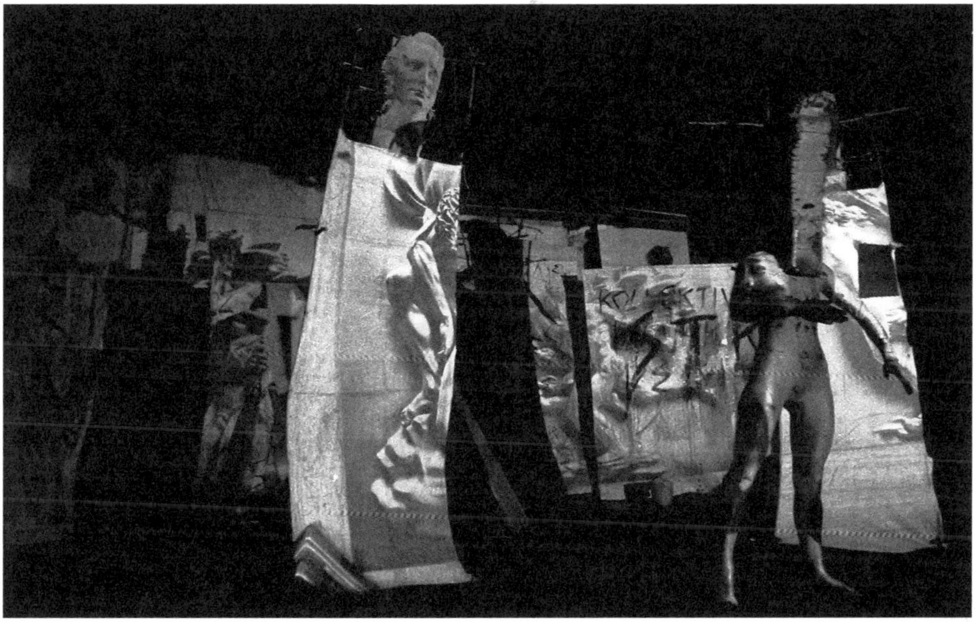

wounds of German fascism. A film projection casts a series of abstract drawings onto Kwiatkowski's small jerking frame, which moves in uncertain union with the agitated strumming of Lothar Fiedler on his guitar. The plastic sheeting both absorbs and projects these images as they bend around her body and the sculptural forms that appear on stage. After quickly swelling to a frantic visual frenzy, the images stop. The stage is dark once again. The next several minutes proceed at an equally unpredictable pace.[2] Slides of images of artworks by the sculptor Breker, family photos, and soundless clips of films produced by and for the Nazis appear as

5.2

Lutz Dammbeck. *Herakles* (*Hercules*). Intermedia I Festival. Klubhaus Coswig, June 1, 1985. Media collage. Photo by Harald Hauswald. Reprinted with the permission of Lutz Dammbeck and VG Bild-Kunst, Bonn; and Harald Hauswald and the OSTKREUZ—Agentur der Fotografen GmbH. © 1985 by Lutz Dammbeck and the OSTKREUZ—Agentur der Fotografen GmbH.

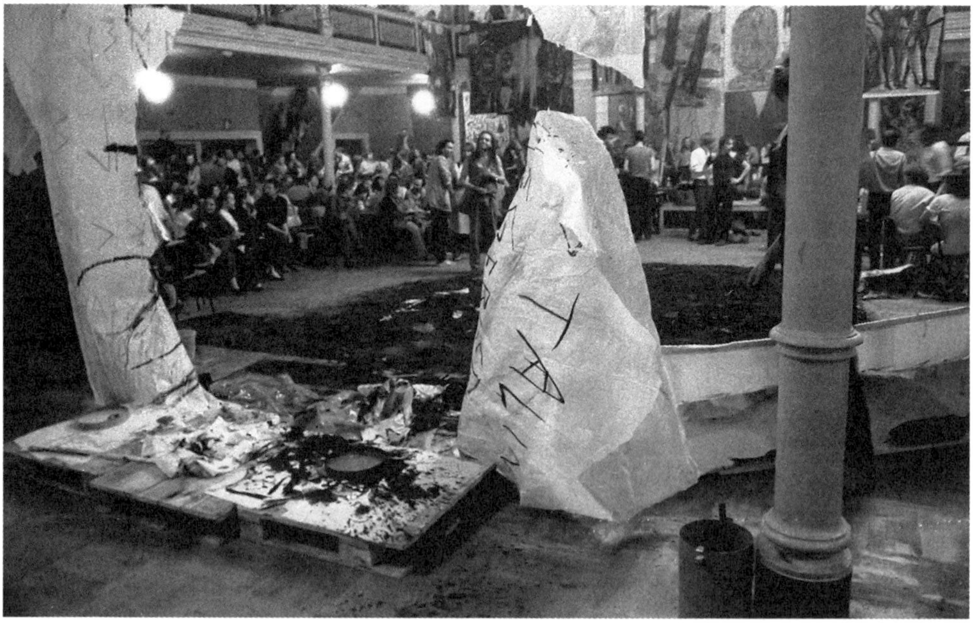

a recitation of the Grimm Brothers' fairy tale "Das eigenwillige Kind" (The willful child) fills the room. A sound collage featuring excerpts read from the East German author Heiner Müller's short-form text "Herakles 2 oder die Hydra" (Hercules 2 or the Hydra) punctuates phases of the performance: "For a long time, he thought he was going through the forest in the stunningly warm wind, which seemed to be blowing from all sides and moving the trees like snakes . . ."

Each part of Dammbeck's project functions together to produce what the artist calls a "Mediencollage" (media collage). The *Hercules* media collage that he

5.3

Lutz Dammbeck. *Herakles* (*Hercules*). Intermedia I Festival. Klubhaus Coswig, June 1, 1985. Media collage. Photo by Harald Hauswald. Reprinted with the permission of Lutz Dammbeck and VG Bild-Kunst, Bonn; and Harald Hauswald and the OSTKREUZ—Agentur der Fotografen GmbH. © 1985 by Lutz Dammbeck and the OSTKREUZ—Agentur der Fotografen GmbH.

presented in Coswig is part of his long-term *Herakles Konzept* (*Hercules Concept*), which he produced and performed internationally from 1979 to 2005.[3] Much can be made of the symbolic power of Dammbeck's *Hercules* media collage. Replete with references to the legacies of Nazism, both cultural and familial, the performance is a portrait of his generation. The first to be raised in the "anti-fascist" Germany, these people were not only the German Democratic Republic's (GDR's) first cohort too young to be implicated in the Nazi past; they were also its first fully "communist" generation. Yet these East Germans were not immune to or recovered from the Nazi past. Its residues linger in personal history.[4] As the Germanist Seth Howes has written, Dammbeck's larger purpose in the *Hercules* series entails both a historical, archival study and a mythical examination of "how the quiescent, disengaged individuals on whom fascism's success depended had failed to protest or resist until it was too late."[5] To be sure, Dammbeck's invocation of Hercules betrays not a condemnation of the average German (either Nazi-era or communist-era), but rather the artist's worry over the repeated manipulations of human capacity in the service of autocratic forms of government. As the art historian Matthias Flügge writes: "The principle theme is the commissioning and shaping of people and their motivations in modern social systems. Or, even more concisely: The shaping of the individual in the interests of present power."[6] Dammbeck's project makes Nazi and state socialist Germany analogous. *Hercules* complicates the agenda of state culture to define a nation by visualizing the tenuous—and recursive—premises of an antidemocratic nation-state. As important as the meaning of this work is the way in which the artist plays with multiple media. This chapter focuses on that materiality. It defines Dammbeck's Intermedia I *Hercules* performance as a signature example of the multimedia and collaborative artworks that characterized the experimental art scene of the 1980s.

PROGRAMMING AN ALTERNATIVE

Hercules appeared several times on stages large and small all over the GDR. What had originally been planned as a film funded by DEFA (Deutsche Film-Aktiengesellschaft) had evolved over years of experimentation, including in response to an official rejection from the national film studio. "This planned film falls short of the potential of the medium for which we produce films, [namely] the cinema screen," Horst Pehnert of the Ministry for Culture explained in his office's definitive disapproval of Dammbeck's request for funding.[7] Of course, the fact that the artist would be permitted to present his project as a media collage (rather than as a film) on some of the GDR's public stages, including at the International Music Festival in Dresden just a few days before the Intermedia I Festival, highlights the inconsistencies in the logic of official culture. In its presentation at Coswig, Dammbeck's work exemplifies the fortitude of artists to pursue and create their own opportunities. And even though Intermedia I would lead to a significant (albeit short-lived) onslaught by state authorities that was largely unexpected by festival organizers, the backlash marked the last time that experimental art would be met with such aggression. In fact, Intermedia I inspired and empowered its public. The festival is emblematic of the calculated risks artists would take to bring their work greater visibility. More importantly, it also demonstrates the waning influence that the state's methods of intimidation had on the very artists it aimed to subdue.

As Intermedia I's inaugural event, the *Hercules* media collage set a tone for a weekend that featured more than eighty artists and musicians who presented artwork or performed live for an audience of more than one thousand onlookers, including visitors from West Germany.[8] Christoph Tannert, one of the two festival organizers, describes the intentional placement of Dammbeck's performance: "[His] media collage got to the point, drawing attention to the urgent need to satisfy the hopes for changing the [artistic and social] conditions in the GDR."[9] Like the Intermedia I Festival itself, Dammbeck was a crossover figure, who worked along the margins of official and unofficial culture. A trained graphic designer,[10] he worked in the animation department at the state's national cinema from 1974 to 1981, where he had a number of successes.[11] DEFA's rejection of his *Hercules* film inspired in Dammbeck an even greater commitment to producing an alternative art form—the media collage—that challenged cinematic convention in both its content and presentation by uniting dance, theater, improvisation, installation, and sound into a single live experience. Despite abandoning his position within the state's culture industry, Dammbeck continued to occupy the realms of both official and unofficial culture. Between June 1984 and the Intermedia I Festival in June 1985, two works in the *Hercules Concept* series—*La Sarraz* and *Herakles*—had appeared four times on official state stages, including at the Bauhaus Theater in Dessau. At the same time, Dammbeck was helping to organize 1984's Erster Leipziger Herbstsalon (First Leipzig Autumn Salon), a three-week exhibition that the journalist Doris Liebermann justifiably calls a "work of piracy."[12] A surprise exhibition at the city's annual international trade fair, the Leipzig salon entailed a clever use of precedent. Essentially, Dammbeck and five other artists identified a loophole in organizational protocols which allowed members of the Union of Fine Artists to rent space at the fair. Officials could find no recourse to shut down the exhibition of experimental paintings and installations, which reached an audience of nearly ten thousand international guests. The bold strategy of organizing an unofficial art exhibition in an official space—though not without its consequences, as Liebermann's book outlines—was broadly influential. In choosing to open Intermedia I with Dammbeck's piece, Tannert and his co-organizer Micha Kapinos maintained a continuity between the First Leipzig Autumn Salon and their own initiative less than one year later. They sent a clear message to their audience, as well as to the cultural functionaries who had granted permission for the unconventional event to take place: multimedia practice represented the ethos of the time, and formed both a mode of practice and a locus point for collaboration and mass gathering.

True to its name, Intermedia I featured an interdisciplinary program of performance art, film screenings, a fashion show, and music. Like *Hercules*, each project combined an improvisational and collaborative aesthetic with multiple central media. For example, opening the second night of the festival were the Dresden painters Andreas Hegewald, Lutz Peter Naumann, Claudia Böttner, Klaus Werner, and others who picked up instruments to form a free jazz group called the Rennbahnband (Racecourse Band). As they played, Jörg Sonntag, Christiane Just, Bodo Münzner, and Michael Hengst painted on a roughly 100-square-foot canvas. Later, the painter Hans-Joachim Schulze, a prolific organizer who founded the Leipzig-based artist collective Gruppe 37,2 (Group 37.2) in the late 1970s, appeared on stage with two others as the noise band Pfff . . . The photographer, sculptor, painter, and musician Klaus Hähner-Springmühl joined his partner Gitte Springmühl and Frank Raßbach to perform saxophone in their legendary improvisation group Kartoffelschälmaschine (Potato Peeler Machine). These three examples especially blurred the lines between music and performance art that were paramount to the Intermedia I Festival.

For the cinematic works featured at Intermedia I, organizers ceded the stage to the improvisational mode of screening that had come to characterize public showcases of Super-8 film. As was typical, filmmaker-artists incorporated live and recorded music, dance, movement, and multiple film projections into their screenings. A kind of "expanded cinema"—to borrow from the media theorist Gene Youngblood—East German experimental film came to fruition before a public audience.[13] The painter and filmmaker Christine Schlegel particularly seized on the opportunity to unite her already improvisational and gestural filmmaking method and concept with live performance. Having worked for some time with Kwiatkowski, Schlegel invited the dancer to move organically between screen and projector at the Coswig festival. Gliding before Schlegel's film *Strukturen* (*Structures*, 1985), Kwiatkowski united herself at once with her own image on the screen while also distancing herself from this representation. For Gabriele Stötzer,[14] who also screened two films at Intermedia I, the Schlegel/Kwiatkowski performance was a festival highlight. She would return home to Erfurt inspired to continue her explorations into the borderlines of gender and sexuality in her solo and collaborative art practices.[15] Intermedia I was also the first time that body-based performance had been showcased so prominently in the GDR. Although sexuality, or even a focus on the body, was not a curatorial concept of the festival, it was one of several cross-currents between artistic practices that Intermedia I inspired or helped to solidify. The fluidity of media, the expressivity, and the lawlessness of the myriad artistic practices and visions put so prominently on display—many for the first time—marked an important point of departure for a large number of East Germany's experimental artists. The effects of Intermedia I might be measured by the surge in multimedia and collaborative practice as well as alternative uses of official spaces for experimental art that would soon follow.

ORGANIZED CHAOS AND SPONTANEOUS COLLECTIVITY

While the Intermedia I Festival is widely regarded as one of the most significant artistic summits to take place in the late GDR, little has been written about how precisely it defined its cultural moment. Tannert describes the influence of the unconventional uses of media as instrumental: "On both evenings, the intermedia concept defined itself in the first place as an affront against the existing, rigid artistic structures. Many of the featured artists made things that no one could have expected from them. They gave in to realms where they would ordinarily not have felt at home."[16] He continues to describe the centrality of exchange and collaboration, concluding that Intermedia I had "enabled young artists to discover themselves and to bind together as a small circle of supporters who were ready to live this new identity together."[17] Given Tannert's proximity to the event, his observations may be critiqued as idealized. However, in her analysis of the festival, the media scholar Barbara Büscher uses the metaphor of the rhizome to interpret Intermedia I as a kind of network that had the ability to build its own organized power: "In such a network—which no apparent institution could or wanted to cultivate—the transitory events, meetings, and exhibitions of the un- or semiofficial sphere became nodes that not only intensified artistic exchange, but allowed artistic activities to be seen."[18] Important for the purpose of linking multimedia and collective practice are Büscher's gestures to the significance of the variegated and unanticipated alliances forged in the space of Intermedia I. The festival is considered to be a rare example of a large-scale union, or at least cohabitation, of at least two fairly distinct milieus in the GDR's experimental scenes: namely, punks and artists. This countered a tendency, which the cultural historians Paul Kaiser and Claudia Petzold identify, for the experimental scene to be fairly stratified, with artists occupying one clique, punks another, and so on.[19] Kaiser and Petzold's assessment of a divided scene emphasizes the significant work undertaken at Intermedia I to bring together hundreds of people invested in various forms of experimental cultural practice. Uniting people working in parallel, if not often intersecting, veins, further underscored the conceptual links between visual artists and musicians, performers and filmmakers, painters and sculptors, which were key to the ontology of independent and experimental cultural practice in the 1980s GDR.

In fact, Intermedia I was officially billed as a jazz festival. Its publicity materials detailed a musical lineup and either omitted the names of participating artists or presented them en masse. Nevertheless, the event's subtitle, *Klangbild/Farbklang* (Noisepicture/Colornoise), could equally describe Dammbeck's media collage, a neoexpressionist painting scrawled on a Roman blind, or the festival's musical performers, who varied from jazz improvisation to punk spontaneity to a clatter of sound. The music—which tended more toward noise or punk than jazz—wedded experimentation to performative elements much in the way that the festival's artworks and performances did. Forging a more tangible link between music and art was particularly significant to Tannert. Just one year earlier, he had published an essay titled "Intermedia: Attempts at Collective Production of Art," in which he considered the significance of multimedia practice to young East German musicians.[20] Appearing in the state-run journal *Musik und Gesellschaft* (Music and society), Tannert's essay argued against rigid uses of media and in favor of the process rather than the product of art making. Identifying constriction as creative fuel, he described the conditions of cultural practice in the East German state: "Creativity arises less out of an aesthetic differentiation from a current trend in music than it does from an unsatisfactory cultural situation."[21] The analogy to the state is plain, though secondary to Tannert's fundamental impulse, which was to introduce the importance of multimedia practice to the readers of one of the GDR's most important cultural publications. In fact, Tannert sought to save state culture by advising it to change, specifically to make room for the needs of an up-and-coming generation of artists: "It is beyond dispute that certain groups of young people develop totally unique needs, which require and warrant accommodation by cultural institutions. If these needs are ignored in the planning of leisure activities, young people—otherwise ready to engage in society—will see their desires unmet and will take their right to enjoyment elsewhere by developing their own forms of expression and group identification."[22] Here the implication is manifold. Tannert not only identifies the real possibility that young artists would feel alienated and thus detach themselves from state culture, but also hints at the increasing allure of the West for them. Artists whose desires the state left unattended to, in short, could choose to leave the GDR. Many would make that choice; many who stayed remained commited to artistic interdisciplinarity.

Tannert's warnings of an official culture doomed to irrelevance went unheeded. Although his analysis had been solicited by the editors of the journal and written while he worked as a secretary in the central management of the Union of Fine Artists, it was ultimately deemed too controversial. Authorities used his *Musik und Gesellschaft* text as grounds to dismiss Tannert from his job in the union. He was nevertheless allowed to continue to work as a freelance art historian with full union accreditation, and continued to publish in the official arts journal *Bildende Kunst* (Fine art). Tannert considers this a strategic move on the part of *Bildende Kunst*'s editor-in-chief Peter Michel, who both needed him to get a sense of the young artistic scene, and who used his texts as a means to test the limits of permissibility: "This was a form of cultural diplomacy—a way of looking toward the future."[23] Such long-term strategizing may also explain why Tannert was allowed to organize the Intermedia I Festival in a state cultural institution just one year after being fired. Permission to organize and publish likewise reveal the foundational vulnerability of state principle in the face of the realities of creative practice in the late GDR. Although Tannert is reluctant to say that Intermedia I produced tangible institutional changes, he allows that the festival empowered its target audience. Attendees came away with "other attitudes" about artistic possibility, including a growing confidence to explore alternative art forms in public forums.[24] The Intermedia I Festival was an opportunity to showcase the cross-disciplinary tendencies that the state's "art history was unwilling to acknowledge."[25] Within a few years of the festival,

Michel's bet on Tannert proved fruitful, as many of the union's art historians began publishing on multimedia practice and other forms of experimental art.[26] By the late 1980s, the Union of Fine Artists regularly held official discussions about incorporating new media practices into its mix. These efforts, led in part by Tannert and the art historian Eugen Blume, culminated in the Permanente Kunstkonferenz (Permanent Art Conference), a Union of Fine Artists-sponsored event that occupied Berlin's most important gallery, the Galerie Weißer Elefant (White Elephant Gallery), for one month in the summer of 1989. The road to this kind of visibility for experimental culture was rocky but fairly speedy—a result of inconsistent policy, and more importantly, an increasingly demanding and risk-taking art world.

AN UNANTICIPATED, BUT SHORT-LIVED, BACKLASH

The Intermedia I Festival in fact maintained a long tradition of interdisciplinary aesthetic experimentation in the GDR. For example, in the 1970s, the Dresden-based Lücke (Gap) group became known for their fusion of music, performance art, and painting. Drawing inspiration from the German expressionist collective Die Brücke (The Bridge), also from Dresden, the five Lücke artists (A. R. Penck, Peter Herrmann, Wolfgang Opitz, Harald Gallash, and Steffen Terk) collaborated on projects and organized exhibitions in Opitz's artist studio between 1971 and 1976. The Lücke group pursued the collaborative ethic of its avant-garde namesake. At the same time that the group's clear reference to the Brücke artists signaled the longevity of autonomous art on German soil, the wordplay in their name "Lücke" likewise underscored the gap or break that Nazi cultural policy had established between German art and a global art movement, and which East Germany's state socialist cultural policies had further entrenched. This kind of reference to Germany's pre-Nazi and precommunist avant-garde surfaced in other contexts. The First Leipzig Autumn Salon of 1984, for example, referred to a 1913 exhibition by Herwarth Walden, who founded the expressionist magazine *Der Sturm* (The Storm) and the gallery of the same name. Commitments to collaborative production and especially publicity in the form of print materials inspired artists like Penck and Herrmann to join the painter Eberhard Göschel, the printer Jochen Lorenz, and the poet Bernhard Theilmann to initiate the Obergrabenpresse (Obergraben Press), which produced graphic works and posters and hosted events from its 1978 founding until its closure three decades later, in 2008. Similarly inspired by this attention to self-production, and with the help of several organizers of the First Leipzig Autumn Salon, Gerd Harry "Judy" Lybke established his still extant gallery EIGEN+ART in 1983.

Also not to be forgotten are the foundational legacies of Karl-Marx-Stadt's Galerie Oben (Above Gallery), founded in 1973, including its relationship to the artists in Clara Mosch, a group and gallery active in the region from 1977 to 1982. The name of this group is derived from the surnames of four of its five central artists: CLA, Carlfriedrich Claus; RA, Thomas Ranft; MO, Michael Morgner; SCH, Gregor-Torsten Schade. The only woman in the group, Dagmar Ranft-Schinke, is not given credit for the name, though as the spouse of Thomas Ranft she may have been folded into the mix by association. Unfortunately, the exclusion of the only woman in the group at the same time that a woman's name was adopted for the collective ought not come as a surprise in a country whose claims to gender equality have been rightly criticized as superficial.[27] Nevertheless, Clara Mosch did embody a collective spirit, perhaps made most clear in the obituary created by the group's photographer Ralf-Rainer Wasse to mark the "death" of the collective in 1982. Over the course of its six years of creative work, Clara Mosch became well known across East Germany for its *plein air* art events, self-run gallery, and prolific printing activities. With several artist portfolios and catalogs, as well as dozens of posters, postcards, and mail art objects, Clara Mosch remains today one of the GDR's best known and most widely exhibited art collectives. Likewise significant to their legacy is the discovery in the 1990s that Wasse had been sharing his documentation and experiences with the secret police (the Ministry for State Security, or Stasi).[28] It is now known that the secret police deployed more than 120 official collaborators not only to observe but to meddle with the Clara Mosch artists, and that these operations contributed to the breakup of the marriage of Ranft and Ranft-Schinke.[29] Without wishing to distract from the inhumane and infantilizing tactics of the Stasi, I believe it matters more that Clara Mosch existed at all, and even more that their efforts with their own gallery and with the Galerie Oben were supported in part by intentional affiliations with state cultural officials. The Galerie Oben, for example, was directed from its opening in 1973 until 1979 by the art collector Georg Brühl, whose influence on the regional chapter of the Union of Fine Artists helped to recast Karl-Marx-Stadt as an enclave for self-taught artists, including those working in experimental forms. Under his direction of the gallery, Brühl featured both jazz concerts and a progressive exhibition agenda.[30] Ironically, Clara Mosch fell apart mostly due to its too cozy relationship with official cultural bureaucracy, which essentially smothered the group's autonomy.

With no clear path or anticipated future for experimental culture, the Intermedia I Festival may seem at first to have been a perilous venture. However, the brief consideration of the history of organizing such projects outlined above reveals that uncertain outcomes may have inspired a stronger commitment among its organizers and participants. Precedent also underscored the necessity for people to be flexible, adaptive, and resourceful. By 1985, the festival organizers Christoph Tannert and Micha Kapinos had both witnessed or experienced firsthand the potential consequences of public-facing experimental art projects. The risks they took when planning the Intermedia I Festival were thus both somewhat reckless and somewhat calculated, both measured against a need for change and an awareness of what had, and had not, worked in the past for experimental culture.

Although by 1985 experimental events were not altogether clandestine, the high profile of Intermedia I was quite special—and deemed a sign of times to come. In fact, more festivals were meant to follow in its path, hence the Roman numeral "I" in the name Intermedia I.[31] Of course, the *First* Leipzig Autumn Salon had also anticipated a second iteration, which never came to pass. Two months after Intermedia I, Wolfgang Zimmerman was fired from his position as the director of the Klubhaus Coswig where the festival had been held. Others, including the artist and musician Hans-Joachim Schulze, were arrested for their involvement in the festival. These repercussions likewise precipitated festival co-organizer Kapinos's emigration to West Berlin, and contributed to the emigration of other Intermedia I artists—including Dammbeck, Fiedler, and Schlegel—in 1986.[32] All three of these artists left the GDR legally with official exit papers, joining a "wave of emigration" (*Ausreisewelle*) that coincided with a revision to national emigration policies.[33] With a high point around 1985, the state's relaxation of these laws effectively drained the country of many of its less desirable citizens, especially artists, writers, and musicians. When artists as important to the scene as Dammbeck applied for an exit permit, they were likely to receive it. When considered within the pantheon of other passive-aggressive strategies of citizen control it employed at this time, the state's relaxation on emigration was certainly deliberate. Since 1976, the Ministry for State Security had employed a strategy known as *Zersetzung* (corrosion), targeting individuals through large-scale enlistment of citizen spies as unofficial collaborators known as *inoffizielle Mitarbeiter*, IMs, as discussed in earlier chapters of this book.[34] *Zersetzung* also entailed sabotaging or destabilizing relationships by seeding deliberately inflammatory gossip, initiating sexual intrigue, or permitting one member of a couple to emigrate to the West while providing no explanation for the other's denial. The harsh reaction to Intermedia I thus was part of a large-scale effort to demoralize and depress East Germany's nonconforming citizens.

On the other hand, it bears mentioning that Dammbeck holds no fond memories of the festival, which he left immediately after presenting his *Hercules* media collage. He recalls, "The atmosphere was depressing . . . and it all felt very hopeless. Coswig was *one* reason for me to leave this 'experimental art scene' behind."[35] Dammbeck's impression sheds light on the necessity to historicize this event with nuance and a critical eye. To be sure, as Tannert has said, "These artists didn't feel good in the 1980s GDR. And they expressed that."[36] A sense of hopelessness, a desire for something new, combined with the appeal and currency of western culture and lifestyles—all of these undermined a coherent collective identity among East Germany's experimental artists. Of course, this feeling was not unique to artists, but rather reflected a national crisis over identity, and in particular a lack of confidence in the government to fulfill its promises to its citizens.

The stringent reaction to Intermedia I by cultural authorities contradicted precedents for bringing experimental practice to public spaces at the Klubhaus Coswig and beyond. A series of free jazz concerts organized under Zimmerman's direction had inspired the choice to bring the Intermedia I Festival there. The Dresden region had seen similar cross-disciplinary acts just a few years earlier at the 1979 International Music Festival. That year, a special program titled *Interferenzen* (Interferences) had included musicians accompanied by dancers who performed before projected images and films. The official program's description of the event seems to welcome interdisciplinarity in the arts:

> Music is a series of supporting layers: The entirety of a piece is comprised simultaneously of a fabric of numerous and varying constellations: The optical responds to music or in the reverse; Dance responds to music or to the optical; Music responds to dance; Musicians respond to each other or to the soundtrack, and so on. . . . The process between media is the process between the authors, and ought to become a (theatrical) process for the audience.[37]

Even with the setback that Tannert had faced in response to his *Musik und Gesellschaft* essay in 1984, the tradition of experimental programming in the region, as well as the accommodation of the cultural center's director, suggests that Intermedia I had been planned well within the new direction that state culture was seemingly willing, even officially advised, to head. Moreover, as the Klubhaus Coswig director, Zimmerman occupied a fairly independent position of luxury, with little oversight by cultural administrators, and already had a track record for hosting unconventional events. Most importantly, he had obtained the requisite official permission to host the festival.

Here the site of the event introduces important inconsistencies in the administration of state culture. The state's vision of creating a culturally (and hence politically) active collective culture manifested in the establishment of regional cultural centers and clubs, such as the Klubhaus Coswig. Reproduced in the introduction to this book, a Stasi-compiled list from the 1980s of the cultural centers that existed in East Berlin notes twenty-two such spaces in the capital city alone.[38] Union of Fine Artists spaces and Freie Deutsche Jugend (FDJ) clubs, which are not on this list, would add another set of options. The creation of cultural clubs formed a critical, and indeed mandatory, component of the GDR's urban and regional planning. High expectations did not necessarily produce an exacting administration of clubs; in fact, quite the opposite was true, particularly in a small town like Coswig. In her study on state-sponsored clubs and leisure activities, the historian Esther von Richthofen demonstrates that East German citizens and local cultural functionaries enjoyed an important degree of autonomy and agency in the shaping of state culture.[39] Through case studies drawn from clubs and cultural centers in the city of Potsdam, Richthofen argues that administrators never strictly followed the country's codes of cultural policy, even during the GDR's ideological high point in the late 1950s and early 1960s. To the contrary, she outlines how, as early as the 1960s, the East German public's preference for "lowbrow, entertaining, and 'hobby' activities . . . forced [the party leadership] to react . . . and to consider broadening the cultural model to address a greater variety of cultural interests."[40] Changes in state films as well as public programs at cultural centers demonstrate that cultural policymakers shifted their attention from ideological to populist aims.[41] Richthofen argues that the intention of this broadening was to consolidate more people into state-sanctioned cultural clubs and activities—a move which, as Paul Kaiser has demonstrated, likewise coincided with an increase in state control over and surveillance of citizen behavior.[42] For example, a hobby film club that filed its production records with the state as a means of legitimating expenditures provided an indirect link between the government and its public, while still maintaining the illusion of the club's autonomy.

Nevertheless, the resulting expansion of cultural possibility unintentionally empowered the East German public. First, an increasingly responsive state led to a more demanding public. If the people wanted free jazz, they now had the means to request it. Second, the growing cultural bureaucracy, which expanded to meet all of those needs, quickly became financially unsustainable. Oversight was severely cut, particularly in the wake of the 1979 oil crisis, which functionally crippled the GDR's already insecure economy.[43] Simultaneous to these changes was a marked increase in personal investment in the direction of cultural centers and other arms of cultural bureaucracy.[44] Rogue cultural administration thus became a norm, especially in smaller-scale places. Because the concentration of cultural bureaucrats was less pronounced in small towns than in big ones, people could take greater risks in places like Coswig than they could in places like East Berlin. By the time Wolfgang Zimmerman took charge of the club in Coswig, it was common for people in his position to work independently, to respond to local need, and to worry little about potential state pushback. And, even though his choice to host an event like Intermedia I certainly required some courage on his part, by 1985 the risks associated with planning something experimental in such a space were far less substantial than they would have been in previous years.

STASI SIGHT

A consideration of the Stasi record offers some insight into why cultural officials were motivated—or pressured—to retroactively punish the supporters and protagonists of Intermedia I. The six-page official secret police report from June 19, 1985, leads with a concern about the lack of information that had been provided to cultural authorities about plans for the event: "Both of the organizers left the director of the Klubhaus Coswig and the regional organs of the state to the fullest extent in the dark, that is to say they deceived them with regard to which groups of people were to participate or be denied participation in the event as well as to what

5.4

Am 1. und 2. 6. 1985 fand im Klubhaus Coswig . . . (On June 1 and 2, 1985 in the Clubhouse Coswig . . .). BStU, MfS, BV Leipzig, Abt. XX, Nr. 0271/08, 2. Reprinted with the permission of the Bundesbeauftragte für die Unterlagen des Staatssicherheitsdienstes der ehemaligen Deutschen Demokratischen Republik via the Stasi Records Act (StUG) § 32.

MINISTERIUM FÜR STAATSSICHERHEIT

Am 1. und 2. 6. 1985 fand im

Klubhaus Coswig
8270 Coswig, Ernst-Thälmann-Str. 29

jeweils von 18.00 - 24.00 Uhr die Veranstaltung "Intermedia I" statt.

Die Organisation der Veranstaltung erfolgte durch den Berliner Kunstwissenschaftler

T a n n e r t , Christoph
wohnhaft: 1035 Berlin, Wühlischstr. 21

und den Ausstellungstechniker des Zentrums für Kunstausstellungen der DDR, Galerie 8060 Dresden, Rähnitzgasse,

[redacted]
geboren am [redacted]
wohnhaft: 8019 Dresden, [redacted]

Durch beide Organisatoren wurden der Leiter des Klubhauses Coswig, Zimmermann, und die territorialen Staatsorgane während der Vorbereitung der Veranstaltung bewußt weitestgehend im Unklaren gelassen bzw. getäuscht, welcher Personenkreis als Mitwirkende die Veranstaltung vorbereitet, bestreitet und welche konkreten Programminhalte vorgesehen sind. [redacted]

An den Veranstaltungen nahmen Personen aus mindestens 12 Bezirken der DDR teil, am 1. 6. ca. 800 Personen und am 2. 6. 1985 ca. nur noch 400 Personen. Außerdem besuchten auch Bewohner der BRD und Westberlins, die mit mindestens 6 Pkw, die in der Nähe des Veranstaltungsortes abgeparkt waren, das Programm des 1. Veranstaltungstages.

Während der Programmfolgen wurden durch verschiedene Besucher Foto- und Video-Aufzeichnungen getätigt. An einem Stand erfolgte der Verkauf von Postkarten mit Motiven, die ihrer Aussage nach in politisch-negativer Weise auszulegen sind und "Mail-Art"-Charakter trugen.

Unter den am 1. Tag Anwesenden waren auch zahlreiche Punker, die durch ihr extremes Äußeres und ihre Verhaltensweisen ihre gesellschaftliche Außenseiterrolle demonstrierten. Inspiriert durch die aggressive Musik der Gruppen "Klick und Aus" und "Pf..." versetzten sie den Saal des Klubhauses in einen unzumutbaren Zustand. Tische und Gestühl wurden teilweise zerbrochen bzw. beschädigt. Glasbruch, Zigarettenreste und anderer Abfall wurden auf dem Fußboden zu Haufen zusammengeschoben und wieder breitgetreten. Die Aufräumungsarbeiten zur Veranstaltung am 2. 6. nahmen mehrere Stunden in Anspruch.

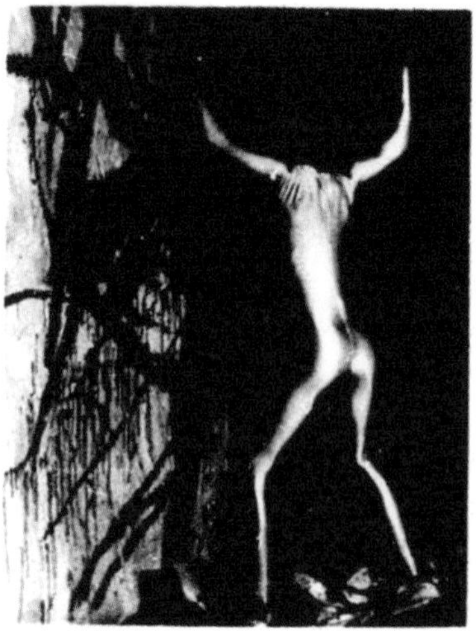

Eindrücke der Aufführung "Herakles"

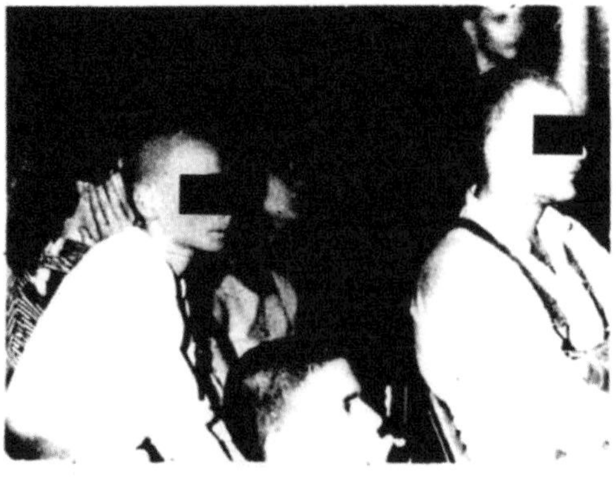

[redacted]

concrete content was being planned for the program."[45] Zimmerman's track record of planning programs of experimental music seems to contradict this claim. The Stasi's report maintains a ruse of authority, which was clearly not true in practice. It suggests that regional authorities were either not aware of or failed to recognize the significance of the jazz concerts that Zimmerman had been bringing to the Coswig club since the late 1970s, including their diverse audiences. In fact, the Intermedia I report obsesses over the public in attendance, with punks a particular concern. Photo documentation dwells on onlookers disproportionately, leaving artwork or performances scarcely recorded. More precisely, out of the thirty-eight photographs that appear in the Stasi dossier, thirteen picture the festival events and twenty-five focus on the audience. It is interesting to note that Kwiatkowski appears twice on one page of the Intermedia I's image report: first, she is pictured performing on stage; in the second photograph, Kwiatkowski (or a person who looks a great deal like her) is captured in profile while seated and observing the scene before her.

The Stasi images reveal the conditions of their making. A shot of legs and beer bottles on a table at first seems to suggest that the spies had to photograph in secret. Captions are often wry, even entertaining, as if consciously written to amuse their intended audience of Stasi officers: "There was nothing unusual about standing on tables on the night of 6/1." In another photograph of a crowd of revelers, the label "Feet up" draws attention to a person seated with their bare feet crossed on a chair in front of them. Immediately to the right of this person appear two other festival-goers who have their feet off the floor and their legs bent on the chairs where they are sitting. Many of the photographs in the Stasi dossier, however, appear as though photographers actively engaged their subjects. Most "spies" were likely unofficial collaborators. Recruited by the Stasi from within the ranks of the scene they were

5.5

Eindrücke der Aufführung 'Herakles' (Impressions of the "Hercules" performance). Intermedia I Festival. Klubhaus Coswig, June 1–2, 1985. Photographer unknown. BStU, MfS, BV Leipzig, Abt. XX, Nr. 0271/08, 10. Reprinted with the permission of the Bundesbeauftragte für die Unterlagen des Staatssicherheitsdienstes der ehemaligen Deutschen Demokratischen Republik via the Stasi Records Act (StUG) § 32.

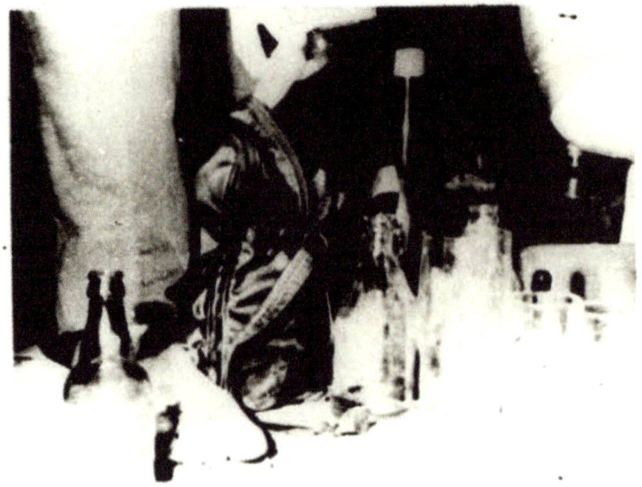

Stehen auf den Tischen war am 1. 6. nichts
außergewöhnliches

5.6

Stehen auf den Tischen war am 1. 6. nichts außergewöhnliches (There was nothing unusual about standing on tables on the night of 6/1). Intermedia I Festival. Klubhaus Coswig, June 1–2, 1985. BStU, MfS, BV Leipzig, Abt. XX, Nr. 0271/08, 15. Reprinted with the permission of the Bundesbeauftragte für die Unterlagen des Staatssicherheitsdienstes der ehemaligen Deutschen Demokratischen Republik via the Stasi Records Act (StUG) § 32.

Beine hoch

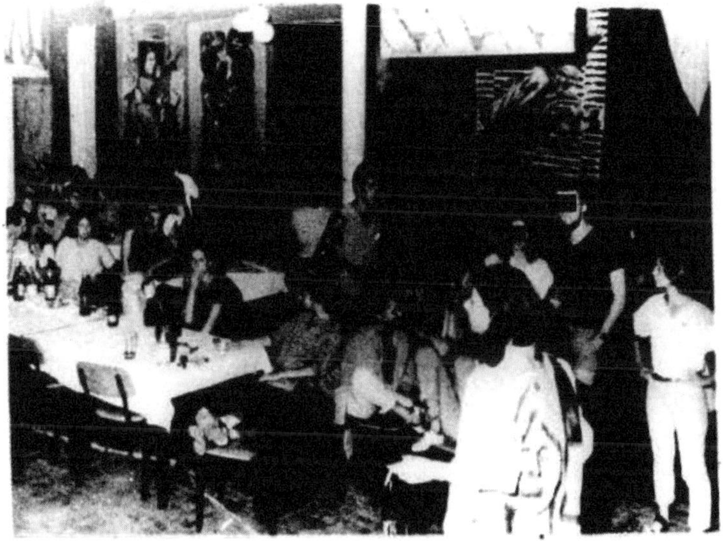

meant to report on, IMs could blend in with their target event. The animated gestures of some attendees in the photographs suggest, in fact, not just recognition, but friendship. Here are reminders on film of how dependent state power was on the participation of its public. The attention to punks may likewise be explained by the fact that spying was particularly pernicious within this scene. Punks were easy targets for authorities looking for a mark. They were also easy recruits for IM positions, whom the state paid in blank cassette tapes and other favors. As Seth

5.7

Beine hoch (Feet up). Intermedia I Festival. Klubhaus Coswig, June 1–2, 1985. Photographer unknown. BStU, MfS, BV Leipzig, Abt. XX, Nr. 0271/08, 23. Reprinted with the permission of the Bundesbeauftragte für die Unterlagen des Staatssicherheitsdienstes der ehemaligen Deutschen Demokratischen Republik via the Stasi Records Act (StUG) § 32.

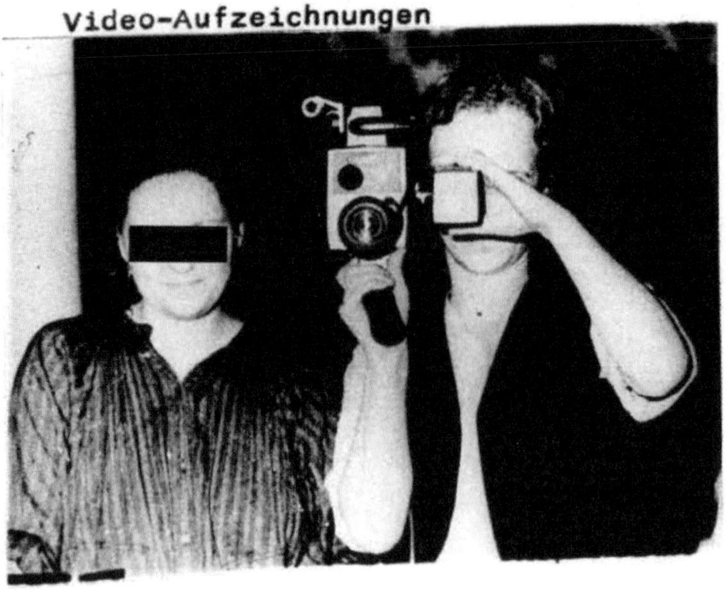

Howes has argued, a "futureless" or anarchic vision defined the punk scene, leaving alliances inherently tenuous.[46] Betrayals went in multiple directions; even punks who willingly collaborated with the Stasi could be subject to extensive censure and imprisonment.[47]

With IM reports gathered, interpreted, and summarized by Stasi officials who were most certainly not at the festival, the text of the report is both much more incisive and much more clinical than the images. The following excerpt is emblematic:

5.8

Video-Aufzeichnungen (Video recordings). Intermedia I Festival. Klubhaus Coswig, June 1–2, 1985. Photographer unknown. BStU, MfS, BV Leipzig, Abt. XX, Nr. 0271/08, 23. Reprinted with the permission of the Bundesbeauftragte für die Unterlagen des Staatssicherheitsdienstes der ehemaligen Deutschen Demokratischen Republik via the Stasi Records Act (StUG) § 32.

5.9

Punker mit "Schlagmanschetten" (Punks with "punchcuffs") and *Punker* (Punks). Intermedia I Festival. Klubhaus Coswig, June 1–2, 1985. Photographer unknown. BStU, MfS, BV Leipzig, Abt. XX, Nr. 0271/08, 13. Reprinted with the permission of the Bundesbeauftragte für die Unterlagen des Staatssicherheitsdienstes der ehemaligen Deutschen Demokratischen Republik via the Stasi Records Act (StUG) § 32.

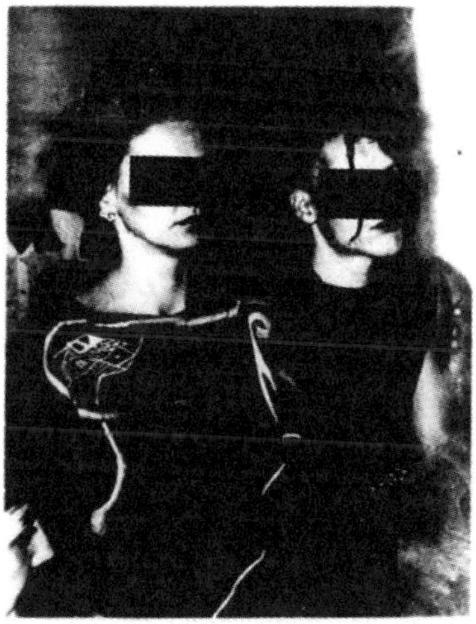

Punker mit Schlagmanschetten

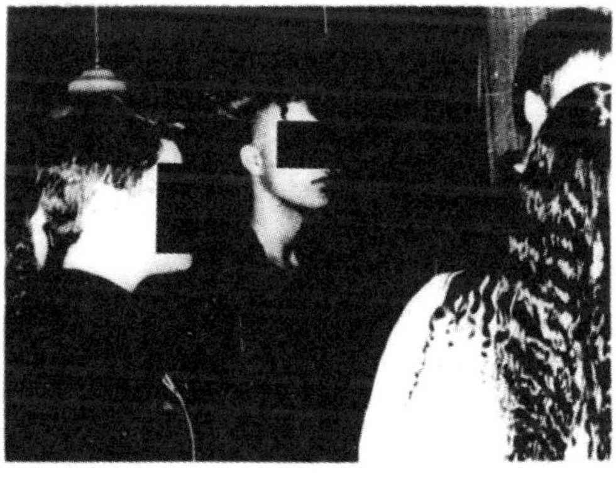

Punker

"Expert evaluation of the entire event has concluded that, owing to their nominal artistic quality and to the presentation of artistic experiments of increasingly socially unacceptable proportions, the individual programs were lacking in impact and appeal."[48] The Stasi's conclusion about the artistic merit of Intermedia I begs the question of artistic evaluation. The drafter interprets through secondhand accounts and documentation (itself not a problem), but filters these artifacts through an ideological lens that measures a work's value based on its clarity and commitment to communist politics. The report's dismissal is generic, moreover—a too easy script that cannot be debated in a country whose cultural politics was quite canned. Nevertheless, the East German government's ability to mandate acceptable and unacceptable culture was a central component of its power. In his[49] report, the Stasi officer recommends that the event be given the fullest consideration by state authorities and that disciplinary actions be taken against all responsible parties. He specifically recommends that the groups Klick und Aus and Pfff . . . receive an official prohibition from performing in public. The report concludes with instruction that the Dresden branch of the Union of Fine Artists redefine its "cultural political concerns" for the Klubhaus Coswig.[50] The directive for more oversight is clear. Blame is shouldered by the clubhouse director Wolfgang Zimmerman, who loses his job. Yet the Stasi hedges. By making Zimmerman both a victim of deception and a person who should have had his "cultural political concerns" in check, the operations of state culture remain secure. This is a problem of the individual and not the system. The Intermedia I Stasi report thus reveals a fundamental frailty in state power. Party leaders had lost control of not only their citizenry but also the armatures established to advocate for, sustain, and monitor mass culture.

PARSING THE TERM "INTERMEDIA": HISTORICAL AND REGIONAL SIGNIFICANCE

The tension between the languages of state and unofficial culture begin already in the festival's title, "Intermedia." The GDR's official *Dictionary of Cultural Politics* (*Kulturpolitisches Wörterbuch*)—a foundational theoretical text—includes within its definition of "Types, Kinds, and Genres of Art" a schematic observation about sense and perception drawn from an early Karl Marx: "To the *eye* an object comes to be other than it is to the *ear*, and the object of the eye *is* another object than it is to the ear."[51] The quotation follows introductory comments by the dictionary's authors on the necessity for a rigid classification system for art: "Concrete artworks always belong to specific types, kinds, that is to say genres of art, which possess their own artistic modes of expression and specific creative possibilities."[52] Implicit in the dictionary's use of the Marx quotation and this framework on medium is a belief that humans are naturally inclined to classify the world. Marx said as much, though he went much further. In the *Economic and Philosophic Manuscripts*, from which his eye/ear distinction derives, he writes, "The peculiarity of each essential power is precisely its *peculiar essence*, and therefore also the peculiar mode of its objectification, of its *objectively actual* living *being*. Thus, man is affirmed in the objective world not only in the act of thinking, but with *all* his senses."[53] These words reveal an early Hegelian Marx seeking to establish the unique capacity of man to both inhabit and control the world. Yet the authors of the dictionary either ignore or misunderstand this nuance. They reduce Marx's subtle observations about sensory perception and subjectivity to a demonstration of the "differences in classification between the types, kinds, and genres of art, as well as the basic possibilities of artistic design."[54] In an ironic twist, their rigid stance toward medium and form mirrored that of high modernism—socialist realism's veritable aesthetic enemy.[55]

The remainder of the dictionary entry continues a strained argument for the necessity of classifying art forms. Yet at times it seems to contradict these claims altogether, calling media the products of dialectics and historical processes—a characterization that renders the "types, kinds, and genres" of art implicitly fluid and fundamentally unnatural.[56] Indeed, the dictionary's team of authors allow that the hierarchy of medium is contingent, a matter of taste and style rather than inherent value. They conclude that communism will neutralize all cultural hierarchies, and assert that equalizing all types, kinds, and genres of art was a "particularly pressing task of cultural politics."[57] Nevertheless, a later definition of "Artistic Experiment" holds that artwork that tests convention is unacceptable unless it is "directed toward the fundamental purpose of socialist cultural politics."[58] Clearly, the need to steer art toward a political end and away from formalism and self-expression remained a central aim of official cultural policy.

Summarizing the state's official stance toward artistic media and genre reveals the uncertainty of the state's cultural authority. If art forms are inherently malleable and meant to change organically, then why suppress these shifts? To that end, the insistence that the authors of the *Dictionary of Cultural Politics* place on achieving equity for all art media, as well as their explicit acknowledgment that new forms of art will—and should—emerge as products of history, contradict the ways in which cultural policy was actually implemented and enforced. Those in power resisted the developments in art that their aesthetic theory actually predicted and deemed necessary. Meanwhile, a significant number of essays in the union-affiliated magazine *Bildende Kunst* had presented arguments in favor of experimental forms of art over the course of several years. Such texts began to appear in the publication's October 1981 issue, with a particularly intense selection in the April to June 1982 issues. In these early debates, which were almost uniformly derisive of performance art, the recent art history graduate Eugen Blume set his support of the medium against the opinions of a reactionary rearguard of art historians. A gradual shift in reporting on performances or other multimedia artworks transpired thereafter. By 1988, editors dedicated an entire issue of *Bildende Kunst* to experimental forms of art, and a year later the Union of Fine Artists enlisted Blume to work with Tannert to organize the pathbreaking Permanent Art Conference. State authorities intent on curtailing the development of new forms of art thus contradicted a vast movement toward a different kind of cultural practice being led by artists and arts professionals.

Christoph Tannert and Micha Kapinos organized their festival around the theme of interdisciplinarity, or intermedia. The use of the word "intermedia" must be taken on its own terms within the GDR's cultural context; any implied references to Fluxus and specifically to Dick Higgins, who devised and theorized the term, must be evaluated secondarily. There are, of course, important parallels between the use of "intermedia" to frame a festival of multimedia, cross-disciplinary, and largely performance-based works and the original Fluxus definition. When Higgins writes, "I would like to suggest that the use of intermedia is more or less universal throughout the fine arts, since continuity rather than categorization is the hallmark of our new mentality," he identifies a fluidity across media that helps to define experimental art in the GDR, as well.[59] Writing in the early—and arguably most ideologically polarized—period of the Cold War, Higgins represents the Fluxus artists' desire for authentic and spontaneous experiences that could combat the era's political and economic coopting of culture. In important ways, that vision also parallels the experience of East Germany's experimental artists at this time.

For most people in the GDR, exposure to Fluxus or other art movements from the West was cursory but not superficial. In fact, East German artists were sincerely interested in expanding their relationship with artists around the world, and especially with those in West Germany, a country with which they of course shared a language and a cultural history. Nevertheless, the frontier that secluded the GDR from outside contact kept most information at bay. Nearly all experience with global contemporary art from other countries was mediated by photographs, catalogs, and secondhand accounts. Artists from the West infrequently crossed into East Germany on day passes. In June 1983, Wolf Vostell, the Fluxus artist and pioneer of the décollage technique, visited the East Berlin collective studio/gallery known as rg,[60] which was led by a group that included the conceptual and performance artist Erhard Monden. Holding court, as it were, Vostell "explained the world" to a legion of East German artists who were introduced, many for the first time, to the artist's media-bending practices.[61] Eugen Blume characterizes Vostell's first audience as intrigued but cautious and overwhelmingly skeptical of this eccentric artist from the West. A list of East Berlin-based performances and artistic actions that Blume and Tannert would later produce as part of their research for the Permanent Art Conference includes Vostell's 1983 trip to the GDR. The text describes it obliquely as a *Gesprächsperformance* (lecture-performance).[62] The term portends an important mode of performance art in the twenty-first century, but it was—as Blume's memory suggests—not necessarily a complimentary description.

More important to the scene was the West German artist Joseph Beuys. Through his involvement in Fluxus, as well as his socially engaged and capitalist-critical practice, he was without question the most important contemporary artist for East Germans. Beuys was first introduced to the GDR by Klaus Werner, the art historian and longtime director of the highly influential state-run Galerie Arkade (Arcade Gallery) in East Berlin.[63] Werner's public lectures on Beuys, both at the Galerie Arkade and at other events affiliated with the Union of Fine Artists, set experimental artists and art historians alike on a course that would forever change the direction of art—unofficial and official—in the GDR. In fact, his advocacy for Beuys and for experimental forms of art resulted in Werner's expulsion from the SED[64] political party, as well as the closure of his gallery; both occurred in 1981. That same year, Blume, then an art history student, would defend a thesis on Beuys.[65] Blume's entry into the Union of Fine Artists, including his vocal defense of Beuys and other experimental art forms and artists (notably, the performance artist Erhard Monden),[66] also contributed to the growing interest in new forms of art and especially in process-oriented art. Blume's advocacy, along with continued efforts by Werner in combination with other leading (and older) Union of Fine Artists art historians, led to eventual acceptance of experimental forms in the GDR's official cultural echelons.

East Germany's experimental artists were especially attached to Beuys's motto "Jeder Mensch Ein Künstler" (Every man is an artist), which plainly contested the GDR's hierarchical relationship to cultural practice, while, ironically, also meeting official culture's vision for a society defined by creative and collective action. Beuys officially visited East Germany just once, in 1981.[67] Even then, he did not technically enter the GDR, but went to West Germany's diplomatic office in East Berlin. More than four hundred intellectuals and artists from across East Germany were in attendance at his exhibition opening that night. Border guards prevented a second visit to the GDR in 1984, when Monden and Blume invited Beuys to participate in a collaborative performance entitled *Sender Empfänger* (*Sender Receiver*). After East German security refused Beuys entry, the project had to take place without the contact its title clearly deemed necessary. With Beuys completing his portion in West Berlin, and Monden and Blume completing theirs in East Berlin, ultimately *Sender Receiver* became a kind of conceptual cable connecting the two Germanys.

In 1988 Beuys would posthumously receive one formal accolade in the GDR when a solo exhibition of 216 of his works produced between 1946 and 1966 was mounted first in East Berlin's Neuer Marstall, a former palace used as an exhibition space by the Union of Fine Artists, and then at the Academy of Fine Arts in Leipzig (Hochschule für Grafik und Buchkunst). The show had been anticipated as a conciliatory gesture by state authorities toward the country's experimental artists. However, the display excluded works made after Beuys turned to social practice and performance in the late 1960s. Authorities sought to conceal this omission, converting the title of the exhibition, which had actually originated in West Germany, from the West German title *Beuys vor Beuys* (*Beuys before Beuys*) to simply *Joseph Beuys*.[68] Artists were disappointed and frustrated, but also activated. The EIGEN+ART gallery—a popular independent space in Leipzig—organized a counterexhibition which opened on the same night as the show at the art academy. With a title that clearly referenced the West German iteration of the Beuys exhibition, *Nach Beuys* (*After Beuys*) featured several weeks of performance projects, including a ten-day durational work by the Auto-Perforation Artists entitled *Allez! Arrest*.[69] On the heels of organizing the exhibition, the EIGEN+ART gallery founder Judy Lybke would reflect, "Against the dead exhibition in the museums we mount living projects! We understand ourselves not as Beuys's youth, but as his survivors [*Überlebende nach Beuys*]."[70] *Nach Beuys* was an answer to and an antidote for the politicking of cultural bureaucrats, who had so obviously strategized their use of such an important figure to placate the youngest generation of East German artists. In 1989, the state reneged again on a promise to this public when it rescinded an earlier commitment to allow West German artists to participate in the Permanent Art Conference, the thirty-one-day festival of performance and other process-oriented *Aktionskunst*. Once again organizers improvised a parallel program by hosting artists from the West at the rg gallery. Importantly, Eugen Blume—who coordinated the Permanent Art Conference with Tannert—was also instrumental in bringing these West German artists to East Berlin; along with Klaus Werner, he was also one of the rg gallery's initiators.

Aside from these rare contacts, seeing artwork—let alone artists—from western countries firsthand was completely impossible for the majority of East Germans. Most could not travel abroad, and restrictions on imports included information deemed potentially inflammatory. Some professors granted students at art academies and universities permission to peruse the library's so-called *Giftschrank* (poison cabinet), which contained censored materials and other books off limits to anyone without a known scholarly interest. Circulation of these texts was monitored, but some instructors obscured student use to protect them. Those with status had easier access to publications. As a Union of Fine Artist-affiliated art historian, Tannert had procured two important catalogs on Fluxus for personal use via contacts in the West, and was certainly aware of the concurrent movement underway in other parts of the Eastern Bloc.[71] Nevertheless, the relationship between his adoption of the term "intermedia" and the use of the term by American (as well as Eastern European)[72] Fluxus artists of the 1960s and 1970s appears to have been somewhat perfunctory. He was less attached to the work of the artists themselves or the significance of the intermedia concept to the global Fluxus movement, than to the implications that such a term could have within the GDR itself.

More convincing than connections that the nomenclature may suggest to western experimental art are the conceptual—if still subliminal—links to contemporary Eastern Bloc artistic practice. East Germany's "intermediality" mirrors performance theorist and artist Bojana Cvejić's description of Yugoslavian experimental art in the 1970s and 1980s as intentionally "unburdened" by aesthetic categories, and made by artists "indifferent to the imperative of branding themselves through the genealogy of medium-specificity or style."[73] She writes, "These practices are delinked from western art traditions in that they are aesthetically 'unburdened': they neglect formalist, craft-oriented and aestheticizing aspects of a work in favor of context, structure, minor stories, non-presence, etc."[74] Here, Cvejić is specifically looking for a way to recuperate this artwork from conventional and western-centered art history. In her view, art historians from the West have been ill-advised in their tendency to apply western theory to the art practices of the Eastern Bloc, because "interpretation in aesthetic terms misrecognizes them by dismissing them as eclectic, nonspecific, nondescript or old-fashioned."[75] She suggests that the art of the Eastern Bloc should be read "parallel" to that made in the West. "Parallelism," she writes, "reveals the difference in the use of art, not in aesthetic categories of form and style."[76] This framework of seeing art as an instrument, rather than a dialectic in conversation with western art practices, defines Eastern Bloc experimental artists as engaged in a process of problem solving or problem posing, which draws from all available artistic modes to articulate, resolve, or simply work through an idea.[77] It places art made in state socialism outside the metrics of aesthetics used to evaluate art from the West, allowing art from the Eastern Bloc to be similar, but different.

While Cvejić seeks a meeting point that might unite the art histories of East and West, the performance art theorist Bojana Kunst offers further insight into the historical specificity of experimental practice in the late Cold War East.[78] Thinking historically helps to explain how different the stakes were for artists working across media in Eastern Bloc states. Kunst draws her examples from the realms of theater, dance, and performance to relate experimental practice specifically to institutionalized forms of state culture. She describes how artists yearning for "radical authenticity" embraced without irony the very claims to representation that western histories of performance art (and conceptual or postmodern practice, more generally) tended to disavow in the post-World War II era.[79] Performance in the East thus represented a defensive or alternative politics set "in relation to the total model of socialist society, which constantly performed itself as the most authentic and at the same time, the must utopian (fictitious) of all."[80] Experimental and mass-media practices were defensive strategies—or "uses," to think with Cvejić[81]—that could confront the state's idealism. These strategies included the manifestations of that vision within cultural policy's prescriptions for art, artificial divisions of medium, and claims to artistic and ideological harmony.

This Eastern Bloc ethos helps explain the significance of the ambition of the Intermedia I Festival organizers to bolster and showcase multimedia practice in a public forum. Indeed, simultaneous to a blending of media was a tendency for artists and their supporters to use art as an excuse and a reason to gather and organize. Each new innovation in creative practice contributed to the cultural drift that brought East Germany's experimental artists ever further away from artistic convention; each gathering solidified that shift, and expanded it. To that end, the experimental art of the late GDR was both media-bending and oriented toward building an audience. Together, these characteristics challenged official state policy's desire to categorize and craft its public through culture. The sense of order and ordering the world through a specific mode and practice of art is not simply a reflection of state socialist cultural policy. Rather, the impulse to compartmentalize artistic practice is the twin of the impulse to delineate the ideal socialist subject. There is, then, a clear relation between medium and control, and even more completely, between the desire to categorize and the production of a specific kind of socialist public—that is to say, the collective. The next chapter of this book turns to a signature example of autonomous collective practice through the work of Erfurt's Künstlerinnengruppe Exterra XX (Women Artists Group Exterra XX) to demonstrate the potential impacts of group work on the creative and even the political realities of the late GDR.

6

THE COLLECTIVE IMPOSSIBLE

Erfurt's Women Artists Group

In theory, the attention—not to mention the money—that the East German state paid to building a collective society around a shared national culture is admirable. Cultural theory clearly defined the ideal "socialist image of man" as requiring "creative and productive physical and spiritual activity."[1] East German citizens were expected to engage actively in a "quest for education and cultural and artistic expression."[2] While the state enabled that quest, artists were meant to guide it. Nevertheless, the sociologist Karl-Siegbert Rehberg has argued that the high priority the German Democratic Republic (GDR) gave to culture in building a socialist society was inherently paternalistic: "The artists were supposed to accept their role as servants of the state, and were not to think of themselves as the masterminds or progenitors of a new world order."[3] The tensions between state demands for creative control and the desire of artists for uninhibited self-expression dogged the GDR from its inception. Artists were not mindless workers but active participants engaged in the creation of a critical culture. A unique, but nevertheless crucial example of a union of art and politics in the experimental art scene is the Künstlerinnengruppe Exterra XX (Women Artists Group Exterra XX) of Erfurt.[4] This collective of several dozen participants first began due to the women's desire to gather and create art, and ultimately contributed to the most significant political action undertaken by East German artists: the storming of Erfurt's Ministry for State Security (Stasi) headquarters in December 1989.

Importantly, the Women Artists Group was not a deviation of social norms. Rather, its formation reflects a widespread grassroots collectivity that emerged across the GDR in the late Cold War era. As the sociologist Wolfgang Engler writes: "Even with all of its mass organizations, the rulers never achieved what they had in other ways achieved, at least in part: activating the society for its purposes. Where organization society [*Organisationsgesellschaft*] failed, the collective society jumped in."[5] By pitting "organization society" against "collective society," Engler underscores the discrepancy between public life in its ideal image and public life as it was actually lived.[6] The comparison also suggests a level of citizen agency, particularly the people's inclination to form independent niches where needs left unmet by government could be fulfilled—whether that meant forming a sophisticated barter system for car maintenance or a collaborative creative practice.[7] While a mutually beneficial "Nischengesellschaft"[8] (niche society) might be construed as a reflection of the GDR's collectively oriented society, its existence actually underscores the government's inability to fulfill the idiosyncratic needs of its public. In fact, with their basic needs met by a heavily subsidized economy, people could more readily pursue private interests. As Engler writes, "Precisely because social life was secure, people could experiment in their personal lives with insecurity, with unusual thoughts, with more open, more spontaneous ways of life."[9] This large-scale view of East German society demonstrates the context within which experimental artists emerged in the 1980s. Although their work was certainly more rebellious than the average citizen's self-actualization in the church, the choral club, or the garden house, artists nevertheless represented a place along a spectrum of society that tended toward independence and autonomy.

SLOW TIME AND SMALL TALK

From its 1984 founding to its dissolution in the early 1990s, the Women Artists Group, a casual and inclusive allegiance of women living and working in the southwestern town of Erfurt, made films, music, and paintings, and organized exhibitions and performances. They also sewed, sold, and presented clothes at fashion shows and street fairs. A loose solidarity network organized around a shared frustration with gender inequality and a desire for more creativity, their first meetings took place in private apartments. The artistic inclinations of several members, as well as the social nature of many of their creative hobbies, eventually inspired collaborative projects. From weaving to sewing, these women brought traditionally feminized forms of culture and handiwork to the group. In fact, the size of a loom had helped

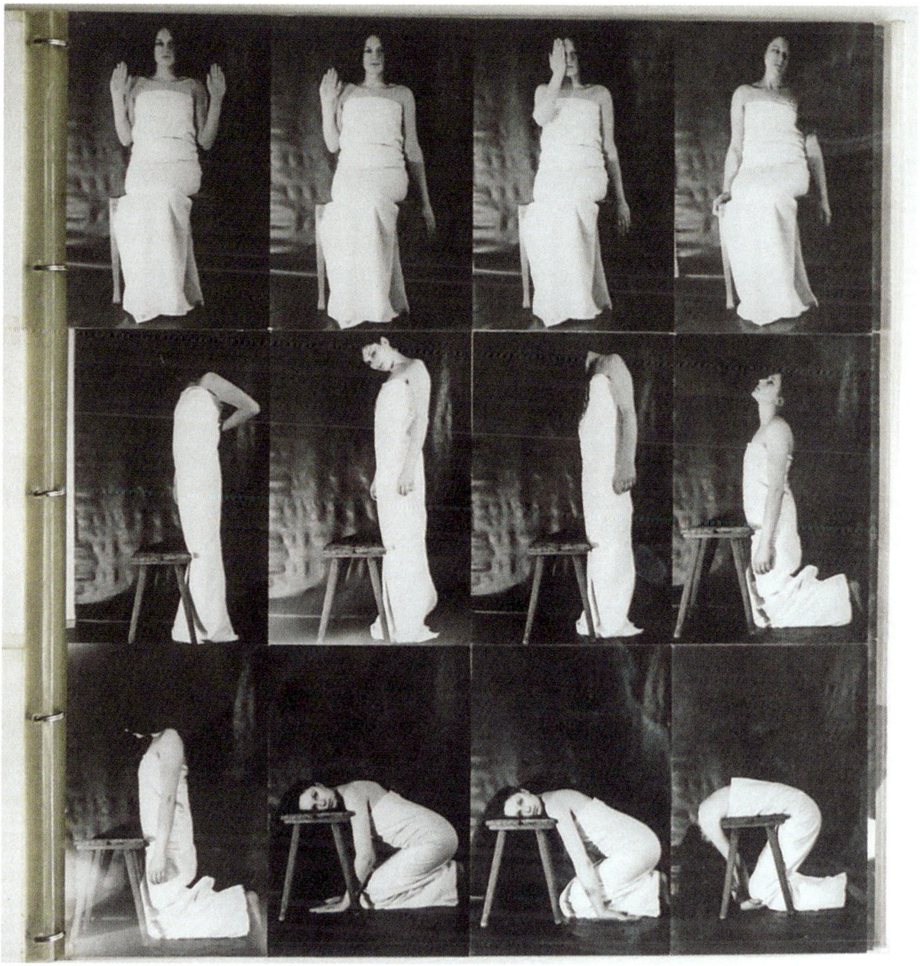

6.1

Gabriele Stötzer. *Göttin* (*Goddess*) from *Gedankensplitter* (*Slivers of Thoughts*). 1984. Black-and-white A4 photographs and India ink on board. Reprinted with the permission of Gabriele Stötzer. © 1984 by Gabriele Stötzer.

to bring the group together after Gabriele Stötzer[10] set up a weaving workshop in an abandoned building in the city center.[11] The Women Artists Group met every few weeks, sometimes to plan collaborative artworks, sometimes just to spend time together in a space that was their own. A few called themselves artists, but others simply enjoyed the creative outlet the community provided. The evolution of the Women Artists Group's collaborative work corresponded with an increasing politicization. As the members grew more comfortable in their collective identification, so too did they become more comfortable contesting social and political norms.

At the same time that group work was a clear objective of the Women Artists Group, so too were the individual creative visions of each member. Stötzer, for example, maintained an active writing, weaving, ceramics, filmmaking, and photography practice, which clearly informed her collaborative work. In fact, the process of making her photo books was highly collaborative and required the trust of sitters to perform and let loose in much the same way that made the collective's films and public performances so successful. From punks to transgender people to the elderly, those imaged in Stötzer's photo books reflect a broader range of East German culture than almost any other experimental artwork from the time. Though not all who appeared in her photographs were members of the Women Artists Group, some of the projects became sketches or raw material for future collective projects. For example, the playful and sculptural portraiture seen throughout Stötzer's photo book *Gedankensplitter* (*Slivers of Thoughts*, 1984) recurs in the group's future films, as well as in the fashion design the women made and sold for extra income. In the image pictured, the "goddess" evokes the wrapped constructions visible toward the end of *Frauenträume* (*Dreams of Women*, 26 min., 1986), the Women Artists Group's first work on Super-8. Group affinity also translated to solidarity for and with individual artists. When in 1989 Verena Kyselka and Monika Andres had a two-person show in the state-run Galerie Nord (Gallery North) in Leipzig, members from the women's group independently organized a public performance that occurred alongside the exhibition.

A blending of individual and group identity came to define the Women Artists Group's core strength. Their collective films, including *Frauenträume* of 1986, especially reveal that union: *Komik—Komisch* (*Comic—Comical*, 25 min., 1988); *Veitstanz/Feixtanz* (*Saint Vitus Dance / Smirk Dance*, 25 min., 1988); *Signale* (*Signals*, 25 min., 1989). Filmmaking necessitated the shared use of a camera, as well as a production team to organize, conceptualize, and execute a project. The first of their four films, *Dreams of Women*, comprises six individually conceived vignettes (dreams) framed by scenes of conceptual and literal unity. A rocking chair bookends the film. In the

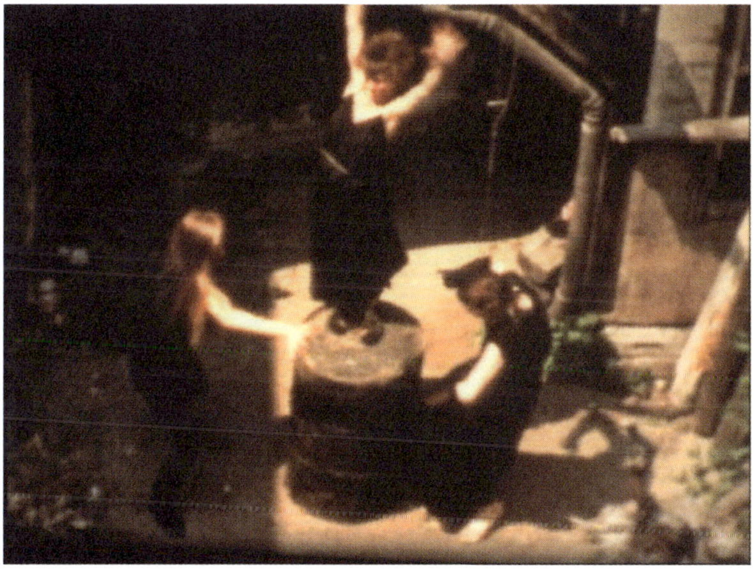

opening sequence, Gabriele Göbel sits on a sidewalk in an urban landscape, gently moving back and forth. She is backlit and turned away from the camera. Cut to a clip of three women (Göbel, Verena Kyselka, and Sylvia Richter) dressed in black, first shot from below and looking forebodingly into the camera; then from above as they writhe in large motions of incantation, as if conjuring spirits—in this case, the dreams of women. The first dream begins. Göbel appears, painted gold. She is bare breasted. She cups her hands gently at her navel. She sits before a tree. The camera examines her now prone body at very close angles. It gazes at her gilded nipple, the tight folds of her belly button, the comparatively sharp angle of her shoulder. An

6.2

Künstlerinnengruppe Exterra XX (Monika Andres, Elke Carl, Monique Förster, Gabriele Göbel, Ina Heyner, Gabriele Stötzer, Verena Kyselka, Ingrid Plöttner, and Sylvia Richter). *Frauenträume* (*Dreams of Women*). 1986. Super-8 film, 26 min. Reprinted with the permission of Gabriele Stötzer. © 1986 by Gabriele Stötzer.

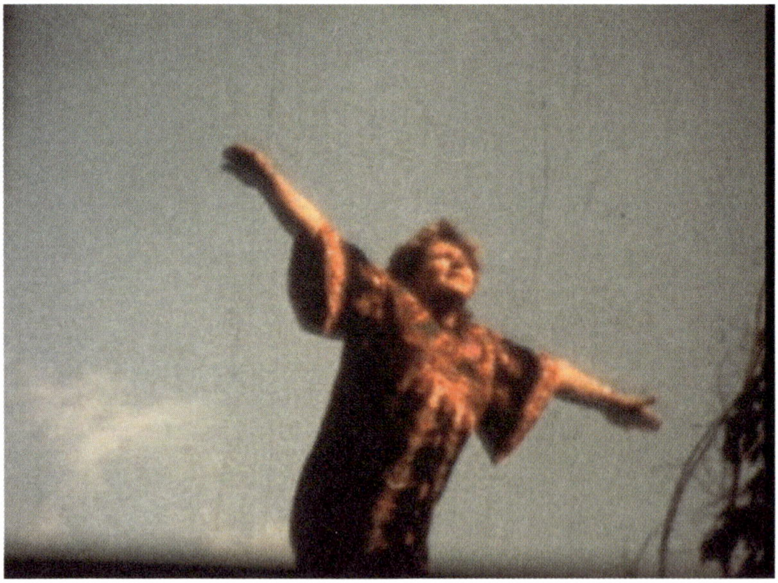

accidental piece of lint briefly dances in and out of the frame from the upper left corner. It is a reminder of the film's amateur production, while also an unintended conceptual addition that accentuates the ethereal, no-place reality imagined in the six dreams on screen. All along, music from Richard Wagner's *Tristan and Isolde* plays. Importantly, the soundtrack described here comes from a recently digitized version of the film; the Super-8 film stock commercially available in the GDR did not record sound. As a result, and as described in the fourth chapter of this book, in addition to employing live experimental sound, filmmakers could "score" their films in advance, and bring recordings to play at the screening.

6.3

Künstlerinnengruppe Exterra XX (Monika Andres, Elke Carl, Monique Förster, Gabriele Göbel, Ina Heyner, Gabriele Stötzer, Verena Kyselka, Ingrid Plöttner, and Sylvia Richter). *Frauenträume* (*Dreams of Women*). 1986. Super-8 film, 26 min. Reprinted with the permission of Gabriele Stötzer. © 1986 by Gabriele Stötzer.

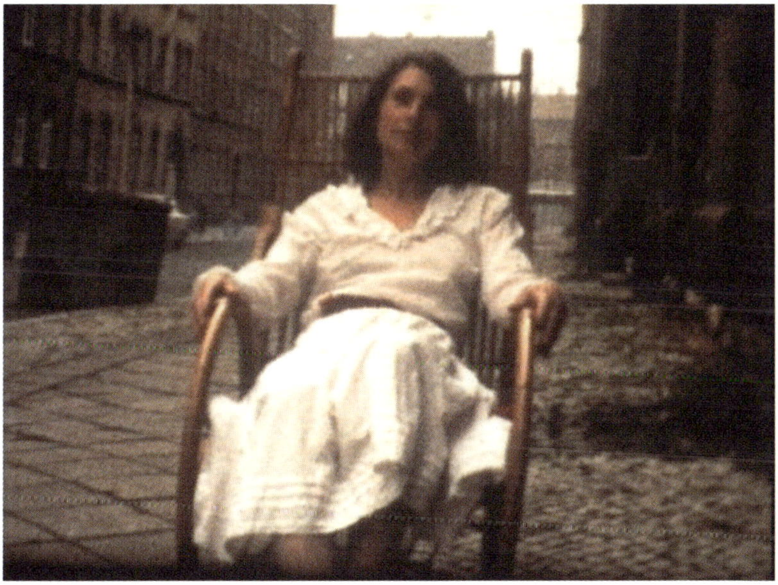

The music shifts for dream number two. Monks' choral voices, a tinny set of strings, and finally a synthesized atmospheric soundtrack accompany Kyselka as she scrambles across a steeply sloped set of stones and scoots herself up a grassy hill lined with a strip of black plastic sheeting. She is suddenly in a park and then on a rooftop. In both places she simulates sex with a silver phallus constructed of cardboard. At ten minutes, Monika Andres appears to begin the third dream. Doused in a stark red light, she walks through a hallway when suddenly a disembodied arm reaches out and presses a hot iron against her left cheek. She appears with friends and opens her shirt. Her left and right shoulders are covered in blood, and she has

6.4

Künstlerinnengruppe Exterra XX (Monika Andres, Elke Carl, Monique Förster, Gabriele Göbel, Ina Heyner, Gabriele Stötzer, Verena Kyselka, Ingrid Plöttner, and Sylvia Richter). *Frauenträume* (*Dreams of Women*). 1986. Super-8 film, 26 min. Reprinted with the permission of Gabriele Stötzer. © 1986 by Gabriele Stötzer.

a third breast. Three friends who have come to her aid alternate between dancing and pretending to punch each other. A woman singing sweetly in an Indo-European language fills the soundtrack. Dream number four begins with Erik Satie's *Gymnopédie No. 2*, which plays as Monique Förster, wearing a long black sleeveless dress carries a black bundle of plastic through a park. She dumps it indiscriminately, and at one point wraps herself in it as if it were a stylish black toga. Later, Förster stuffs the material voraciously into her mouth. In the next dream—number five—Ingrid Plöttner, dressed in a kaftan, moves her arms and legs joyfully in gestures of flying. She lies on a white sheet and gently swims through the air. She appears on a rooftop and extends herself upward and outward. Elke Carl's dream, the last, represents the film's most pensive moments. She walks wistfully through a park, balances along a water's edge, and steps along small wooden planks. She stands on top of a building and drops the black plastic sheeting over the ledge, allowing it to float in the air before she proceeds to wrap herself in it. The material is a suture, linking several of the women's dreams. The film's concluding minutes also bring several sequences together. Joyful wordless pop and sax-heavy jazz set a whimsical tone. The clips of the women cavorting together are at once unions of the various dreams and insights into the working process of the filmmaking team. A closing sequence shows the *Dreams of Women* protagonists. They take turn rocking in the wicker chair and face the camera, talking and smiling, as if taking a bow.

In recounting the process of making *Dreams of Women*, Stötzer describes the candidness of her collaborators as well as their need for reconciliation and unity: "When the women were fighting, we would make a film."[12] She explains that collaborative work helped to unite the group of upward of twenty-five people, many of whom had joined the circle out of frustration with the status of women in East German society, including its impact on their views of themselves and of other women.[13] This included people working through complicated relationships with their mothers, as well as those seeking a forum to articulate and confront the rampant misogyny of the GDR.[14] The collective grew fairly spontaneously. Stötzer would meet women on the street or at events and invite them to join the circle. The ambition of the group reflected that spontaneity. Although big projects—especially as the years progressed—required coordinated effort, the fundamental mission remained the exchange of ideas, "a safe space and a protection against outside forces."[15] The group included one man, Frank Zieris, who was group member Kyselka's boyfriend. Zieris, responsible for some of the music and technical work during the group's performances and fashion and object shows, turned out to have been spying on them for the Stasi.[16] At the risk of downplaying the betrayal of a friend and collaborator—an all-too-common complaint of the GDR's experimental artists—it is, nevertheless, significant that Stötzer, an aggressive target of the Stasi, thought of the Women Artists Group as a protective shield against the state. In particular, the group's public solidarity became its greatest tactic: "For me," Stötzer said, "the most important ruse was always to be in public view, to make everything public, to not remain alone. After all, the strategy of the Stasi was to disintegrate groups, to isolate people, to make them feel insecure, to drive them into seclusion."[17] In contrast, the artist collective empowered its members through group work that differentiated them from the status quo—giving them purpose and identity. If practicalities brought them together, for Stötzer the time they spent making their group projects made all the difference. In point of fact, she allows, "the more we made, the better we got along."[18] Stötzer names "small talk" in particular as a significant element of the Women Artists Group's group work.[19] Making things—from planning a film to sewing clothes for sale at a weekend market, whether in collaboration or simply side by side—eased the inevitable tension that grew out of a group of people drawn together by a shared intensity and passion for life, particularly within a context hostile to the changes their work proposed.[20] The process of working together was thus as important as any product the group created.

Of course, the women could skill-share, as well. For example, Stötzer's interest in photography inspired her to experiment with friends, setting them up in the kinds of free-form vignettes that appear in her photo books and presage the Women Artists Group's Super-8 projects. The handiwork skills of several women translated to the elaborate fashion and art objects that populate the group films, as well. As Stötzer reflects in her 1995 work of fiction *erfurter roulette*, "We were poor and bartered with ourselves. Woman for woman, flesh for flesh, object for object."[21] Her description of barter usefully equates the group's collective labor as a kind of alternative economy, which could also threaten the stability of the state. By engaging in unproductive labor, the artists implicitly rejected the strategic plans that the East German government had devised to serve—which is to say, mold—its collective.

Sometimes members joined forces to earn a living. Many people in the Women Artists Group made money ad hoc by selling clothing, prints, or an annual group calendar at local markets. This was often a legal practice. Stötzer, for example, had a *Preisgenehmigung* (permit giving permission to sell), which enabled her to earn up to 2,000 East German marks per year on her hand-made clothing.[22] Others picked up day labor, earning both money and official security against the threat of being accused of "antisocial" behavior. For artists in the Union of Fine Artists, life was even less precarious. A monthly allowance, also allotted during the two- to three-year candidate status, plus free studio space made it easier to live outside the system while still living within the law. It is puzzling that someone like Stötzer, who had been a political prisoner and who the Stasi monitored over years of very invasive—and certainly expensive—surveillance operations that ultimately amounted to nothing, could receive official permission to work freelance. Perhaps this was all a part of the state's fantasy that all citizens, regardless of their history, could somehow be shunted artificially into the collective mass. Governmental authority depended, after all, on employment statistics that seemed to turn rhetoric into reality. By this logic, Stötzer may have actually been doing the state a service simply by doing work that went on the books. On the other hand, maybe the artists were actually serving as a sign of the "freedom" the state supposedly allowed them.

In what may be considered a tandem resistance to the institutionalization of the body—a theme discussed in detail in the second chapter of this book—artists across the Eastern Bloc likewise actively worked to be unproductive. The performance art theorist Bojana Kunst calls this a form of "radical authenticity."[23] In the same way that others have theorized "laziness" in a positive sense—from the nineteenth-century French poet Charles Baudelaire to the renowned Croatian conceptual artist Mladen Stilinović[24]—Kunst proposes delay as a resistance strategy: "Delay in the sense of taking time, delaying productivity, delaying effect. Delay as a continuous resistance to accumulation."[25] Here Kunst is both speaking historically and offering a pathway for artists in Central and Eastern Europe today to claim their outsider status as an alternative to capital accumulation and the market forces that drive the art world and polarize its artists. Her concept of delay likewise describes the prioritization of the working process over a finished artistic product: "Delay is a specific working attitude, which doesn't subjugate the working processes to the acceleration of time."[26] Within a collaborative environment, it is then the work that happens between outcomes—the slow time and small talk—that matters the most.

THE "ANTISOCIAL" SOCIAL LIFE OF GABRIELE STÖTZER

The success of the Women Artists Group is clearly indebted to Stötzer's own innovative vision for autonomous culture, as well as to her commitment to advancing the cause of female solidarity through creative and collaborative practice. Her work with women began in 1982 when she first led the effort to illegally turn a condemned house in Erfurt into a creative workshop. Stötzer's commitment to experimental culture had begun two years earlier when she took over the leadership of Erfurt's popular independent arts space, the Galerie im Flur (Gallery in the Corridor). Given the gallery's popularity, city officials initially sought to strike a compromise with her. They offered to allow the operation to continue if Stötzer incorporated it into official city cultural programming. When she refused, the Stasi quickly swept in. The gallery, which had opened its doors three years earlier, shut for good in 1981.[27]

Stötzer originally honed her refusal to compromise in the face of state intimidation during her yearlong imprisonment in 1976–1977, which included seven months in Hoheneck, the GDR's prison for women.[28] She had been incarcerated for engaging in a fairly low-stakes political action. While still a university student, and following the lead of major cultural figures in East Germany, she and her friend Thomas Werner had gathered a few dozen signatures to protest the expatriation of the singer-songwriter Wolfgang Biermann, who had been kicked out of the country for unsubstantiated acts of treason.[29] As discussed in this book's introduction, more than one hundred people from the cultural scene, including prominent members of the Writers Union, signed a letter protesting Biermann's expatriation. The political scientist and historian Klaus Schroeder writes that while high-profile figures like Jurek Becker were expelled from the SED[30] party and others, like Volker Braun, were given stern (but ultimately ineffectual) warnings, the "lower-profile signatories" were the ones who received the brunt of the fallout from this collective action and faced imprisonment.[31] Stötzer was charged with *Staatsverleumdung* (defamation of the state) under §220 in the GDR's penal code, and was sentenced to one year in prison. She spent the first five months in pretrial custody in the Erfurt jail before being moved to the Hoheneck prison one hundred miles away in the Ore Mountains. During her incarceration, she experienced extreme physical and emotional abuse, including a forced surgery to treat a misdiagnosed ectopic pregnancy, which turned out to be kidney stones. More impressive for Stötzer than this physical injustice, however, was witnessing the mistreatment of women who had been thrown into prison for being "antisocial." The so-called *Assi-Paragraph* (Antisocial Paragraph), §249 in the GDR's penal code, punished all able-bodied and jobless citizens with upward of two years' imprisonment. The law could also be used against people exhibiting nonconformist behavior.[32] Given no rehabilitation, "antisocial" women could only protect their futures if they conformed to the will of the state. Stötzer also watched as the government sold its political prisoners to the West for huge sums of money—an option she had also been offered, but refused. The realization that political action and citizen dissent could lead to a financial transaction that would actually benefit the East German state broke any remaining illusions Stötzer had about the government's investment in its own ideology.[33] The experience also made her question the effectiveness of conventional forms of political dissent. Her incarceration for such a minor infraction likewise led Stötzer to conclude that artistic activity could act as a shield against the arm of the law. She reflects, "In prison I thought: I'll do art, because with art they don't jail you right away."[34] Stötzer went into prison an activist and came out an artist—committed to the belief that the best course to democratic reform, as well as personal expression and claims to autonomy, was through creative and collective projects.

If imprisonment had not been enough, Stötzer was actively observed by the Stasi after being released, though she does not profess to have experienced any psychic worry or physical harm as a result. Her lack of concern about the perceived threats of state power was actually fairly typical of East Germany's experimental artists at this time. There was always an option to apply for an exit visa, and many did so. In fact, Stötzer seemed to be one of the most likely candidates expected to have applied for (and to have received) an exit visa during the GDR's so-called *Ausreisewelle* (wave of emigration) of the 1980s.[35] People like her stayed in the GDR in part out of a commitment to the desire to forge a better country from the grassroots, and especially through creative production.

Skeptical but resourceful, Stötzer carefully steered both her own practice and that of her fellow artists toward a sustainable vision. Part of that sustenance lay in working flexibly across artistic media, as we saw in the example of the Intermedia I Festival analyzed in the previous chapter. This was also the case for several other collectives that arose at the time, including the Leipzig-based Gruppe 37,2 (Group 37.2) and the SUM Theater, a Dresden-based performance collective, which was active from 1982 to 1984. SUM members included the painter and filmmaker Christine Schlegel and the dancer Fine Kwiatkowski, as well as the filmmaker Helge Leiberg and the musician, writer, and independent publisher Lothar Fiedler. Their group's name, which translates to the Latin "I am," may be interpreted as a reference to the autonomy of the artist, as well as to the group's identification with the creative process: "I make, therefore I am." Importantly, as Schlegel recalls, SUM performed for an audience only a few times.[36] "It was more about trying to work something out, like Artaud," she reflects, summoning the memory of one of Europe's most significant avant-garde dramatists.[37] In fact, Schlegel's showing of her film with the interactive performance by Kwiatkowski at the Intermedia I Festival in 1985 was one of the few times she presented her performance practice in public. In contrast to the SUM Theater, the Women Artists Group strove for greater exposure. And, as their engagement with wider publics grew, so too did their political agenda.

FEMINISM AND THE STATE, FEMINISM AND THE COLLECTIVE

The Women Artists Group made their first major public appearance as part of the Frauenforum (Women's Forum), which took place from June 10 to 12, 1988, at Saint Augustine's Monastery in Erfurt. Organized by Heino Falcke, a theologian and the long-serving Protestant provost of Erfurt, the three-day event brought together activist groups, artists, and progressive preachers to represent some of the most pressing issues facing women in the GDR. One group present advocated for the right to stay at home with children—a controversial subject in a country that defined a woman's emancipation by her participation in the workforce. Certainly, the official rhetoric of gender equality only thinly veiled the economic needs of a country dependent on a predictable and active labor force. Another group at the Women's Forum contested the newly passed national law that laid the groundwork for compulsory military service for women ages eighteen to fifty.[38] Lesbian groups likewise made a formidable public appearance, representing the GDR's burgeoning grassroots gay rights movement. An article in the local newspaper listed no fewer than twelve themes: abortion, genetic technologies, feminist theology, the peace movement, women in rural areas, lesbians, developmentally disabled children, rights of future generations, rape, women in professions, sexism in language, and contraception.[39] The range of these interests helps explain why the Women's Forum would come to represent the increasingly intersectional nature of East Germany's feminist movement.[40]

Creative projects were interspersed among the debates, sermons, and discussions. A highpoint came on the afternoon of the second day when a fashion show put on by eighteen women in the Women Artists Group began at four o'clock. The women had been meeting for weeks to sew clothing and plan the event. Eleven would take about three minutes each to put their fashions on display. A jazz group made up of women from the town of Gießen accompanied their presentations. Kyselka and her models donned the modular series of bullfighter-inspired fashions she had constructed with red and green blocks of fabric. Stötzer presented a line of

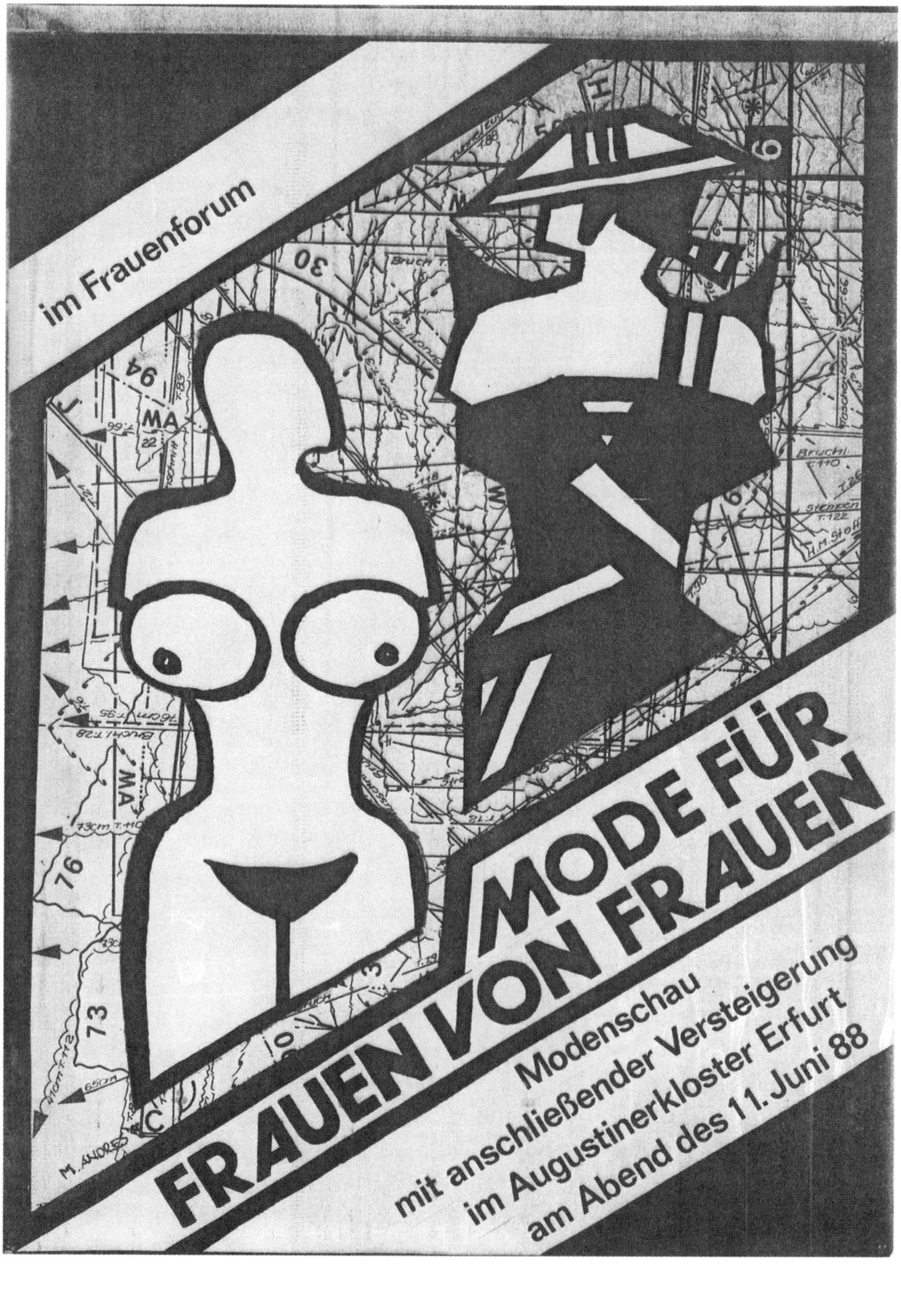
im Frauenforum
MODE FÜR
FRAUEN VON FRAUEN
Modenschau
mit anschließender Versteigerung
im Augustinerkloster Erfurt
am Abend des 11. Juni 88

boxy black-and-white clothing, whose fabric she had painstakingly woven on her loom from scrap materials scavenged from a state-run clothing factory. Fashion-forward looks by professional tailors disgruntled by the state's centrally controlled industry appeared between avant-garde experiments, including Andres's raincoat-like constructions made of red and clear plastic sheeting and newspapers. Three paintings collaboratively made by Kyselka, Stötzer, and Andres formed a backdrop to the weekend's closing discussion. Plans were made, alliances forged.

The Women's Forum marked a clear turning point for the collective. Future projects would be even more public-facing as the group's modus operandi of strength in numbers and "escape into the public" took on a greater meaning.[41] Creative empowerment coincided with political empowerment. Gay rights activists who met the group at the forum joined their ranks, appearing in the final group film, *Signals* (1989), a work that visualizes an emboldened collective. In the film, more bodies appear nude, others perform in eccentric handmade clothing or wearing objects that seem to represent the externalization of internal conflict. The choreography is similarly more agitated, but also more sophisticated and practiced than in previous films. Actions take place more assertively in public places. Stötzer walks through the city streets wearing a beastlike mask she has woven by hand. She leaps around the central cathedral steps—a place where only a few years previously she had been nearly arrested for photographing a punk on a large wooden cross. (The altercation had, of course, come on the heels of—and across a public square from—her 1976 incarceration in the Erfurt city jail.) Elsewhere in the film, several women occupy a public bridge. They walk across it in sync. They lay down a piece of white paper drawn with the outline of a body, like a murder victim chalked out on the ground. They pretend to joust. Angelika Andres sets up an installation and speaks to a mannequin's head

6.5

Monika Andres. Poster for the Mode für Frauen von Frauen (Fashions by Women for Women) fashion show at the Frauenforum (Women's Forum). Augustinerkloster, Erfurt, June 11, 1988. Ormig-Print. Reprinted with the permission of Monika Andres. © 1988 by Monika Andres.

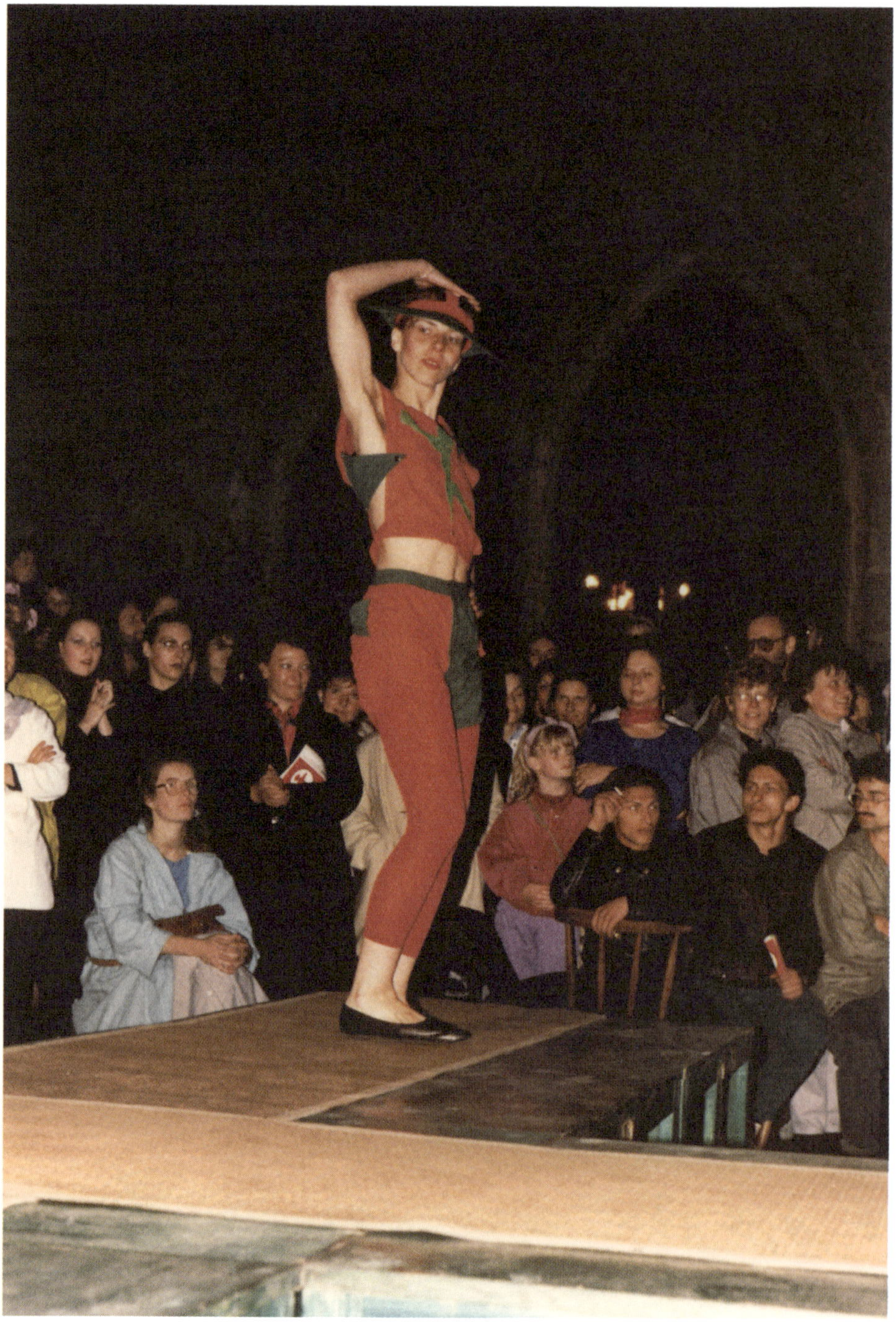

painted red. The improvisational sound of the Women Artists Group's offshoot noise group eog (erweiterter orgasmus gruppe [extended orgasm group]) comes through in its full range in *Signals*.[42] The noise contrasts with the smoothness of the film's edits. Conceptual flows emerge from its montage, and differ substantially from the choppiness of the earlier *Dreams of Women*. In its form, *Signals* is more coherently collaborative. Its message is also more concise—somewhere between confrontation and deep disinterest in the audience they know they have captured for nearly a half hour of performance-cum-fashion-show-cum-city-romp on Super-8.

Around the time that they made *Signals*, and in collaboration with other activists they met at the Women's Forum, several of the Women Artists Group members helped to initiate the activist group Frauen für Veränderung (Women for Change). The coalition joined a movement of local feminist initiatives then emerging all across East Germany. These groups formed partially in response to a continued marginalization of women's voices within the country's largely male-dominated human rights groups.[43] The Erfurt-based Women for Change organized its biggest action—a kind of group performance of democracy—in December 1989. Just weeks after the fall of the Berlin Wall, five women (including Stötzer and two other core members of the artist collective, Tely Büchner and Claudia Bogenhardt) stormed the Stasi headquarters in the center of Erfurt to stop the destruction of the state's surveillance files. This action set off a chain of similar building occupations across the GDR, and also brought the state's invasive practices to an international stage. The impact of the women's action cannot be overstated. The objective of the 1989 political movement had been to improve, not to dismantle the East German state. Few people knew the extent of citizen surveillance that the Stasi files would reveal. Efforts by the Ministry for State Security to destroy its surveillance files were thus prophetic. The world saw with great clarity the lengths to which a now vulnerable East German government would go to cover up its own past. This severely damaged

6.6

Verena Kyselka. *Torero*, part of the self-made fashion objects made and performed by the artist. Fashion show at the Frauenforum (Women's Forum). Augustinerkloster, Erfurt, June 11, 1988. Model: Verena Kyselka. Photographer unknown. Reprinted with the permission of Verena Kyselka. Image courtesy of the Fotoarchiv Verena Kyselka. © 1988 by Verena Kyselka.

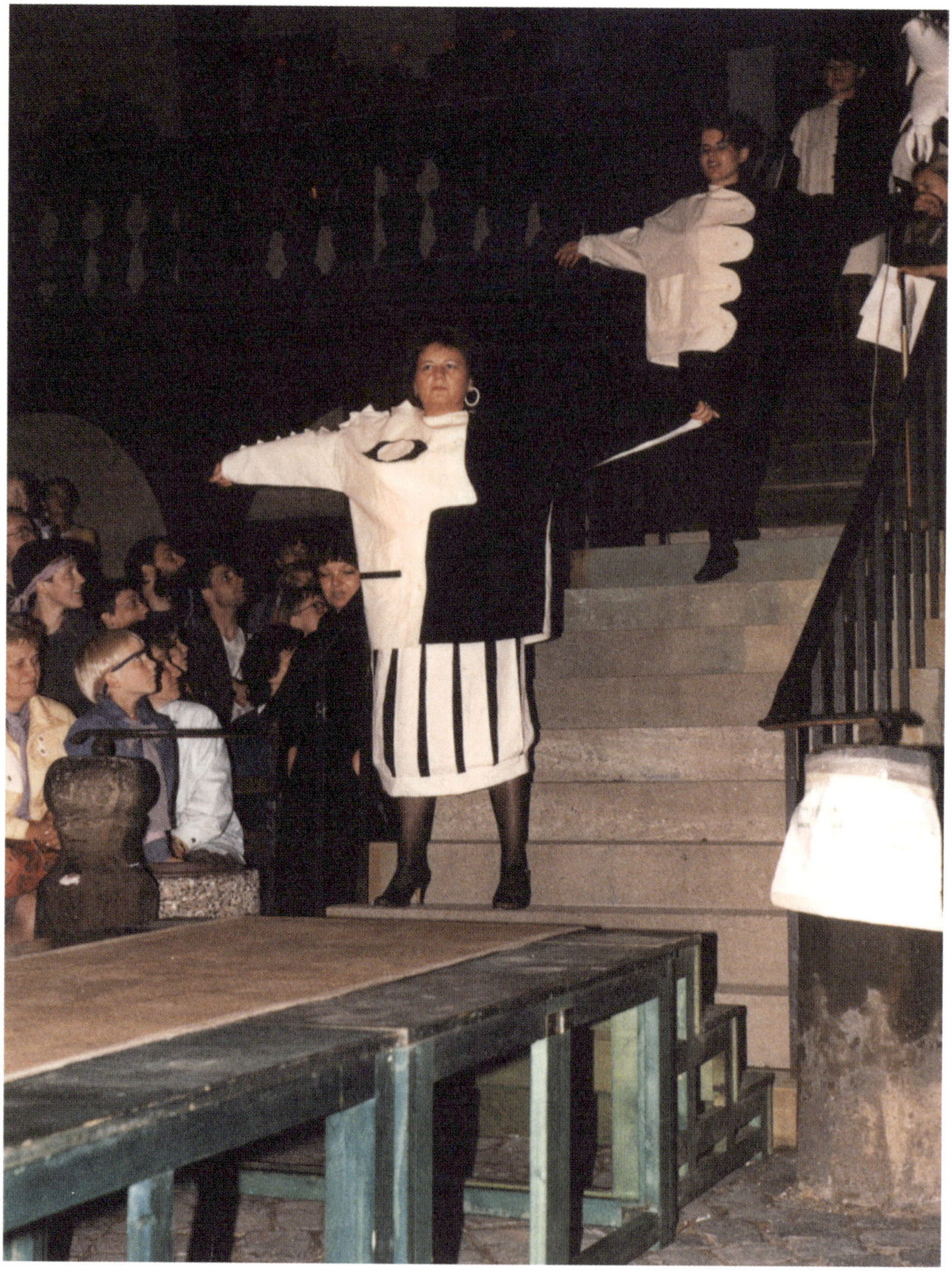

the country's reputation, and laid bare its unwillingness to reform or cede power in the name of civil rights.

The core presence of artists at the Stasi building occupation in Erfurt represents an exception to the typical makeup of citizens engaged in direct political action at this time. Indeed, some lament the lack of artistic participation in the GDR's 1989 revolution at both the state and unofficial levels.[44] Others discredit this critique, suggesting it misinterprets the political activity of experimental artists who consistently confronted the state by pointing out its hypocrisies and limitations.[45] The point here is not to debate the political merits of artistic action or inaction. In fact, recent scholarship on the art and cultural history of the Eastern Bloc, including by the art historian Klara Kemp-Welch, draws attention to a decisive turn to "anti-political politics," a concept first advanced by the Czech poet, performance artist, and future politician Václav Havel.[46] The idea essentially holds that by divesting themselves from state politics, artists helped to redefine what politics could mean in the Eastern Bloc at the grassroots level. To be antipolitical was not to be apolitical. Rather it describes a position that set a person apart from the official definitions of politics. The collective political activity that emerged out of collective creative activity at Erfurt's Stasi headquarters in December 1989 offers a compelling history while simultaneously demonstrating the potential power of alternative group work to reveal the false premises of GDR society and take effective action against it.

To draw out the political (or antipolitical) direction of experimental collective practice in the GDR, it is valuable to look more closely at the politics of the Women Artists Group, which were far from simple. Indeed, they do not conform to western definitions of "identity politics," which might seem an obvious choice in a context where difference was criminalized. It is worth debating whether a latent feminism inspired the work of the collective. As an outspoken feminist, Stötzer represented

6.7

Gabriele Stötzer. *Schwarz-Weiß-Serie* (Black-and-White series). Fashion show at the Frauenforum (Women's Forum). Augustinerkloster, Erfurt, June 11, 1988. Models: Ingrid Plöttner, Angelika Andres, and Anita Ritter. Photograph by Verena Kyselka. Reprinted with the permission of Gabriele Stötzer and Verena Kyselka. Image courtesy of the Fotoarchiv Verena Kyselka. © 1988 by Gabriele Stötzer.

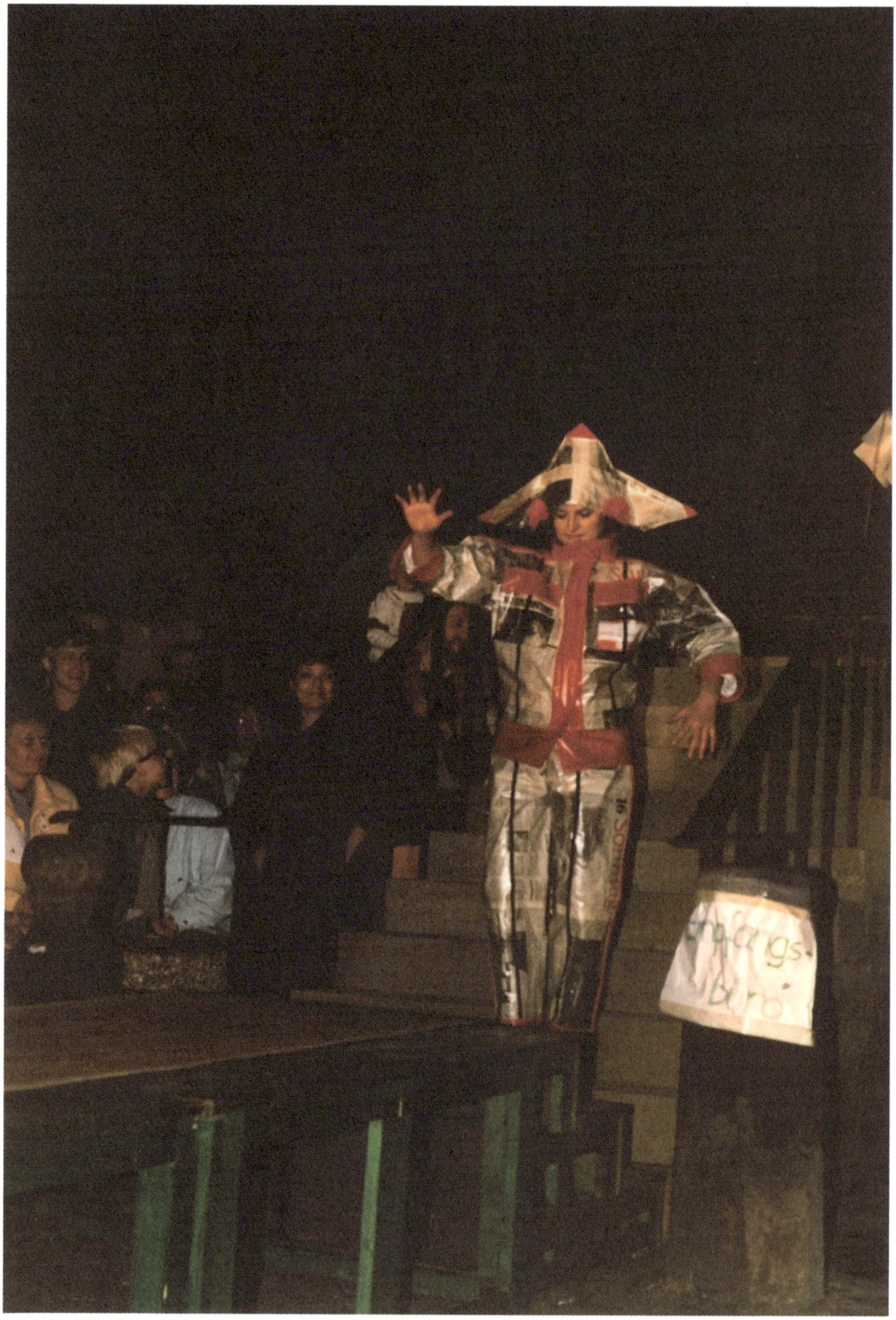

an often hard-line gender politics that was actually quite unusual for women artists in the GDR's experimental arts scene. In fact, most artists, including those in her group, associated feminism with the ruse of gender equality propagated in the state's socialist image. For many, the purported egalitarianism promised by the East German state reflected an institutionalized form of feminism rather than a social reality. On the surface, population statistics do seem to bear out the equality that party officials proclaimed. Official demographics from 1982 indicate that women constituted 49.3 percent of students in higher education and 49.6 percent of the workforce.[47] However, in terms of leadership in professions and government, even though women made up more than half of all doctors and dentists, and nearly 70 percent of pharmacists, by 1982 women still represented a minority of the national legislature, the Volkskammer (People's Chamber) at 30.8 percent.[48] These figures demonstrate a crucial ambivalence toward female authority, and reveal a continued imbalance between the roles and duties of women in East German society. As the sociologist Myra Marx Ferree has demonstrated, the gendered power differential contributed greatly to the formation of the feminist movement in the late GDR, because "the prevailing model of men making politics on women's behalf became a significant grievance in its own right."[49] Women looked to create their own political channels "through which [they] could express their interests and formulate alternatives."[50]

In her analysis of popular publications from the GDR, the sociologist Irene Dölling offers a nuanced example of the visualization of women's roles in a supposedly equal society. She argues that photographs of women in the workplace reveal not only that a hierarchy of gender continued to subordinate women to men, but

6.8

Monika Andres. *Zeitungskostüm* (Newspaper Dress) *Name, Stadt, Land, Fluss* (Name, City, Country, River). Fashion show at the Frauenforum (Women's Forum). Augustinerkloster, Erfurt, June 11, 1988. Model and dancer: Elizabeth Kaufmann. Photograph by Verena Kyselka. Reprinted with the permission of Monika Andres and Verena Kyselka. Image courtesy of the Fotoarchiv Verena Kyselka. © 1988 by Monika Andres.

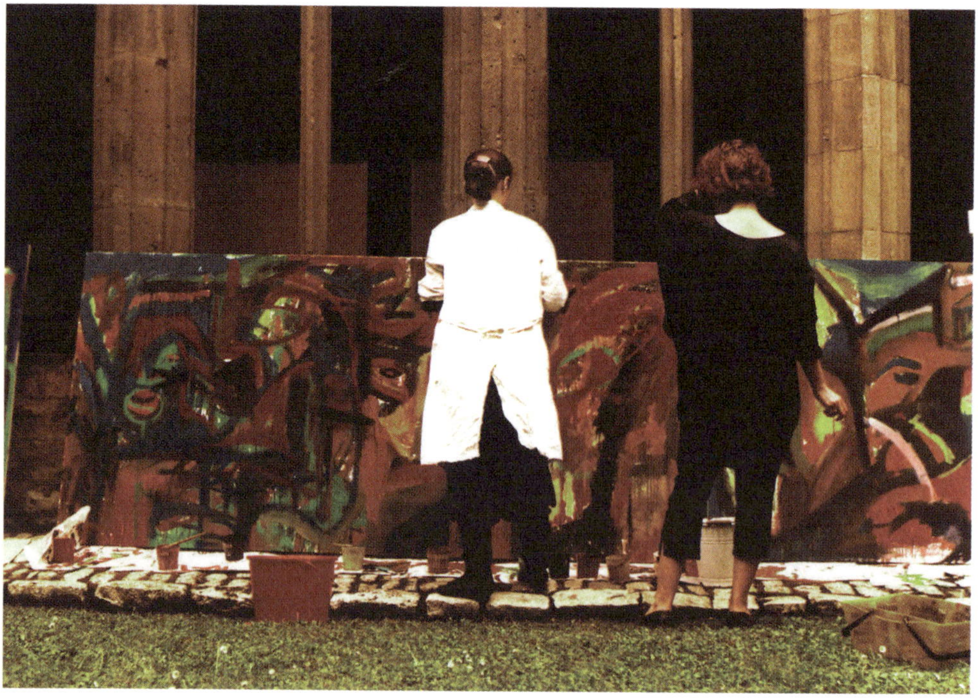

6.9

Monika Andres, Gabriele Stötzer, and Verena Kyselka. Untitled group painting. Frauenforum (Women's Forum). Augustinerkloster, Erfurt, June 11, 1988. Reprinted with the permission of Monika Andres, Gabriele Stötzer and Verena Kyselka.

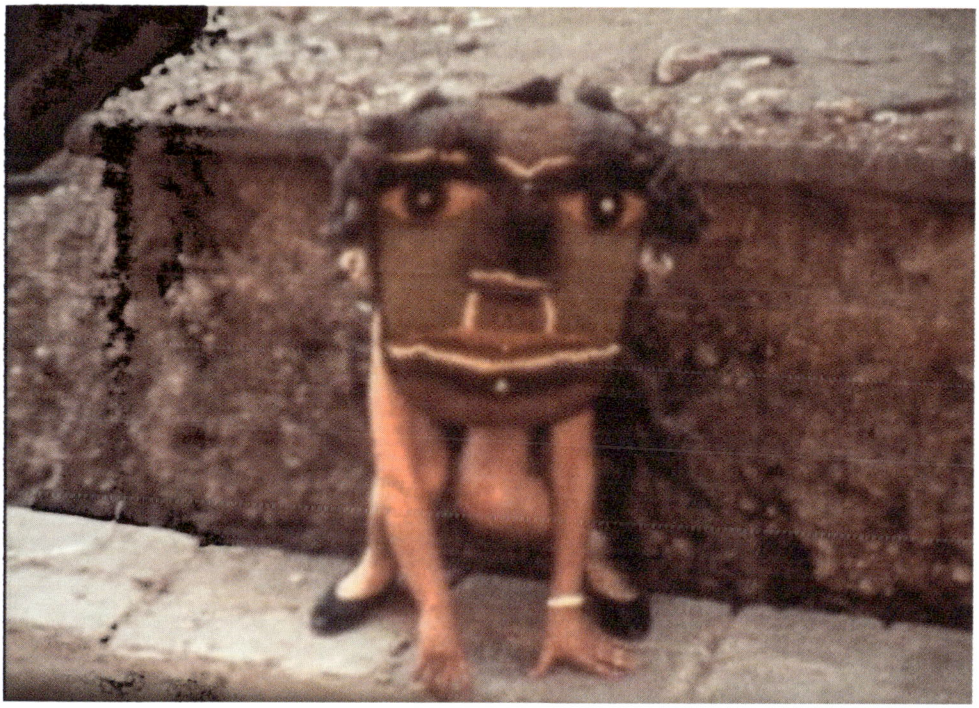

6.10

Künstlerinnengruppe Exterra XX (Angelika Andres, Monika Andres, Claudia Bogenhardt, Gabriele Göbel, Michaela Hopf, Gabriele Stötzer, Verena Kyselka, Ingrid Plöttner, and Harriet Wollert). *Signale* (*Signals*). 1989. Super-8 film, 25 min. Reprinted with the permission of Gabriele Stötzer. © 1989 by Gabriele Stötzer.

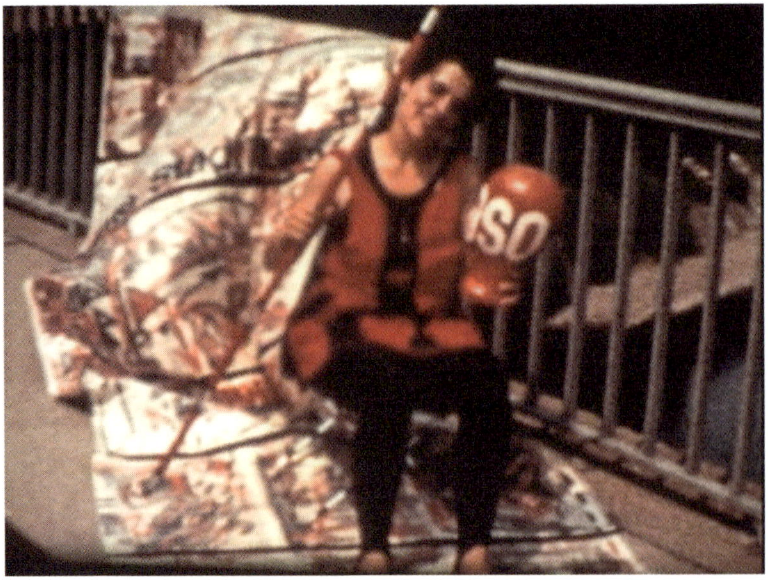

that working women were regularly accused of compromising their femininity. She writes, "Although the photographs convey that holding a profession was a normal part of women's everyday experience, they also give the impression that work did not really tap into her 'womanliness.'"[51] Dölling concludes that official representations of working women still showed their labor in the workforce as secondary to their domestic roles. The message on gender was clearly inconsistent. While some scholars estimate a 90 percent rate of eligible women in education or the workforce,[52] this figure misleads in that it does not account for discrepancies in leadership positions, let alone the disproportionate amount of unpaid labor women

6.11

Künstlerinnengruppe Exterra XX (Angelika Andres, Monika Andres, Claudia Bogenhardt, Gabriele Göbel, Michaela Hopf, Gabriele Stötzer, Verena Kyselka, Ingrid Plöttner, and Harriet Wollert). *Signale* (*Signals*). 1989. Super-8 film, 25 min. Reprinted with the permission of Gabriele Stötzer. © 1989 by Gabriele Stötzer.

with families conducted in the home. According to Ferree, some important policy changes were developed from the 1970s onward with the hope of resolving this disparity.[53] These reforms included greater access to childcare and contraception, and the legalization of first-trimester abortion. Nevertheless, the social attitude about women as primary caregivers remained largely unchanged, and likewise remained a serious point of contention. In an open letter published in October 1989, the Women for Change identified these contradictions as a reason many citizens were choosing to leave the GDR: "The [current] mass emigration is a clear expression of the persisting contradictions of our society."[54] The members identified gender inequality not as a women's problem but as a collective problem. To that end, they presented their network as an alliance with the growing civil rights, environmental, and antinuclear movements of the time, and not simply as a group focused on gender-based politics.

A similar attention to social equality is evident in the creative activity of the Women Artists Group. Important to the women was the creation of a space where they could work and talk seriously about their artwork and intellectual interests.[55] Many wanted to get away from their identification as mothers. For example, Harriett Wollert, whose child custody was threatened by the state, sought a coalition of support.[56] Some found respite from abusive relationships. Others simply wanted to do something new. At the same time that it set itself apart from the political machinations of the East German government, the Women Artists Group also confronted the hostility and misogyny of the experimental art scene, which—as Stötzer recalls—"treated women like mattresses."[57] The collective served a dual purpose for its members: it allowed them to differentiate themselves from normative definitions of femininity and gender, and it emphasized that the creative capacities of women are equal to those of men. For the members of the Women Artists Group, one of their best options was to collectivize and to thus enact a new form of public life in which they could thrive, create, and remain autonomous.

A UNITED FRONT: COLLECTIVE PRACTICE IN EAST GERMANY

Like the term "intermedia," the term "collective" requires some contextualization. Collective art practice had been a mainstay of European modernism, including in Germany. From the secessionist movement of the late nineteenth century, in which artists combatted the authority of the national academy, to the Brücke (Bridge) or

Blaue Reiter (Blue Rider) artists, who skill-shared across media to produce a mass of similarly minded, yet aesthetically distinct artworks, to the post-World War I materialization of performance, photographic montage, and overtly politicized sculpture in Dada, historical examples of collective art practice were abundant in the 1980s—even for East Germans, whose access to such work was considerably limited. An important exception is the Bauhaus (1919–1933), a utopian and visionary project and arts academy that united the fine arts, design, dance, performance, and architecture. Bauhaus received a renewed profile as part of East Germany's socialist cultural heritage in the mid-1970s, particularly in 1975 when the country celebrated the fiftieth anniversary of the opening of the Bauhaus in Dessau.

The post-World War II collectives of the West such as the Situationist International, Fluxus, or Arte Povera were likewise clearly indebted to the institutional and media critiques of these and other German predecessors. As a core part of their analysis of collectivism in the Cold War West, the art historian Blake Stimson and the artist Gregory Sholette argue that the turn to collective practice after World War II reflects a desire among artists to develop new modes of civic participation through the arts in the wake of European fascism and Stalinism.[58] In other words, collectivism after modernism reveals a dramatic shift in the ways that people understood or related to mass culture. Not communist, but also not *not* communist, western artists in the late Cold War period returned to the pre-World War II vision of collective creative power in a renewed hope for grassroots and socially oriented forms of culture that resisted the trappings of ideology into which culture had so dramatically fallen. Stimson and Sholette characterize a break in collective practice from World War II onward as ideological: "The old modernist collectivism was indissolubly linked with a bigger ism, a bigger ideal that had failed—communism—and it had little choice but to distance itself."[59] In other words, artists in the West felt compelled to redefine collectivism in the post-World War II period because communism had given mass (read: collective) culture such a bad reputation.

Stimson and Sholette historicize collectivism as something that emerged out of a conscious rejection of modernism's latent communism. Absent from this assessment is the reality of a collectivist *present* that defined art in state socialist countries, and with which all of East Germany's artists—both state and experimental—had to contend. In fact, acknowledging this reality actually helps to cohere artists along the two sides of the Cold War's metaphorical Iron Curtain. Just as Stimson and Sholette claim that it took several decades for western artists to return to collectivization after observing the direction that communist forms of art could head, East

Germany's experimental artists of the 1980s came to group work with a similar degree of skepticism rooted in actual experience. Their collectivism reflects a culture of disillusionment, in which the antidote for a corrupted national collective was an autonomous one. In short, collectivism in the Eastern Bloc was an outcome of autonomous citizen action in concert with the communist political agenda, which had sought—but failed—to create a public cohered around national culture. Certainly, when official culture is defined as a kind of armature of state power, its impacts come to seem singularly oppressive. Yet the examination of the art of the Women Artists Group, as well as the related political work of some of its group members, suggests that collectivism as a social ethic may have influenced and inspired a kind of autonomous collectivity that is similar to but different from that of the West. The turn to group activities was thus equally a critique of state aesthetic principles, which favored the division of media and the collectively bound artist, as it was a way of confronting the state by deploying its own method of unity in culture, unity in the collective.

The Women Artists Group represents a mutual insistence on group work as a means to transcend, augment, and repurpose the possibilities of East German culture in public life. Even more explicitly, the multimedia practices represented by this group demonstrate the demand, even necessity, for bringing together a wide array of artists, musicians, and supporters in order to produce a critical practice in the late GDR. Quite simply, no one single person could have created the kinds of projects produced by the Women Artists Group. Multimedia practices relied on collectivity, including its attendant dependence on distributive authorship and shared respect. These were practices invested in working together, wherein the principle of collective action could produce more dynamic outcomes.

Embedded within the dependence on collective labor that defined the multimedia practices of the late GDR is a fundamental irony. Namely, artists' interest in working together and strengthening creative bonds through side-by-side or mutually beneficial action in fact actualized the East German state's own credo for a society premised in collective culture. One of the threats of that interdisciplinarity (or intermediality, to think with this book's previous chapter) was its realization of the significance of the collective—not for something utopian, state-designated, or prescribed but for the sake of building, from within, alternatives that could, and ultimately did, dismantle state authority.

7

DIY PUBLIC SPHERE

A Counterdiscourse in the Publication *Anschlag* and the Gallery EIGEN+ART

Two Styrofoam egg cartons folded out, pressed flat, and adhered to stiff cardboard adorn the front and back covers of the ninth issue of the independent magazine *Anschlag* (Attack/Strike) released in 1987. Designed by the bookbinder Wiebke Müller, the cover materializes the conditions of consumption that surrounded the production of this technically illegal publication. The label "12 FRISCHEIER B" appears stamped in large chartreuse block letters across the carton's flattened top, indicating that the packaging once housed a dozen fresh—albeit grade-B quality—eggs. Other than a few small, friendly logos, including a rather cute hybrid chick-egg, the carton is plain and austere. Its use in the unlikely space of German Democratic Republic (GDR) samizdat[1] makes an immediate reference to the country's centralized economic planning, as well as the resourceful do-it-yourself culture it both inspired and in fact depended upon. The eighty egg cartons required for the full forty-issue run of this *Anschlag* edition harken back to a consumer culture defined by limited options that satisfied need rather than desire and where an excess of one good often came at the expense of shelf variety. Their "EVP" price tags (4.08M on one cover; 4.68M on another) reveal the state's promise to provide the public with low-priced staple foods.[2] Two basic instructions underscore the planned economy's parallel dependence on a culture of reuse: *RÜCKGABEVERPACKUNG* (RETURNABLE PACKAGING) and *Vorsicht! Nicht verbrennen!* (Caution! Do not burn!). Neither returned nor burned, but nevertheless no longer usable as intended, Müller's smashed cartons have been made into a durable surface—a protective casing fashioned out of the recycled resources of a state intent on predefining the consumer

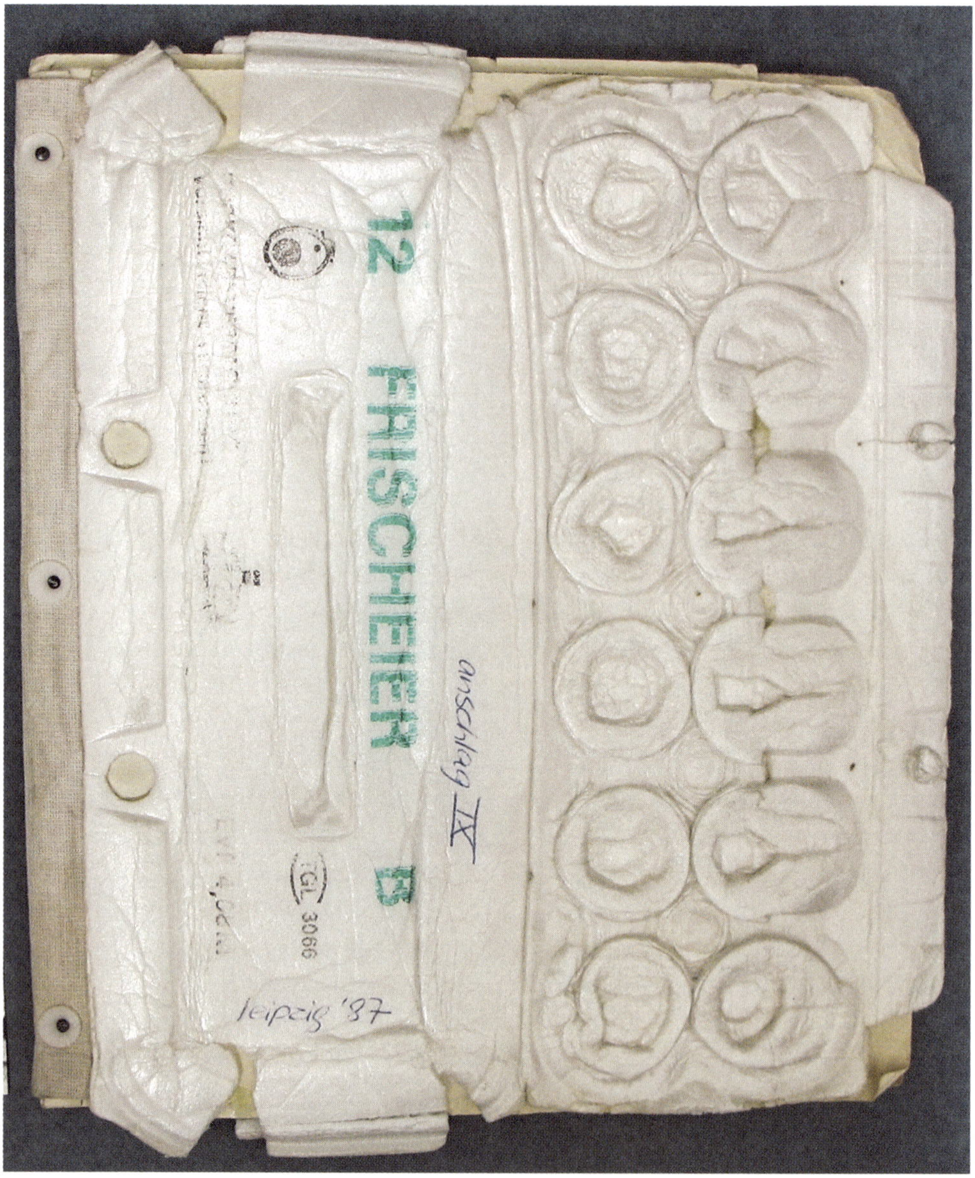

7.1

Wiebke Müller. *Anschlag*, no. 9 (1987). Cover design. Egg carton and book binding. Reprinted with the permission of Wiebke Müller. © 1987 by Wiebke Müller.

habits of its citizenry, from foodstuffs to culture. In short, in these forty issues of *Anschlag*, the excess of the 960 subpar eggs becomes a poignant metaphor for state culture. For, though abundant and state-subsidized, the cultural goods meant to define and transform the GDR's public had long since expired.

Karim Saab, one of *Anschlag*'s three core editors, reflects that "Wiebke Müller's covers caused quite a stir. She picked up ordinary products and upcycled materials from our everyday world: used sandpaper, the Leipzig city map, Jacquard loom cards, flattened egg cartons, or paint trays."[3] The commonplace material grounded the often esoteric or theoretical contents of *Anschlag* in a more quotidian reality—unsubtle reminders of the context that made this experimental form of publication a necessity. Contained within issue number nine's unusual packaging are eighty-two pages of original artist prints and photographs, carbon-copied typewritten texts, and computer printouts. *Anschlag*'s editorial team painstakingly gathered and bound each issue individually from copies of texts and images that the contributors themselves supplied. This method of assembly is as resourceful—and improvisational—as the bookbinder's use of random materials for the magazine's covers. No single theme unifies the publication's ten regular issues. The ninth edition leads with a German translation of the Czech activist and writer Václav Havel's "Politics and Conscience." The text, which Havel wrote in 1984, helped to galvanize the civil rights movements that spread across the Eastern Bloc in the late Cold War period. Some conceptual union may be interpreted between Müller's upcycled cover and Havel's political treatise, which centers regularly on his concern for the environmental destruction that the Eastern Bloc's industrialization had caused but willfully ignored. More important, however, is the use of this text, at all, in the pages of *Anschlag*. Because Havel was persona non grata in the GDR, the reproduction of his essay challenged the state's monopoly on print culture, and especially on political discourse. In fact, each page of *Anschlag* may be understood as an enactment of citizen agency. The poets included in the volume dismantle hegemonic culture through experiments with language. Essays on the intersections of aesthetics and politics challenge the state's scripted vision of socialist aesthetics. Each page asserts its own intentionality—a kind of equity of voice within the issue's discourse, itself a small sampling of the conversations taking place in the GDR's creative underbelly. Importantly, *Anschlag*'s contents consistently reveal the conditions of everyday living that many of East Germany's experimental artists sought to address in their work. The project is thus not a hermetically sealed enactment of creative autonomy; rather, it illustrates that artists and writers saw themselves as participants in and contributors to a counterpublic that was more dialogical, honest, and authentic than the public sphere provided (that is to say, orchestrated) by the state.

Anschlag is one of approximately thirty independent publications produced in the GDR between 1979 and 1990.[4] Its ninth issue, including its motley form and content, is representative of a larger print phenomenon that emerged in the GDR in the 1980s. The magazine, produced between 1984 and 1989 in Leipzig, is likewise emblematic of the ways in which alternative cultures—from the artistic to the literary, and to a lesser extent, the more overtly political—commingled in the pages of East German samizdat. These were all collaborative efforts, involving artists and creative writers, journalists and bookmakers, gallerists and art historians who organized prolific projects in a state marked by material privation, as well as political and creative censorship. Some publications recurred as many as eight times per year; many appeared as special editions organized around thematic concepts; some focused primarily on textual works; others highlighted photography, graphic arts, even film. All violated the government's demand for universal control of print culture, itself an armature of state power. The DIY aesthetic of these publications reflect that subversion. From methods of duplication to quality of paper to distribution strategies, publishers were as resourceful as their contributors were inventive.

Independent gallery spaces emerged simultaneous to the expansion of alternative publications in the mid-1980s.[5] This chapter analyzes galleries and publications together to demonstrate how they functioned co-constitutively to host and promulgate the experimental culture's autonomous public sphere. Examining in particular the relationship between the Leipzig-based magazine *Anschlag* and the independent gallery EIGEN+ART (literally, OWN+ART),[6] which was established by Gerd Harry "Judy" Lybke in 1983 in Leipzig, this chapter demonstrates that both entities functioned side by side, and sometimes in direct collaboration, to produce a multivalent and durable platform for the presentation and dissemination of artwork and ideas.

Anschlag produced ten regular issues, as well as two special issues, including "Foto-Anschlag," a box set of thirty-two original photographs with as many texts. The other special issue, which focused on EIGEN+ART, will be examined closely in the second half of this chapter. Although both functioned independently, the gallery would play a supportive and at times symbiotic role in the production of the magazine. In addition to providing *Anschlag* with a conduit between writers and artists, the gallery offered it a physical space, both for its editorial meetings, which were open to the public, and as a point of distribution for this and a number of other samizdat. Poets and other writers featured in the magazine presented their work at readings held in the gallery. Essays by art historians written for EIGEN+ART exhibitions regularly appeared in *Anschlag*. The texts on EIGEN+ART artists and events regularly appeared alongside more political or theoretical ones, thus rendering the gallery a political dimension that Lybke claims he deliberately avoided. Nevertheless, he admits that even though his gallery "was never about politics, but about living, that alone made it political."[7] The relationship between *Anschlag* and EIGEN+ART demonstrates, moreover, that interdisciplinarity and a networked community both defined and fortified East Germany's independent platforms.

While the statistical impacts of any samizdat publication or independent gallery are difficult to ascertain, anecdotal evidence as well as reports made by the secret police (Ministry for State Security, or Stasi) reveal that the reach and impact of *Anschlag* and EIGEN+ART were not insignificant. Anticipated readership could be multiplied by a factor of ten to twenty people per issue.[8] Issues 1 through 4 (1984–1985) came out in editions of twenty-five; issues 5 through 10 (1986–1989) appeared in editions of forty. Over the course of its five-year run, the publication reached anywhere from 250 to 800 readers multiple times a year. According to Saab, *Anschlag* achieved a mythic status that well exceeded its most immediate milieu. As he recalls, "Once some neighbors from a nearby town reported to [Müller's] parents—who lived in the Ore Mountains—that there were apparently some brave people in Leipzig who were publishing a magazine called *Anschlag*."[9] The anecdote reveals a cross-generational and cross-GDR presence for the publication. If a middle-aged couple living a few hundred kilometers away from the heart of the action had heard of *Anschlag*, then certainly the interests of others closer to its production center (not to mention more immediately invested in its contents) must have been quite profound. Given that the magazine was technically an illegal undertaking, no formal statistical data on the consumption of this or any other autonomous publication from the East Germany is available. It is nevertheless quite telling that a few of the GDR's libraries, including the State Library of Saxony, actively collected East German samizdat from 1986 onward.[10] Whereas this may of course be explained as a form of surveillance and control, the attention paid to such publications by the state likewise signals that authorities valued them as more than countercultural anomalies.

EIGEN+ART achieved an even greater level of notoriety, both across the GDR and in West Germany. The gallery, which is today one of Germany's most successful commercial spaces, was a revelation in the late GDR. EIGEN+ART was originally conceived as a kind of ad hoc space in Lybke's shared Leipzig apartment (the "Galerie am Körnerplatz") for, as he recounts, "losers like me."[11] This is modest shorthand for the gallerist's status as an unemployable artist type who lost educational and career opportunities after a series of choices that effectively left him as a social outcast. First, during his obligatory military service, Lybke wrote "Make love, not war" on an army barracks. The punishment for the act of vandalism—which he describes as "foolish"[12]—led to his expulsion from military exercises and veritable internment in the library on his base. Soon after, his refusal to study power plant technology (*Kraftwerkstechnik*) in Moscow left him without any other educational opportunities. He realized he had lost his ability to lead the "normal life" he had anticipated, even hoped for.[13] Once he accepted his fate, Lybke found himself freed: "I thought, ok, then I am antisocial [*asozial*], and I suddenly realized that a lot of people in the city were just as antisocial as I was."[14] He entered and quickly passionately commited himself to Leipzig's parallel world of artists. Including those held at the Galerie am Körnerplatz, EIGEN+ART's seventy-two exhibitions held between 1983 and 1990, which involved easily three times as many artists, were risk-taking and ambitious. From painting to installation to performance art, the Leipzig gallery became a locus for the dissemination and consumption of experimental art in the GDR.

Reflecting the scholarly consensus on the subject of East Germany's experimental culture, the historian Yvonne Fiedler calls its network of publications, galleries, and events a "parallel infrastructure," which ran alongside official culture.[15] Experimental culture augmented the deficits of the status quo and over time did so with increasing visibility. In short, the experimental art scene was effectively a part of—and not apart from—public life. To that end, rather than providing an exhaustive look at the content of either the publication or the gallery, this chapter focuses on how *Anschlag* and EIGEN+ART functioned as conduits for the distribution of ideas. Focusing on these two case studies facilitates a deeper examination of the ways in which the creators and supporters of experimental culture produced their own form of public life. Both demonstrate the necessity and the viability of autonomous production as an alternative to the limited opportunities that state culture afforded. Their invitations to critique, which will be explored below, likewise demonstrate the attention that members of the experimental scene paid to improving their ventures through open dialogue and greater visibility.

ANSCHLAG'S PROACTIVE VISION

Anschlag's original editorial team of Angelika Klüssendorf and Wiebke Müller first established the magazine in 1984. Dedicated activists in the solidarity movement

Hoffnung Nicaragua (Hope for Nicaragua), which first formed in 1981, the duo initially solicited artists and writers to donate artworks and texts to be bound and sold in the service of a school in Managua.[16] After the first issue, the *Anschlag* co-founders no longer coordinated the publication with their activism for Nicaragua.[17] This origin nevertheless demonstrates that a worldly impulse and external orientation were foundational to the publication. It also suggests that *Anschlag*'s audience of readers, as well as its contributors, comprised a larger population than the scene of artists that samizdat ordinarily engaged with. When Klüssendorf emigrated to West Germany, Karim Saab took her place on the editorial board. He explains that coming across the Dresden-based independent magazine *Und* (And) inspired in him a desire to use a creative media platform to grow the networks of artists and writers already organizing a counterpublic sphere. "We wanted to 'dare for democracy,'" Saab reflects.[18] *Anschlag* thus evolved from grassroots organizing defined by global politics, and quickly narrowed in on more immediate, local needs.

The East German context significantly influenced production and distribution decisions for this and all other samizdat. Censorship laws, including those which restricted the numbers of photocopies an individual could make to five, meant that for each issue, editors asked all contributors to provide enough reproductions of their work to satisfy the full print run. Uwe Warnke, the co-founder and editor of *Entwerter/Oder* (Cancelation/other,[19] 1982–present), nevertheless describes a simple and effective act of subterfuge that allowed a person to receive more than their five-copy allocation: "If a person wanted more copies, they could go around the block once, and return to the copy shop after maybe five minutes, and stand before the same employee as before. If you needed twenty-five copies, they would say, come back three more times. With a good attitude—and in the view of only four eyes—the desired copies would be immediately completed."[20] Importantly, Warnke does not describe any gain for the copy shop employee. The anecdote reveals a human-to-human camaraderie that recognized and then exceeded the unreasonable limitations of bureaucracy. Certainly, for some the GDR's hierarchical culture will have amplified a desire to undermine authority.

The multisourced reproduction process continued throughout *Anschlag*'s eight-year history, which—in its fifth issue—increased production from twenty-five to forty issues. By this time, the editors shrank the number of contributors from essentially a limitless set to a more manageable dozen or so selected or invited by them for each regular issue. In general, each contributor received one issue free of charge, and could also sell two copies for about 50 East German marks (about 12.50 West German marks, or $8) to people both in the GDR and beyond, partially via the

EIGEN+ART gallery's connections to the West. These prices appear in the Stasi's surveillance files on EIGEN+ART, a fact that demonstrates that state authorities maintained an awareness of the publication on a granular level.[21] Such insight, however, did not lead to effective action to shut down the publication, or the gallery for that matter.

Anschlag's contributor-driven reproduction process and improvisational approaches to sales and distribution were standard practice among East Germany's unofficial publications. Crucial was the necessity to work around the Fine Arts Censorship Law (*Honorarordnung "Bildende Kunst"*), which stipulated that print runs of artworks that exceeded one hundred pages receive official authorization from cultural authorities.[22] Technically, *Anschlag* named itself an *Originalgrafik* (artistic portfolio), a clever nomenclature that skirted the necessity for official printing permission.[23] The portfolio status proved to be a surprisingly impenetrable defense against the laws of print. In general, although some were forced to close (only to form again under new names),[24] no samizdat publishers or contributors faced criminal charges in the late GDR. Certainly, as demonstrated above, the secret police were aware of the publications. It is also well known that the writers Sascha Anderson and Rainer Schedlinski—who also co-produced the samizdat *Ariadnefabrik* (Ariadne factory)—aggressively informed the Stasi on the inner workings of the Prenzlauer Berg scene in East Berlin.[25] Nevertheless, in a country that defined itself as constitutional, even the duplicitous Ministry for State Security could not find a way to permanently stop independent publishers, whose tactics and community-oriented strategies were simply too adaptive.

Stasi observation of *Anschlag* public meetings, which often took place in EIGEN+ART, dwelled on summary and information gathering rather than direct action. Surveillance reports often read more like meeting minutes than assessments

7.2

"Operativinformation Nr. 245/86" (Operational Information No. 245/86). BStU, MfS, BV Leipzig, ZMA, AKG, Nr. 4974, 44. Reprinted with the permission of the Bundesbeauftragte für die Unterlagen des Staatssicherheitsdienstes der ehemaligen Deutschen Demokratischen Republik via the Stasi Records Act (StUG) § 32.

BV für Staatssicherheit Leipzig
Kreisdienststelle Leipzig-Stadt

Leipzig, 02. Juli 1986
Ref. XX/2/koß-hg

Operativinformation Nr. 245/86

Sachverhaltskomplex: 1.   Sachverhaltsart: 1.4.

Am 24. 6. 1986 nahm eine inoffizielle, bisher noch nicht überprüfte Quelle der DE an der Veranstaltung des Redaktionskollegiums der Untergrundzeitschrift "Anschlag" unter dem Thema "Anschlag stellt sich vor" in

7030 Leipzig, ...Fritz-Austel-Str. 31
Ausstellungsräume des
.....Lybke.. ....Gerd.. ([redacted])

teil. Insgesamt waren ca 20 Personen anwesend. Ziel der Veranstaltung war die Konzipierung der weiteren Gestaltung der Untergrundzeitschrift. Die Veranstaltung war in vorangegangenen Redaktionssitzungen insbesondere durch den Einfluß des

[redacted].. (erf. Abt. XX, BV Leipzig)

vorbereitet worden. Der Quelle ist bekannt, daß der [redacted] die weitere Arbeit mit der Zeitschrift "Anschlag" unter das Thema "Jenseits der Möglichkeiten" stellen will. Er hat zu diesem Thema für die nächste Ausgabe ein 30 Seiten umfassendes Essay geschrieben, über dessen Inhalt noch nichts bekannt ist. Der [redacted] war zur Eröffnung der Veranstaltung am 24. 6. 1986 nicht anwesend. Nach der Begrüßung und wenigen einleitenden Worten durch L.ybke.. wurde durch die [redacted], Härtel.... (Vorname nicht bekannt) ein literarischer Beitrag gehalten, der sich inhaltlich mit der Problematik "Verfolgter Priester in Rußland" beschäftigte. Der Vortrag wurde ohne Kommentar in den Raum gestellt und auch nicht diskutiert.

Im Anschluß sprach sich ein Mathematiker der KMU (ca. 40 Jahre, kantiger Haarschnitt) gegen die einseitige und tendenziöse Darstellung der Probleme in den bisherigen Ausgaben von "Anschlag" aus. Auch das Thema "Jenseits der Möglichkeiten" läßt wieder viel Spielraum für Spekulationen und tendenziöse Darstellungen. Die zur Veranstaltung erwartete Berliner Schriftstellerin

.....[redacted](erf.: nicht bekannt)

war nicht anwesend. Eine Grafikerin aus Berlin kritisierte den Verlauf der Zusammenkunft betreffs der fehlenden Konzeption und zeigte sich in hohem Maße enttäuscht.

Die Beiträge liegen von der inhaltlichen Seite unter ihren Erwartungen.

In der Diskussion wurde versucht, einen gemeinsamen Standpunkt zur weiteren Gestaltung von "Anschlag" zu finden. Es wurde vorgeschlagen, die Redaktionszugehörigkeit ständig zu wechseln. Befriedigt wurde die Mitgestaltung durch den Leipziger Maler Heisig an einer der letzten Ausgaben aufgenommen.

Die Zahl von 32 herzustellenden Exemplaren soll nicht überschritten werden. Beid der Auswahl dereinzelnen Beiträge soll deren mögliche strafrechtliche Relevanz geprüft werden. Die verstärkte Einbeziehung von grafischen Zeichnungen usw. bei der Gestaltung ist vorgesehen.

Als Teilnehmer der Veranstaltung konnten als weitere Personen identifiziert werden:

......[redacted] (erf. BV Leipzig, Abt. XX)

....[redacted] (erf. -"- -"-)

.....[redacted] (erf. KD Leipzig-Stadt)

....[redacted] (erf. BV Leipzig, Abt.XX)

Durch die Abwesenheit von [redacted] verlief die Veranstaltung teilweise ohne Konzeption. Weitere Entscheidungen zur Arbeit der Redaktion "Anschlag" sollen Ende Juli 1987 getroffen werden. Die [redacted] hatte eine Satire auf den abwesenden [redacted] vorbereitet, in welcher sie ihr Unverständnis zu der inhaltlichen Gestaltung der Zeitschrift zum Ausdruck bringt und den [redacted] persönlich angreift. Der Vortrag wurde jedoch aufgrund der Abwesenheit nicht verlesen.

Maßnahmen

- Weiterer Einsatz des IM-Vorlaufes zur Erarbeitung von Informationen über Pläne und Absichten der Redaktion von "Anschlag"

- Es werden weitere Informationen erarbeitet, um festzustellen, welche Rolle der [redacted] ([redacted]) im Zusammenhang mit der "Anschlag" - Veröffentlichung spielt

- Seitens der Quelle wird versucht, ein Exemplar der nächsten Ausgabe von "Anschlag" zu erwerben.

Leiter der DE

Schmidt
Oberst

Verteiler
Abt. XX/BV Leipzig
AKG
KD Leipzig-Stadt AuI
KD Leipzig-Stadt Ref. XX/2

or strategies. For example, the "plans of action" listed in a July 1986 report on an *Anschlag* editorial meeting—written after a full five issues had already been produced—illustrate a security system essentially spinning its wheels.[26] The report (1) demanded continued deployment of informants to gather more information; (2) requested more information about the role that gallerist Lybke played in the production of the magazine; and (3) advised that attempts should be made to secure a copy of the forthcoming issue. This third plan of action clearly begs the question of state power, namely: To what extent did the Stasi conspire against itself in its attempts to be inconspicuous yet still omnipresent? At least in the context of *Anschlag*, the question of the Stasi's influence may then be a moot point. The collaborative production plan combined with the state's own inability to act secured the publication's autonomy.

Dwelling on Stasi presence when evaluating the content of publications reinforces state authority that seems to have largely been ineffectual. More interesting may be a consideration of the *quality* of their contents. In short, a sustained, and arguably more interesting, critique of *Anschlag* and other independent publications is that they lacked a cohesive theme or argument. This judgment articulates a central problem in the purpose of such publications: their most important goal was to create an alternative platform that was free from state-imposed restrictions. This led to a defining paradox: Was it enough that the samizdat publishers produced a venue, or should their objective have been more additive, that is, more strategically attentive to outcomes beyond the artistic or literary milieus their publications served? Did they do enough by producing an autonomous discourse? *Anschlag* faced this problem from inception. The first four issues placed no editorial constraints on content, resulting in what Saab diplomatically describes as a "lively, qualitatively quite diverse spectrum of mostly apolitical texts."[27] The tentativeness of its original issues countered the magazine's assertive title.

7.3

"Operativinformation Nr. 245/86" (Operational Information No. 245/86). BStU, MfS, BV Leipzig, ZMA, AKG, Nr. 4974, 45. Reprinted with the permission of the Bundesbeauftragte für die Unterlagen des Staatssicherheitsdienstes der ehemaligen Deutschen Demokratischen Republik via the Stasi Records Act (StUG) § 32.

Lpzg., den 26.

Liebe Angelika Klüssendorf,

ich habe hoffentlich nicht zu lange gewartet und bringe hoffentlich nichts zum Einstürzen in Bezug auf Euer Vorhaben: "Anschlag", wofür ich sehr zu haben wäre, aber es ist leider kein wirklicher Ansdhlag aufs Gehabte. Auch nicht, wenn ich reiflich überlege und alles mögliche an Anfangsschwierigkeiten usw. bedenke. Ich fand ja die gesamte Gestaltung des Hefts ziemlich gut, überraschend gut und besser als das meiste, was ich da sonst schon gesehen habe. Und wollte aus diesem Grund sehr gerne mitmachen, nicht etwa, weil ich besonders viel Wert auf Verpackung legte, - im Gegenteil: aber das ist es, die Gestaltung ist, scheint mir, in diesem Fall leider nur die Verpackung.
Ich habe nun jüngst auch die Texte gelesen, und habe sie intensiv gelesen, bereit, siehe oben, alles mögliche an Anfangsschwierigkeiten zu tolerieren, ich hatte sogar den Vorschuß der wirklich guten Gestaltung im Hinterkopf. Nun habe ich leider, zu meiner Enttäuschung, herausfinden müssen, daß keiner der Texte so ist, das er diesen Transport lohnt. Ich sage keiner: außer einem natürlich, das ist selbstverständlich der Text von Gert Neumann (...), nochmal:`diesen Text, man kann dagegen sein oder nicht sein, muß man natürlich transportieren. Aber nicht die anderen!
Die Konzeption müßte meines Erachtens folgende sein: Da man hier in dem Land die Veröffentlichungspolitik ... die Äußerungsmöglichkeiten der Kunst, die Verbreitung eigenständigen, unvorgedachten Gedanken- und Sprachvorkommens als eingeschränkt, zensiert, verboten, ja fast vernichtet ansehen muß, sind derartige Publikationsformen, wie ich sie in "Anschlag" vermutete, eine äußerst wertvolle, unumgängliche und mit allem Ernst und mit Behutsamkeit zu unternehmende Art, uns vor weiteren Verlusten an Stimmen oder Texten zu bewahren, die nicht in irgendeiner Form dem Banalitätsgebot der Bewußtseinsindustrie die Hand reichen. - Aber ich kann in diesem ersten Versuch leider keinen Text finden, der meines Erachtens ein weitergehendes Interesse, als das des Selbstgenügens des jeweiligen Autors, verdient. Ich muß sogar sagen, daß die "künstlerischen Ergüsse" (was Euer Wort ist) des vorgedachten, oder nachempfundenen Denkens, wie es in etwa das Poetenseminar-Poesiealbum bringt - und damit die Druckerschwärze verbraucht, die Euch zustehen könnte - besser gearbeitet sind, teilweise, als die Euren, wenn auch dieses Bessere keines ist, weil es in Wirklichkeit die Schmalheit der zerebralen Frustration ist.
So, nun bitte ich Euch, diese wirklich außerordentliche Kritik - die womöglich auf den ersten Blick zuviel verlangt: aber dem Ansatz nach müßte Euer Vorhaben doch von solchen Vorstellungen ausgehen - kühl zu überdenken. Glaubt mir, ich will und kann nicht mitmachen, weil ich die Konzeption ~~da~~ für von Grund auf verfehlt halte. Wenn ich das zweite Heft vor die Augen kriegen sollte, und ich sehe dann etwas anderes, dann reden wir weiter.
...
Ansonsten wünsche ich Euch natürlich Erfolg und ... bessere Texte. Aber die kann man nicht zaubern.

Herzliche Grüße, Wolfgang Hilbig

Anschlag's equivocation was not missed by its ostensible allies. Issue two (1984), for example includes the reproduction of a scathing letter from the influential experimental writer Wolfgang Hilbig. Expressing regrets that he could not provide the magazine with a contribution, he writes, "Though I would so much like to support your efforts, unfortunately I see nothing new here."[28] He continues: "Believe me, I cannot and will not participate, because the concept [of this publication] has so miserably failed." Hilbig closes his letter with a meaningful ellipsis: "I definitely wish you success and . . . better texts." The editors of *Anschlag* reprinted the fifty-line letter in full. In this—an effectively illegal operation's second attempt—the editors elected to put themselves in the sightlines of critique. Why not succumb to Hilbig's wounding assessment? And why reproduce it, rather than disregard its mean accusations of naiveté and lack of talent? The editors provided no commentary to contextualize or defend the journal against this letter. Future issues likewise do not reveal the discussions or frustrations of the authors, let alone the magazine's editorial team. *Anschlag* does not document these discussions, but nevertheless its evolution in concept and content suggest a heady dialogue off page. In general, among East German samizdat, the norm seems to have been to weather the storm and publish critique. This vulnerability differentiated these independent publications from the ideological texts offered in the official press, which by and large served only to unquestionably propagate the government's ideology.

Nevertheless, even though *Anschlag* published critique, it did not publish debate until it produced a special issue on EIGEN+ART in 1988 entitled "EIGEN+ART im Gespräch" (EIGEN+ART in conversation). This lack of debate is fairly consistent across East German samizdat, where an absence of dialogical texts is conspicuous. Yet this absence certainly does not imply that the scene was more cohesive or internally resilient than any equivalent counterpublics in other contexts. To the contrary, competition and individuation were manifest, perhaps partly in reaction to the experience of being socialized in a country that emphasized the heroism of the communally minded individual while simultaneously maintaining clear

7.4

Wolfgang Hilbig. "Liebe Angelika Klüssendorf" (Dear Angelika Klüssendorf). *Anschlag*, no. 2 (1984). Image courtesy of the Beinecke Rare Book and Manuscript Library, Yale University. Reprinted with fair use.

hierarchies that prioritized individual action. Less cynically, the experimental arts scene of the GDR was preoccupied with a somewhat naïve idea of "authenticity," where the goal was to express oneself unimpeded by the social or political structure. For some, authenticity meant unrestricted access to a public platform. On his magazine, Warnke reflects that "*Entwerter/Oder* was an attempt to independently bring the writing made 'for the drawer only' to an end, both for itself and in order to open up and assert a free space for others."[29] Although he adapted his publication over time, Warnke's wish to produce a platform for unrestricted self-expression represented a formative impulse for his and similar initiatives, particularly in the early 1980s when the independent publication movement began in earnest. As one young writer put it: "I already grew up in a frustrated society. For me disappointment is no longer something to be experienced; rather it is a precondition of life."[30] For others, authenticity could be achieved only through debate. They believed that a critical culture required some level of exclusion. Indeed, Karim Saab's "dare for democracy" was predicated on a visionary editorial team, "which could debate and discuss the quality of texts."[31] The curator Christoph Tannert represents a second impulse that advocated for a more selective form of experimental culture when he laments that "the majority of the subcultural and agitating artists in the GDR had no desire to flee the embrace of one side for the embrace of the other side. The interest to conspiratorially conceive of a political and social change was quite small. People satisfied themselves with spontaneous protests and were otherwise happy with receiving praise from like-minded people."[32] Even though both *Anschlag* and EIGEN+ART began as projects that erred on the side of inclusivity, they would soon become more discerning. Ultimately, as both projects became more established in the scene, they began to embrace the more selective, arguably more confrontational, approach that Tannert's observation deems necessary.

By 1986 *Anschlag* would no longer publish just any submission. Saab, actually citing Hilbig's critique as an influence, explains that three issues after they printed his letter, the editorial team decided to increase production "so that we would no longer act like criminals in fear of the state."[33] They also adopted a more selective editorial vision. The magazine immediately faced criticism from contributors who interpreted the new submission policy as a form of censorship. *Anschlag* defector Torsten Ziesche would begin his own aptly titled publication *Glasnost* in protest, "for which we were very grateful," Saab reflects.[34] In fact, in 1987—the year after *Anschlag*'s new submission policy went into effect—two other independent magazines began production in Leipzig, thus quadrupling the total number of publications

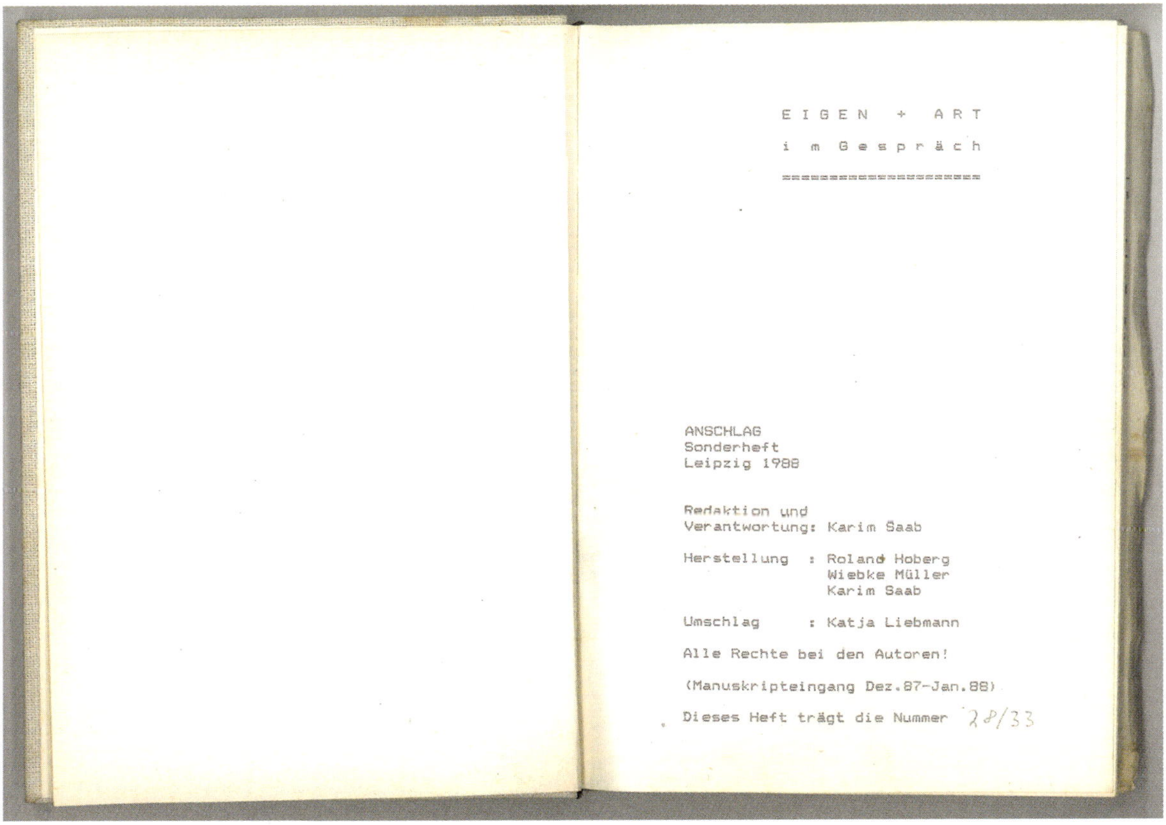

E I G E N + A R T

i m G e s p r ä c h

ANSCHLAG
Sonderheft
Leipzig 1988

Redaktion und
Verantwortung: Karim Saab

Herstellung : Roland Hoberg
Wiebke Müller
Karim Saab

Umschlag : Katja Liebmann

Alle Rechte bei den Autoren!

(Manuskripteingang Dez.87-Jan.88)

Dieses Heft trägt die Nummer 28/33

7.5

"EIGEN+ART im Gespräch" (EIGEN+ART in conversation), front matter. Special issue of *Anschlag* (1988). Reprinted with the permission of the Archiv EIGEN+ART, Potsdam and Gerd Harry "Judy" Lybke. © 2020 by the Archiv EIGEN+ART.

based in the city from one to four. The first peak production of East German samizdat also occurred in 1987, with sixteen distinct publications nationwide, up nine from the year prior.[35]

Lybke faced similar criticism in 1985 when he moved EIGEN+ART from his apartment, an essentially clandestine location, to a larger and more public-facing space in a former chemical workshop. It soon became clear that he would run the gallery with a selective, curatorial approach, rather than as a team-led *Produzentengalerie* (collective gallery), as some had expected. The controversy around the gallery is particularly well documented in "EIGEN+ART in Conversation," *Anschlag*'s special issue from 1988. One exchange between Saab and Lybke from a seventeen-page interview provides an introductory frame to both the motivation for the issue and the parallel contexts within which the magazine and the gallery emerged:

KARIM SAAB: Being an *Anschlag* collaborator, your situation is all too familiar to me. We too are often criticized and asked why we have not taken this or that text. This is always accompanied by the accusation that we are no different from the state institutions. But it is not our intention to make a quickly produced publication, but rather to produce edited volumes on our terms. And the E+A walls are certainly also not meant to be bulletin boards for just anybody. Because we strive to be selective—and feel we are obligated to do so—people like to contest our alternative status.

JUDY LYBKE: Nevertheless, you are in a better situation. In the GDR, there are still other venues where people can publish. E+A is out on a limb all by itself. I think it is really, really unfortunate that the example of E+A has not caught on, and that up until now there are not comparable projects in other cities. Certainly, we cannot forget that the Galerie fotogen flourished in Dresden until the city council shut it down. Unfortunately, other activities are only happening on smaller scales, and this activity is pretty inconsistent.[36]

Lybke identifies a resounding crisis—the lack of autonomous galleries—and laments the recent loss of the Galerie fotogen. This was Claudia "Wanda" Reichardt's side project to the groundbreaking work she did at the student club at the Dresden Academy of Fine Arts (Hochschule für Bildende Künste) in the mid to late 1980s. Significantly, Reichardt continued programming in Galerie fotogen for another three years after officials ordered its closure in 1987. Thereafter the gallery went essentially back into the underground until Reichardt closed it for good in 1990.[37] The kind of independently run and public-facing spaces Lybke desired were indeed rare.

Elsewhere in the interview with Saab, Lybke comments on a need for competition both to inspire better exhibitions and to fortify the autonomous scene. Strength in numbers was a necessity in a country that disincentivized private cultural initiatives. The fact that EIGEN+ART was one of the GDR's few successful and lasting autonomous galleries reflects as much Lybke's unique blend of improvisation and careful preparation as it does the reality of a creative subculture that had yet to become secure.

A FUTURE IN THE MAKING: EIGEN+ART'S ARCHIVE DREAMS

Ample attention has been paid to EIGEN+ART's formative history, as well as to its vast and energetic exhibition and programming schedule.[38] To summarize briefly, in 1983 after meeting artists through his work as a nude model at the Academy of Fine Arts in Leipzig (Hochschule für Grafik und Buchkunst), Lybke decided to turn the home he shared with his friend Torsten Schilling into a gallery. For his first exhibition opening, on April 10, 1983, at the then-named Galerie am Körnerplatz (Gallery on Koernerplace), Lybke greeted his guests at the door naked (electing later to don his bathrobe). He tied his messy mop of red curls to the top of his head and stuck three eggs in it as if it were a nest. The eccentricity was actually a fairly intricate ruse. Because it was illegal to host large non-work-related gatherings in private homes, Lybke could, if necessary, claim that his immodest clothing was his work attire, and his hairstyle some sort of drawing challenge.[39] Two years and sixteen exhibitions later, more carefully plotted subterfuge would allow him to establish an essentially legal gallery in a more professional space; the gallery would adopt the handle EIGEN+ART at this time. By formally registering his gallery as the studio of Akos Novaky, a member of the Union of Fine Artists, Lybke circumvented a long list of laws that left autonomous galleries vulnerable to state closure. These laws included prohibitions against public assembly without prior permission (*Veranstaltungsverordnung*), laws against noise and disturbance (*Ordnungswidrigkeiten*), misuse of living space (*Lenkung des Wohnraums*), and a prohibition against privately run businesses (*Gewerbetätigkeit*).[40] Technically, EIGEN+ART was not a gallery but a workshop that artists could legally rent and open up to the public for exhibitions. Here, it is important to recall that *Anschlag* also found an alternative legal means to create a more innovative publication when it named itself an artist portfolio. Lybke faced only one precondition when he formally registered

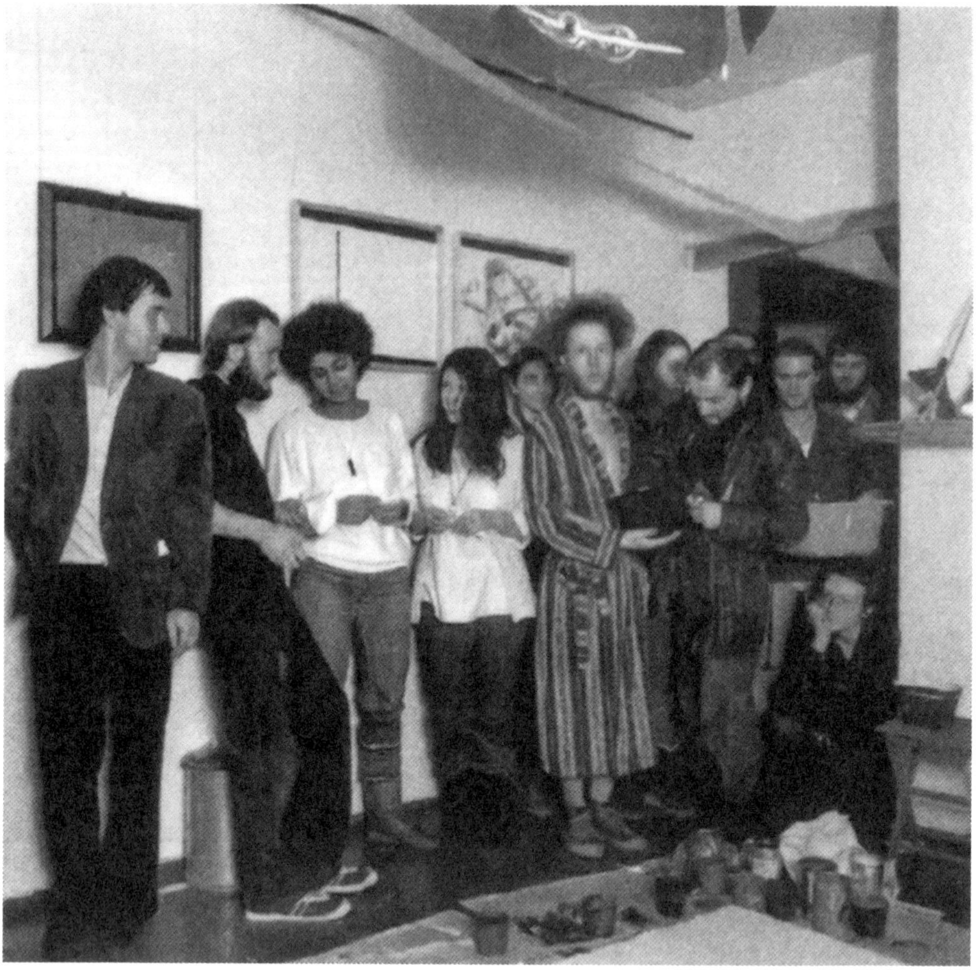

7.6

Gerd Harry "Judy" Lybke greets his guests at an opening at the Galerie am Körnerplatz, 1983. Photograph by Thomas Steinert. Reprinted with the permission of the Archiv EIGEN+ART, Potsdam, Gerd Harry "Judy" Lybke and the Josef Fillipp Gallery. © 1983 by Thomas Steinert.

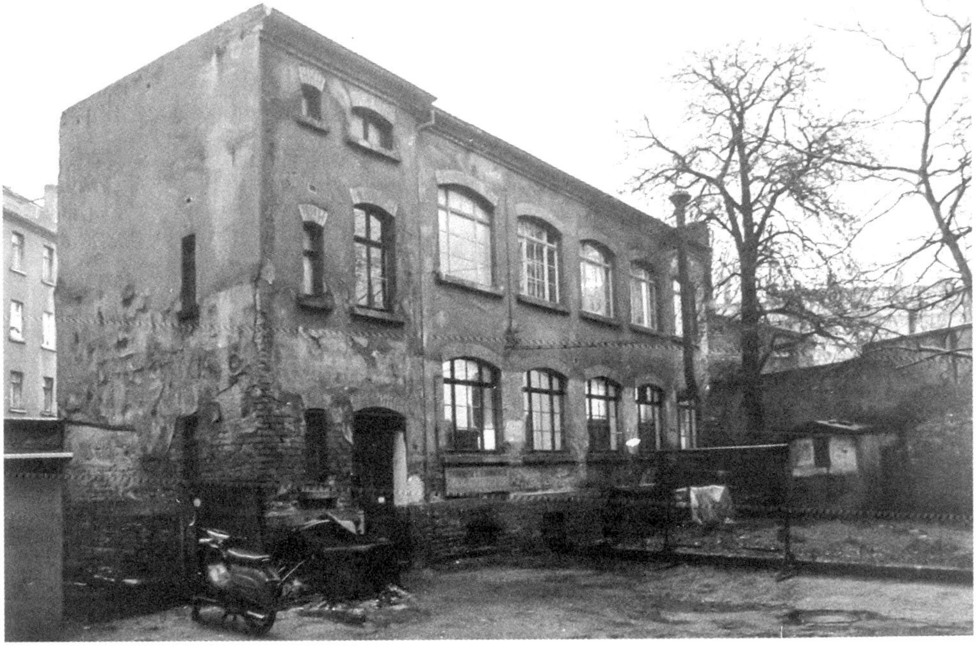

7.7

Gallery EIGEN+ART façade. Ca. 1985. Located in the interior courtyard of the Fritz-Austel-Straße 31, Leipzig. Photograph by Christian Günther. Reprinted with the permission of Christian Günther. Image provided by Uta Grundmann. © 1985 (?) by Christian Günther.

EIGEN+ART as a workshop: the artists had to keep open hours for the public to visit. This requirement actually proved another formal protection. The GDR's vision of a nation united by culture idealized contact between everyday citizens and artists. In theory, then, EIGEN+ART performed a kind of community and state socialist service by granting public access to its artists.

Lybke, who ran his gallery singlehandedly, was both inventive and truly indefatigable. The exhibitions at EIGEN+ART were nearly continuous, with an average of only four days scheduled in between each show. Artists came and went with complicated projects. The gallery's open-door policy and its ancillary events resulted in an average of three to six hundred visitors per exhibition.[41] Certainly other galleries and exhibition projects during this period were equally ambitious. The Erster Leipziger Herbstsalon (First Leipzig Autumn Salon) of 1984 had been the inspiration for Lybke's move to this more public gallery space in 1985. A truly ingenious deception, the salon involved a group of union artists (Lutz Dammbeck, Günter Firit, Hans-Hendrick Grimmling, Frieder Heinze, Günther Huniat, and Olaf Wegewitz) who took advantage of an overlooked bureaucratic loophole in the Leipzig Trade Fair that allowed anyone in the Union of Fine Artists to officially rent a thousand-square-meter exhibit hall. It was only after the work of the six artists was already installed that officials at the fair caught wind of the exhibition, which featured experimental forms of art—from installation to conceptual works and abstract painting. Over the next four weeks, nearly ten thousand visitors from in and outside of the GDR saw the show.[42] EIGEN+ART's first exhibition, the *Stifterausstellung* (donor show), featured the First Leipzig Autumn Salon artists, who sold their work in support of the new gallery, which they believed would follow the collaborative spirit their trade fair show had embodied. Thereafter, Lybke abandoned any official affiliation with the group of older artists, much to their dismay. Indeed, EIGEN+ART's quick evolution from a collective gallery to a one-man operation became a serious point of contention between Lybke and the Autumn Salon artists and many others.

Equal to the EIGEN+ART exhibitions was the exhaustive archive that Lybke maintained. The gallery's network of artists gained traction internationally in the surfeit of EIGEN+ART documentation as well as the distribution of that archive in a series of annual publications.[43] Though productions were small, these books were precisely crafted, simultaneously sharing the work of the EIGEN+ART artists and establishing the gallery's name, both in the GDR and beyond. More than a marketing ploy, however, Lybke describes the documentation as "important to us. If we were kicked out of the GDR, we would always have something to show for ourselves."[44] His attention to documentation echoes the drive to self-historicize that the curator Zdenka Badovinac identifies as foundational to the experimental culture of the late Eastern Bloc period. Specifically, she stresses that artists of the 1980s felt compelled to prove their actions to outsiders, and especially to future audiences.[45] By consciously engaging in the act of "historicizing their own traditions," artists actively shaped a public record.[46] The Eastern Bloc artist's archive is deliberately oriented toward two temporalities. Self-archiving reflected the related impulses to be accountable in the present and to preserve something for the future. A material mark of an artistic practice—such as a poster, a documentary photograph, or a publication—could establish a person in their own time, as well as in the times to come. Badovinac explains that artists in the Eastern Bloc were preoccupied with the future because they anticipated the imminent failure of the socialist cultural landscape and wanted to prove that they had done something with their lives independent of a soon-to-be-irrelevant official culture. For Lybke, his fastidious archival practice extended the presence and influence of his gallery beyond the spatiotemporal limitations of a country walled in, both literally and figuratively, politically and culturally. The archive was a symptom of his larger ambition; its dissemination in publications a means of realizing that dream.

In 1986, EIGEN+ART released its first annual yearbook. Two members of *Anschlag*'s core team—Karin Wieckhorst (who organized photography for the magazine) and Wiebke Müller (an editor and also the *Anschlag* bookbinder)—also collaborated with the Leipzig gallery on documenting, archiving, and distributing its work in publication form. Many of Wieckhorst's photographs appear in the yearbooks, as well. From her solo exhibition *Begegnungen in Ateliers* (*Studio Visits*, 1987), in which she recorded the work of many of the experimental scene's most influential painters, to her documentation of performances and exhibition openings at EIGEN+ART, the gallery's comprehensive archive is clearly indebted to this photographer, who received no remuneration for her efforts. Müller bound the yearbooks, which as opposed to *Anschlag*'s characteristic whimsy and DIY material makeup, followed an austere format of single-sided dot matrix texts and black-and-white photographs housed in a simple, unmarked cover. The yearbooks consist primarily of a chronological overview of the shows that had taken place in the previous year. Each exhibition is represented in a several-page spread that contains a series of photographs—including a portrait of each artist and installation shots—followed

by artist statements and biographies. Often, copies of the speeches read at gallery openings appeared in the yearbooks. Less frequently, other mostly editorial texts or press clippings were gathered from over the course of the year. Lybke also produced annual portfolios of original artworks made by the artists who had been exhibited in the gallery. He sold the portfolios and yearbooks abroad, particularly to West Germans who were drawn to what one reporter in the *Frankfurter Allgemeine Zeitung* described as the romantic illusion of the GDR's "poor dissidents."[47] By all accounts, these western contacts provided EIGEN+ART both notoriety and necessary financial support.

In fact, Lybke's extensive Stasi file reveals that authorities were more preoccupied with the potential money he was making from supporters abroad than they were with the outlandish exhibitions that he programmed in his gallery. The following excerpt is exemplary: "The MfS [Ministerium für Staatssicherheit, or Stasi] is aware that substantial portions of the catalog, in particular the texts, were printed in West Germany. In that case, the L.[48] is using his extensive contacts to citizens in the NSW [*nichtsozialistische Wirtschaft*, nonsocialist economic zone]. It may be assumed that the L. is making a living through the sale of these catalogs, and in so doing is breaking and working around existing laws for the production and distribution of printed goods."[49] The report demonstrates that the state security apparatus relied on legalese, rather than a moral authority, to control experimental culture. Appeals to socialism's claim to a higher cultural order clearly rang hollow, even to those in power. In fact, sales to the West not only brought financial support to the gallery but also granted Lybke a kind of diplomatic immunity; the East German state's fear of what the Germanist David Bathrick calls the "power of speech"[50] extended to bad press abroad.[51] It is thus not surprising that Lybke would be admitted into the Union of Fine Artists as an autodidact art historian in 1988.

7.8

Vier Jahre EIGEN+ART (Four years of EIGEN+ART). 1989. A2 paper, bound with string. Reprinted with the permission of Gerd Harry "Judy" Lybke. Image courtesy of the Beinecke Rare Book and Manuscript Library, Yale University. © 1989 by Gerd Harry "Judy" Lybke.

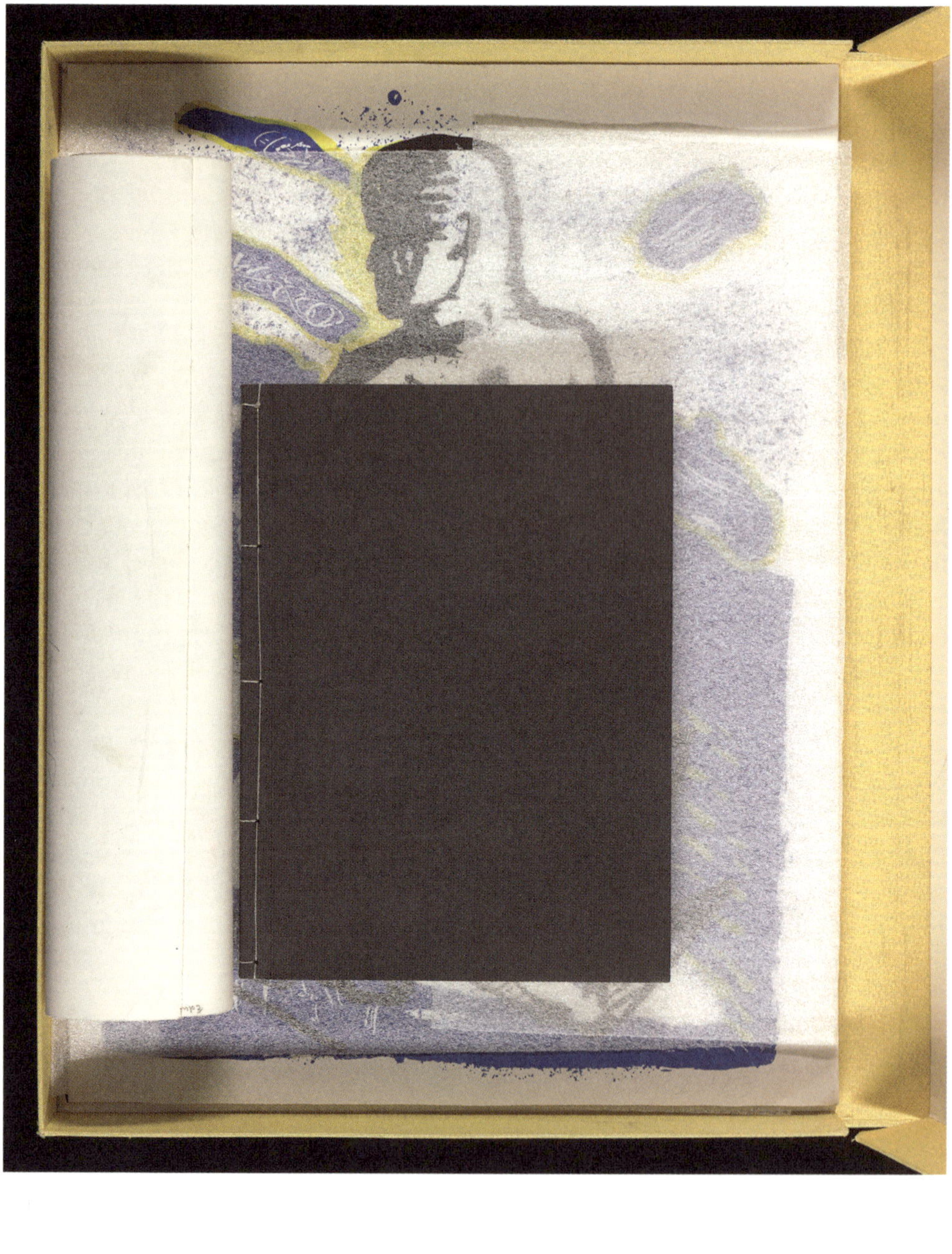

SUI GENERIS: "EIGEN+ART IM GESPRÄCH"

In 1988, EIGEN+ART partnered with *Anschlag* to produce "EIGEN+ART in Conversation." The special issue—the first and last of its kind—is important because it represents a turning point in East German samizdat. Rarely before had unofficial magazines published the experimental art scene's debate culture so candidly. Its criticality reflected the burgeoning ethos of newly established publications, which embraced the more selective vision of authenticity that both *Anschlag* and EIGEN+ART championed.

Cloth-bound and unmarked, "EIGEN+ART in Conversation" is visually quite understated within the scope of *Anschlag*'s production. Looking more like a paperback than a piece of samizdat, the issue matches the EIGEN+ART style of publication. About forty reports[52] by artists, writers, gallery visitors, art historians, and even West Germans on the topic of EIGEN+ART fill the issue's several dozen pages. All texts appear on single sides of paper, and are typed in a uniform font printed out on a dot matrix printer. The replacement of typewritten texts with computer-processed ones achieves a new visual uniformity in the *Anschlag* format that conforms to the look and design of the gallery's own publications. The interview quoted earlier between *Anschlag*'s editor Karim Saab and EIGEN+ART gallerist Judy Lybke closes the issue. Wiebke Müller, as always, bound the volume, which appeared in a run of ninety-nine.

Seven black-and-white snapshots inserted at random in the issue trace the route from Leipzig's main train station to the EIGEN+ART gallery south of the city center. The trip takes about a half hour and is delineated by digital time stamps that begin the journey from the station at 2:53 PM and end at the gallery's front door at 3:21 PM. Conspicuously placed, though unacknowledged in the text, the series is not creative but documentary. The photographs are candid and unassuming signposts or guides that visually map a route from the city center to the gallery. For

7.9

Various artists. EIGEN+ART *Kassette* (Portfolio). 1988–1989. Dimensions and material variable. Reprinted with the permission of Gerd Harry "Judy" Lybke. Image courtesy of the Beinecke Rare Book and Manuscript Library, Yale University. © 1989 by Gerd Harry "Judy" Lybke.

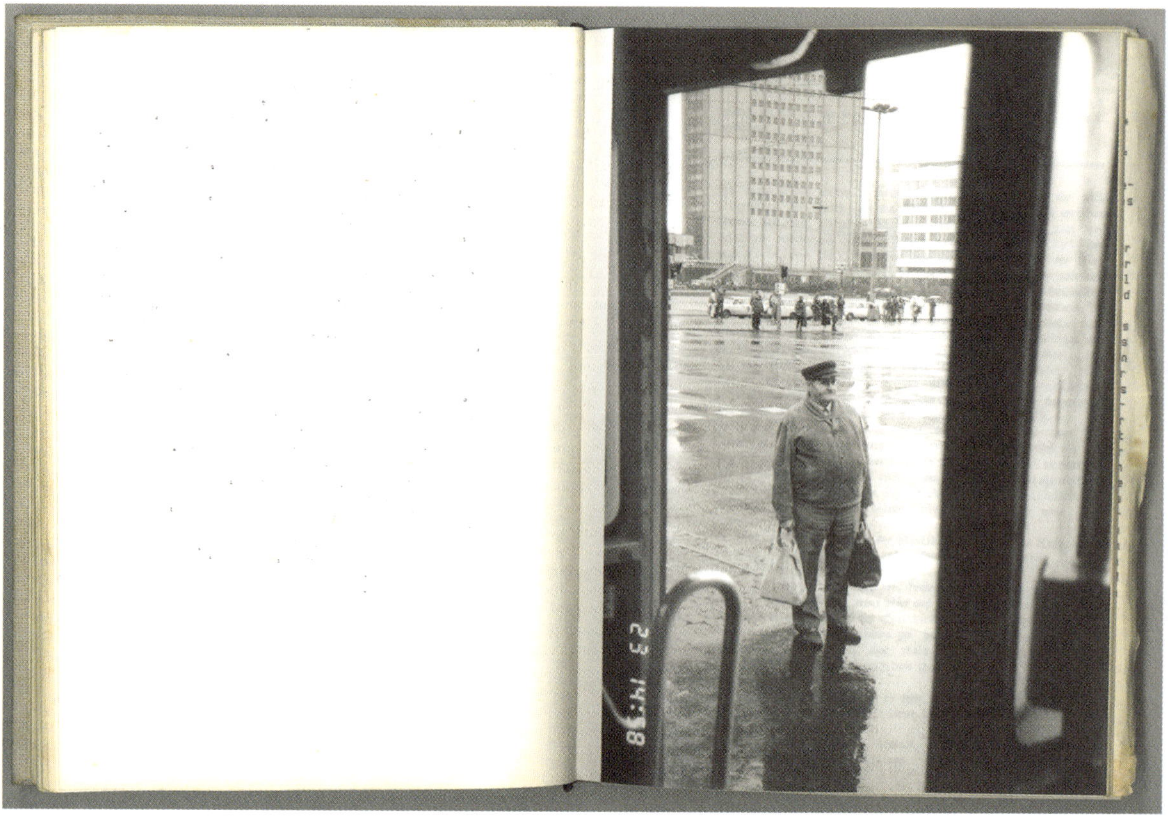

7.10

Unknown photographer. Photograph #3 of seven in "EIGEN+ART im Gespräch" (EIGEN+ART in conversation). *Anschlag* special issue (1988). Reprinted with the permission of the Archiv EIGEN+ART, Potsdam and Gerd Harry "Judy" Lybke. Image courtesy of the Archiv EIGEN+ART, Potsdam. © 1988 by the Archiv EIGEN+ART.

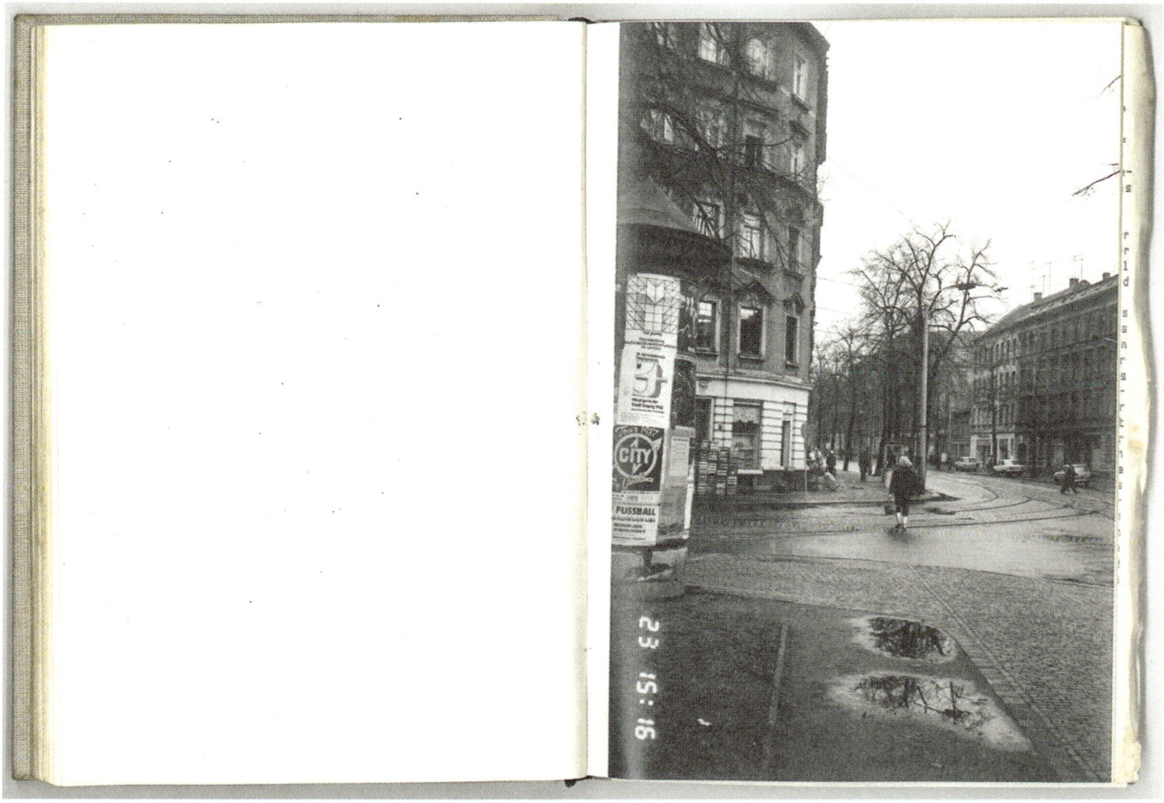

7.11

Unknown photographer. Photograph #4 of seven in "EIGEN+ART im Gespräch" (EIGEN+ART in conversation). *Anschlag* special issue (1988). Reprinted with the permission of the Archiv EIGEN+ART, Potsdam and Gerd Harry "Judy" Lybke. Image courtesy of the Archiv EIGEN+ART, Potsdam. © 1988 by the Archiv EIGEN+ART.

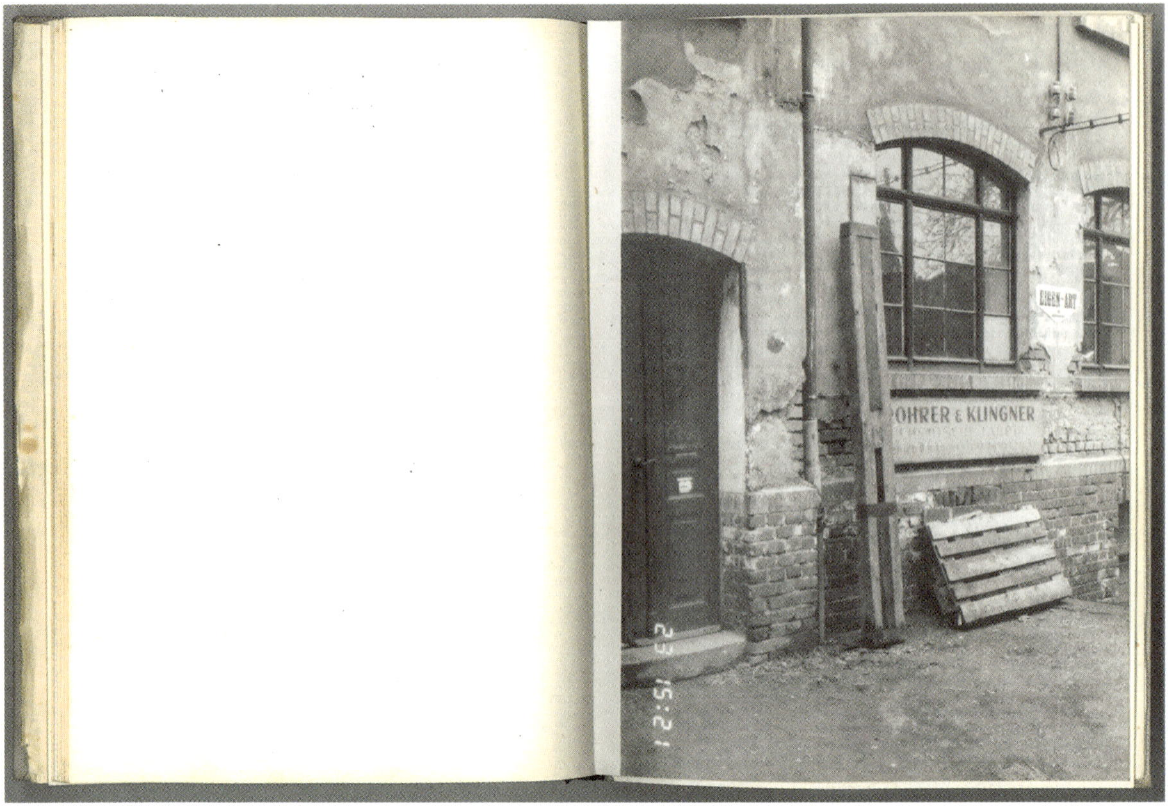

7.12

Unknown photographer. Photograph #6 of seven in "EIGEN+ART im Gespräch" (EIGEN+ART in conversation). *Anschlag* special issue (1988). Reprinted with the permission of the Archiv EIGEN+ART, Potsdam and Gerd Harry "Judy" Lybke. Image courtesy of the Archiv EIGEN+ART, Potsdam. © 1988 by the Archiv EIGEN+ART.

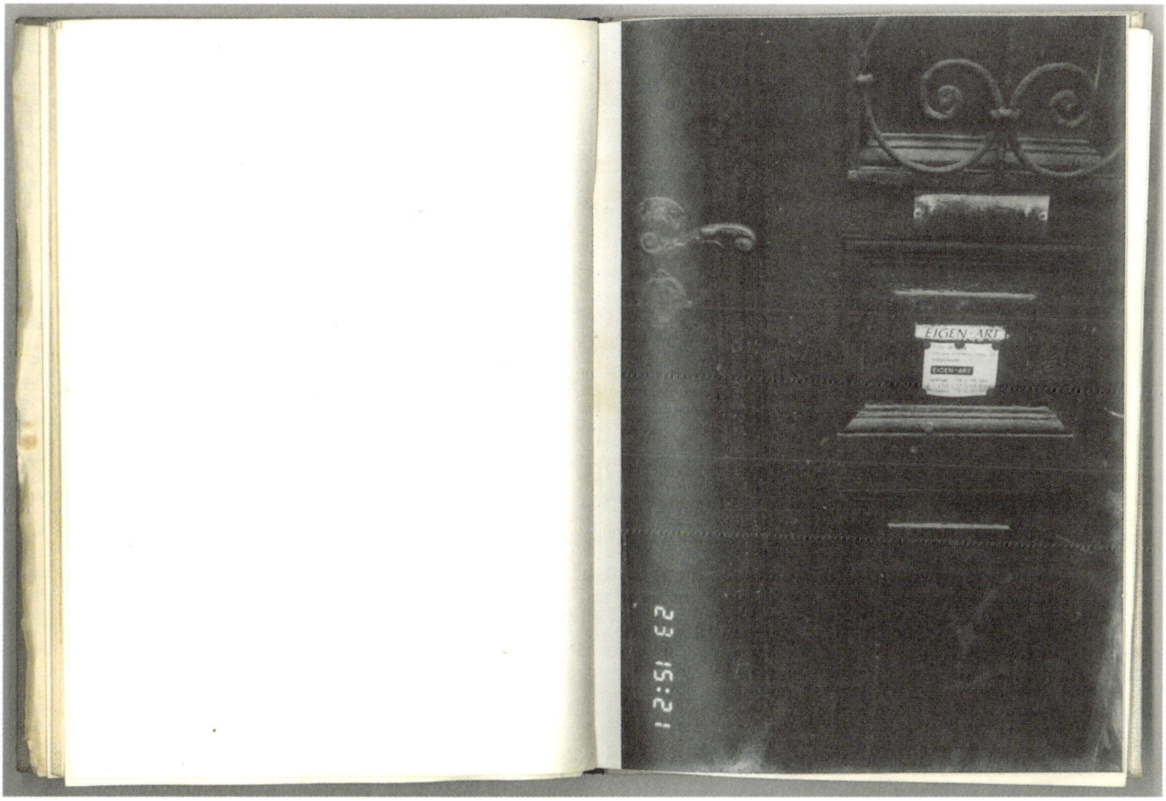

7.13

Unknown photographer. Photograph #7 of seven in "EIGEN+ART im Gespräch" (EIGEN+ART in conversation). *Anschlag* special issue (1988). Reprinted with the permission of the Archiv EIGEN+ART, Potsdam and Gerd Harry "Judy" Lybke. Image courtesy of the Archiv EIGEN+ART, Potsdam.

example, in image number three, a portly gentleman stands in a wet plaza carrying two plastic shopping bags. The doors to a tram (entered sometime after image number two) frame his rotund figure as he stares into the distance, unaware of his observer. Image number four is shot about twenty minutes later, off the tram and on a rain-dampened street. The photographer trails behind a woman carrying a parcel. She crosses a street, and is flanked by tall unrenovated apartment buildings in the working-class neighborhood of Connewitz. The sixth and seventh images show, first, the door to the gallery from an angled approach, and then finally, a close-up on the white EIGEN+ART nameplate. The seven-part path maps an easy-to-follow trail from the train station to the artistic enclave, bringing the out-of-town guest safely to the EIGEN+ART doorstep. In this regard, the mapping system contributes quite literally to the material-based network that spread the word about the experimental art scene.

The reports on the gallery that fill the majority of "EIGEN+ART in Conversation" reflect the expectations and tensions that surrounded Lybke's gallery. This is no glorified celebration of an autonomous gallery. Rather, the special issue of *Anschlag* represents a full spectrum of opinion from laudatory encouragement—"EIGEN+ART in its humanistic-pluralistic character knows no bounds"[53]—to cautious optimism—"E+A is not flawless, and is as such vital"[54]—to unambiguous censure: "E+A is an esoteric business for Judy, a kind of masturbation."[55] Saab, who initiated and edited the issue, had envisioned that it would serve as a kind of open forum for debate. He reflects, "I am particularly proud of this issue, which practiced a kind of democratic expression that was not possible in the GDR outside the church. It was meant to be a discussion platform. There were no models for this kind of work."[56] In fact, Lybke explains in the interview with Saab that "EIGEN+ART in Conversation" arose as a direct response to the state's confiscation of the gallery's visitor book in 1986. To a small extent, the publication remedied the loss of this platform, an ostensible host for sharing sentiments about the space with a broader—and, to some extent, unanticipated—public. It is significant that "EIGEN+ART in Conversation" was *Anschlag*'s highest print run. At ninety-nine (and with an estimated ten to twenty readers per issue), the audience was sizable. These numbers certainly exceeded the confines of the experimental art scene's few hundred most active members.

Many contributors to the issue reported a skeptical but supportive attitude. They urged the gallery to take more risks, to facilitate more debate, and to exhibit a broader range of artists. Christoph Tannert's sharp-tongued observations reflect the ambivalence of many of the gallery's supporters: "Will E+A continue to bumble along as before, without competition, as a sterile test site, sooner or later coming dangerously close to the edge of self-satisfaction?"[57] He synthesizes the greatest problematic of the period. Although many artists in the GDR yearned for greater artistic autonomy, many understood that creative sovereignty was meaningless in a vacuum. This problem is ultimately a reflection of the lack of variety afforded by the East German public sphere. While publications like *Anschlag* provided a space to host open debate and dialogue about art and its intersections with politics and aesthetic philosophy, a gallery like EIGEN+ART assumed the role of an autonomous commons. This was the space where debate took place in person and, more importantly, was enacted through the assembly of bodies (and artworks) excluded from official culture.

Nevertheless, Lybke would be the first to admit the failure of his gallery—or, better said, its inadequacy. In his conversation with Saab, he returns frequently to the dialogical vision he had for EIGEN+ART, and the inability to achieve that vision without other people willing to take the same kind of risks he had taken. Although the workshop status of the gallery had been a good initial strategy to navigate the GDR's cultural bureaucracy, Lybke clearly wanted the experimental scene to become more consistent and less improvisational. For him, that power resided in the hands of his gallery visitors and artists, whom he urges to use the space for open exchange, dialogue, and debate. In "EIGEN+ART in Conversation," Lybke laments that few artists used the open gallery hours as a time to engage with visitors, who themselves did not grab the opportunity to read the many magazines, including *Anschlag*, that he laid out for them: "Maybe it is just a typical phenomenon under our current circumstances that open spaces are used too little." There is something generous in this perspective, which suggests that perhaps the East German public needed a little more time to grow accustomed to autonomous space before they would really know how to engage. Similarly, a reticence to interact with one another reveals a kind of traumatic acculturation; turning inward had become a defensive strategy in a country whose public sphere was more ritualistic and superficial than sincere in its collectivity.[58]

Lybke eventually summarizes the need: "Taking inventory is important, whereby I mean more than documentation. This interview is for me the kind of inventory that I mean, and should continue." What are needed, he continues, are "interviews in which the voiceless can develop their voices and the ideologues do not abuse their dominance and everyone seeks to acknowledge the uniqueness of the other."

To which, Saab asks, "A world at home, instead of being at home in the world?" Lybke offers a candid response: "This question is not at all funny. E+A cannot be complacent." The interview concludes quickly thereafter, with Lybke emphasizing a necessity for more publications like "EIGEN+ART in Conversation": "The model must be made even more public, so that people can see that this is working, and so that it will be adopted in other places." To an important extent, that kind of dialogue was beginning to happen in the publications of the late 1980s. In 1989, its second and final year, *Liane*—notable for its coverage of the visual arts as well as its pointed thematic issues—dedicated its final publication to the subject of alternative galleries. EIGEN+ART was one of six spaces analyzed. Were it not for the fall of the Berlin Wall in November 1989—the same month that the issue of *Liane* came out—perhaps this text would have contributed to the movement Lybke envisioned. And yet the signs of a sustainable (let alone sustained) alternative culture continued to be uncertain. *Liane* had already lost at least one ally when *Anschlag* abruptly ended in May 1989 after Saab became the third and last of its editors to leave the country. Three special issues of *Anschlag* were in the planning stage at that time. One was to have reported on visits to West Germany by East Germans, an option newly extended to more of the GDR's citizens. Two other issues were to have looked at the citizen opposition movements in Poland and Czechoslovakia. The lure of the West had, however, outweighed the possibilities of the walled-in East for Saab. What is left, then, is the significant role that the writing of history plays in shaping the understanding of what was once possible. Such narratives reveal what citizens did to make a world for themselves that was meaningful, so they could both build a world at home and be at home in the world.

CODA

There Is No East German Art without East Germany

An implied contextual necessity foregrounds GDR-era art practices. Namely, the photography, performance art, films, events, collaborations, publications, and galleries described in this book were all products of the German Democratic Republic (GDR), both implicitly and explicitly. This quality does not come at the exclusion of the globally or historically minded work pursued by the members of the experimental scene (or by state artists, for that matter). The defining attachment of the art of East Germany to the state is particularly evident in the ways in which the practices of individual artists changed in the wake of the GDR's opening to the West in 1989. Although all members of the cast of characters in this book pursued creative lives after this point—and many did so without leaving their homes in the former East German states—the directions they took and the range of their success varied considerably.

Many artists, including the photographer Thomas Florschuetz and the painter Cornelia Schleime, had already left the GDR well before the massive social movement that led to the country's rapid demise in 1989. After moving to West Berlin in 1988, Florschuetz developed his already quiet, introspective, and almost scientific photography into even deeper camera-enabled close examinations of the world, particularly in moments of transition, such as water droplets condensing on a glass or light passing through skin or flower petals. After state-imposed prohibitions prevented her from exhibiting her paintings in the GDR, Schleime, a 1984 émigré, quickly returned to painting in her new environment in West Berlin. Like Florschuetz, she seized the opportunity to travel and conduct artist residencies abroad. Gino Hahnemann, who chose to remain in the GDR, also enjoyed the improved mobility afforded by open borders, but his film practice never returned to its mid-1980s fever pitch. In fact, according to his longtime partner, Matthias Fischer, Hahnemann had some difficulty adjusting to the new competitive realities of the newly "freed" East.[1] Many of his new friends who came from West Germany also could not quite grasp the significance of the East German background, including the nuances of governmental control and artistic freedom described throughout this book. In short, it was difficult for Hahnemann to find people who saw him (or any other artist who had lived in East Germany, for that matter) as an independent producer. Attendance at screenings, exhibitions, and readings also waned as a seemingly limitless world of options suddenly oversaturated the scene, making its erstwhile coherence no longer necessary, or even relevant.

Few collective projects or independently run galleries and publications continued after reunification. The German term for the dissolution of East Germany is the *Wende*, the turn; in many ways, that turn has been a turn away. Karim Saab, for example, betrays an apocryphal impulse when describing the significance of his work with the independent magazine *Anschlag*: "After '89 I just didn't deal with that anymore. Back then it was just important to do something. This was part of my self-worth."[2] The rapid end to most of the GDR's samizdat may be attributed to a lack of perceived necessity for such alternatives in a democratic context where the free exchange of ideas is a central tenet (albeit often in name only). That being said, Uwe Warnke, who began publishing the magazine *Entwerter/Oder* (Cancelation/other)[3] in 1982, continues to produce new issues. He also participates in the historicization of samizdat, as well as photography, in scholarly texts and art exhibitions.[4]

The shift from a socialist to a capitalist economic system was for some an existential shock, for others an opportunity. Gundula Schulze Eldowy,[5] upon the invitation of her mentor, the photographer Robert Frank, moved immediately to New York City after the wall fell. She experienced notable successes, including gallery representation at PACE gallery, exhibitions in the United States and worldwide, and sales to the Museum of Modern Art's photography collection. Within a few years, however, she left the United States, electing to call first Egypt and then Peru her new home. Gerd Harry "Judy" Lybke of EIGEN+ART readily dove into the newly opened art market. He moved his Leipzig gallery from a courtyard workshop in a working-class neighborhood to a more visible space in the city center. A second space in Berlin's Mitte district soon followed. In fact, Lybke's efforts to reinvigorate this former East Berlin neighborhood helped to establish it as the gallery and boutique hotspot it is today. Similar efforts to expand his EIGEN+ART enterprise internationally—with forays in New York City and Tokyo—ultimately failed. Nevertheless, the continued success of EIGEN+ART, which is one of Germany's top commercial galleries today, is clearly indebted to the marketing acumen of its director. Of course, as described in this book's previous chapter, Lybke's notable efforts to document and publicize EIGEN+ART originated well before the GDR's collapse.

Most who remained in the former East German states did not see the kind of financial or international successes that EIGEN+ART has enjoyed. Nevertheless, for people like Gabriele Stötzer,[6] this does not seem to have been the point. Her creative pursuits in the GDR fluidly connect to her post-reunification practice. In addition to her solo writing and art practices, she has continued to work with some of the original women in her artist group, including in the establishment of a contemporary art space. The Kunsthaus Erfurt (Art House Erfurt) still exists and is managed by Monique Förster of the Künstlerinnengruppe Exterra XX (Women Artists Group Exterra XX). Though not comparable to the international success that the EIGEN+ART gallery has enjoyed, the continued accomplishments of the former members of the Erfurt-based group may be attributed to their foundational identification with concerns that exceeded the GDR's own material and contextual framework, specifically issues of gender and sexual equality. Stötzer has subsequently become one of the most vocal witnesses to secret police (Ministry for State Security, or Stasi) and other forms of state oppression, experiences that she relates to the country's deficient and contradictory policies on women's rights. Similarly, the curator Christoph Tannert has achieved notable success in the post-Wende period, not least in his work as the project coordinator (1991–2000) and now director (2000–present) of one of Berlin's leading contemporary art spaces, the Künstlerhaus Bethanien. Eugen Blume, who was also a vocal and influential advocate for East Germany's experimental art in the 1980s and a regular collaborator with Tannert, directed Berlin's Hamburger Bahnhof, a globally recognized contemporary art space, from 2001 to 2016. In his high-profile position, Blume never organized an exhibition of East German art at the museum. He did, however, contribute to large and important exhibitions on the theme elsewhere, including at the Martin-Gropius-Bau in Berlin, where he co-curated the *Gegenstimmen* (*Voices of Dissent*) exhibition with Tannert in 2016, and as part of a larger team for the two-part exhibition *Klopfzeichen. Kunst und Kultur der 80er in Deutschland* (*Knocking on the Door: Art and Culture in the 1980s Germany*), held in Leipzig and Essen in 2002.

EULOGIES FOR THE EAST GERMAN STATE: CONFRONTING FRUSTRATION, EXCEEDING ARCHIVES

East Germany remains a condition against which each of the artists, curators, publishers, and gallerists described in this book continue to contend. Are they East German artists, or artists from East Germany? Is their work GDR art or art of the GDR? In contrast to other Eastern Bloc contexts, these questions are especially complicated by the fact that East Germany no longer exists, and that it has no independent cultural history that precedes the Cold War era. Certainly, Czechoslovakia is now the Czech Republic and Slovakia, and the Socialist Federal Republic of Yugoslavia has also been divided into separate nation-states. Nevertheless, those who study the history of these countries contend with a very different set of historical and cultural variables, including a pre-Cold War era legacy, that is not comparable to the situation of the former East German territory.

In her book *What Does It Mean to Be Post-Soviet?*, Madina Tlostanova describes the experience of living through the Soviet Union's collapse as one of awakening "to find ourselves in a new condition that was chosen for us by someone else."[7] She compares the new post-Soviet condition to postcolonialism: "We woke up to a new reality of multiple dependencies and increased unfreedoms in which the previous Soviet unfreedom was not at all lifted, but, on the contrary soon acquired new forms that combined economic exploitation with the lack of rights and renewed ideological control. That is, although the external forms changed, conditions remained the same in their repressive essence."[8] Tlostanova describes a society grappling with a precarious economic condition, and offers in this an explanation for the current surge of xenophobia and anti-refugee politics in the regions of the former Eastern Bloc.[9] These shifts have, of course, also taken place in the eastern part of Germany, where the anti-Islam movement Pegida[10] formed in Dresden in October 2014, exactly twenty-five years after the peaceful protests of the fall of 1989 began. Support for the alt-right political party Alternative für Deutschland (Alternative for Germany, AfD) has consistently been at its highest in the former East German states. Importantly, the country's lowest household incomes and rates of production have disproportionately affected the area.[11] Germany's postsocialist landscape thus follows both social and economic trends witnessed across the territories of the former Eastern Bloc.[12]

Many citizens in Eastern and Central Europe have begun to blame their chronic financial and social insecurity on refugees, particularly those originating in the

Muslim world. In contrast, artists from these countries have begun to explore pre-Soviet-era ethnicities as a means of demonstrating the longevity of globalism's impact on the loss of regional identities. In other words, whereas many are nostalgic for a geographically and ethnically isolated Soviet past, artists diagnose a deeper problem in the roots of global orders, even those that were communist in name. Characteristic of contemporary art from the former Eastern Bloc region is a tendency to consider the contours of a post-Soviet identity through a reckoning with regional difference as well as the homogenizing effects of a globalism twice experienced—first, under Soviet communism and now in postsocialism's neoliberalism (see, for example, the work of the collective Slavs and Tatars).

Germany has yet to see a similar wave of interest in East German identity—and most likely never will, because its Cold War experience coincided with a post-Nazi recovery. Quite simply, it is more difficult to blame the era's new world order on the mission of the Soviet Union, given that Germany needed a major revision after the Second World War. In fact, artists had already begun in the 1980s to disassociate themselves from an East German identity, and saw themselves instead as simply German, or global, artists. For them, reunification meant a return to the more permissive and international cultural environment that Germany had been renowned for in the lead up to its National Socialist takeover. Nevertheless, today museum professionals and scholars alike advocate for a more critical review of the legacies of communism in eastern Germany. Paul Kaiser, a leading expert on the art of East Germany, argues for the inclusion of this work in the collections of major museums located in the former East German territory, so that it can be valued aesthetically as well as historically, including as evidence of an artistic tradition during (and in spite of) communism. In December 2017, Kaiser accused Dresden's Albertinum museum of politicizing their displays of East German art. Noting that the institution's leadership had consistently ignored his suggestions for a stronger investment in East German art, he critiqued their willingness to quickly address the AfD's demands for a stronger "German" legacy in the region's public museums.[13]

It may strike readers as ironic that some of the earliest supporters of East German art have sought to place it within a narrative of German culture, wanting to demonstrate it as a national, specifically *German*, treasure. These advocates argue that art from the GDR maintained the aesthetic and philosophical traditions of Germany more authentically than art made in the more globally oriented Federal Republic of Germany. This perspective has a long history. In 1982, West German author and future Nobel Prize winner Günter Grass observed that "people paint in a more German manner in the GDR. This country and its citizens clearly bear a weightier and less compromising relationship to the German past."[14] In its time, Grass's observation promoted a more discerning and inclusive view of the art of East Germany, but today his words are a strange bedfellow to the nationalistic and isolationist rhetoric of Germany's alt-right movement. East Germany, in short, has been returned to Germany, but its own instantiation of a German (or communist) cultural history remains tentative at best, contradictory at worst.

A defining quality of the GDR, which unites it with the rest of the Eastern Bloc, is its excessive bureaucratic trace. A cumulative and well-collated material mass, the East German archive is vast, comprising mountains of documents left behind by the GDR's exacting institutions, from its Union of Fine Artists to its Ministry for State Security. If the archive, as Jacques Derrida writes, "speak[s] the law,"[15] then these material effects serve to reaffirm the power of the governing over citizens both in their time and for posterity. Authority requires the trace of its power. Who can contest the staggering statistic that in 1988–1989, in addition to its regular employees, the Stasi could count on information from approximately 173,000 unofficial collaborators?[16] The seventy miles of observation files that still remain in the archive certainly attest to the work of an unremitting bureaucracy.

This book closes with these figures not to reinstate the authority of the East German state, but as a reminder that perceived power does not equal actual power. It closes, moreover, with a conscious reminder of Stasi surveillance, which inspired—or engendered—the art with which the book opened. These reminders serve to underscore the centrality of state authority, even as they demonstrate the profound impotence that defined its core. For the artists and organizers working in experimental forms of culture in late East Germany, the government was almost harmless. May the ever-advancing success of these artists who worked independently be both a measure of state harm and a sign of its negation.

ACKNOWLEDGMENTS

I am completing this book in northern Minnesota in late November 2020, at the height of the second wave of the COVID-19 pandemic. A pandemic is no antidemocratic state; and let me be clear: I am by any measure extremely fortunate in my circumstances. Nevertheless, I am struck by how much this global health crisis has given me a sense of what it means to "live through history"—to be *subject to*, rather than *a subject in*, a place and time. *Parallel Public* describes a generation of people who were "born into" socialism, who had no choice but to live where they did, and yet who made something of the experience. Although I believe their work speaks for itself, I have done my best to speak for it.

I would like to first acknowledge the subjects of my study: the artists, art historians, curators, organizers, publishers, and other interesting people who shared their stories and often their objects with me. My bibliography notes the cast of people who have supported and facilitated my research in very tangible ways. Among these, I extend especially heartfelt appreciation to Claus Löser, Gabriele Stötzer, and Christoph Tannert; as well as to Judy Lybke, Frank Eckart, and the EIGEN+ART gallery staff in Berlin and Leipzig; and to Roland Berbig at the Humboldt University in Berlin. I also thank Lutz Dammbeck, Matthias Fischer, Thomas Florschuetz, Reimund Frentzel, Else Gabriel, Eckhart Gillen, Andreas Hüneke, John P. Jacob, Paul Kaiser, Andreas Ludwig, Claudia Reichardt, Karim Saab, Christine Schlegel, Cornelia Schleime, Gundula Schulze Eldowy, Silke Wagler, Uwe Warnke, and Karin Wieckhorst for granting me their time and access to knowledge, material, and personal experience. Thank you to Monika Andres, Micha Brendel, Christiane Bühling-Schultz, Josef Fillipp and the Josef Fillipp Galerie, Uwe Frauendorf, Rainer Görß, Uta Grundmann, Christian Günther, Harald Hauswald and OSTKREUZ—Agenteur der Fotografen, Jörg Herold, Thomas Kläber, Verena Kyselka, Via Lewandowsky, Wiebke Müller, Andreas Rost, Antonia Schlegel, Hiltrud Schultz of the DEFA Film Library, and Jochen Wermann for responding with such rapid speed to my requests for materials and other information. Thank you also to Karen Rosenflanz for providing me with translations of the permissions forms; these certainly contributed to the speed of my receipt of interview and image permissions.

I am also grateful to Elena Alzate at the Stasi archive in Berlin as well as to Raphaela Schröder—also of the BStU—for her recent support, and to Michael Kresja, Romy Kleiber, Elfe Raasch, Wolfgang Lux, Franziska Galek, and Helga Neumann at the archive of the Academy of Fine Arts in Berlin. Although the material from its archive is not present here, I also worked extensively at the Wende Museum and am grateful to its team, current and past, including Justin Jampol, Joes Segal, Christina Cuevas-Wolf, Patrick Mansfield, Christine Rank, Kate Dollenmeyer, and John Ahouse. I received additional archival support from Simone Fugger von dem Rech at the Dresden Academy of Fine Arts and Kathleen M. Smith at Stanford's Germanic collections, as well as from the Getty Research Library, Paul Civitelli at the Beinecke Library of Rare Books and Manuscripts at Yale University, and from staff at the Federal Foundation for the Reappraisal of the SED Dictatorship in Berlin.

My current institution, the University of Minnesota Duluth, has provided me consistent financial and in-kind support. I am especially grateful to Robert Kase, the last dean of our School of Fine Arts, for advocating on my behalf to grant me a single-semester leave for the fall of 2020. This time away from teaching fundamentally led to the success of my book revisions. I received generous financial support that contributed to this book from Dean Kase, as well as from Jeremy Youde, dean of the College of Arts, Humanities, and Social Sciences, of which I am glad to be a new faculty member. Thank you also to the CLA Research and Creative Activity Committee for image reproduction support. I am also grateful to the University of Minnesota's Imagine Fund for awarding me funds to support my research on a number of occasions.

The following funders enabled me to conduct the extensive field and archival research in Germany that made this book possible: the German Academic Exchange Service (DAAD), the College Art Association, the Rosa Luxemburg Foundation, the Coalition of Women in German, and the University of California, Santa Cruz's Graduate Division and Arts Division.

I would also like to acknowledge the incredible experience of completing my PhD in Visual Studies at the University of California, Santa Cruz. I was lucky to work on this research first as a dissertation under the guidance of Jennifer González, and with support from Hunter Bivens and Jenny Horne (both also at UCSC), as well as Julia Bryan-Wilson (of UC Berkeley) and Joes Segal (of the Wende Museum). The environment at UCSC gave me the chance to forge lifelong collegial bonds with scores of graduate student allies. I extend my gratitude to Lorraine Affourtit, Erin Gray, Amber Hickey, Aubrey Hobart, Alex Johnston, Rachel Nelson, Ian Alan Paul,

Kathleen Reinhardt, and Benjamín Schultz-Figueroa for their insights and support. Another note of gratitude is owed to a few other friends in Santa Cruz who reminded me to take breaks and have fun: Ben and Cait, Kit and Alex—you are so missed.

This work could not have been done without the support of the colleagues and friends I have met along the way. Jennifer Webb in the Department of Art and Design has been central to my success at UMD since I joined the faculty in 2017. Jennifer is a model leader, educator, and friend. I wish to extend a special note of gratitude to Seth Howes and Sarah James, who both seem to possess a magical ability to invent time for a "quick" read. I am also grateful to April Eisman, Megan Hoetger, Anna Horakova, Angelika Richter, and Briana Smith for their readership and heady collegial exchange, as well as to Jill Casid, Paula Derdiger, Daniela Sandler, and Marquard Smith for their support and advice. It bears mentioning that the confluence of this book with new monographs by Sarah James (*Paper Revolutions: An Invisible Avant-Garde*) and Briana Smith (*Free Berlin: Art, Urban Politics, and Everyday Life*), also with the MIT Press, affords an extraordinary opportunity for the research on experimental forms of art in the GDR.

I am grateful to Victoria Hindley at the MIT Press for her trust and confidence in my book, as well as for our consistent and easy working relationship. Thank you also to Gabriela Bueno Gibbs and Matthew Abbate at the MIT Press for additional support. I am very grateful to the three anonymous peer reviewers, whose thoughtful commentary on this project helped me to refine it to its present state. Finally, thank you to Paula Woolley whose copyedits on this manuscript were extraordinarily helpful.

Of course, I could not have completed this dissertation without the support of a generous and encouraging family. Thank you especially to my mom, Elke Kurpiers, who modeled for me the spirit of adventure that fuels this book, and Russ Blaylock, whose diligence and focus I am grateful to have inherited. Thank you also to my big sister Kristina Trybek, my *Tante* Peggy Kurpiers, and my *Onkel* Martin Roger, as well as to Patty Feld, Barry Feld, and my dear *Schwägerin* Julia Strand.

While completing this research and writing, I also began the journey of parenting. Thank you to Benesh, Sula, and Frank for completing our wolf pack. My most profound gratitude is owed to my partner, Ari Feld, a heroic advocate, an enduring editor, an exceptional interlocutor, and a remarkable person.

NOTES

INTRODUCTION

1. Christoph Tannert, "Intermedia. Versuche kollektiver Kunstproduktion," *Musik und Gesellschaft*, no. 34 (1984): 349–353.
2. Sozialistische Einheitspartei Deutschland, the Socialist Unity Party of Germany. The SED was the GDR's governing political party.
3. Eugen Blume and Christoph Tannert, "Dokumentation zur Aktionskunst in Berlin-DDR," February 1989, Verband-Bildender-Künstler-Archiv, Berlin, no. 36, Akademie der Künste, Berlin.
4. "Rg" has been said to stand for both *rot-grün* (red-green) and *Raumgemeinschaft* (literally, "space collective"). Eugen Blume lists the people who initiated the rg gallery as Erhard Monden, Mario Monden, Wolfram Adalbert Scheffler, Robert Rehfeldt, Horst Bartnig, Klaus Werner, and himself. Eugen Blume, "Außerhalb der Ordnung," in *Klaus Werner: Für die Kunst*, ed. Gabriele Muschter et al. (Köln: Verlag der Buchhandlung Walther König, 2000), 14–16.
5. Eugen Blume in conversation with Angelika Richter, October 14, 2016, cited in Angelika Richter, *Das Gesetz der Szene. Genderkritik, Performance Art und zweite Öffentlichkeit in der späten DDR* (Bielefeld: transcript Verlag, 2019), 178.
6. Stötzer went by the surname Kachold or Kachold-Stötzer in the 1980s.
7. Boris Groys, *The Total Art of Stalinism* (Princeton: Princeton University Press, 1992).
8. Clement Greenberg, "'Avant-Garde and Kitsch' 1939," in *Art in Theory, 1900–2000. An Anthology of Changing Ideas*, ed. Charles Harrison and Paul Wood (Malden, MA: Blackwell Publishing, 2003), 539–549.
9. See, for example, Paul Kaiser, "Symbolic Revolts in the 'Workers' and Peasants' State': Countercultural Art Programs in the GDR and the Return of Modern Art," in *Art of Two Germanys: Cold War Cultures*, ed. Stephanie Barron and Sabine Eckmann (New York: Abrams, 2009), 170–185.
10. Wolfgang Emmerich, *Kleine Literaturgeschichte der DDR* (Leipzig: Kiepenheuer, 1996), especially 119 and 404.
11. Uwe Kolbe, *Hineingeboren: Gedichte, 1975–1979* (Frankfurt am Main: Suhrkamp, 1982).
12. For more on the way the wall figured in East German culture, see Charity Scribner, "August 1961: Christa Wolf and the Politics of Disavowal," *German Life and Letters* 55, no. 1 (January 2002): 61–74.
13. Seán Allan, "DEFA: An Historical Overview," in *DEFA: East German Cinema, 1946–1992*, ed. Seán Allan and John Sandford (New York: Berghahn Books, 1999), 1–21.

14. Sebastian Heiduschke, "Film Censorship, the East German *Nouvelle Vague*, and the 'Rabbit Films': *Das Kaninchen bin ich* (*The Rabbit Is Me*, Kurt Maetzig, 1965)," in his *East German Cinema: DEFA and Film History* (New York: Palgrave MacMillan, 2013), 77–83.

15. Erich Honecker, speech at the Fourth Meeting of the Central Committee of the Socialist Unity Party, December 17, 1971, quoted in Paul Kaiser and Claudia Petzold, "Perlen vor die Säue. Eien Boheme im Niemandsland," *Boheme und Diktatur in der DDR: Gruppen, Konflikte, Quartiere 1970–1989*, exhibition catalog (Berlin: Fannei & Walz, 1997), 24.

16. Quoted in Klaus Schroeder, "The SED's Fear of the Big Bad Wolf," in *Ende vom Lied*, ed. Christoph Tannert, exhibition catalog (Berlin: Künstlerhaus Bethanien, 2016), 243.

17. For more on the Biermann affair, see Ian Wallace, "The Politics of Confrontation: The Biermann Affair and Its Consequences," *German Monitor*, no. 29 (1992): 68–80.

18. Václav Havel, quoted in Klara Kemp-Welch, *Antipolitics in Central European Art: Reticence as Dissidence under Post-Totalitarian Rule, 1956–1989* (London: I. B. Tauris, 2014), 8. Original citation: Václav Havel, "The Anatomy of Resistance (1985)," in *Václav Havel, Living in Truth: Twenty-two Essays Published on the Occasion of the Award of the Erasmus Prize to Václav Havel* (London: Faber and Faber 1987), 193.

19. See, for example, Esther von Richthofen, *Bringing Culture to the Masses: Control, Compromise, and Participation in the GDR* (New York: Berghahn Books, 2009); and Alexei Yurchak, *Everything Was Forever, Until It Was No More: The Last Soviet Generation* (Princeton: Princeton University Press, 2006).

20. Régine Robin, *Socialist Realism: An Impossible Aesthetic* (Stanford: Stanford University Press, 1992), 57. Emphasis in the original.

21. For more on the history of establishing the GDR's cultural foundation, see Wolfgang Schivelbusch, *In a Cold Crater: Cultural and Intellectual Life in Berlin, 1945–1948* (Berkeley: University of California Press, 1998).

22. Ibid., 42.

23. This phrase is said to have originated in a meeting between Joseph Stalin and a group of Communist Party writers on October 26, 1932. The artist-as-engineer metaphor became a signature phrase for socialist realism. For a review of its primacy in communism's foundational aesthetic theory, see Leonid Maximenkov, "Stalin's Meeting with a Delegation of Ukrainian Writers on 12 February 1929," *Harvard Ukrainian Studies* 16, no. 3/4 (December 1992): 361.

24. Yurchak, *Everything Was Forever*, 25.

25. Mary Fulbrook, *The People's State: East German Society from Hitler to Honecker* (New Haven: Yale University Press, 2005), 12.

26. Richthofen, *Bringing Culture to the Masses*.

27. Ibid., 3.

28. Yurchak, *Everything Was Forever*, 27.

29. Ibid., 29 and 25.

30. Richthofen, *Bringing Culture to the Masses*, 176.

31. Jens Gieseke, *The History of the Stasi: East Germany's Secret Police, 1945–1990* (New York: Berghahn Books, 2014), 147.

32. The art schools were Hochschule für Bildende Künste Dresden, Hochschule für Grafik und Buchkunst Leipzig, Burg Giebichenstein Kunsthochschule Halle, and Weißensee Kunsthochschule Berlin.

33. Paul Kaiser, *Boheme in der DDR. Kunst und Gegenkultur im Staatsozialismus* (Dresden: Dresdner Institut für Kulturstudien, 2016), 69.

34. April Eisman, *Bernhard Heisig and the Fight for Modern Art in East Germany* (Rochester, NY: Camden House, 2018).

35. Hans-Joachim Schluze, quoted in Uta Grundmann, Klaus Michael, and Susanna Seufert, "Die Akademie als Experimentierfeld. Hartwig Ebersbach und die Folgen," in *Revolution im geschlossenen Raum. Die andere Kultur in Leipzig 1970–1990*, ed. Uta Grundmann, Klaus Michael, and Susanna Seufert (Leipzig: Verlag Faber & Faber, 2002), 42–43. All translations from this text by the author.

36. See Katalin Cseh-Varga and Adam Czirak, *Performance Art in the Second Public Sphere: Event-Based Art in Late Socialist Europe* (New York: Routledge, 2018), especially the text's introduction.

37. Bojana Cvejić, "A Parallel Slalom from BADco: In Search of a Poetics of Problems," *Representations*, no. 136 (Fall 2016): 23.

38. Bojana Cvejić, "Problems That Aesthetically 'Unburden' Us," in *Parallel Slalom: A Lexicon of Non-aligned Poetics*, ed. Bojana Cvejić and Goran Sergej Pristaš (Belgrade: Walking Theory, 2013), 325.

39. Tannert, quoted in Elisabeth Jappe, *Performance, Ritual, Prozeß* (Munich: Prestel-Verlag, 1993), 61. All translations from this text by the author.

40. See Alexei Yurchak's discussion on this topic in *Everything Was Forever*, 6–7. Studies on consumer culture in the GDR, such as Katherine Pence and Paul Betts's *Socialist Modern: East German Everyday Culture and Politics* (Ann Arbor: University of Michigan Press, 2008), or Mary Fulbrook's recent histories of the GDR (i.e., *The People's State*, 2005), likewise carefully nuance the distinctions between official and unofficial culture.

41. Anna Horakova, "Mimicry as Critique: New Perspectives on the Prenzlauer Berg, Avantgarde Aesthetics and Communist Cultures of Dissidence" (doctoral thesis, Cornell University, 2016), 9.

42. Ibid.

43. Two texts that argue for a more nuanced approach to the use of Stasi records, in particular, are Konrad Jarausch, "Between Myth and Reality: The Stasi Legacy in German History," *German Historical Institute Bulletin* 9 (2014): 73–83; and Julia Hell, "Loyal Dissidents and Stasi Poets: Sascha Anderson, Christa Wolf, and the Incomplete Project of GDR Research," *German Politics and Society* 20, no. 4 (Winter 2002): 82–118.

44. Jarausch, "Between Myth and Reality," 74.

45. Karl-Siegbert Rehberg, "Verkörperungs-Konkurrenzen. Aktionskunst in der DDR zwischen Revolte und 'Kristallisation,'" in *Ohne uns! Kunst und alternative Kultur in Dresden vor und nach '89*, ed. Frank Eckhardt and Paul Kaiser (Dresden: Efau Verlag, 2009), 269. All translations from this text by the author.

46. Gieseke, *History of the Stasi*, 112.

47. Ann Laura Stoler, *Along the Archival Grain: Epistemic Anxieties and Colonial Common Sense* (Princeton: Princeton University Press, 2010).

48. See, for example, David Bathrick, *The Powers of Speech: The Politics of Culture in the GDR* (Lincoln: University of Nebraska Press, 1995), as well as the films *Betrayal* (*Verrat*), directed by Fredrik von Krusenstjerna and Björn Cederberg (Stockholm: Charon Film, 1994), VHS, and *Anderson*, directed by Annekatrin Hendel (Berlin: Salzgeber & Co. Medien, 2015), DVD.

49. For a discussion of this shift, see Andrew I. Port, "The Banalities of East German Historiography," in *Becoming East German: Socialist Structures and Sensibilities after Hitler*, ed. Mary Fulbrook and Andrew I. Port (New York: Berghahn Books, 2013), 16–24.

50. A few recent examples include Klara Kemp-Welch, *Networking the Bloc: Experimental Art in Eastern Europe, 1965–1981* (Cambridge, MA: MIT Press, 2018); Beáta Hock and Anu Allas, eds., *Globalizing East European Art Histories, Past and Present* (New York: Routledge, 2018).

51. During the period being discussed, Schulze Eldowy went simply by "Schulze." She added the name "Eldowy" from the Arabic word *el dowy* (the light) in the mid-1990s.

CHAPTER 1

1. Hübchen, quoted in Jens Gieseke, *The History of the Stasi: East Germany's Secret Police, 1945–1990* (New York: Berghahn Books, 2014), 218. Original citation: Susanne Sturm, "Hart, aber herzlich. Interview mit Henry Hübchen," *Stern TV Magazin*, no. 23 (June 1, 2006): n.p.

2. Ibid.

3. Stötzer went by the surname Kachold or Kachold-Stötzer in the 1980s.

4. An exception to this is Alison Lewis, "En-Gendering Remembrance: Memory, Gender and Informers for the Stasi," *New German Critique*, no. 86 (2002): 103–134.

5. Angelika Richter, *Das Gesetz der Szene. Genderkritik, Performance Art und zweite Öffentlichkeit in der späten DDR* (Bielefeld: transcript Verlag, 2019), 33. All translations from this text by the author.

6. Myra Marx Ferree, "The Rise and Fall of 'Mommy Politics': Feminism and Unification in (East) Germany," *Feminist Studies* 19, no. 1 (Spring 1993): 92.

7. Gabriele Stötzer, "Überwachung von Kunst und Kultur. Der lange Arm der Staatssicherheit" in *Zwischen Ausstieg und Aktion. Die Erfurter Subkulture der 1960er, 1970er und 1980er Jahre*, ed. Tely Büchner and Susanne Knorr, exhibition catalog (Bielefeld: Kerber Verlag, 2014), 159. All translations from this text by the author.

8. For more on the controversies surrounding the public opening of the Stasi archives, as well as the reasons for opening them, see Konrad Jarausch, "Between Myth and Reality: The Stasi Legacy in German History," *German Historical Institute Bulletin* 9 (2014): 77–78.

9. Gieseke, *History of the Stasi*, 205.

10. Ibid., 213.

11. Ibid., 213–214.

12. Sozialistische Einheitspartei Deutschland, the Socialist Unity Party of Germany. The SED was the GDR's governing political party.

13. Jarausch, "Between Myth and Reality," 79.

14. Ibid., 80.

15. Gieseke, *History of the Stasi*, 213.

16. Verena Kyselka, "Pigs Like Pigments," accessed May 7, 2021, https://verena-kyselka.de/pigs-like-pgments/.

17. Ibid.

18. Christine Schlegel and Trude Trunk, "Hautlos," in *Hautlos. Eingeschweißte Überwachung* (Berlin: Janus Press, 2011), 40. All translations from this text by the author.

19. Richter, *Das Gesetz der Szene*, 319.

20. Schlegel and Trunk, "Hautlos," 40.

21. See, for example, David Bathrick, *The Powers of Speech: The Politics of Culture in the GDR* (Lincoln: University of Nebraska Press, 1995), and Dominic Boyer, "Foucault in the Bush: The Social Life of Post-Structuralist Theory in East Berlin's Prenzlauer Berg," *Ethnos* (*Estoclomo*) 66, no. 2 (2001): 207–236, as well as the films *Betrayal* (*Verrat*), directed by Fredrik von Krusenstjerna and Björn Cederberg (Stockholm: Charon Film, 1994), VHS, and *Anderson*, directed by Annekatrin Hendel (Berlin: Salzgeber & Co. Medien, 2015), DVD.

22. Julia Hell, "Loyal Dissidents and Stasi Poets: Sascha Anderson, Christa Wolf, and the Incomplete Project of GDR Research," *German Politics and Society* 20, no. 4 (Winter 2002): 85.

23. Ibid., 112.

24. Ibid.

25. Schlegel and Trunk, "Hautlos," 45.

26. Boyer, "Foucault in the Bush," 224.

27. Cornelia Schleime, *Weit Fort* (Regensburg: Hoffmann und Campe, 2008). All translations from this text by the author.

28. Von Krusenstjerna and Cederberg, *Betrayal* (*Verrat*).

29. Cited in Boyer, "Foucault in the Bush," 224.

30. Gerd Harry "Judy" Lybke in Ulrike Knöfel, "Du fühlst dich unsterblich," *Der Spiegel*, no. 34 (August 18, 2014): 114. All translations from this text by the author.

31. Gieseke, *History of the Stasi*, 81.

32. I have written previously on this project; the following text will duplicate some of my published descriptions of Schleime's *Stasi Series*. Rather than elaborate on its individual parts, as I have done before, here I am interested in using the project as an example of the ways that artists, in general, reflect a bemused, rather than a victimized, response to their Stasi files. See Sara Blaylock, "La femme de leurs rêves: Cornelia Schleime et les archives de la Stasi," *Gradhiva*, no. 24 (December 2016): 21–49; Sara Blaylock, "Being the Woman They Wanted Her to Be: Cornelia Schleime Performs Her Stasi File," *Third Text* 35, no. 2 (March 2021): 227–247.

33. Cornelia Schleime, personal interview, February 25, 2015. All translations from this interview by the author.

34. Ibid.

35. Cornelia Schleime, "Stasi Serie," in *In der Liebe und in der Kunst weiß ich genau, was ich nicht will* (Bielefeld: Kerber Verlag, 2010), 74. All translations from this text by the author.

36. Ibid., 75.

37. Schleime, personal interview.

38. Schleime, *Weit Fort*, 37.

39. The artist Simon Menner has recently published a compilation of Stasi disguises; see Simon Menner, *Top Secret. Bilder aus den Archiven der Staatssicherheit/Images from the Stasi Archives* (Ostfildern: Hatje Cantz Verlag, 2013).

40. See also the ways the Stasi sought to destabilize the relationships of the Clara Mosch group, as described in Claudia Mesch, *Modern Art at the Berlin Wall: Demarcating Culture in the Cold War Germanys* (London: I. B. Tauris, 2006), 196.

41. Gieseke, *History of the Stasi*, 215. Another 30 percent originated in the 1970s, leaving only 10 percent to account for the GDR's first two decades—a time when, according to Gieseke, "the worst crimes of this secret apparatus were committed."

42. Ibid., 112.

43. Bundesbeauftragte für die Unterlagen der Staatssicherheitsdienstes der ehemaligen Deutschen Demokratischen Republik, ed., *"Eingeschränkte Freiheit." Der Fall Gabriele Stötzer* (Berlin: BStU, 2014).

44. Sylvia Sasse, "Stasi-Dada: How Artists Work with Their Stasi Records," *Performance Art in Eastern Europe* (March 2016), accessed May 7, 2021, http://www.performanceart.info/blog/stasi-dada-how-artists-work-with-their-stasi-records/.

45. Ibid.

46. DW Euromaxx, "In Prison in the GDR—Fighting against the Regime with Art: Witnessing the Fall of the Wall," YouTube video, 8:07, October 29, 2019, https://www.youtube.com/watch?v=aQejyOVZgdU. An "IMB" is an *Inoffizieller Mitarbeiter der Abwehr mit Feindverbindung bzw. zur unmittelbaren Bearbeitung im Verdacht der Feindtätigkeit stehender Personen.* This translates to "unofficial collaborators [working toward] the defense of enemy connections and for the immediate processing of people suspected of enemy connections," and effectively identifies IMs who had direct connections to people identified by the Stasi as "negative-hostile" (*feindlich-negative*). IMBs were considered particularly valuable to the state's secret security.

47. Ibid.

48. Gabriele Stötzer, email message to author, April 29, 2021. All translations from this message by the author.

49. BStU, MfS, BV Erfurt Abt. XX, Nr. 1753/86, Band 4, 87: "Information zu Gabi Kachold," September 21, 1984.

50. Stötzer, email to author.

51. Ibid.

52. Stötzer in DW Euromaxx, *"In Prison in the GDR."*

53. Stötzer seemingly refers to this man as an "IM" in her interview with DW Euromaxx (see ibid.). However, she disputed this categorization in an April 29, 2021 email message. Stasi reports she supplied me also suggest that he was not working for the Stasi.

54. Gieseke, *History of the Stasi*, 147.

55. Bundesbeauftragte für die Unterlagen der Staatssicherheitsdienstes der ehemaligen Deutschen Demokratischen Republik, ed., "Zersetzung," in *Das MfS-Lexicon*, accessed May 7, 2021, https://www.bstu.de/mfs-lexikon/detail/zersetzung/.

56. Alison Lewis, *Die Kunst des Verrats: Der Prenzlauer Berg und die Staatssicherheit* (Würzburg: Königshausen & Neumann, 2003), 179.

57. Stötzer, "Überwachung von Kunst und Kultur," 154.

58. See Seth Howes, "Pessimism and the Politics of the Future in East German Punk," *Journal of Popular Culture* 49, no. 1 (February 2016): 77–96, as well as Seth Howes, "'*Killersatellit*' and *Randerscheinung*: Punk and the Prenzlauer Berg," *German Studies Review* 36, no. 3 (October 2013): 579–601.

59. Ulrike Bestgen, "'. . . ein anderes stück leibverantwortung.' Lebensthema Haft in Sprache und Bild bei Gabriele Stötzer," in *Gabriele Stötzer. Schwingungskurve Leben*, ed. Ulrike Bestgen and Wolfgang Holler, exhibition catalog (Weimar: Klassik Stiftung Weimar, 2013), 26. All translations from this text by the author.

CHAPTER 2

1. See, for example, Eckhart Gillen, "Wiederkehr der Geschichte und des Realismus: Die Leipziger Schule," in Gillen, *Feindliche Brüder?: Der Kalte Krieg und die deutsche Kunst, 1945–1990* (Berlin, Nicolai: 2009), 327–350; Karl-Siegbert Rehberg, "Apotheose des Schreckens. Leipziger Geschichtsbilder," in *Abschied von Ikarus. Bildwelten in der DDR—neu gesehen*, ed. Karl-Siegbert Rehberg, Wolfgang Holler, and Paul Kaiser, exhibition catalog (Cologne: Walter König, 2012), 259–271.

2. The series is also referred to as the *Körperstücke*, which may translate as *Body Pieces* or *Body Fragments*. In an interview on May 12, 2015, Thomas Florschuetz explained to me that he neither prefers nor differentiates these names.

3. Micha Brendel, Else Gabriel, Rainer Görß, and Via Lewandowsky composed the core of this group. Other regular collaborators are not considered Auto-Perforation Artists.

4. Thomas Florschuetz, personal interview, May 12, 2015. All translations from this interview by the author.

5. Sarah James, *Common Ground: German Photographic Cultures across the Iron Curtain* (New Haven: Yale University Press, 2013), 42.

6. Berthold Beiler, *Die Gewalt des Augenblicks* (Leipzig: VEB Fotokinoverlag, 1969), 9. All translations from this text by the author.

7. Ibid.

8. I have written previously on this topic; the following text will duplicate some of that description as it appears in Sara Blaylock, "Aufstand des Materials. Körperbilder im Prenzlauer Berg der 1980er Jahre" / "A Material Revolt: Body portraits in the Prenzlauer Berg of the 1980s," in *Gegenstimmen. Kunst in der DDR 1976–1989 / Voices of Dissent: Art in the GDR*, ed. Christoph Tannert, exhibition catalog (Berlin: Deutsche Gesellschaft and Künstlerhaus Bethanien, 2016), 394–401.

9. Florschuetz, personal interview.

10. *The Painter Came from a Foreign Land*, dir. Lutz Dammbeck, disc 2 of *Art Unleashed: Experiments on Film by Lutz Dammbeck* (Amherst, MA: DEFA Film Library, 2019), DVD.

11. Gerhard Wolf, "gegen sprache mit sprache, mit-sprache gegen-sprache. Thesen mit Zitaten und Notizen zu einem literarischen Prozeß," in *Die andere Sprache. Neue DDR-Literatur der 80er Jahre*, ed. Heinz Ludwig Arnold and Gerhard Wolf (Munich: Edition Text + Kritik, 1990), 15–25. All translations from this text by the author.

12. See Anna Horakova, "Mimicry as Critique: New Perspectives on the Prenzlauer Berg, Avant-garde Aesthetics and Communist Cultures of Dissidence" (doctoral thesis, Cornell University, 2016).

13. György Lukács, "Reification and the Consciousness of the Proletariat (1923)," in *History and Class Consciousness* (1967; Georg Lukács Archive on Marxists.org, n.d.), https://www.marxists.org/archive/lukacs/works/history/hcc05.htm.

14. Ibid.

15. Michel Foucault, "Docile Bodies," in his *Discipline and Punish: The Birth of the Prison* (New York: Pantheon Books, 1977), 135–169.

16. Walter Ulbricht, then the First Secretary of the leading Socialist Unity Party of Germany, presented an explicit set of guidelines entitled the "Ten Commandments of the New Socialist Man" in 1958. The text wove instructions for proper physical appearance into instructions for good behavior.

17. Greg Eghigian, "Homo Munitus: The East German Observed," in *Socialist Modern: East German Everyday Culture and Politics*, ed. Katherine Pence and Paul Betts (Ann Arbor: University of Michigan Press, 2008), 42.

18. Sozialistische Einheitspartei Deutschland, the Socialist Unity Party of Germany. The SED was the GDR's governing political party.

19. Eghigian, "Homo Munitus," 43.

20. W. P. Jefanow (Secretary of the Union of Soviet Fine Artists), interview in *Fotografie* (December 1953): 331, quoted in John P. Jacob, *Recollecting a Culture: Photography and the Evolution of a Socialist Aesthetic in East Germany* (Boston: Photographic Resource Center at Boston University, 1998), 6.

21. Eghigian, "Homo Munitus," 43.

22. Karin Thomas, "Thomas Florschuetz. Körperbilder," *European Photography* 8, no. 4 (December 1987): 16. All translations from this text by the author.

23. Peter Dittmer and the dancer Hanne Wandtke also participated in this project, though their contributions are not included in the narratives of the project. One group photo of all six, taken before or after one of the three performances, exists. Here Wandtke appears with her head clean-shaven and a metallic pigment covering all of her exposed skin, including her hands. Dittmer sits in a chair with his legs splayed open. His entire body is covered in bits of paper. Even his face is obscured, making him look like a rogue scarecrow. What Wandtke and Dittmer did in the performance is unknown. See Christoph Tannert, ed., *Autoperforationsartistik*, exhibition catalog (Nuremberg: Verlag für modern Kunst, 1991), 21. All translations from this text by the author.

24. Christoph Tannert, "Ereignisgeschichte," in *Autoperforationsartistik*, 8.

25. Durs Grünbein, "Protestantische Rituale. Zur Arbeit der Autoperforationsartisten," in *Kunst in der DDR*, ed. Eckhart Gillen and Rainer Haarmann (Cologne: Kiepenheuer & Witsch, 1990), 312. All translations from this text by the author.

26. Ibid.

27. See Else Gabriel, quoted in Seth Howes, *Moving Images on the Margins: Experimental Film in Late Socialist East Germany* (Rochester, NY: Camden House, 2019), 124 n99. Original citation: Else Gabriel, "FLU—(Virus und Werk): Über Performance, Publikum, Peinlichkeit, Konserven und ein Mittel gegen alles in der eigenen Arbeit," in *Performance im medialen Wandel*, ed. Petra Maria Meyer (Munich: William Fink, 2006), 361–377.

28. Claudia Mesch, *Modern Art at the Berlin Wall: Demarcating Culture in the Cold War Germanys* (London: I. B. Tauris, 2006), 202–203.

29. Ibid., 203.

30. Tannert, "Ereignisgeschichte," 8.

31. For more on Lewandowsky and other examples of artists from the Eastern Bloc who identify as male and explore gender, see Piotr Piotrowski, "Male Artist's Body: National Identity vs. Identity Politics," in *Gender Check, A Reader: Art and Theory in Eastern Europe*, ed. Bojana Pejić (Cologne: Walther König, 2010), 127–136; and Bojana Pejić, "Proletarians of All Countries, Who Washes Your Socks? Equality, Dominance and Difference in Eastern European Art," in *Gender Check: Femininity and Masculinity in the Art of Eastern Europe*, exhibition catalog (Cologne: Walther König, 2009), 19–29.

32. Micha Brendel, quoted in *Ohne Uns! Kunst und alternative Kultur in Dresden vor und nach '89*, ed. Frank Eckhardt and Paul Kaiser (Dresden: Efau Verlag, 2009), 269. All translations from this text by the author.

33. Else Gabriel, personal interview, June 24, 2015. All translations from this interview by the author.

34. Hochschule für Bildende Künste, Dresden, Bestand 03, Nr. 1235: "Fasching 1986 'Vogelgewetter'," January 21, 1986.

35. The title for the group performance is noted in the artists' individual academic records as *Die wunderbare Hervorbringung des Biegsamen* (*The Wondrous Birthing of the Bendable*), but the artists used the title *Herz Horn Haut Schrein* in their publicity for the event. Seth Howes explains that the title refers to roles each artist played in the performance, with Gabriel as the heart, Lewandowsky as the bone, and Brendel as the skin. Based on extensive archival research and interviews, Howes's lengthy description of the work provides an even more vivid picture of the performance than its extensive (and fairly esoteric) film and photographic documentation can offer. See Howes, *Moving Images on the Margins*, 122–130.

36. Joseph Beuys's 1969 piece was entitled *Ja Ja Ja Ja Ja, Nee Nee Nee Nee* (Yes Yes Yes Yes Yes, No No No No).

37. Grünbein, "Protestantische Rituale," 312.

38. Ibid.

39. For a description of the versions of the performance film, see Howes, *Moving Images on the Margins*, 126–130.

40. Ibid., 120–121.

41. Gabriel, personal interview.

42. Ibid.

43. Howes, *Moving Images on the Margins*, 130.

44. Micha Brendel, Else Gabriel, and Via Lewandowsky, "Schreiben an den Ministerrat der DDR, 30.2.1987," reprinted in *Grauzone 8mm. Materialien zum autonomen Künstlerfilm in der DDR*, ed. Dieter Daniels and Jeannette Stoschek (Ostfildern, Germany: Hatje Cantz Verlag, 2007), 69–70. All translations from this text by the author.

45. Seth Howes, "Cultures Grow Exponentially: An Interview with Rainer Görß," in *Imperfect Recall: Re-collecting the GDR*, Otago German Studies 30, ed. Cecilia Novero (Dunedin: University of Otago, 2020), 175–176.

46. Christoph Tannert [Anita Kenner, pseud.], "Avantgarde in der DDR heute? Ein Panorama der Kunst-, Literatur-, und Musikszene," in "Avantgarde," special issue, *Niemandsland* 2, no. 5 (1988): 107. Translation by the author.

47. Grünbein, "Protestantische Rituale," 309–318.

48. See Mary Fulbrook, "Render unto Caesar? The Pivotal Role of the Protestant Churches," *Anatomy of a Dictatorship: Inside the GDR 1949–1989* (Oxford: Oxford University Press, 1995), 87–128.

49. Hans-Joachim Maaz, *Behind the Wall: The Inner Life of Communist Germany* (New York: W. W. Norton, 1995), 51. Maaz's book originally appeared in 1990 as *Der Gefühlsstau. Ein Psychogramm der DDR*.

50. Ibid., 84.

51. Else Gabriel, *Vom Ebben und Fluten* (Dresden: Leonhardi-Museum, 1988), quoted in Eckhart Gillen, "Fear of Germany," in *German Art from Beckmann to Richter: Images of a Divided Country*, ed. Eckhart Gillen, exhibition catalog (Cologne: DuMont Buchverlag, 1997), 324.

52. Gillen, "Fear of Germany," 324.

53. Ibid.

54. Ibid.

55. One month into the exhibition, the artists hosted two nights of performances. On February 1, Micha Brendel appeared with Else Gabriel in *Lacheisen II* (a play on words that means something like "Laughing Iron II"). The following night featured the collaborative reading/performance *Verlesung der Befehle* (Reading of the Orders) with Via Lewandowsky and the writer Durs Grünbein.

56. Jens Gieseke, *The History of the Stasi: East Germany's Secret Police, 1945–1990* (New York: Berghahn Books, 2014), 205.

57. Steege is listed as an IMS, which stands for *Inoffizieller Mitarbeiter zur politisch-operativen Durchdringung und Sicherung des Verantwortungsbereiches*, which may be translated as "unofficial collaborator for political-operative penetration and for protection of responsibility areas." The Stasi categorized the majority of IMs as "IMS."

58. BStU, MfS, BV Dresden AOP, Nr. 2784/90/2, 391: "Information des IMS "Nora Steege" zur Ausstellung 'MENETEKEL'," February 22, 1989. All translations from this text by the author.

59. Ibid.

60. Gabriel, personal interview. See also Tannert, "Ereignisgeschichte," 11.

61. BStU, MfS, BV Dresden AOP, Nr. 2784/90/1, 143–146: "Nachwuchskünstler, die sich durch ihre Verhaltensweisen dem gesellschaftlichen Einfluß entziehen und Aktivitäten entwickeln, die einen provokativen politischen Charakter tragen," n.d. (February 1989?). All translations from this text by the author.

62. Ibid., 145–146.

63. Micha Brendel, Else Gabriel, and Via Lewandowsky, "Schreiben an den Ministerrat der DDR, 30.2.1987," 69–70.

64. The name might indicate either the conference's literal thirty-one-day contiguous programming, or it may ironically refer to the impermanence of the artwork presented, or perhaps the permanent introduction of the genre into East German official culture. Claudia Mesch has also suggested that the title refers to a 1979 quotation from Joseph Beuys. See Mesch, *Modern Art at the Berlin Wall*, 201.

65. This event followed a several-year public debate on performance art among the Union of Fine Artists, which also appeared in its official arts journal, *Bildende Kunst*, particularly in the issues of October 1981 and April to June 1982. After these debates, which were almost uniformly derisive of the medium, reporting on performances or other multimedia artworks both increased and became less uniformly critical.

66. Gabriel, personal interview.

67. In East Germany, Schulze Eldowy went simply by "Schulze." She added the name "Eldowy" from the Arabic word *el dowy* (the light) in the mid-1990s.

CHAPTER 3

1. During the period being discussed, Schulze Eldowy went simply by "Schulze." She added the name "Eldowy" from the Arabic word *el dowy* (the light) in the mid-1990s.

2. For an extended engagement with this argument about sitter agency, see Sara Blaylock, "The Subject Who Knows: Photographers and the Photographed in the Late East Germany," in *The Oxford Handbook of Communist Visual Cultures*, ed. Aga Skrodzka, Xiaoning Lu, and Kasia Marciniak, 500–518. (Oxford: Oxford University Press, 2020). See also Michel Foucault, "Docile Bodies," in his *Discipline and Punish: The Birth of the Prison* (New York: Pantheon Books, 1977), 135–169.

3. Gundula Schulze Eldowy, "The Times are Fleeing from the Memories," in *Der große und der kleine Schritt* (Leipzig: Lehmstadt Verlag, 2012), 12.

4. For more on hobby photography and scrapbooking, see Cristina Cuevas-Wolf, "Making the Past Present: GDR Photo Albums and Amateur Photographs," *Visual Resources* 30, no. 1 (2014): 33–56.

5. Schulze Eldowy, "The Times are Fleeing from the Memories," 13.

6. Ibid.

7. Gundula Schulze Eldowy, personal interview, July 27, 2015. All translations from this interview by the author.

8. Gundula Schulze Eldowy, "In the Autumn Leaves of Oblivion," in *Berlin in einer Hundenacht* (Leipzig: Lehmstadt Verlag, 2011), 20.
9. Schulze Eldowy, personal interview.
10. Ibid.
11. Schulze Eldowy, "In the Autumn Leaves of Oblivion," 24.
12. Schulze Eldowy, personal interview.
13. Josie McLellan, "Visual Dangers and Delights: Nude Photography in East Germany," *Past and Present* 205, no. 1 (November 2009): 163.
14. Gundula Schulze Eldowy, "Halt die Ohren Steif. Robert Frank und Gundula Schulze Eldowy in New York," in Kunstmuseen Erfurt (2018), accessed May 7, 2021, https://kunstmuseen.erfurt.de/km/de/service/aktuelles/ausstellungen/2018/128389.html.
15. For more on the relationship between East and West German photography, see Sarah James, *Common Ground: German Photographic Cultures across the Iron Curtain* (New Haven: Yale University Press, 2013).
16. For more on this history, see Jana Duda, Gabriele Muschter, and Uwe Warnke, *Geschlossene Gesellschaft. Künstlerische Fotografie in der DDR 1945–1989*, exhibition catalog (Bielefeld: Kerber Verlag, 2012).
17. Nicholas Mirzoeff, *The Right to Look: A Counterhistory of Visuality* (Durham: Duke University Press, 2011).
18. Ibid., 1.
19. Ibid.
20. Gundula Schulze Eldowy, "Die Plaudereien des Scharfschützen," in *Am fortgewehten Ort* (Leipzig: Lehmstadt Verlag, 2011), 192–193. All translations from this text by the author.
21. See, for example, Eckhart Gillen, *Feindliche Brüder? Der Kalte Krieg und die deutsche Kunst, 1945–1990* (Berlin: Nicolai, 2009), 160–174.
22. This and the following two sentences duplicate a description of this program that I wrote in "The Subject Who Knows," 510.
23. In film, for example, the works of this period inaugurated the so-called East German New Wave cinema; see, for example, Joshua Feinstein, "Straddling the Wall: Socialist Realism Meets the Nouvelle Vague in *Der geteilte Himmel*," in *The Triumph of the Ordinary: Depictions of Daily Life in the East German Cinema, 1949–1989* (Chapel Hill: University of North Carolina Press, 2002), 110–136.
24. Schulze Eldowy, personal interview.
25. For my discussion of this image, see Blaylock, "The Subject Who Knows," 510–512.
26. Schulze Eldowy, "Die Plaudereien des Scharfschützen," 129–221.
27. Ibid., 194.
28. James, *Common Ground*, 200.
29. Ibid.
30. In *Antlitz der Zeit*, Sander used these men to visualize the social schematics of "Revolutionaries" and "Communist Leader."
31. James, *Common Ground*, 201.

32. Wolfgang Engler describes this as "the phenomenon of the 'beer belly.'" Wolfgang Engler, *Die Ostdeutschen. Kunde von einem verlorenen Land* (Berlin: Aufbau Taschenbuch Verlag, 2002), 200. All translations from this text by the author.

33. Hans-Wulf Kunze, "Eine Bewährungsprobe für Fotografen," *Fotografie* (March 1986): 90. All translations from this text by the author.

34. Christoph Tannert, personal interview, May 11, 2015. All translations from this interview by the author.

35. Mary Fulbrook, *The People's State: East German Society from Hitler to Honecker* (New Haven: Yale University Press, 2005), 214.

36. Importantly, the demand for better working conditions and greater transparency in government united East Germans in the protests that brought down the Berlin Wall in the fall of 1989.

37. Engler, *Die Ostdeutschen*, 194.

38. Sozialistische Einheitspartei Deutschland, the Socialist Unity Party of Germany. The SED was the GDR's governing political party.

39. Schulze Eldowy, personal interview.

40. Schulze Eldowy, personal interview.

41. Susan Sontag, *On Photography* (New York: Rosetta Books, 2003), 4.

42. Stötzer went by the surname Kachold or Kachold-Stötzer in East Germany.

43. Angelika Richter, *Das Gesetz der Szene. Genderkritik, Performance Art und zweite Öffentlichkeit in der späten DDR* (Bielefeld: transcript Verlag, 2019), 307. All translations from this text by the author.

44. Ibid.

45. Cornelia Schleime, "Immer wenn das Leben so intensive wurde, griff ich zum Film," in *Gegenbilder. Filmische Subversion in der DDR, 1976–1996*, ed. Karin Fritzsche and Claus Löser (Berlin: Janus Press, 1996), 66. All translations from this text by the author.

46. Claus Löser, the foremost expert on the GDR's experimental film scene, provides these figures. Löser also possesses the world's most complete collection of these works in his ex.oriente.lux archive, which is located in Berlin. See also Claus Löser, *Strategien der Verweigerung. Untersuchungen zum politisch-ästhetischen Gestus unangepasster filmischer Artikulationen in der Spätphase der DDR* (Berlin: DEFA-Stiftung, 2011), 13.

47. *In der Sanduhr* (*In the Hourglass*, 11 min., 1982), *Die Spiegelfalle* (*Mirror Trap*, unknown duration, 1982); *Unter weißen Tüchern* (*Draped in White*, 9 min., 1983), *Das Nierrenbett* (*Bed of Kidneys*, 12 min., 1983), and *Das Puttennest* (*Den of Cherubs*, 12 min., 1984). All film titles have been translated by the author.

48. Listed in Claus Löser's encyclopedic text *Strategien der Verweigerung* (2011) as a "double projection," *Zwischen Gold und Gelb kann nur noch Licht fallen* (*Between Gold and Yellow Comes Only Light*) features animations of the artist's image-filled journals, 456. All translations from this text by the author.

49. For more on this discussion, see the first chapter of this book, as well as Sara Blaylock, "Being the Woman They Wanted Her to Be: Cornelia Schleime Performs Her Stasi File," *Third Text* 35, no. 2 (March 2021): 227–247.

50. Claus Löser, "Urge for Movement and Mobility: On Cornelia Schleime's Super 8 Films," in *Cornelia Schleime. Ein Wimpernschlag. A Blink of an Eye*, ed. Thomas Köhler and Stefanie Heckmann, exhibition catalog (Bielefeld: Kerber Verlag, 2016), 33.

51. *The Painter Came from a Foreign Land*, DVD, directed by Lutz Dammbeck (Amherst, MA: DEFA Film Library, 2019).

52. Löser, *Strategien der Verweigerung*. 14.

53. Rüdiger Thomas, "Selbst-Behauptung," in *Jenseits der Staatskultur. Traditionen autonomer Kunst in der DDR*, ed. Gabriele Muschter and Rüdiger Thomas (Munich: Hanser, 1992), 38. All translations from this text by the author.

54. Schleime, "Immer wenn das Leben," 67.

55. Löser, *Strategien der Verweigerung*, 183.

56. Schleime, "Immer wenn das Leben," 67.

57. Ibid., 68.

58. Ibid., 69.

59. Ibid.

60. McLellan, "Visual Dangers and Delights," 162. See also Quinn Slobodian, "Socialist Chromatism: Race, Racism, and the Racial Rainbow in East Germany," in *Comrades of Color: East Germany in the Cold War World*, ed. Quinn Slobodian (New York: Berghahn Books, 2015), 23–39.

61. Schleime, quoted in Löser, *Strategien der Verweigerung*, 187.

62. Claus Löser speculates that these sculptures were taken from the scattered ruins of the City Palace of Berlin, which was demolished in 1950. Löser, "Urge for Movement and Mobility," 36 n18.

63. Schleime, quoted in Löser, *Strategien der Verweigerung*, 189–190.

64. For more on punks in the GDR, see Seth Howes, "Pessimism and the Politics of the Future in East German Punk," *Journal of Popular Culture* 49, no. 1 (February 2016): 77–96, as well as Seth Howes, "'*Killersatellit*' and *Randerscheinung*: Punk and the Prenzlauer Berg," *German Studies Review* 36, no. 3 (October 2013): 579–601.

65. As of May 2021, this video is available online. Bundesbeauftragte für die Unterlagen des Staatssicherheitsdienstes der ehemaligen DDR, *Farewell Comrades! Stasi Watching Punks*, YouTube video, posted by "Farewell Comrades," February 23, 2012, 1:36, accessed May 3, 2021, https://www.youtube.com/watch?v=sLehmoEH7lE.

66. Cornelia Schleime, "Immer wenn das Leben," 66.

CHAPTER 4

1. See, for example, Rüdiger Thomas, "Selbst-Behauptung," in *Jenseits der Staatskultur. Traditionen autonomer Kunst in der DDR*, ed. Gabriele Muschter and Rüdiger Thomas (Munich: Hanser, 1992), 11–42.

2. Seth Howes, *Moving Images on the Margins: Experimental Film in Late Socialist East Germany* (Rochester, NY: Camden House, 2019), 30.

3. Claus Löser, "Das Phänomen des Schmalfilmbooms," in *Gegenbilder. Filmische Subversion in der DDR, 1976–1996*, ed. Karin Fritzsche and Claus Löser (Berlin: Janus Press, 1996), 81. All translations from this text by the author.

4. Claus Löser, the foremost expert on the GDR's experimental film scene, provides these figures. Löser also possesses the world's most complete collection of these works in his ex.oriente.lux archive, which is located in Berlin. See also Claus Löser, *Strategien der Verweigerung. Untersuchungen zum politisch-ästhetischen Gestus unangepasster filmischer Artikulationen in der Spätphase der DDR* (Berlin: DEFA-Stiftung, 2011), 13.

5. Cornelia Schleime, "Immer wenn das Leben so intensive wurde, griff ich zum Film," in Fritzsche and Löser, *Gegenbilder*, 67. All translations from this text by the author.

6. Ibid., 66.

7. Howes, *Moving Images on the Margins*, 30. See also Löser, "Das Phänomen des Schmalfilmbooms," 81.

8. Hahnemann reproduced several of these film treatments in his book *Exogene Zerrinerung* (Berlin: Gerhard Wolf Janus Press, 1994).

9. Hahnemann, quoted in Löser, "Das Phänomen des Schmalfilmbooms," 84.

10. The film's official name is *Die Täuschung verträgt die Realität nicht* (*Illusion Cannot Bear Reality*). All film titles have been translated by the author.

11. Thomas Naumann in conversation with Gino Hahnemann, Berlin, November 21, 1990, transcript of unpublished (?) interview, Gino-Hahnemann-Archiv, no. 76, Akademie der Künste, Berlin. All translations from this text by the author.

12. Gino Hahnemann, "RÖMISCHE BÄDER," 1, Gino-Hahnemann-Archiv, no. 22, Akademie der Künste, Berlin. All translations from this text by the author.

13. Ibid.

14. Sergei Eisenstein, quoted in Giuliana Bruno, "Geography of the Moving Image," in *Atlas of Emotion: Journeys in Art, Architecture, and Film* (New York: Verso, 2002), 59. Original citation: Sergei Eisenstein, "Piranesi, or the Fluidity of Forms [1947/1964]," *Oppositions*, no. 11 (Winter 1977): 98.

15. Bruno, "Geography of the Moving Image," 56.

16. Ibid., 55.

17. Ibid., 56.

18. Ibid., 55.

19. Ibid., 57.

20. Sozialistische Einheitspartei Deutschland, the Socialist Unity Party of Germany. The SED was the GDR's governing political party.

21. Christoph Dieckmann, "Der König der DDR," *ZEIT Geschichte*, no. 4 (November 22, 2011), accessed May 7, 2021, https://www.zeit.de/zeit-geschichte/2011/04/Friedrich-der-Grosse-DDR/komplettansicht.

22. Ibid.

23. For more on Maaß's ceramics studio, see Henryk Gericke and Ingeborg Quaas, eds., *Brennzeiten: die Keramikwerkstatt Wilfriede Maass 1980–1989–1998: ein Zentrum des künstlerischen Offgrounds in Ost-Berlin*, exhibition catalog (Berlin: Lukas, 2014).

24. Claus Löser, "Der Spion, der aus dem Kino kam," *tip* (November 1995): 47.

25. For more on this, see Elaine Kelly, "Late Beethoven and Late Socialism," in *Composing the Canon in the GDR: Narratives of Nineteenth-Century Music* (Oxford: Oxford University Press, 2014), 144–191.

26. Löser, "Das Phänomen des Schmalfilmbooms," 82–83.

27. For more on the growth of this annual festival, see Howes, *Moving Images on the Margins*, 30.

28. Note, as with all civil rights groups in the GDR, as evident in its name, the *Kirchlicher Arbeitskreis Homosexualität Dresden* (Church working group for homosexuals in Dresden) organized itself within the church. For more information on the ostensible political immunity that churches (largely evangelical) had in the GDR, see Mary Fulbrook, "Render unto Caesar? The Pivotal Role of the Protestant Churches," in her *Anatomy of a Dictatorship: Inside the GDR 1949–1989* (Oxford: Oxford University Press, 1995), 87–128. For a more critical evaluation of the church, see Hans-Joachim Maaz, *Behind the Wall: The Inner Life of Communist Germany* (New York: W. W. Norton, 1995), 48–52. For the source of the quotations, see Ulrich Zieger, "Info Brief," 1985, Gino-Hahnemann-Archiv, no. 280. All translations from this text by the author.

29. "Zwischen Fantasie und Wirklichkeit," November 27 and 28, 1987, Gino-Hahnemann-Archiv, no. 283. All translations from this text by the author.

30. "Wir alle sind nur in dem Maß Menschen geworden, in welchem wir Menschen liebten oder Gelegenheit sie zu lieben hatten." Source of quotation unknown. Translation by the author.

31. Quoted in Jeffrey M. Peck and Jürgen Lemke, "Being Gay in Germany: An Interview with Jürgen Lemke," in "German Unification," special issue of *New German Critique*, no. 52 (Winter 1991): 153.

32. Thomas Naumann in conversation with Gino Hahnemann, Gino-Hahnemann-Archiv.

33. Kelly, *Composing the Canon in the GDR*, 2.

34. Ibid., 6 and 2.

35. In the *GINO-KINO* DVD liner notes, Hahnemann cites Jahnn from a 1967 interview with Walter Muschig. The citation from the DVD is as follows: "Gespräche mit Hans Henny Jahnn, aufgezeichnet von Walter Muschg" [sic!], *Europäische Verlagsanstalt*, Frankfurt/Main, 1967, Seite 32. From the liner notes to *GINO-KINO. Filme von Gino Hahnemann 1982–1985* (Berlin: Produktion Geld ohne Ende, 2006), DVD, 4. All translations from this text by the author.

36. Harald Bühl, Dieter Heinze, Hans Koch, and Fred Staufenbiel, "Realismus," *Kulturpolitisches Wörterbuch* (Berlin: Dietz Verlag, 1970), 447. All translations from this text by the author.

37. Patricia Herminghouse, "Die Wiederentdeckung der Romantik: zur Funktion der Dichterfiguren in der neueren DDR-Literatur," in *DDR-Roman und Literaturgesellschaft*, ed. Jos Hoogeveen and Gerd Labroisse (Amsterdam: Rodopi, 1981), 219. Friedrich Schiller was the closest equal to Goethe. Hahnemann addresses him in his film by visualizing Goethe drawing Schiller's house.

38. Claudia Knetsch, "Betrachtungen zur Rezeption Goethes und Schillers in der SBZ/DDR (1949–59)," *Uni-Journal Jena* (April 2000). All translations from this text by the author.

39. Kelly, *Composing the Canon in the GDR*, 109.

40. *GINO-KINO* DVD liner notes, 4.

41. Ibid.

42. Ibid.

43. Stötzer is called by her married name, Gabi Kachold, in the program shown in figure 4.13.

44. "Interfilm 3 (26.9.—29.9.1985, West Berlin)," Gino-Hahnemann-Archiv, no. 279, Akademie der Künste, Berlin. All translations from this text by the author.

45. "Deutsche Demokratische Republik," in ibid.

46. Claus Löser, "Vorab," in Fritzsche and Löser, *Gegenbilder*, 17 and 17n19.

47. Ibid., 18.

48. Cornelia Klauß, "Die Stand der Dinge oder wie ich Schmalfilm lieben lernte," *KOMA-KINO*, no. 1 (1987): n.p. All translations from this text by the author.

49. Ibid.

50. Cornelia Schleime in "DEFA 50—Die Sechste. 17.10.1986. Filmische Subversion—Das andere Kino" (panel discussion with Schleime and others, moderated by Knut Elstermann), in *DEFA 50: Gespräche aus acht Filmnächten; Protokolle*, ed. Ingrid Poss (Potsdam, Germany: Brandenburgische Landeszentrale für Politische Bildung, 1997), 157. All translations from this text by the author.

51. Ibid.

52. Christoph Tannert, quoted in Elisabeth Jappe, *Performance, Ritual, Prozeß* (Munich: Prestel Verlag, 1993), 61. All translations from this text by the author.

53. Klauß, "Die Stand der Dinge," n.p.

54. See, for example, Elisabeth Jappe, who describes the lack of interest in the Auto-Perforation Artists in relation to the Viennese Actionists: "These are such superficial rejections; even if these works . . . share a similar aesthetic, completely different artistic motivations background them; in the time they produced this work, the artists had barely any knowledge of these alleged exemplars." Jappe, *Performance, Ritual, Prozeß*, 61.

55. The program appeared on Kanal 4 and was produced by the Cologne-based production team named KAOS, also affiliated with a gallery of the same name, and was facilitated by Gerd Harry "Judy" Lybke via his gallery EIGEN+ART in Leipzig. The filmmakers included Mario Achsnick, Thomas Werner, Yana Milev, and Cornelia Klauß. The program was titled "Bericht über Super-8-Filmszene in der DDR," which translates to "A Report on the Super-8 Film Scene in the GDR." An exact broadcast date is unknown, but an excerpted copy of the program is in the EIGEN+ART archive in Potsdam, Germany. See EIGEN + ART 1988-045 [Videoarchiv].

56. Wolfgang Engler, *Die Ostdeutschen. Kunde von einem verlorenen Land* (Berlin: Aufbau Taschenverlag, 2002), 169.

57. John Cunningham, *Hungarian Cinema: From Coffee House to Multiplex* (London: Wallflower Press, 2004).

58. Amos Vogel, *Film as a Subversive Art* (New York: Distributed Art Publisher; United Kingdom: C.T. Editions, 1974), accessed May 7, 2021, https://monoskop.org/File:Vogel_Amos_Film_as_a_Subversive_Art.pdf, 192.

59. Ibid.

60. On this history, see, for example, Sebastian Heiduschke, "Film Censorship, the East German *Nouvelle Vague*, and the 'Rabbit Films': *Das Kaninchen bin ich* (*The Rabbit Is Me*, Kurt Maetzig, 1965)," in his *East German Cinema: DEFA and Film History* (New York: Palgrave MacMillan, 2013), 77–83.

61. There are a few important cases of experimental films made within the GDR's state film house, DEFA. These include Jürgen Böttcher's triptych *Verwandlungen: I. Potters Stier; II. Venus nach Giorgione; III. Frau am Klavichord* (1981) and Lutz Dammbeck's animations, including the narrative short *Einmart* (1981). See Claus Löser's chapter on painting and experimental film, which discusses both of these filmmakers at length: "Malerfilme der ersten Generation," in his *Strategien der Verweigerung*, 97–169. See also Sara Blaylock, "*Verwandlungen* (Strawalde, 1981)," in *The Handbook of East German Cinema: The DEFA Legacy*, ed. Henning Wrage and Evan Torner (Berlin: De Gruyter, anticipated 2022).

62. I am indebted to Amelia Jones, who honors the "life" of the archived object. See, for example, Amelia Jones, "'Presence' in Absentia: Experiencing Performance as Documentation," in "Performance Art: (Some) Theory and (Selected) Practice at the End of this Century," special issue of *Art Journal* 56, no. 4 (Winter 1997): 11–18.

63. Löser, *Strategien der Verweigerung*, 82.

CHAPTER 5

1. The band was made up of Lothar Fiedler, Hans-Jürgen Noack, and Gottfried Rössler

2. The length of the 1985 *HERAKLES* performance in Coswig is unrecorded, but a video of a 1984 performance (ostensibly its own independent 4D work) archived on the Herakles Konzept website is listed at 10 minutes and 28 seconds. Lutz Dammbeck, "Video Herakles (1984)," Adobe Flash video, 10:28, Herakles Konzept, accessed May 7, 2021, http://herakleskonzept.de/material/index.php/video-herakles.html.

3. Dammbeck formally adopted the name *Herakles Konzept* in 1984 for the first performance of a media collage at the Klubhaus Nationale Front in Leipzig on June 24 of that year. The idea to make a Hercules-inspired film originated in 1979.

4. For more on East Germany's desire to divide itself from its World War II-era past, as well as to differentiate itself from West Germany, see Jeffrey Herf, *Divided Memory: The Nazi Past in the Two Germanys* (Cambridge, MA: Harvard University Press, 1997).

5. Seth Howes, *Moving Images on the Margins: Experimental Film in Late Socialist East Germany* (Rochester, NY: Camden House, 2019), 48.

6. Matthias Flügge, "Von der Erfindung zum Dokument—das HERAKLES KONZEPT von Lutz Dammbeck," Herakles Konzept, accessed May 7, 2021, http://www.herakleskonzept.de/material/index.php/herakles-konzept-95.html. All translations from this text by the author.

7. February 3, 1984, letter quoted in Howes, *Moving Images on the Margins*, 62. Original citation: Lutz Dammbeck, *REALFilm: Arbeitsmaterialien und Texte, 1985–1986* (Hamburg: LDI Produktion, 2008), n.p.

8. The attendance figure is taken from a Stasi report, which estimates that 800 people attended the first night and 400 people attended the second night of the festival. BStU, MfS, BV Berlin AKG 2008, 2: "Information über die Veranstaltung 'Intermedia I' am 1. und 2. 6. 1985 im Klubhaus Coswig, Kreis Meißen," June 19, 1985. For a comprehensive list of artists, musical acts, and more, see Barbara Büscher, "Intermedia DDR 1985—Ereignis und Netzwerk," *media archive performance*, no. 2 (2010), accessed May 7, 2021, http://www.perfomap.de/map2/geschichte/intermedia-ddr.

9. Christoph Tannert, "'Intermedia I' in Coswig 1985," in *Ohne uns! Kunst und alternative Kultur in Dresden vor und nach '89*, ed. Frank Eckhardt and Paul Kaiser, exhibition catalog (Dresden: Efau Verlag, 2009), 318. All translations from this text by the author.

10. Dammbeck first took evening classes from 1965 to 1967 before studying full-time from 1967 to 1972 at the Hochschule für Grafik und Buchkunst (Academy of Fine Arts) in Leipzig, with a specialization in book design.

11. Successes include the animations *Der Mond* (*The Moon*, 6 min., 1975), *Der Schneider von Ulm* (*The Tailor from Ulm*, 14 min., 1979), and *Einmart* (15 min., 1981).

12. Doris Liebermann, *Ein Piratenstück: Der 1. Leipziger Herbstsalon 1984, seine Vorgeschichte und seine Protagonisten* (Halle (Saale), Germany: Mitteldeutscher Verlag, 2014).

13. Gene Youngblood, *Expanded Cinema* (New York: Dutton, 1970).

14. Stötzer went by the surname Kachold or Kachold-Stötzer in East Germany.

15. Gabriele Stötzer, email message to author, February 27, 2017.

16. Tannert, "'Intermedia I' in Coswig 1985," 313–314.

17. Ibid., 315.

18. Büscher, "Intermedia DDR 1985."

19. Paul Kaiser and Claudia Petzold, *Boheme und Diktatur in der DDR: Gruppen, Konflikte, Quartiere 1970–1989* (Berlin: Fannei & Walz, 1997), 148.

20. Christoph Tannert, "Intermedia. Versuche kollektiver Kunstproduktion," *Musik und Gesellschaft*, no. 34 (1984): 349–353. All translations from this text by the author.

21. Ibid., 349.

22. Ibid.

23. Christoph Tannert, personal interview, January 26, 2015. All translations from this interview by the author.

24. Ibid.

25. Ibid.

26. See, for example, Barbara Barsch, "'Ist das noch Kunst?' Zu einigen Aspekten intermedialer Arbeit junger Künstler der DDR," *Bildende Kunst* (September 1989): 31–34.

27. See, for example, Myra Marx Ferree, "The Rise and Fall of 'Mommy Politics': Feminism and Unification in (East) Germany," *Feminist Studies* 19, no. 1 (Spring 1993): 89–115.

28. Claudia Mesch, *Modern Art at the Berlin Wall: Demarcating Culture in the Cold War Germanys* (London: I. B. Tauris, 2006), 197.

29. Uta Grundmann, "Die Künstlergruppe Clara Mosch," Bundeszentrale für politische Bildung, September 6, 2012, accessed May 7, 2021, https://www.bpb.de/geschichte/deutsche-geschichte/autonome-kunst-in-der-ddr/55822/clara-mosch.

30. Mesch, *Modern Art at the Berlin Wall*, 193–194.

31. Christoph Tannert, personal interview, November 3, 2014. All translations from this interview by the author.

32. See, for example, Lutz Dammbeck's comment that "At the end of 1985 everything in Leipzig had fizzled out; it was all over." He put in exit papers, which were granted in September 1986. Lutz Dammbeck, "Vorlauf. Die Mediencollagen (1984–1988)," Herakles Konzept, accessed May 7, 2021, http://www.herakleskonzept.de/material/index.php/vorlauf.html. All translations from this text by the author.

33. Between 1980 and 1985, roughly four hundred artists and art historians left the GDR. Werner Schmidt, ed., *Ausgebürgert. Künstler aus der DDR und aus dem Sowjetischen Sektor Berlins 1949–1989*, exhibition catalog (Berlin: Argon Verlag, 1990), 65–72.

34. Jens Gieseke, *The History of the Stasi: East Germany's Secret Police, 1945–1990* (New York: Berghahn Books, 2014), 147.

35. Lutz Dammbeck, email message to author, September 29, 2020. Emphasis in the original. All translations from this message by the author.

36. Christoph Tannert, personal interview, May 11, 2015. All translations from this interview by the author.

37. Program flyer entitled "workshop I. Interferenzen," Dresden, Kulturpalast, May 23, 1979, reprinted in Matthias Herrmann, "Zweite Realität. Avancierte Musik in Dresdner Institutionen zwischen 1950 und 1989," in Eckhardt and Kaiser, *Ohne uns!*, 140. All translations from this text by the author.

38. BStU, MfS, HA II, Nr. 33928, 1–2: "Inhaltsverzeichnis," n.d. All translations from this text by the author.

39. Esther von Richthofen, *Bringing Culture to the Masses: Control, Compromise, and Participation in the GDR* (New York: Berghahn Books, 2009). See also Alexei Yurchak's discussion of mass organizations and their autonomy from state politics in *Everything Was Forever, Until It Was No More: The Last Soviet Generation* (Princeton: Princeton University Press, 2006).

40. Richthofen, *Bringing Culture to the Masses*, 149.

41. Ibid., 179.

42. Paul Kaiser, *Boheme in der DDR. Kunst und Gegenkultur im Staatssozialismus* (Dresden: Dresdner Institut für Kulturstudien, 2016), 74.

43. Richthofen, *Bringing Culture to the Masses*, 193.

44. Ibid., 54 and 75.

45. BStU, MfS, BV Leipzig Abt. XX, Nr. 0271/08, 2: "Am 1. und 2. 6. 1985 fand im Klubhaus Coswig . . . ," n.d. (June 1985?). All translations from this text by the author.

46. Seth Howes, "Pessimism and the Politics of the Future in East German Punk," *Journal of Popular Culture* 49, no. 1 (February 2016): 77–96

47. See, for example, Howes's description of Schleimkeim frontman Dieter "Otze" Ehrlich, who faced Stasi intimidation and legal punishment despite his eighteen-month collaboration as an IM. Ibid., 84–85.

48. BStU, MfS, BV Leipzig Abt. XX, Nr. 0271/08, 6: "Am 1. und 2. 6. 1985 fand im Klubhaus Coswig . . . ," n.d. (June 1985?). All translations from this text by the author.

49. I use the pronoun "his" without qualification. Leadership positions were overwhelmingly held by men, not just in the Stasi, but across professions in the GDR. On men in the Stasi, see Gabriele Stötzer, "Das künstliche Frauenbild der Stasi konzentriert auf Stasi-Aktivitäten in der Thüringer Provinz in den 80iger Jahren," presentation, Tübingen, Germany, 2014.

50. BStU, MfS, BV Leipzig Abt. XX 0271/08, 7: "Am 1. und 2. 6. 1985 fand im Klubhaus Coswig . . . ," n.d. (June 1985?). All translations from this text by the author.

51. Harald Bühl, Dieter Heinze, Hans Koch, and Fred Staufenbiel, "Arten, Gattungen und Genres der Kunst," in *Kulturpolitisches Wörterbuch* (Berlin: Dietz Verlag, 1970), 35. Emphasis in the original. All translations from this text by the author.

52. Ibid., 34.

53. Karl Marx, *Economic and Philosophic Manuscripts of 1844* (Mineola, NY: Dover, 2007), 108. Emphasis in the original.

54. Bühl et al., "Arten, Gattungen und Genres der Kunst," 35.

55. See, for example, Clement Greenberg, "Towards a Newer Laocoon," *Partisan Review* 7, no. 4 (July–August 1940): 296–310.

56. Bühl et al., "Arten, Gattungen und Genres der Kunst," 37.

57. Ibid., 38.

58. Bühl et al., "Experiment, künstlerisches," in *Kulturpolitisches Wörterbuch*, 139. All translations from this text by the author.

59. Richard C. Higgins, "Intermedia (1965)," *Horizons: The Poetics and Theory of the Intermedia* (Carbondale and Edwardsville: Southern Illinois University Press, 1984), 22.

60. "Rg" stands for both *rot-grün* (red-green) and *Raumgemeinschaft* (space collective).

61. Eugen Blume, "Laborismus gegen Kapitalismus und Kommunismus im Dunkeln: Joseph Beuys," in *Wahnzimmer/Klopfzeichen. Kunst und Kultur der 80er Jahre in Deutschland*, ed. Eugen Blume, Hubertus Gaßner, Eckhart Gillen, and Hans-Werner Schmidt, exhibition catalog (Leipzig: Faber & Faber Verlag, 2002), 49. All translations from this text by the author.

62. Eugen Blume and Christoph Tannert, "Dokumentation zur Aktionskunst in Berlin-DDR," 1989, Verband-Bildender-Künstler-Archiv, Berlin, no. 36, Akademie der Künste, Berlin. All translations from this text by the author.

63. For a comprehensive overview of Klaus Werner's contribution, see *Klaus Werner: Für die Kunst*, ed. Gabriele Muschter et al. (Köln: Verlag der Buchhandlung Walther König, 2000).

64. Sozialistische Einheitspartei Deutschland, the Socialist Unity Party of Germany. The SED was the GDR's governing political party.

65. Blume reflects on Werner's influence on his thesis on Beuys in Eugen Blume, "Außerhalb der Ordnung," in *Klaus Werner*, 14–16.

66. Eugen Blume, "Das Ergebnis ist ein Prozess," *Bildende Kunst* 4 (1982): 202.

67. Blume, "Laborismus gegen Kapitalismus und Kommunismus im Dunkeln," 49.

68. Uta Grundmann, Klaus Michael, and Susanne Seufert, eds., *Revolution im geschlossenen Raum. Die andere Kultur in Leipzig 1970–1990* (Leipzig: Verlag Faber & Faber, 2002), 93.

69. For more on this project, see Constanze Fritzsch, "Allez! Arrest: Gelebte Wirklichkeit gegen tote Realität," *OwnReality* 25 (2016): 1–26.

70. Gerd Harry "Judy" Lybke, quoted in Karim Saab, "Gespräch mit Judy Lybke," in "EIGEN+ART im Gespräch," special issue of *Anschlag*, ed. Karim Saab (Leipzig, 1988), n.p. All translations from this text by the author.

71. Christoph Tannert, email message to author, February 19, 2017. These catalogs were Hanns Sohm, ed., *Happening und Fluxus* (Cologne: Kölnischer Kunstverein, 1970), and *Fluxus: Aspekte eines Phänomens* (Wuppertal: Kunst- und Museumsverein, 1982).

72. For more on this, see Petra Stegmann, ed., *Fluxus East: Fluxus-Netzwerke in Mittelosteuropa / Fluxus Networks in Central Eastern Europe* (Berlin: Künstlerhaus Bethanien, 2007).

73. Bojana Cvejić, "Introductory Note," in *Parallel Slalom: A Lexicon of Non-aligned Poetics*, ed. Bojana Cvejić and Goran Sergej Pristaš (Belgrade: Walking Theory, 2013), 12.

74. Bojana Cvejić, "Problems That Aesthetically 'Unburden' Us," in Cvejić and Pristaš, *Parallel Slalom*, 324.

75. Ibid.

76. Bojana Cvejić, "A Parallel Slalom from BADco: In Search of a Poetics of Problems," *Representations*, no. 136 (Fall 2016): 23.

77. Cvejić, "Problems That Aesthetically 'Unburden' Us," 325.

78. Bojana Kunst, "Politics of Affection and Uneasiness," in Cvejić and Pristaš, *Parallel Slalom*, 341–352.

79. Ibid., 342.

80. Ibid.

81. Cvejić, "Parallel Slalom from BADco," 23

CHAPTER 6

1. Harald Bühl, Dieter Heinze, Hans Koch, and Fred Staufenbiel, "Menschenbild, sozialistisches," *Kulturpolitisches Wörterbuch* (Berlin: Dietz Verlag, 1970), 358. All translations from this text by the author.

2. Ibid.

3. Karl-Siegbert Rehberg, "Die verdrängte Abstraktion. Feind-Bilder im Kampfkonzept des 'Sozialistischen Realismus,'" in *Abstraktion im Sozialismus. Feindsetzungen und Freiräume im Kunstsystem der DDR*, ed. Karl-Siegbert Rehberg and Paul Kaiser (Weimar: Verlag und Datenback für Geistwissenschaften, 2003), 18. All translations from this text by the author.

4. The group would use a number of different names. From "Undine" to "Atlantis" to "Exterra XX," these names seemed to be randomly selected. Gabriele Stötzer suggested that I combine the original name *Künstlerinnengruppe* and *Exterra XX*. Gabriele Stötzer, email message to author, February 27, 2017. All translations from this message by the author.

5. Wolfgang Engler, *Die Ostdeutschen. Kunde von einem verlorenen Land* (Berlin: Aufbau-Verlag, 2002), 281. All translations from this text by the author. The term "*Organisationsgesellschaft*" was first applied by the sociologist Detlef Pollack to describe the GDR. See, for example, Detlef Pollack, "Das Ende einer Organisationsgesellschaft: systemtheoretische Überlegungen zum gesellschaftlichen Umbruch in der DDR," *Zeitschrift für Soziologie* 19, no. 4 (1990): 292–307.

6. Engler, *Die Ostdeutschen*, 61.

7. Engler writes on the significance of people working together; see, especially, "Eine arbeiterliche Gesellschaft" in ibid., 173–208.

8. Günter Gaus, *Wo Deutschland liegt: Eine Ortsbestimmung* (Hamburg: Hoffmann und Campe, 1983), 156–233.

9. Engler, *Die Ostdeutschen*, 61.

10. Stötzer went by the surname Kachold or Kachold-Stötzer in East Germany.

11. Stötzer and her friends used a house at Pergamentergasse 41 from about 1982 onward. In 1990, several women in the collective, including Stötzer, purchased a house at Michaelisstraße 34 and turned it into an official arts space called the Kunsthaus Erfurt (Art House of Erfurt). At the time of this book's publication, Monique Förster still directs the space.

12. Gabriele Stötzer, personal interview, May 3, 2015. All translations from this interview by the author.

13. A 2014 exhibition catalog about Erfurt's subculture lists the following members: Angelika Andres, Monika Andres, Eve Bach, Claudia Bogenhardt, Tely Büchner, Monique Förster, Gabriele Göbel, Anke Hendrich, Ina Heyer, Angelika Hummel, Elisabeth Kaufhold, Dorothea Krug, Verena Kyselka, Ines Lesch, Bettina Neumann, Ingrid Plöttner, Karina Popp, Birgit Quehl, Jutta Rauchfuß, Anita Ritter, Marlies Schmidt, Susanne Schmidt, Gabriele Stötzer, Susanne Trockenbrodt, Harriet Wollert, as well as one man, Frank Zieris. I have drawn this list from Claus Löser, "Die Geister Berühren. Undergroundfilme von Erfurter Frauen," in *Zwischen Ausstieg und Aktion. Die Erfurter Subkultur der 1960er, 1970er und 1980er Jahre*, ed. Tely Büchner and Susanne Knorr (Bielefeld: Kerber Verlag, 2014), 105 n7. Löser also lists Dirk Schütz as a second man in the group, but Gabriele Stötzer names Zieris as the only man in the group; he reported to the Stasi on their activities under the name Udo. Stötzer, email to author.

14. Gabriele Stötzer, personal interview, May 4, 2015. All translations from this interview by the author.

15. Gabriele Stötzer quoted in Claus Löser, "Super-8 als soziale Plastik. Die Schmalfilme Gabriele Stötzers im Kontext der unabhängigen DDR-Filmszene," in *Gabriele Stötzer. Schwingungskurve Leben*, ed. Ulrike Bestgen, Wolfgang Holler, and Gabriele Stötzer-Kachold, exhibition catalog (Weimar: Klassik Stiftung Weimar, 2013), 57. The original citation was from Monique Förster, ed., *Künstlerinnengruppe Exterra XX* (Erfurt: Kunsthaus Erfurt, 2001), 21. All translations from this text by the author.

16. Gabriele Stötzer, "Überwachung von Kunst und Kultur. Der lange Arm der Staatssicherheit," in Büchner and Knorr, *Zwischen Ausstieg und Aktion*, 159. Stötzer names the IM "Udo" as "the only man who appeared as a musician and a performer with the *Women Artists Group*." Other people, including a man named Peter Krause (IM alias Breaky), were also sent as Stasi spies to observe the group's activities. See the first chapter of this book for a description of Krause's relationship to Stötzer's art practice, as well as her memories of him. Stötzer, email to author.

17. Gabriele Stötzer quoted in Claus Löser, *Strategien der Verweigerung. Untersuchungen zum politisch-ästhetischen Gestus unangepasster filmischer Artikulationen in der Spätphase der DDR* (Berlin: DEFA-Stiftung, 2011), 292. All translations from this text by the author.

18. Stötzer, personal interview, May 3, 2015.

19. Ibid.

20. For more on the process of collaboration and its impacts on group cohesion, see Gabriele Stötzer, "Frauenträume ändern das Leben in der geschlossenen Gesellschaft," *Horch und Guck*, no. 65 (March 2009): 28–31.

21. Gabriele Stötzer, *erfurter roulette* (Munich: Peter Kirchheim Verlag, 1995), 18. All translations from this text by the author.

22. Stötzer, personal interview, May 4, 2015.

23. Bojana Kunst, "Delay," in *Parallel Slalom: A Lexicon of Non-aligned Poetics*, ed. Bojana Cvejić and Goran Sergej Pristaš (Belgrade: Walking Theory, 2013), 352–353.

24. Mladen Stilinović, "In Praise of Laziness," in Cvejić and Pristaš, *Parallel Slalom*, 335–340.

25. Kunst, "Delay," 352.

26. Ibid.

27. For more on this history, see Yvonne Fiedler, "Die Galerie im Flur in Erfurt," in *Kunst im Korridor. Private Galerien in der DDR zwischen Autonomie und Illegalität* (Berlin: Christoph Links Verlag, 2013), 106–135.

28. Ines Geipel, "Der Preis war hoch," *Emma* (1 November 2009), accessed May 7, 2021, https://www.emma.de/artikel/ueberlebende-der-preis-war-hoch-264201.

29. A 2016 exhibition curated by Christoph Tannert at the Künstlerhaus Bethanien in Berlin focused on the significance of the so-called Biermann Affair to East Germany's artists. Christoph Tannert, ed., *Ende vom Lied*, exhibition catalog (Berlin: Künstlerhaus Bethanien, 2016).

30. Sozialistische Einheitspartei Deutschland, the Socialist Unity Party of Germany. The SED was the GDR's governing political party.

31. Klaus Schroeder, "The SED's Fear of the Big Bad Wolf," in Tannert, *Ende vom Lied*, 245.

32. A good visual example of how citizens deemed antisocial could be treated is in the character of Stella in Christian Petzold's film *Barbara* (2012).

33. Stötzer, personal interview, May 3, 2015.

34. DW Euromaxx, "In Prison in the GDR—Fighting against the Regime with Art: Witnessing the Fall of the Wall," YouTube video, 8:07, October 29, 2019, https://www.youtube.com/watch?v=aQejyOVZgdU.

35. Between 1980 and 1985, roughly four hundred artists and art historians left the GDR. Werner Schmidt, ed., *Ausgebürgert. Künstler aus der DDR und aus dem Sowjetischen Sektor Berlins 1949–1989*, exhibition catalog (Berlin: Argon Verlag, 1990), 65–72.

36. For more on SUM, see Harald Schluttig, "Christine Schlegel—Ich bin—SUM," YouTube video, 14:28, March 4, 2013, https://www.youtube.com/watch?v=mmN8lMmzLwA.

37. Christine Schlegel, personal interview, June 29, 2015. All translations from this interview by the author.

38. Marlies Menge, "Wo schöne Träume verboten werden," *Die Zeit* (April 2, 1982).

39. Christine Lässig, "Frauen stellten ihre eigenen Fragen," *Thüringer Tagesblatt*, no. 142 (June 17, 1988).

40. Myra Marx Ferree, "The Rise and Fall of 'Mommy Politics': Feminism and Unification in (East) Germany," *Feminist Studies* 19, no. 1 (Spring 1993): 96.

41. Stötzer, personal interview, May 3, 2015.

42. eog formed in 1986 and included Ina Heyner, Gabriele Stötzer (then Kachold), and Verena Kyselka.

43. Ferree, "Rise and Fall of 'Mommy Politics,'" 98.

44. See, for example, Wolfgang Mattheuer's response to Eckhart Gillen and Rainer Haarmann, eds., "Fragen an Politiker, Künstler und Kunstkritiker zum 9. November 1989," in *Kunst in der DDR*, ed. Eckhart Gillen and Rainer Haarmann (Cologne: Kiepenheuer & Witsch, 1990), 48. All translations from this text by the author.

45. Gabriele Muschter in ibid., 42–43. All translations from this text by the author.

46. Klara Kemp-Welch, *Antipolitics in Central European Art: Reticence as Dissidence under Post-Totalitarian Rule, 1956–1989* (London: I. B. Tauris, 2014). See also Václav Havel, "Politics and Conscience" (1985; UnivForum, 2015), http://www.univcongress.info/static/2015/10/Politics-conscience.pdf.

47. G. E. Edwards, *GDR Society and Social Institutions* (London: Macmillan, 1985), 68 and 77: table 2.7, "Percentage of women in universities and colleges of higher education in 1982," and table 2.11, "Female population and female employees (in 1000s)," respectively.

48. Ibid., 81 and 101: table 2.15, "Women in the professions, as percentage," and table 2.24, "Percentage of men and women in the Peoples Chamber."

49. Ferree, "Rise and Fall of 'Mommy Politics,'" 96.

50. Ibid.

51. Irene Dölling, "Frauen- und Männerbilder. Eine Analyse von Fotos in DDR-Zeitschriften," *Feministische Studien*, 8, no. 1 (1990): 40. All translations from this text by the author.

52. Marilyn Rueschemeyer, "Women in East Germany: From State Socialism to Capitalist Welfare State," in *Democratic Reform and the Position of Women in Transitional Economies*, ed. Valentine M. Moghadam (Oxford: Clarendon Press, 1993), 78.

53. Ferree, "Rise and Fall of 'Mommy Politics,'" 93–94.

54. Frauen für Veränderungen Bürgerinneninitiative (Kerstin Schön, Mechthild Ziegenhagen, Michaela Hopf, Sabine Fabian, Gabi Kachold [Stötzer], Susanne Keßler, Barbara Weisshuhn,

Verena Kyselka, Elisabeth Kaufhold, Almuth Falcke, Christiane Dietrich, Andrea Richter, Heidi Malz, Uta Schmidt, and Petra Streit), "Offener Brief," October 2, 1989. Gabriele Stötzer personal archive, Erfurt, Germany. All translations from this text by the author.

55. Stötzer, personal interview, May 3, 2015.

56. Harriet Wollert, "Wer ist Gabriele Stötzer? Ein Versuch" in *Schwingungskurve Leben*, 62.

57. Stötzer, personal interview, May 3, 2015.

58. Blake Stimson and Gregory Sholette, eds., *Collectivism after Modernism: The Art of Social Imagination after 1945* (Minneapolis: University of Minnesota Press, 2007).

59. Ibid., xii.

CHAPTER 7

1. I use the term "samizdat," which literally translates to "self-published" in Russian, as a means of generalizing East German independent publications within a larger Eastern Bloc print phenomenon of the late Cold War period. I follow the lead of other scholarship, including the Humboldt University-produced *Berliner Hefte zur Geschichte des literarischen Lebens*, which, in an issue with a key focus on East German artist publications, contextualizes these texts as "Eastern European 'Samizdat-culture.'" See, for example, Ilona Schäkel, "ANSCHLAG, HERZATTACKE und andere SCHADENsfälle. Grundriß einer Typologie der originalgraphischen Zeitschriften aus der DDR," *Berliner Hefte zur Geschichte des literarischen Lebens*, no. 4 (2001): 118. It is important to note that the Germanist David Bathrick advises against the use of the term "samizdat" to describe independent publications from the GDR, because the Russian context from which it derives was far different from that of East Germany. See David Bathrick, *The Powers of Speech: The Politics of Culture in the GDR* (Lincoln: University of Nebraska Press, 1995), 59–61.

2. Katherine Pence, "Eat, Drink & Smoke," in *Beyond the Wall: Art and Artifacts from the GDR/Jenseits der Mauer. Kunst und Alltagsgegenstände aus der DDR*, ed. Justinian Jampol, Benedikt Taschen, and Ina Pfitzner (Cologne: Taschen, 2014), 28.

3. Karim Saab, email message to author, February 23, 2016. All translations from this message by the author.

4. For a complete index of independent publications from the GDR, see Frank Eckart, ed., *Eigenart und Eigensinn. Alternative Kulturszenen in der DDR (1980–1990)* (Bremen: Edition Temmen, 1993).

5. Yvonne Fiedler, *Kunst im Korridor. Private Galerien in der DDR zwischen Autonomie und Illegalität* (Berlin: Christoph Links Verlag, 2013), 55, table 1. All translations from this text by the author.

6. The name also refers to the word "eigenartig," which means "peculiar" or "strange."

7. Ulrike Knöfel, "Du fühlst dich unsterblich," *Der Spiegel*, no. 34 (August 18, 2014): 113. All translations from this text by the author.

8. Saab, email to author.

9. Ibid.

10. See Frank Eckart's description of the state's collections of independent publications and artists books, etc., in *Eigenart und Eigensinn*, 94.

11. Katharina Hegewisch, "Im Dienste der Unsterblichkeit. Gerd Harry Lybke," accessed May 7, 2021, http://eigen-art.com/files/text_khegewisch.pdf, 8. All translations from this text by the author.

12. Knöfel, "Du fühlst dich unsterblich," 113.

13. Ibid.

14. Ibid.

15. Fiedler, *Kunst im Korridor*, 48.

16. Florian Berg, "Literarische Zeitschriften: Anschlag," *Berliner Hefte zur literarischen Lebens* 4 (2001): 128.

17. For more on the Hoffnung Nicaragua history, see Karim Saab, "Initiative 'Hoffnung Nicaragua,'" in *Revolution im geschlossenen Raum. Die andere Kultur in Leipzig 1970–1990*, ed. Uta Grundmann, Klaus Michael, and Susanne Seufert (Leipzig: Verlag Faber & Faber, 2002), 67–69.

18. Saab, email to author.

19. This is a play on the words *entweder/oder*, which means "either/or."

20. Uwe Warnke, "Viermal um den Block. Alternatives Publizieren von Fotografie in der späten DDR," June 19, 2013, accessed May 7, 2021, https://uwewarnke.wordpress.com/2013/06/19/uwe-warnke-viermal-um-den-block/. All translations from this text by the author.

21. BStU, MfS, BV Leipzig ZMA AKG, Nr. 4974, 65–66: "Operativinformation Nr. 241/86," n.d. (June 1986?). All translations from this text by the author.

22. See Helgard Sauer's description quoted in Frank Eckart, "Nie überwundener Mangel an Farben. . . . Über ein Kapitel der Kulturentwicklung in der DDR der achtziger Jahre," in Eckart, *Eigenart und Eigensinn*, 38.

23. Saab, email to author.

24. Under pressure from authorities, Lothar Fiedler abandoned his Dresden-based magazine *Und* in May 1985. He re-formed under the title *USW*, which had already begun producing publications in 1984. On this history, see Klaus Michael and Thomas Wolfhart, eds., *Vogel oder Käfig sein. Kunst und Literatur aus unabhängigen Zeitschriften in der DDR 1979–1989* (Berlin: Druckhaus Galrev, 1991), 412.

25. See, for example, Dominic Boyer, "Foucault in the Bush: The Social Life of Post-Structuralist Theory in East Berlin's Prenzlauer Berg," *Ethnos (Estoclomo)* 66, no. 2 (2001): 207–236.

26. BStU, MfS, BV Leipzig ZMA, AKG, 4974, 45: "Operativinformation Nr. 245/86," July 2, 1986. All translations from this text by the author.

27. Saab, email to author.

28. Wolfgang Hilbig, "Liebe Angelika Klüssendorf," *Anschlag*, no. 2 (Fall 1984): n.p. All translations from this text by the author.

29. Uwe Warnke, "Entwerter-Material (den Umständen entsprechend)," in Uwe Warnke and Ingeborg Quaas, *Die Addition der Differenzen. Die Literaten- und Künstlerszene Ostberlins 1979 bis 1989* (Berlin: Verbrecher Verlag, 2009), 94 n1. All translations from this text by the author.

30. Fritz Hendrik Melle in Antonia Grunenberg, "'Vogel oder Käfig sein'. Zur 'zweiten' Kultur und zu den inoffiziellen Zeitschriften in der DDR," in Eckart, *Eigenart und Eigensinn*, 82. All translations from this text by the author.

31. Saab, email to author.

32. Christoph Tannert, quoted in Gerrit Gohlke, "Ein Interview mit Christoph Tannert. In der Charybde Geheul. Über die Kontinuität kultureller Schulmeisterei," in Warnke and Quaas, *Die Addition der Differenzen*, 200. All translations from this text by the author.

33. Saab, email to author.

34. Ibid.

35. Only 1989 would see more unique titles with 18 publications. The vast majority of them dissolved in the wake of the GDR's 1990 dissolution.

36. Karim Saab and Judy Lybke quoted in Karim Saab, "Gespräch mit Judy Lybke," in "EIGEN+ART im Gespräch," special issue of *Anschlag*, ed. Karim Saab (Leipzig, 1988), n.p. All translations from this text by the author.

37. For more on Reichardt's gallery, see Claudia Reichardt, *Die Galerie bleibt während der Öffnungszeit geschlossen. Wanda und die Villa Marie 1982–1990* (Berlin: Martin Schmitz Verlag, 2010).

38. See, for example, Herbert Lange, *EIGEN+ART. Die Geschichte der Galerie im Spiegel der Quellen* (Leipzig: Leipziger Universitätsverlag, 2013), and Grundmann, Michael, and Seufert, eds., *Revolution im geschlossenen Raum*, 69–101.

39. Gerd Harry "Judy" Lybke, personal interview, March 17, 2015.

40. For an explanation of all laws used against private galleries, see Fiedler, *Kunst im Korridor*, 49–53.

41. Saab, "Gespräch mit Judy Lybke," n.p.

42. Uta Grundmann, "Der '1. Leipziger Herbstsalon,'" Bundeszentrale für politische Bildung website, September 6, 2012, accessed May 7, 2021, http://www.bpb.de/geschichte/deutsche-geschichte/autonome-kunst-in-der-ddr/55829/herbstsalon. See also Doris Liebermann, *Ein Piratenstück: Der 1. Leipziger Herbstsalon 1984, seine Vorgeschichte und seine Protagonisten* (Halle (Saale), Germany: Mitteldeutscher Verlag, 2014).

43. EIGEN+ART also produced at least one special publication for an exhibition inspired by the dancer and performance artist Fine Kwiatkowski, "FINE," April 28 to May 21, 1989. EIGEN+ART archive, Potsdam, H 80 (1989).

44. Knöfel, "Du fühlst dich unsterblich," 114.

45. Zdenka Badovinac, quoted in Sven Spieker and Nataša Petrešin-Bachelez, "Creating Context: Zdenka Badovinac on Eastern Europe's Missing Histories," interview with Zdenka Badovinac in ARTMargins [online], August 31, 2009, accessed May 7, 2021, https://artmargins.com/creating-context-zdenka-badovinac-on-eastern-europes-missing-histories-interview/.

46. Ibid.

47. Uwe Wittstock, "Überall lauert Kunst. Die private Galerie EIGEN+ART in Leipzig," *Frankfurter Allgemeine Zeitung*, no. 94 (April 22, 1989), quoted in Lange, *EIGEN+ART*, 73. Translation by the author.

48. Stasi reports frequently referred to subjects by the first letters of their last names, preceded by a definite article. Elsewhere I have argued that this shorthand suggests an attempt by the East German state to make their reports appear more objective or scientific. See Sara Blaylock, "La femme de leurs rêves: Cornelia Schleime et les archives de la Stasi," *Gradhiva*, no. 24 (December 2016): 24; and Sara Blaylock, "Being the Woman They Wanted Her to Be: Cornelia Schleime Performs Her Stasi File," *Third Text* 35, no. 2 (March 2021): 231.

49. BStU, MfS, BV Leipzig ZMA AKG, Nr. 4974, 79: "Vorliegende Erkentnisse zur staatlich nicht genehmigten Galerie 'Eigen-Art'," March 17, 1987. Translation by the author.

50. Bathrick, *The Powers of Speech.*

51. Knöfel, "Du fühlst dich unsterblich," 115.

52. My research in the EIGEN+ART archive as well as at the Humboldt University Archiv für Regionalliteratur/Insititut für deutsche Literatur indicates that some copies of the issue had fewer contributors.

53. Klaus Rudolf, "die von us zu gründende, multimediale dadistische kunstbewegung EIGEN+ART in ihrem humanistisch-pluralistischem charakter kennt keine grenzen," in "EIGEN+ART im Gespräch," n.p.

54. Gabriel Muschter, "20 eigene Sätze über EIGEN+ART," in "EIGEN+ART im Gespräch," n.p.

55. Günther Huniat, "Das läuft mir alles eine Nummer zu zahm ab!," in "EIGEN+ART im Gespräch," n.p.

56. Saab, email to author. For more on the unique role that the Protestant church played in East German society, see Mary Fulbrook, "Render unto Caesar? The Pivotal Role of the Protestant Churches," in her *Anatomy of a Dictatorship: Inside the GDR, 1949–1989* (New York: Oxford University Press, 1995), 87–128.

57. Christoph Tannert, "Als ob alles alright wäre," in "EIGEN+ART im Gespräch," n.p.

58. See Alexei Yurchak on what he describes as the "performative shift" in the late Soviet Union, in Yurchak, *Everything Was Forever, Until It Was No More* (Princeton: Princeton University Press, 2006), 25.

CODA

1. Matthias Fischer, personal interview, November 28, 2016. All translations from this interview by the author.

2. Quoted in Florian Berg, "Initiativgruppe Hoffnung DDR. Gespräch mit Karim Saab," *Berliner Hefte zur literarischen Lebens* 4 (2001): 135. All translations from this text by the author.

3. This is a play on the words *entweder/oder*, which means "either/or."

4. See, for example, Uwe Warnke and Ingeborg Quaas, *Die Addition der Differenzen. Die Literaten- und Künstlerszene Ostberlins 1979 bis 1989* (Berlin: Verbrecher Verlag, 2009); Jana Duda, Gabriele Muschter, and Uwe Warnke, *Geschlossene Gesellschaft. Künstlerische Fotografie in der DDR 1945–1989*, exhibition catalog (Bielefeld: Kerber Verlag, 2012).

5. In East Germany, Schulze Eldowy went simply by "Schulze." She added the name "Eldowy" from the Arabic word *el dowy* (the light) in the mid-1990s.

6. Stötzer went by the surname Kachold or Kachold-Stötzer in East Germany.

7. Madina Tlostanova, *What Does It Mean to Be Post-Soviet? Decolonial Art from the Ruins of the Soviet Empire* (Durham: Duke University Press, 2018), 8.

8. Ibid., 9.

9. Ibid., 4.

10. Pegida stands for *Patriotische Europäer gegen die Islamisierung des Abendlandes*, or Patriotic Europeans Against the Islamization of the Occident.

11. Deutschland.de, "Federal States of Germany," accessed May 7, 2021, https://www.deutschland.de/en/topic/politics/germany-europe/federal-states.

12. European Commission, "GDP per Capita, Consumption per Capita and Price Level Indices," accessed May 7, 2021, https://ec.europa.eu/eurostat/statistics-explained/index.php/GDP_per_capita,_consumption_per_capita_and_price_level_indices.

13. Paul Kaiser, "Vortragsmanuskript/Vortrag, Der Dresdner Bilderstreit,'" lecture held at the Lingner Castle in Dresden, December 7, 2017, accessed May 7, 2021, http://www.kulturstudien-dresden.de/wa_files/Vortrag_20Kaiser.pdf, 17.

14. Günter Grass, "Sich ein Bild machen," in *Zeitvergleich: Malerei und Grafik aus der DDR*, ed. Axel Hecht and Hanne Reinecke (Hamburg: Gruner & Jahr, 1982), 12. All translations from this text by the author.

15. Jacques Derrida, *Archive Fever: A Freudian Impression* (Chicago: University of Chicago Press, 1996), 2.

16. Jens Gieseke, *The History of the Stasi: East Germany's Secret Police, 1945–1990* (New York: Berghahn Books, 2014), 81.

BIBLIOGRAPHY

ARCHIVAL SOURCES

FROM THE AKADEMIE DER KÜNSTE, BERLIN:

Gino-Hahnemann-Archiv, nos. 1–5, 22, 76, 211, 251, 279, 280, and 283

Lutz-Dammbeck-Archiv, no. 14/2

Verband-Bildender-Künstler-Archiv, Zentral-Vorstand, no. 1086

Verband-Bildender-Künstler-Archiv, Berlin, no. 36

FROM THE ARCHIV EIGEN+ART, POTSDAM:

1988-045 [Videoarchiv]

A 1984 0010

H 10 (1987)

H 20 (1987)

H 70 (1989)

H 80 (1989)

FROM THE HOCHSCHULE FÜR BILDENDE KÜNSTE DRESDEN ARCHIV:

Bestand 03, Nr. 1235

FROM THE OFFICE OF THE BUNDESBEAUFTRAGTE FÜR DIE UNTERLAGEN DES STAATSSICHERHEITSDIENSTES DER EHEMALIGEN DDR:

BStU, MfS, BV Berlin, AKG, Nr. 2008

BStU, MfS, BV Dresden, AKG Pl, Nr. 69/89

BStU, MfS, BV Dresden, AOP, Nr. 2784/90/1

BStU, MfS, BV Dresden, AOP, Nr. 2784/90/2

BStU, MfS, BV Erfurt, Abt. XX, Nr. 1753/86

BStU, MfS, BV Leipzig, Abt. XX, Nr. 0271/08

BStU, MfS, BV Leipzig, ZMA, AKG, Nr. 4974

BStU, MfS, HA II, Nr. 33928

ADDITIONAL ARCHIVES CONSULTED

Archiv Cornelia Schleime, Berlin

Archiv für Regionalliteratur / Institut für deutsche Literatur der Humboldt Universität

Beinecke Rare Book and Manuscript Library, Yale University

Bundesstiftung zur Aufarbeitung der SED-Diktatur

DDR Collection, Getty Research Institute

ex.oriente.lux—Experimental-Filmarchiv-Ost

Gabriele Stötzer, personal archive

Gino Hahnemann, personal archive (in custody of Matthias Fischer)

Special Collections, Stanford University

The Wende Museum of the Cold War

INTERVIEWS

Roland Berbig, personal interview, October 20, 2014

Lutz Dammbeck, email message to author, September 29, 2020

Frank Eckart, personal interview, January 19, 2015

Frank Eckart, personal interview, February 24, 2015

Matthias Fischer, email message to author, November 11, 2020

Matthias Fischer, personal interview, November 28, 2016

Thomas Florschuetz, email message to author, February 22, 2017

Thomas Florschuetz, personal interview, May 12, 2015

Reimund Frentzel, personal interview, March 13, 2015

Else Gabriel, email message to author, May 29, 2019

Else Gabriel, personal interview, June 24, 2015

Eckhart Gillen, personal interview, July 30, 2012

Elke Hannemann, personal interview, July 25, 2015

Andreas Hüneke, personal interview, July 25, 2012

John P. Jacob, personal interview, February 5, 2016

Paul Kaiser, personal interview, July 16, 2012

Romy Kleiber, personal interview, July 9, 2012

Michael Kresja, personal interview, July 9, 2012

Claus Löser, personal interview, October 20, 2014

Claus Löser, personal interview, February 23, 2015

Claus Löser, personal interview, March 5, 2015

Claus Löser, personal interview, June 9, 2015

Andreas Ludwig, personal interview, July 26, 2012

Gerd Harry "Judy" Lybke, email message to author, July 19, 2019

Gerd Harry "Judy" Lybke, personal interview, March 17, 2015

Gerd Harry "Judy" Lybke, personal interview, March 25, 2015

Claudia "Wanda" Reichardt, personal interview, June 2, 2015

Karim Saab, email message to author, February 23, 2016

Christine Schlegel, email message to author, November 7, 2020

Christine Schlegel, personal interview, June 29, 2015

Christine Schlegel, telephone interview, July 20, 2015

Cornelia Schleime, email message to author, November 19, 2016

Cornelia Schleime, telephone interview, February 25, 2015

Gundula Schulze Eldowy, personal interview, July 27, 2015

Gabriele Stötzer, email message to author, February 27, 2017

Gabriele Stötzer, email message to author, April 29, 2021

Gabriele Stötzer, personal interview, May 3, 2015

Gabriele Stötzer, personal interview, May 4, 2015

Christoph Tannert, email message to author, February 19, 2017

Christoph Tannert, personal interview, October 14, 2014

Christoph Tannert, personal interview, November 3, 2014

Christoph Tannert, personal interview, January 26, 2015

Christoph Tannert, personal interview, May 11, 2015

Christoph Tannert, personal interview, October 17, 2016

Silke Wagler, personal interview, July 17, 2012

Uwe Warnke, personal interview, April 15, 2015

Karin Wieckhorst, personal interview, June 26, 2015

MULTIMEDIA

Cederberg, Björn, and Fredrik von Krusenstjerna, dir. *Berlin DDR Hintergrund*. Sweden: Ausendrehs, 1985. 16mm film.

Dammbeck, Lutz, dir. *Art Unleashed: Experiments on Film by Lutz Dammbeck*. Amherst, MA: DEFA Film Library, 2019. DVD.

Dammbeck, Lutz, dir. *The Painter Came from a Foreign Land*. Disc 2 of *Art Unleashed: Experiments on Film by Lutz Dammbeck*. Amherst, MA: DEFA Film Library, 2019. DVD.

Dammbeck, Lutz, dir. *Video Herakles (1984)*. Adobe Flash video, 10:28. Accessed May 7, 2021. http://herakleskonzept.de/material/index.php/video-herakles.html.

DW Euromaxx. "In Prison in the GDR—Fighting against the Regime with Art: Witnessing the Fall of the Wall." YouTube video, 8:07. October 29, 2019. https://www.youtube.com/watch?v=aQejyOVZgdU.

Farewell Comrades. "Farewell Comrades! Stasi Watching Punks." YouTube video, 1:36, from a 1989 Stasi surveillance video. February 23, 2012. https://www.youtube.com/watch?v=sLehmoEH7lE.

Frydetzk, Thomas, Gino Hahnemann, Helge Leiberg, Via Lewandowsky, Claus Löser, Cornelia Klauß, Ramona Köppel-Welsh, Tohm di Roes, Cornelia Schleime, and Thomas Werner, dirs. *Counter Images: GDR Underground Films 1983–1989*. Amherst, MA: DEFA Film Library, 2008. DVD.

GINO-KINO. Filme von Gino Hahnemann 1982–1985. Berlin: Produktion Geld ohne Ende, 2006. DVD.

Henckel von Donnersmarck, Florian, dir. *Das Leben der Anderen* (*The Lives of Others*). Culver City, CA: Sony Pictures Home Entertainment, 2007. DVD.

Hendel, Annekatrin, dir. *Anderson*. Berlin: Salzgeber & Co. Medien, 2015. DVD.

Kroske, Gerd, dir. *La Villette*. Amherst, MA: DEFA Film Library, 2012. DVD.

Lutz Dammbeck: Filme und Mediencollagen 1975–1986. Edited by the Film Museum, Potsdam, in collaboration with the Goethe Institute. Munich: film & Kunst GmbH, 2008. DVD.

Petzold, Christian. *Barbara*. New York: Kino Lorber Home Video, 2013. DVD.

Schluttig, Harald. "Christine Schlegel—Ich bin—SUM." YouTube video, 14:28. March 4, 2013. https://www.youtube.com/watch?v=mmN8lMmzLwA.

Schumann, Dieter, dir. *flüstern und SCHREIEN—Ein Rockreport*. New York: First Run Features, 2010. DVD.

von Krusenstjerna, Fredrik, and Björn Cederberg, dir. *Verrat*. Stockholm: Charon Film, 1994. VHS.

PUBLISHED SOURCES

Allan, Seán. "DEFA: An Historical Overview." In *DEFA: East German Cinema, 1946–1992*, edited by Seán Allan and John Sandford, 1–21. New York: Berghahn Books, 1999.

Altmann, Susanne. *Entdeckt! Rebellische Künstlerinnen in der DDR*. Exhibition catalog. Mannheim: Kunsthalle Mannheim, 2011.

Badovinac, Zdenka, ed., *Body and the East: From the 1960s to the Present*. Exhibition catalog. Cambridge, MA: MIT Press, 1999.

Barron, Stephanie, and Sabine Eckmann, eds. *Art of Two Germanys: Cold War Cultures*. Exhibition catalog. New York: Abrams, 2009.

Barsch, Barbara. "'Ist das noch Kunst?' Zu einigen Aspekten intermedialer Arbeit junger Künstler der DDR." *Bildende Kunst* (September 1989): 31–34.

Bathrick, David. *The Powers of Speech: The Politics of Culture in the GDR*. Lincoln: University of Nebraska Press, 1995.

Bátorová, Andrea. "Interview with Katalin Cseh and Adam Czirak about the Second Public Sphere in the Former Eastern Bloc." ARTMargins [online]. Web. October 23, 2014. Accessed May 7, 2021. https://artmargins.com/interview-with-katalin-cseh-and-adam-czirak-about-the-second-public-sphere-in-the-former-eastern-bloc/.

Beiler, Berthold. *Die Gewalt des Augenblicks*. Leipzig: VEB Fotokinoverlag, 1969.

Berg, Florian. "Initiativgruppe Hoffnung DDR. Gespräch mit Karim Saab." *Berliner Hefte zur literarischen Lebens*, no. 4 (2001): 131–135.

——. "Literarische Zeitschriften: Anschlag." *Berliner Hefte zur literarischen Lebens*, no. 4 (2001): 128–130.

Berghahn, Daniela. "The Re-evaluation of Goethe and the Classical Tradition in the Films of Egon Günther and Siegfried Kühn." In *DEFA: East German Cinema 1946–1992*, edited by Seán Allan and John Sandford, 222–244. Oxford: Berghahn Books, 1999.

Bestgen, Ulrike. "'. . . ein anderes stück leibverantwortung.' Lebensthema Haft in Sprache und Bild bei Gabriele Stötzer." In *Gabriele Stötzer. Schwingungskurve Leben*, edited by Ulrike Bestgen and Wolfgang Holler, 21–31. Exhibition catalog. Weimar: Klassik Stiftung Weimar, 2013.

Bestgen, Ulrike, and Wolfgang Holler, eds. *Gabriele Stötzer. Schwingungskurve Leben*. Exhibition catalog. Weimar: Klassik Stiftung Weimar, 2013.

Blaylock, Sara. "Aufstand des Materials. Körperbilder im Prenzlauer Berg der 1980er Jahre" / "A Material Revolt: Body Portraits in the Prenzlauer Berg of the 1980s." In *Gegenstimmen. Kunst in der DDR 1976–1989 / Voices of Dissent: Art in the GDR*, edited by Christoph Tannert, 394–401. Exhibition catalog. Berlin: Deutsche Gesellschaft and Künstlerhaus Bethanien, 2016.

——. "Authenticity's Visual Turn." Afterword to *Politics of Authentic Subjectivity: Countercultures and Radical Movements Across the Iron Curtain (1968–1989)*, edited by Joachim C. Häberlen, Mark Keck-Szajbel, and Kate Mahoney, 278–286. New York: Berghahn Books, 2018.

——. "Being the Woman They Wanted Her to Be: Cornelia Schleime Performs Her Stasi File." *Third Text* 35, no. 2 (March 2021): 227–247.

——. "Bringing the War Home to the United States and East Germany: *In the Year of the Pig* and *Pilots in Pajamas*." *Cinema Journal* 56, no. 4 (Summer 2017): 26–50.

———. “La femme de leurs rêves: Cornelia Schleime et les archives de la Stasi.” *Gradhiva*, no. 24 (December 2016): 21–49.

———. “The Subject Who Knows: Photographers and the Photographed in the Late East Germany.” In *The Oxford Handbook of Communist Visual Cultures*, edited by Aga Skrodzka, Xiaoning Lu, and Katarzyna Marciniak, 500–518. Oxford: Oxford University Press, 2020.

———. “*Verwandlungen* (Strawalde, 1981).” In *The Handbook of East German Cinema: The DEFA Legacy*, edited by Henning Wrage and Evan Torner. Berlin: De Gruyter, forthcoming.

Blume, Eugen. “Das Ergebnis ist ein Prozess.” *Bildende Kunst* 4 (1982): 202.

———. “Laborismus gegen Kapitalismus und Kommunismus im Dunkeln: Joseph Beuys.” In *Wahnzimmer/Klopfzeichen. Kunst und Kultur der 80er Jahre in Deutschland*, edited by Eugen Blume, Hubertus Gaßner, Eckhart Gillen, and Hans-Werner Schmidt, 45–51. Exhibition catalog. Leipzig: Faber & Faber Verlag, 2002.

Blume, Eugen, Hubertus Gaßner, Eckhart Gillen, and Hans-Werner Schmidt, eds. *Wahnzimmer/Klopfzeichen. Kunst und Kultur der 80er Jahre in Deutschland*. Exhibition catalog. Leipzig: Faber & Faber Verlag, 2002.

Boehlke, Michael, and Henryk Gericke, eds. *Ostpunk! Too Much Future: Punk in der DDR 1979–89*. Exhibition catalog. Berlin: Künstlerhaus Bethanien, 2005.

Boyer, Dominic. “Foucault in the Bush: The Social Life of Post-Structuralist Theory in East Berlin’s Prenzlauer Berg.” *Ethnos (Estoclomo)* 66, no. 2 (2001): 207–236.

Bruno, Giuliana. “Geography of the Moving Image.” In *Atlas of Emotion: Journeys in Art, Architecture, and Film*. New York: Verso, 2002.

Bryzgel, Amy. *Performance Art in Eastern Europe since 1960*. Manchester, UK: Manchester University Press, 2017.

———. *Performing the East: Performance Art in Russia, Latvia and Poland since 1980*. London: I. B. Tauris, 2013.

Buchloh, Benjamin. “How German Was It?” *Artforum International* 47, no. 10 (Summer 2009): 294–299.

Büchner, Tely, and Susanne Knorr, eds. *Zwischen Ausstieg und Aktion. Die Erfurter Subkulture der 1960er, 1970er und 1980er Jahre*. Exhibition catalog. Bielefeld: Kerber Verlag, 2014.

Bühl, Harald, Dieter Heinze, Hans Koch, and Fred Staufenbiel. *Kulturpolitisches Wörterbuch*. Berlin: Dietz Verlag, 1970.

Bundesbeauftragte für die Unterlagen des Staatssicherheitsdienstes der ehemaligen DDR, ed. *Das MfS-Lexicon*. Web. Accessed May 7, 2021. https://www.bstu.de/mfs-lexikon/.

———. *Eingeschränkte Freiheit. Der Fall Gabriele Stötzer*. Berlin: BStU, 2014.

Burchkardt, Liane, and André Meier. *Bemerke den Unterschied*. Exhibition catalog. Nuremberg: Verlag für moderne Kunst, 1991.

Büscher, Barbara. “Intermedia DDR 1985—Ereignis und Netzwerk.” *media archive performance*, no. 2 (2010). Web. Accessed May 7, 2021. http://www.perfomap.de/map2/geschichte/intermedia-ddr.

Caute, David. *The Dancer Defects: The Struggle for Cultural Supremacy during the Cold War*. Oxford: Oxford University Press, 2003.

Cseh-Varga, Katalin, and Adam Czirak, *Performance Art in the Second Public Sphere: Event-Based Art in Late Socialist Europe*. New York: Routledge, 2018.

Cuevas-Wolf, Cristina. "Making the Past Present: GDR Photo Albums and Amateur Photographs." *Visual Resources* 30, no. 1 (2014): 33–56.

Cunningham, John. *Hungarian Cinema: From Coffee House to Multiplex*. London and New York: Wallflower Press, 2004.

Cvejić, Bojana. "A Parallel Slalom from BADco: In Search of a Poetics of Problems." *Representations*, no. 136 (Fall 2016): 21–35.

——. "Problems That Aesthetically 'Unburden' Us." In *Parallel Slalom: A Lexicon of Non-aligned Poetics*, edited by Bojana Cvejić and Goran Sergej Pristaš, 322–334. Belgrade: Walking Theory, 2013.

Cvejić, Bojana, and Goran Sergej Pristaš, eds. *Parallel Slalom: A Lexicon of Non-aligned Poetics*. Belgrade: Walking Theory, 2013.

Dammbeck, Lutz. "Vorlauf. Die Mediencollagen (1984–1988)." Herakles Konzept. Web. Accessed May 7, 2021. http://www.herakleskonzept.de/material/index.php/vorlauf.html.

——. "Vorlauf: Der Film *HERAKLES* (1979–1984)." Herakles Konzept. Web. Accessed May 7, 2021. http://www.herakleskonzept.de/material/index.php/vorlauf-6.html.

Daniels, Dieter, and Jeannette Stoschek, eds. *Grauzone 8mm. Materialien zum autonomen Künstlerfilm in der DDR*. Ostfildern, Germany: Hatje Cantz Verlag, 2007.

Derrida, Jacques. *Archive Fever: A Freudian Impression*. Chicago: University of Chicago Press, 1996.

Deutschland.de. "Federal States of Germany." Web. Accessed May 7, 2021. https://www.deutschland.de/en/topic/politics/germany-europe/federal-states.

Dieckmann, Christoph. "Der König der DDR." *ZEIT Geschichte*, no. 4 (November 22, 2011). Web. Accessed May 7, 2021. https://www.zeit.de/zeit-geschichte/2011/04/Friedrich-der-Grosse-DDR/komplettansicht.

Dobvrenko, Evgeny. *Political Economy of Socialist Realism*. New Haven: Yale University Press, 2007.

Dölling, Irene. "Frauen- und Männerbilder. Eine Analyse von Fotos in DDR-Zeitschriften." *Feministische Studien* 8, no. 1 (1990): 35–49.

Duda, Jana, Gabriele Muschter, and Uwe Warnke. *Geschlossene Gesellschaft. Künstlerische Fotografie in der DDR 1945–1989*. Exhibition catalog. Bielefeld: Kerber Verlag, 2012.

Eckart, Frank, ed. *Eigenart und Eigensinn. Alternative Kulturszenen in der DDR (1980–1990)*. Bremen: Edition Temmen, 1993.

——. "Zwischen Verweigerung und Etablierung." Doctoral thesis, University of Bremen, 1995.

Eckhardt, Frank, and Paul Kaiser, eds. *Ohne uns! Kunst und alternative Kultur in Dresden vor und nach '89*. Exhibition catalog. Dresden: Efau Verlag, 2009.

Edwards, G. E. *GDR Society and Social Institutions*. London: Macmillan, 1985.

Eghigian, Greg. "Homo Munitus: The East German Observed." In *Socialist Modern: East German Everyday Culture and Politics*, edited by Katherine Pence and Paul Betts, 37–70. Ann Arbor: University of Michigan Press, 2008.

Eisman, April. *Bernhard Heisig and the Fight for Modern Art in East Germany*. Rochester, NY: Camden House, 2018.

Emmerich, Wolfgang. *Kleine Literaturgeschichte der DDR*. Leipzig: Kiepenheuer, 1996.

Engler, Wolfgang. *Die Ostdeutschen. Kunde von einem verlorenen Land*. Berlin: Aufbau Taschenbuch Verlag, 2002.

——. *Die Ostdeutschen als Avantgarde*. Berlin: Aufbau-Verlag, 2002.

Erjavec, Aleš, ed. *Postmodernism and the Postsocialist Condition: Politicized Art under Late Socialism*. Berkeley: University of California Press, 2003.

European Commission. "GDP per Capita, Consumption per Capita and Price Level Indices." Web. Accessed May 7, 2021. https://ec.europa.eu/eurostat/statistics-explained/index.php/GDP_per_capita,_consumption_per_capita_and_price_level_indices.

Feinstein, Joshua. *The Triumph of the Ordinary: Depictions of Daily Life in the East German Cinema, 1949–1989*. Chapel Hill: University of North Carolina Press, 2002.

Feist, Günter, and Eckhart Gillen. *Kunstkombinat DDR. Daten und Zitate zur Kunst und Kunstpolitik der DDR 1945–1990*. Berlin: Verlag Dirk Nishen, 1990.

Felsmann, Barbara, and Annett Gröschner, eds. *Durchgangszimmer Prenzlauer Berg: eine Berliner Künstlersozialgeschichte in Selbstauskünften*. Berlin: Lukas, 1999.

Fenemore, Mark. *Sex, Thugs, and Rock 'n' Roll: Teenage Rebels in Cold-War East Germany*. New York: Berghahn Books, 2007.

Ferree, Myra Marx. "The Rise and Fall of 'Mommy Politics': Feminism and Unification in (East) Germany." *Feminist Studies* 19, no. 1 (Spring 1993): 89–115.

——. *Varieties of Feminism: German Gender Politics in Global Perspective*. Stanford: Stanford University Press, 2012.

Fiedler, Yvonne. *Kunst im Korridor. Private Galerien in der DDR zwischen Autonomie und Illegalität*. Berlin: Christoph Links Verlag, 2013.

Flügge, Matthias. "Von der Erfindung zum Dokument—das HERAKLES KONZEPT von Lutz Dammbeck." Herakles Konzept. Web. Accessed May 7, 2021. http://www.herakleskonzept.de/material/index.php/herakles-konzept-95.html.

Foucault, Michel. "Docile Bodies." In *Discipline and Punish: The Birth of the Prison*, 135–169. New York: Pantheon Books, 1977.

Fraser, Nancy. "Rethinking the Public Sphere: A Contribution to the Critique of Actually Existing Democracy." *Social Text*, no. 25/26 (1990): 56–80.

Fritzsch, Constanze. "Allez! Arrest: Gelebte Wirklichkeit gegen tote Realität." *OwnReality* 25 (2016): 1–26.

Fritzsche, Karin, and Claus Löser, eds. *Gegenbilder. Filmische Subversion in der DDR, 1976–1996*. Berlin: Janus Press, 1996.

Fulbrook, Mary. *Anatomy of a Dictatorship: Inside the GDR, 1949–1989*. New York: Oxford University Press, 1995.

———. *The People's State: East German Society from Hitler to Honecker*. New Haven: Yale University Press, 2005.

———. "Render unto Caesar? The Pivotal Role of the Protestant Churches." In *Anatomy of a Dictatorship: Inside the GDR 1949–1989*, 87–128. Oxford: Oxford University Press, 1995.

Galenza, Ronald, and Heinz Havemeister, eds. *Wir wollen immer artig sein: Punk, New Wave, HipHop, Independent-Szene in der DDR 1980–1990*. Berlin: Schwarzkopf & Schwarzkopf, 1999.

Gaus, Günter. *Wo Deutschland liegt: Eine Ortsbestimmung*. Hamburg: Hoffmann und Campe, 1983.

Geipel, Ines. "Der Preis war hoch." *Emma* (1 November 2009). Web. Accessed May 7, 2021. https://www.emma.de/artikel/ueberlebende-der-preis-war-hoch-264201.

Gericke, Henryk, and Ingeborg Quaas. *Brennzeiten: Die Keramikwerkstatt Wilfriede Maaß 1980–1989–1998. Ein Zentrum des künstlerischen Offgrounds in Ost-Berlin*. Exhibition catalog. Berlin: Lukas Verlag, 2014.

Gesetzblatt der Deutschen Demokratischen Republik 1949–1990. Edited by Carmen Adam, Petra Biering, and Gudrun Lucks. Berlin: November 2010. Web. Accessed May 7, 2021. http://www.bundesarchiv.de/findbuecher/sapmo/b_gblddr/.

Gieseke, Jens. *The History of the Stasi: East Germany's Secret Police, 1945–1990*. New York: Berghahn Books, 2014.

Gillen, Eckhart. *Feindliche Brüder? Der Kalte Krieg und die Deutsche Kunst 1945–1990*. Berlin: Nicolai, 2009.

——, ed. *German Art from Beckmann to Richter: Images of a Divided Country*. Exhibition catalog. Cologne: DuMont Buchverlag, 1997.

——. *Das Kunstkombinat DDR: Zäsuren einer gescheiterten Kunstpolitik*. Cologne: DuMont, 2005.

Gillen, Eckhart, and Rainer Haarmann, eds. "Fragen an Politiker, Künstler und Kunstkritiker zum 9. November 1989." In *Kunst in der DDR*, edited by Eckhart Gillen and Rainer Haarmann, 38–48. Cologne: Kiepenheuer & Witsch, 1990.

——. *Kunst in der DDR*. Cologne: Kiepenheuer & Witsch, 1990.

Goeschen, Ulrike. *Vom sozialistischen Realismus zur Kunst im Sozialismus*. Berlin: Duncker & Humblot, 2001.

Grass, Günter. "Sich ein Bild Machen." In *Zeitvergleich: Malerei und Grafik aus der DDR*, edited by Axel Hecht and Hanne Reinecke, 10–13. Hamburg: Gruner & Jahr, 1982.

Greenberg, Clement. "'Avant-Garde and Kitsch' 1939." In *Art in Theory, 1900–2000: An Anthology of Changing Ideas*, edited by Charles Harrison and Paul Wood, 539–539. Malden, MA: Blackwell, 2003.

——. "Towards a Newer Laocoon." *Partisan Review* 7, no. 4 (July–August 1940): 296–310.

Groys, Boris. *The Total Art of Stalinism: Avant-Garde, Aesthetic Dictatorship, and Beyond*. Princeton: Princeton University Press, 1992.

Grünbein, Durs. "Protestantische Rituale. Zur Arbeit der Autoperforationsartisten." In *Kunst in der DDR*, edited by Eckhart Gillen and Rainer Haarmann, 309–318. Cologne: Kiepenheuer & Witsch, 1990.

Grundmann, Uta. "Der '1. Leipziger Herbstsalon.'" Bundeszentrale für politische Bildung. September 6, 2012. Web. Accessed May 7, 2021. http://www.bpb.de/geschichte/deutsche-geschichte/autonome-kunst-in-der-ddr/55829/herbstsalon.

——. "Die Galerie Arkade." Bundeszentrale für politische Bildung. September 6, 2012. Accessed May 7, 2021. https://www.bpb.de/geschichte/deutsche-geschichte/autonome-kunst-in-der-ddr/55802/galerie-arkade.

——. "Die Künstlergruppe Clara Mosch." Bundeszentrale für politische Bildung. September 6, 2012. Web. Accessed May 7, 2021. https://www.bpb.de/geschichte/deutsche-geschichte/autonome-kunst-in-der-ddr/55822/clara-mosch.

——. "'Nach Beuys'—eine Hommage." Bundeszentrale für politische Bildung. September 6, 2012. Web. Accessed May 7, 2021. https://www.bpb.de/geschichte/deutsche-geschichte/autonome-kunst-in-der-ddr/55833/nach-beuys.

Grundmann, Uta, Klaus Michael, and Susanne Seufert, eds. *Revolution im geschlossenen Raum. Die andere Kultur in Leipzig 1970–1990*. Leipzig: Verlag Faber & Faber, 2002.

Habermas, Jürgen. *The Structural Transformation of the Public Sphere: An Inquiry into a Category of Bourgeois Society*. Cambridge, MA: MIT Press, 1989.

Hahnemann, Gino. *Exogene Zerrinerung*. Berlin: Gerhard Wolf Janus Press, 1994.

Hamelin, Candace. "The Diversification of East Germany's Visual Culture." In *The Ethics of Seeing: Photography and Twentieth-Century German History*, edited by Jennifer Evans, Paul Betts, and Stefan-Ludwig Hoffmann, 227–249. New York: Berghahn Books, 2018.

Harsch, Donna. *Revenge of the Domestic: Women, the Family, and Communism in the German Democratic Republic*. Princeton: Princeton University Press, 2007.

Havel, Václav. "Politics and Conscience." Reprint of the 1985 *Salisbury Review* translation, UnivForum, 2015. http://www.univcongress.info/static/2015/10/Politics-conscience.pdf.

Hecht, Axel, and Alfred Welti. "Ein Meister, der Talent verschämt. Interview mit Georg Baselitz." *Art. Das Kunstmagazin*, no. 6 (1990): 54–72.

Hegewisch, Katharina. "Im Dienste der Unsterblichkeit. Gerd Harry Lybke." Web. Accessed May 7, 2021. http://eigen-art.com/files/text_khegewisch.pdf.

Heiduschke, Sebastien. "Film Censorship, the East German *Nouvelle Vague*, and the 'Rabbit Films': *Das Kaninchen bin ich* (*The Rabbit Is Me*, Kurt Maetzig, 1965)." In *East German Cinema: DEFA and Film History*, 77–83. New York: Palgrave MacMillan, 2013.

Hell, Julia. "Loyal Dissidents and Stasi Poets: Sascha Anderson, Christa Wolf, and the Incomplete Project of GDR Research." *German Politics and Society* 20, no. 4 (Winter 2002): 82–118.

Herf, Jeffrey. *Divided Memory: The Nazi Past in the Two Germanys*. Cambridge, MA: Harvard University Press, 1997.

Herminghouse, Patricia. "Die Wiederentdeckung der Romantik: zur Funktion der Dichterfiguren in der neueren DDR-Literatur." In *DDR-Roman und Literaturgesellschaft*, edited by Jos Hoogeveen and Gerd Labroisse, 217–248. Amsterdam: Rodopi, 1981.

Herrmann, Matthias. "Zweite Realität. Avancierte Musik in Dresdner Institutionen zwischen 1950 und 1989." In *Ohne uns! Kunst und alternative Kultur in Dresden vor und nach '89*, edited by Frank Eckhardt and Paul Kaiser, 136–145. Exhibition catalog. Dresden: Efau Verlag, 2009.

Hickley, Catherine. "East German 'Arseholes' Are Reappraised." *Art Newspaper*, February 23, 2018. Accessed May 7, 2021. https://www.theartnewspaper.com/preview/east-german-arseholes-are-reappraised.

Higgins, Richard C. "Intermedia (1965)." In *Horizons: The Poetics and Theory of the Intermedia*. Carbondale and Edwardsville: Southern Illinois University Press, 1984.

Hilbig, Wolfgang. "Liebe Angelika Klüssendorf." *Anschlag*, no. 2 (Fall 1984): n.p.

Hlavajova, Maria, and Simon Sheikh, eds. *Former West: Art and the Contemporary after 1989*. Utrecht: BAK; Cambridge, MA: MIT Press, 2016.

Hock, Beáta, and Anu Allas, eds. *Globalizing East European Art Histories, Past and Present*. New York: Routledge, 2018.

Horakova, Anna. "Mimicry as Critique: New Perspectives on the Prenzlauer Berg, Avantgarde Aesthetics and Communist Cultures of Dissidence." Doctoral thesis, Cornell University, 2016.

Howes, Seth. "Cultures Grow Exponentially: An Interview with Rainer Görß." In *Imperfect Recall: Re-collecting the GDR*. Otago German Studies 30, edited by Cecilia Novero, 174–198. Dunedin: University of Otago, 2020.

——. "'Killersatellit' and *Randerscheinung*: Punk and the Prenzlauer Berg." *German Studies Review* 36, no. 3 (October 2013): 579–601.

——. *Moving Images on the Margins: Experimental Film in Late Socialist East Germany*. Rochester, NY: Camden House, 2019.

——. "Pessimism and the Politics of the Future in East German Punk." *Journal of Popular Culture* 49, no. 1 (February 2016): 77–96.

Jacob, John P. *Recollecting a Culture: Photography and the Evolution of a Socialist Aesthetic in East Germany*. Boston, MA: Photographic Resource Center at Boston University, 1998.

James, Sarah. *Common Ground: German Photographic Cultures across the Iron Curtain*. New Haven: Yale University Press, 2013.

——. *Paper Revolutions: An Invisible Avant-Garde*. Cambridge, MA: MIT Press, 2022.

Janevski, Ana, Roxana Marcoci, and Ksenia Nouril, eds. *Art and Theory of Post-1989 Central and Eastern Europe: A Critical Anthology*. New York: Museum of Modern Art, 2018.

Jappe, Elisabeth. *Performance, Ritual, Prozeß*. Munich: Prestel-Verlag, 1993.

Jarausch, Konrad. "Between Myth and Reality: The Stasi Legacy in German History." *German Historical Institute Bulletin* 9 (2014): 73–83.

Jones, Amelia. *Body Art: Performing the Subject*. Minneapolis: University of Minnesota Press, 1998.

——. "'Presence' in Absentia: Experiencing Performance as Documentation." In "Performance Art: (Some) Theory and (Selected) Practice at the End of this Century." Special issue, *Art Journal* 56, no. 4 (Winter 1997): 11–18.

Kaiser, Paul. *Boheme in der DDR. Kunst und Gegenkultur im Staatsozialismus*. Dresden: Dresdner Institut für Kulturstudien, 2016.

——. "Suggestion und Recherche. Eine quellenkritische Fallstudie zur Aktenlage um Willi Sitte." In *Politik und Kunst in der DDR. Der Fonds Willi Sitte im Germanischen Nationalmuseums*, edited by Ulrich Großmann, 96–107. Nuremberg: Verlag des Germanischen Nationalmuseums, 2003.

——. "Symbolic Revolts in the 'Workers' and Peasants' State': Countercultural Art Programs in the GDR and the Return of Modern Art." In *Art of Two Germanys: Cold War Cultures*, edited by Stephanie Barron and Sabine Eckmann, 170–185. Exhibition catalog. Abrams, New York: 2009.

——. "Von Mülltonnen, Frühlingssalons und Brunnenfröschen. Ein Gespräch mit Ingo Sandner, HfBK-Rektor (1982–1988)." In *Ohne uns! Kunst und alternative Kultur in Dresden vor und nach '89*, edited by Frank Eckhardt and Paul Kaiser, 162–169. Exhibition catalog. Dresden: Efau Verlag, 2009.

——. "Vortragsmanuskript/Vortrag 'Der Dresdner Bilderstreit.'" Lecture held at the Lingner Castle in Dresden, December 7, 2017. Web. Accessed May 7, 2021. http://www.kulturstudien-dresden.de/wa_files/Vortrag_20Kaiser.pdf.

Kaiser, Paul, and Claudia Petzold. *Boheme und Diktatur in der DDR: Gruppen, Konflikte, Quartiere 1970–1989*. Exhibition catalog. Berlin: Fannei & Walz, 1997.

Katzengruber, Werber. "Wir machen Kunstgeschichte mit dem Ziel, unsterblich zu werden—Interview mit Gerd Harry Lybke, 16. Februar. 2010." In *Mythos Führungskraft*, 230–244. Weinheim: Wiley-VCH, 2010.

Kelly, Elaine. *Composing the Canon in the GDR: Narratives of Nineteenth-Century Music*. Oxford: Oxford University Press, 2014.

Kelly, Elaine, and Amy Lynn Wlodarski, eds. *Art outside the Lines: New Perspectives on GDR Art Culture*. Amsterdam: Rodopi, 2011.

Kemp-Welch, Klara. *Antipolitics in Central European Art: Reticence as Dissidence under Post-Totalitarian Rule, 1956–1989*. London: I. B. Tauris, 2014.

——. *Networking the Bloc: Experimental Art in Eastern Europe, 1965–1981*. Cambridge, MA: MIT Press, 2018.

Klauß, Cornelia. "Die Stand der Dinge oder wie ich Schmalfilm lieben lernte." *KOMA-KINO*, no. 1 (1987): n.p.

Knaup, Bettina, Angelika Richter, and Beatrice E. Stammer, eds. *Und jetzt: Künstlerinnen aus der DDR*. Exhibition catalog. Nuremberg: Verlag für moderne Kunst, 2009.

Knetsch, Claudia. "Betrachtungen zur Rezeption Goethes und Schillers in der SBZ/DDR (1949–59)." *Uni-Journal Jena* (April 2000).

Knöfel, Ulrike. "Du fühlst dich unsterblich." *Der Spiegel*, no. 34 (August 18, 2014): 112–116.

Köhler, Thomas, and Stefanie Heckmann, eds. *Cornelia Schleime. Ein Wimpernschlag*. Exhibition catalog. Bielefeld: Kerber Verlag, 2016.

Kolbe, Uwe. *Hineingeboren: Gedichte*, 1975–1979. Frankfurt am Main: Suhrkamp, 1982.

Kunst, Bojana. "Delay." In *Parallel Slalom: A Lexicon of Non-aligned Poetics*, edited by Bojana Cvejić and Goran Sergej Pristaš, 352–353. Belgrade: Walking Theory, 2013.

——. "Politics of Affection and Uneasiness." In *Parallel Slalom: A Lexicon of Non-aligned Poetics*, edited by Bojana Cvejić and Goran Sergej Pristaš, 341–351. Belgrade: Walking Theory, 2013.

Kunze, Hans-Wulf. "Eine Bewährungsprobe fur Fotografen." *Fotografie* (March 1986): 90–95.

Kyselka, Verena. "Pigs Like Pigments." Accessed May 7, 2021. https://verena-kyselka.de/pigs-like-pgments/.

Lange, Herbert. *EIGEN+ART. Die Geschichte der Galerie im Spiegel der Quellen*. Leipzig: Leipziger Universitätsverlag, 2013.

Lässig, Christine. "Frauen stellten ihre eigenen Fragen." *Thüringer Tagesblatt*, no. 142 (June 17, 1988), n.p.

Lemke, Jürgen. *Ganz Normal Anders. Auskünfte schwuler Männer*. Berlin & Weimar: Aufbau-Verlag, 1989.

Lenin, Vladimir Il'ich. *State and Revolution: Marxist Teaching about the Theory of the State and the Tasks of the Proletariat in the Revolution*. Westport, CT: Greenwood Press, 1978.

Lewis, Alison. "En-Gendering Remembrance: Memory, Gender and Informers for the Stasi." *New German Critique*, no. 86 (2002): 103–134.

——. *Die Kunst des Verrats. Der Prenzlauer Berg und die Staatssicherheit*. Würzberg, Germany: Königshausen & Neumann, 2003.

Liebermann, Doris. *Ein Piratenstück: Der 1. Leipziger Herbstsalon 1984, seine Vorgeschichte und seine Protagonisten*. Halle (Saale), Germany: Mitteldeutscher Verlag, 2014.

Lindner, Bernd, and Rainer Eckert, eds. *Mauersprünge: Klopfzeichen. Kunst und Kultur der 80er Jahre in Deutschland*. Exhibition catalog. Leipzig: Faber & Faber Verlag, 2002.

Löser, Claus. "Das Phänomen des Schmalfilmbooms." In *Gegenbilder. Filmische Subversion in der DDR, 1976–1996*, edited by Karin Fritzsche and Claus Löser, 80–99. Berlin: Janus Press, 1996.

——. "Der Spion, der aus dem Kino kam." *tip* (November 1995): 46–48.

——. *Strategien der Verweigerung: Untersuchungen zum politisch-ästhetischen Gestus unangepasster filmischer Artikulationen in der Spätphase der DDR*. Berlin: DEFA-Stiftung, 2011.

——. "Urge for Movement and Mobility: On Cornelia Schleime's Super 8 Films." In *Cornelia Schleime. Ein Wimpernschlag. A Blink of an Eye*, edited by Thomas Köhler and Stefanie Heckmann, 33–37. Exhibition catalog. Bielefeld: Kerber Verlag, 2016.

——. "Vorab." In *Gegenbilder. Filmische Subversion in der DDR, 1976–1996*, edited by Karin Fritzsche and Claus Löser, 5–23. Berlin: Janus Press, 1996.

Lukács, György. "Reification and the Consciousness of the Proletariat (1923)." In *History and Class Consciousness*. Reprint of the 1967 Merlin Press edition, Georg Lukács Archive on Marxists.org, n.d. https://www.marxists.org/archive/lukacs/works/history/hcc05.htm.

Lybke, Judy. *EIGEN+ART Jahrbuch 1986*. Leipzig: EIGEN+ART, 1986.

——. *EIGEN+ART Jahrbuch 1987*. Leipzig: EIGEN+ART, 1987.

——. *EIGEN+ART Jahrbuch 1989*. Leipzig: EIGEN+ART, 1989.

Maaz, Hans-Joachim. *Behind the Wall: The Inner Life of Communist Germany*. New York: W. W. Norton, 1995.

Marlin, Constanze von, ed. *Ordnung durch Störung. Auto-Perforations-Artistik*. Exhibition catalog. Nuremberg: Verlag für moderne Kunst, 2006.

Martin, Anne, ed. *Foto-Anschlag: Vier Generationen ostdeutscher Fotografen*. Leipzig: Seemann, 2001.

Marx, Karl. *Economic and Philosophic Manuscripts of 1844*. Mineola, NY: Dover, 2007.

Maximenkov, Leonid. "Stalin's Meeting with a Delegation of Ukrainian Writers on 12 February 1929." *Harvard Ukrainian Studies* 16, no. 3/4 (December 1992): 361–431.

McLellan, Josie. *Love in the Time of Communism: Intimacy and Sexuality in the GDR*. Cambridge: Cambridge University Press, 2011.

——. "Visual Dangers and Delights: Nude Photography in East Germany." *Past and Present*, no. 205 (November 2009): 143–174.

Meier, André. "Die Werkstatt-Galerie EIGEN+ART." In *Kunst in der DDR*, edited by Eckhart Gillen and Rainer Haarmann, 415–417. Cologne: Kiepenheuer & Witsch, 1990.

Menge, Marlies. "Wo schöne Träume verboten werden." *Die Zeit*, April 2, 1982.

Menner, Simon. *Top Secret. Bilder aus den Archiven der Staatssicherheit/Images from the Stasi Archives*. Ostfildern: Hatje Cantz Verlag, 2013.

Mesch, Claudia. *Modern Art at the Berlin Wall: Demarcating Culture in the Cold War Germanys*. London: I. B. Tauris, 2006.

Messmer, Arwed. *Reenactment MfS*. Ostfildern: Hatje Cantz Verlag, 2014.

Michael, Klaus. "Unabhängige Literatur in der DDR." Bundeszentrale für politische Bildung. September 6, 2012. Web. Accessed May 7, 2021. https://www.bpb.de/geschichte/deutsche-geschichte/autonome-kunst-in-der-ddr/55789/unabhaengige-literatur-in-der-ddr#footnodeid13-13.

Michael, Klaus, and Thomas Wohlfart, eds. *Vogel oder Käfig sein. Kunst und Literatur aus unabhängigen Zeitschriften in der DDR 1979–1989*. Berlin: Druckhaus Galrev, 1991.

Mirzoeff, Nicholas. *The Right to Look: A Counterhistory of Visuality*. Durham: Duke University Press, 2011.

Muschter, Gabriele, ed. *DDR Frauen fotografieren. Lexikon und Anthologie*. Berlin: ex pose verlag, 1989.

——. "Eigen+Art ist eigen." *Bildende Kunst* (January 1988): 43.

——. "Frauen fotografieren—anders." *Bildende Kunst* (February 1988): 50–53.

Muschter, Gabriele, Barbara Barsch, Lothar Hirlemann, Kathleen Krenzlin, Hartmut Pätzke, Jens Schlechte, and Joachim Sommermeier, eds. *Klaus Werner: Für die Kunst*. Cologne: Walther König, 2000.

Muschter, Gabriele, and Rüdiger Thomas, eds. *Jenseits der Staatskultur. Traditionen autonomer Kunst in der DDR*. Munich: Hanser, 1992.

Peck, Jeffrey M., and Jürgen Lemke. "Being Gay in Germany: An Interview with Jürgen Lemke." In "German Unification." Special issue, *New German Critique*, no. 52 (Winter 1991): 144–154.

Pejić, Bojana. "Proletarians of All Countries, Who Washes Your Socks? Equality, Dominance and Difference in Eastern European Art," in *Gender Check: Femininity and Masculinity in the Art of Eastern Europe*, ed. Bojana Pejić, 19–29. Exhibition catalog. Cologne: Walther König, 2009.

Pejić, Bojana, ed. *Gender Check: Femininity and Masculinity in the Art of Eastern Europe*. Exhibition catalog. Cologne: Walther König, 2009.

——. *Gender Check, A Reader: Art and Theory in Eastern Europe*. Cologne: Walther König, 2010.

Pence, Katherine. "Eat, Drink & Smoke." In *Beyond the Wall: Art and Artifacts from the GDR / Jenseits der Mauer. Kunst und Alltagsgegenstände aus der DDR*, edited by Justinian Jampol, Benedikt Taschen, and Ina Pfitzner, 27–28. Cologne: Taschen, 2014.

Pence, Katherine, and Paul Betts, eds. *Socialist Modern: East German Everyday Culture and Politics*. Ann Arbor: University of Michigan Press, 2008.

Piotrowski, Piotr. *Art and Democracy in Post-Communist Europe*. London: Reaktion, 2012.

——. *In the Shadow of Yalta: Art and the Avant-garde in Eastern Europe, 1945–1989*. London: Reaktion Books, 2009.

——. "Male Artist's Body: National Identity vs. Identity Politics." In *Gender Check, A Reader: Art and Theory in Eastern Europe*, edited by Bojana Pejić, 127–136. Cologne: Walther König, 2010.

Pollack, Detlef. "Das Ende einer Organisationsgesellschaft: systemtheoretische Überlegungen zum gesellschaftlichen Umbruch in der DDR." *Zeitschrift für Soziologie* 19, no. 4 (1990): 292–307.

Port, Andrew I. "The Banalities of East German Historiography." In *Becoming East German: Socialist Structures and Sensibilities after Hitler*, edited by Mary Fulbrook and Andrew I. Port, 16–24. New York: Berghahn Books, 2013.

Poss, Ingrid, ed. *DEFA 50: Gespräche aus acht Filmnächten: Protokolle*. Potsdam, Germany: Brandenburgische Landeszentrale für Politische Bildung, 1997.

Pracht, Erwin. *Ästhetik der Kunst*. Berlin: Dienst Verlag, 1987.

Rehberg, Karl-Siegbert. "Die verdrängte Abstraktion. Feind-Bilder im Kampfkonzept des 'Sozialistischen Realismus.'" In *Abstraktion im Sozialismus. Feindsetzungen und Freiräume im Kunstsystem der DDR*, edited by Karl-Siegbert Rehberg and Paul Kaiser, 15–67. Weimar: Verlag und Datenback für Geistwissenschaften, 2003.

Rehberg, Karl-Siegbert, Wolfgang Holler, and Paul Kaiser, eds. *Abschied von Ikarus. Bildwelten in der DDR—neu gesehen*. Exhibition catalog. Cologne: Walter König, 2012.

Rehberg, Karl-Siegbert, and Paul Kaiser, eds. *Bilderstreit und Gesellschaftsumbruch. Die Debatten um die Kunst aus der DDR im Prozess der deutschen Wiedervereinigung*. Berlin: Siebenhaar Verlag, 2013.

Reichardt, Claudia. *Die Galerie bleibt während der Öffnungszeit geschlossen: Wanda und die Villa Marie 1982–1990*. Berlin: Schmitz, 2010.

Richter, Angelika. *Das Gesetz der Szene. Genderkritik, Performance Art und zweite Öffentlichkeit in der späten DDR*. Bielefeld: transcript Verlag, 2019.

Richthofen, Esther von. *Bringing Culture to the Masses: Control, Compromise, and Participation in the GDR*. New York: Berghahn Books, 2009.

Robin, Régine. *Socialist Realism: An Impossible Aesthetic*. Stanford: Stanford University Press, 1992.

Rueschemeyer, Marilyn. "Women in East Germany: From State Socialism to Capitalist Welfare State." In *Democratic Reform and the Position of Women in Transitional Economies*, edited by Valentine M. Moghadam, 75–91. Oxford: Clarendon Press, 1993.

Saab, Karim. "Gespräch mit Judy Lybke." In "EIGEN+ART im Gespräch," ed. Karim Saab. Special issue, *Anschlag* (Leipzig, 1988).

——, ed. "EIGEN+ART im Gespräch." Special issue, *Anschlag* (Leipzig, 1988).

Sasse, Sylvia. "Stasi-Dada: How Artists Work with Their Stasi Records." *Performance Art in Eastern Europe* (March 2016). Accessed May 7, 2021. http://www.performanceart.info/blog/stasi-dada-how-artists-work-with-their-stasi-records/.

Schäkel, Ilona. "ANSCHLAG, HERZATTACKE und andere SCHADENsfälle. Grundriß einer Typologie der originalgraphischen Zeitschriften aus der DDR." *Berliner Hefte zur Geschichte des literarischen Lebens*, no. 4 (2001): 117–127.

Schivelbusch, Wolfgang. *In a Cold Crater: Cultural and Intellectual Life in Berlin, 1945–1948*. Berkeley: University of California Press, 1998.

Schlegel, Christine. *Hautlos. Eingeschweißte Überwachung*. Berlin: Janus Press, 2011.

Schlegel, Christine, and Trude Trunk. "Hautlos." In *Hautlos. Eingeschweißte Überwachung*, 40–81. Berlin: Janus Press, 2011.

Schleime, Cornelia. "Ich sagte, ich trete in den Hungerstreik." Interview by Herlinde Koelbl, *ZEITmagazin*, no. 35 (August 25, 2011). Web. Accessed May 7, 2021. http://www.zeit.de/2011/35/Rettung-Cornelia-Schleime.

——. "Immer wenn das Leben so intensive wurde, griff ich zum Film." In *Gegenbilder. Filmische Subversion in der DDR, 1976–1996*, edited by Karin Fritzsche and Claus Löser, 66–74. Berlin: Janus Press, 1996.

——. *In der Liebe und in der Kunst weiß ich genau, was ich nicht will.* Bielefeld: Kerber Verlag, 2010.

——. "Jeder Satellit hat einen Killersatelliten," Hätten wir es nur wörtlich genommen." In *Ostpunk! Too Much Future: Punk in der DDR 1979–89*, edited by Michael Boehlke and Henryk Gericke, 177–190. Exhibition catalog. Berlin: Künstlerhaus Bethanien, 2005.

——. *Weit Fort.* Regensburg: Hoffmann und Campe, 2008.

Schmidt, Werner, ed. *Ausgebürgert. Künstler aus der DDR und aus dem Sowjetischen Sektor Berlins 1949–1989*. Exhibition catalog. Berlin: Argon Verlag, 1990.

Schroeder, Klaus. "The SED's Fear of the Big Bad Wolf." In *Ende vom Lied*, edited by Christoph Tannert, 243–247. Berlin: Künstlerhaus Bethanien, 2016.

Schulze Eldowy, Gundula. *Am fortgewehten Ort. Berliner Geschichten.* Leipzig: Lehmstadt Verlag, 2011.

——. *Berlin in einer Hundenacht.* Leipzig: Lehmstadt Verlag, 2011.

——. *Der große und der kleine Schritt.* Leipzig: Lehmstadt Verlag, 2012.

——. "Halt die Ohren Steif. Robert Frank und Gundula Schulze Eldowy in New York." In *Kunstmuseen Erfurt* (2018). Accessed May 7, 2021. https://kunstmuseen.erfurt.de/km/de/service/aktuelles/ausstellungen/2018/128389.html.

——. "In the Autumn Leaves of Oblivion." In *Berlin in einer Hundenacht*, 20–25. Leipzig: Lehmstadt Verlag, 2011.

——. "Die Plaudereien des Scharfschützen." In *Am fortgewehten Ort. Berliner Geschichten*, 129–221. Leipzig: Lehmstadt Verlag, 2011.

——. "The Times are Fleeing from the Memories." In *Der große und der kleine Schritt*, 11–17. Leipzig: Lehmstadt Verlag, 2012.

Scribner, Charity. "August 1961: Christa Wolf and the Politics of Disavowal." *German Life and Letters* 55, no. 1 (January 2002): 61–74.

Shaul, Matthew, ed. *Do Not Refreeze: Photography behind the Berlin Wall.* Exhibition catalog. Manchester, UK: Cornerhouse, 2007.

Silberman, Marc. "Problematizing the 'Socialist Public Sphere': Concepts and Consequences." In *What Remains? East German Culture and the Postwar Public*, edited by Marc Silberman, 1–23. Washington, DC: American Institute for Contemporary German Studies, 1997.

Slobodian, Quinn. "Socialist Chromatism: Race, Racism, and the Racial Rainbow in East Germany." In *Comrades of Color: East Germany in the Cold War World*, edited by Quinn Slobodian, 23–39. New York: Berghahn Books, 2015.

Smith, Briana J. "Experimental Art and Cultural Exchange in Late Cold War Berlin." In *Cold War Berlin: Confrontations, Cultures, Identities*, edited by Konrad H. Jarausch, Stefanie Eisenhuth, and Scott H. Krause, 151–164. London: I. B. Tauris, 2021.

——. *Free Berlin: Art, Urban Politics, and Everyday Life*. Cambridge, MA: MIT Press, 2022.

——. "Grassroots Glasnost: Experimental Art, Participation, and Civic Life in 1980s East Berlin." *American Historical Review*, forthcoming June 2021.

Sontag, Susan. *On Photography*. New York: Rosetta Books, 2003.

Spieker, Sven, and Nataša Petrešin-Bachelez. "Creating Context: Zdenka Badovinac on Eastern Europe's Missing Histories." Interview with Zdenka Badovinac in ARTMargins [online]. August 31, 2009. Web. Accessed May 7, 2021. https://artmargins.com/creating-context-zdenka-badovinac-on-eastern-europes-missing-histories-interview/.

Stegmann, Petra, ed. *Fluxus East: Fluxus-Netzwerke in Mittelosteuropa / Fluxus Networks in Central Eastern Europe*. Exhibition catalog. Berlin: Künstlerhaus Bethanien, 2007.

Stilinović, Mladen. "In Praise of Laziness." In *Parallel Slalom: A Lexicon of Non-aligned Poetics*, edited by Bojana Cvejić and Goran Sergej Pristaš, 335–340. Belgrade: Walking Theory, 2013.

Stimson, Blake, and Gregory Sholette, eds. *Collectivism after Modernism: The Art of Social Imagination after 1945*. Minneapolis: University of Minnesota Press, 2007.

Stoler, Ann Laura. *Along the Archival Grain: Epistemic Anxieties and Colonial Common Sense*. Princeton: Princeton University Press, 2010.

Stötzer, Gabriele. *erfurter roulette*. Munich: P. Kircheim Verlag, 1995.

——. "Frauenträume ändern das Leben in der geschlossenen Gesellschaft." *Horch und Guck*, no. 65 (March 2009): 28–31.

——. "Das künstliche Frauenbild der Stasi konzentriert auf Stasi-Aktivitäten in der Thüringer Provinz in den 80iger Jahren." Presentation, Tübingen, Germany, 2014.

——. "Überwachung von Kunst und Kultur. Der lange Arm der Staatssicherheit." In *Zwischen Ausstieg und Aktion. Die Erfurter Subkulture der 1960er, 1970er und 1980er Jahre*, edited by Tely Büchner and Susanne Knorr, 150–169. Bielefeld: Kerber Verlag, 2014.

Tack, Anja. "Kunstdebatte und Vereinigungskrise. Der Bilderstreit um die Kunst aus der DDR." In *Jahresbericht des ZZF 2010*, 75–83. Potsdam: ZZF, 2011.

Tannert, Christoph, ed. *Autoperforationsartistik*. Exhibition catalog. Nuremberg: Verlag für moderne Kunst, 1991.

——[Anita Kenner, pseud.]. "Avantgarde in der DDR heute? Ein Panorama der Kunst-, Literatur-, und Musikszene." In "Avantgarde." Special issue, *Niemandsland* 2, no. 5 (1988): 94–110.

——, ed. *Ende vom Lied*. Exhibition catalog. Berlin: Künstlerhaus Bethanien, 2016.

——, ed. *Gegenstimmen. Kunst in der DDR 1976–1989 / Voices of Dissent: Art in the GDR*. Exhibition catalog. Berlin: Deutsche Gesellschaft and Künstlerhaus Bethanien, 2016.

——. "'Intermedia I' in Coswig 1985." In *Ohne uns! Kunst und alternative Kultur in Dresden vor und nach '89*, edited by Frank Eckhardt and Paul Kaiser, 308–319. Exhibition catalog. Dresden: Efau-Verlag, 2009.

——. "Intermedia. Versuche kollektiver Kunstproduktion." *Musik und Gesellschaft*, no. 34 (1984): 349–353.

——. “Keine Chance für niemand.” In *Bilderstreit und Gesellschaftsumbruch. Die Debatten um die Kunst aus der DDR im Prozess der deutschen Wiedervereinigung*, edited by Karl-Siegbert Rehberg and Paul Kaiser, 350–353. Berlin and Kassel: Siebenhaar Verlag, 2013.

——, et al. “Offener Brief gegen die Einbeziehung von Bernhard Heisig bei der künstlerischen Ausgestaltung des Berliner Reichstages (1998).” In *Bilderstreit und Gesellschaftsumbruch. Die Debatten um die Kunst aus der DDR im Prozess der deutschen Wiedervereinigung*, edited by Karl-Siegbert and Paul Kaiser, 425. Berlin and Kassel: Siebenhaar Verlag, 2013.

Thomas, Karin. “Thomas Florschuetz. Körperbilder.” *European Photography* 8, no. 4 (December 1987): 16–17.

Thomas, Rüdiger. “Selbst-Behauptung.” In *Jenseits der Staatskultur. Traditionen autonomer Kunst in der DDR*, edited by Gabriele Muschter and Rüdiger Thomas, 11–42. Munich: Hanser, 1992.

Thomas, Stefan. *Das Programm der SED*. Cologne: Verlag Wissenschaft und Politik, 1963.

Tlostanova, Madina. *What Does It Mean to Be Post-Soviet? Decolonial Art from the Ruins of the Soviet Empire*. Durham: Duke University Press, 2018.

Vesić, Jelena. “Post-Research Notes: (Re)Search for the True Self-Managed Art.” In *Art and Theory of Post-1989 Central and Eastern Europe: A Critical Anthology*, edited by Ana Janevski, Roxana Marcoci, and Ksenia Nouril, 40–49. New York: Museum of Modern Art, 2018.

Vogel, Amos. *Film as a Subversive Art*. New York: Distributed Art Publisher; United Kingdom: C.T. Editions, 1974. Web (PDF). Accessed May 7, 2021. https://monoskop.org/File:Vogel_Amos_Film_as_a_Subversive_Art.pdf.

Wallace, Ian. “The Politics of Confrontation: The Biermann Affair and Its Consequences.” *German Monitor*, no. 29 (1992): 68–80.

Walther, Joachim. *Sicherungsbereich Literatur. Schriftsteller und Staatssicherheit in der Deutschen Demokratischen Republik*. Berlin: Ch. Links Verlag, 1996.

Warnke, Uwe. “Viermal um den Block. Alternatives Publizieren von Fotografie in der späten DDR.” June 19, 2013. Web. Accessed May 7, 2021. https://uwewarnke.wordpress.com/2013/06/19/uwe-warnke-viermal-um-den-block/.

Warnke, Uwe, and Ingeborg Quaas. *Die Addition der Differenzen. Die Literaten- und Künstlerszene Ostberlins 1979 bis 1989*. Berlin: Verbrecher Verlag, 2009.

Wichner, Ernst, and Herbert Wiesner, eds. *Zensur in der DDR. Geschichte, Praxis, und ‘Ästhetik’ der Behindering von Literatur*. Berlin: Literaturhaus Berlin, 1991.

Woods, Roger. *Opposition in the GDR under Honecker, 1971–85: An Introduction and Documentation*. Basingstoke: Macmillan, 1986.

Wolf, Gerhard. “gegen sprache mit sprache, mit-sprache gegen-sprache. Thesen mit Zitaten und Notizen zu einem literarischen Prozeß.” In *Die andere Sprache. Neue DDR-Literatur der 80er Jahre*, edited by Heinz Ludwig Arnold and Gerhard Wolf, 15–25. Munich: Edition Text + Kritik, 1990.

Youngblood, Gene, *Expanded Cinema*. New York: Dutton, 1970.

Yurchak, Alexei. *Everything Was Forever, Until It Was No More: The Last Soviet Generation*. Princeton: Princeton University Press, 2006.

WEBSITES

Bundeszentrale für politische Bildung, "Autonome Kunst in der DDR." Accessed May 7, 2021. https://www.bpb.de/geschichte/deutsche-geschichte/autonome-kunst-in-der-ddr/.

The Calvert Journal. Accessed May 7, 2021. https://www.calvertjournal.com/.

Former West. Accessed May 7, 2021. http://www.formerwest.org/Front.

Kunst in der DDR. Accessed May 7, 2021. https://www.bildatlas-ddr-kunst.de/.

Museum of Modern Art: Contemporary and Modern Art Perspectives (C-MAP). Accessed May 7, 2021. https://www.moma.org/research-and-learning/international-program/globalresearch.

Performing the East. Accessed May 7, 2021. http://performingtheeast.com/.

re.act.feminism, a Performing Archive. Accessed May 7, 2021. http://www.reactfeminism.org/.

INDEX